NOMAD
Journeys from Samburu

NOMAD

Journeys from Samburu

MARY ANNE FITZGERALD

VIKING

VIKING
Published by the Penguin Group
Penguin Books USA Inc., 375 Hudson Street,
New York, New York 10014, U.S.A.
Penguin Books Ltd, 27 Wrights Lane,
London W8 5TZ, England
Penguin Books Australia Ltd, Ringwood,
Victoria, Australia
Penguin Books Canada Ltd, 10 Alcorn Avenue,
Toronto, Ontario, Canada M4V 3B2
Penguin Books (N.Z.) Ltd, 182–190 Wairau Road,
Auckland 10, New Zealand

Penguin Books Ltd, Registered Offices:
Harmondsworth, Middlesex, England

First American Edition
Published in 1993 by Viking Penguin,
a division of Penguin Books USA Inc.

1 3 5 7 9 10 8 6 4 2

LIBRARY OF CONGRESS CATALOGING IN PUBLICATION DATA
Fitzgerald, Mary Anne.
Nomad/Mary Anne Fitzgerald.
p. cm.
ISBN 0-670-84846-8
1. Africa, Sub-Saharan — Description and travel.   2. Africa, Sub-
Saharan — Description and travel — 1981-   3. Fitzgerald, Mary Anne —
Journeys — Africa, Sub-Saharan.   I. Title.
DT352.F58   1993
967.03′2′092 — dc20   92-50741

Printed in the United States of America
Set in Ehrhardt

To my friends
Tara and Petra

Acknowledgements

Nomad was created by many people, not just the author. There were those in the bush who treated a stranger as a friend such as Ingrid and Jean-Marc Froment, Theresa and Jose Tello, and Marta and Mario Lopes. Some gave me the courage to start such as Brian Wolfson, and others the enthusiasm to keep going such as Jane Turnbull and Christopher Sinclair-Stevenson. Kathy and Amy Eldon provided a home and laughter in London in between safaris. Andy Hill took me into his house during a Cyprus summer where I literally sweated in front of a word processor. Jeremy and Brett Richdale, Anthony and Yvonne Constance, and Anthony and Roseanne Fitzgerald were always there when I needed them, which was often. And Luigi Guarino carefully pencilled in 'rubbish' across much of the manuscript, although he was more sparing towards the end. My thanks go to them and to the many friends in Africa and elsewhere who gave me encouragement and support during difficult times.

Contents

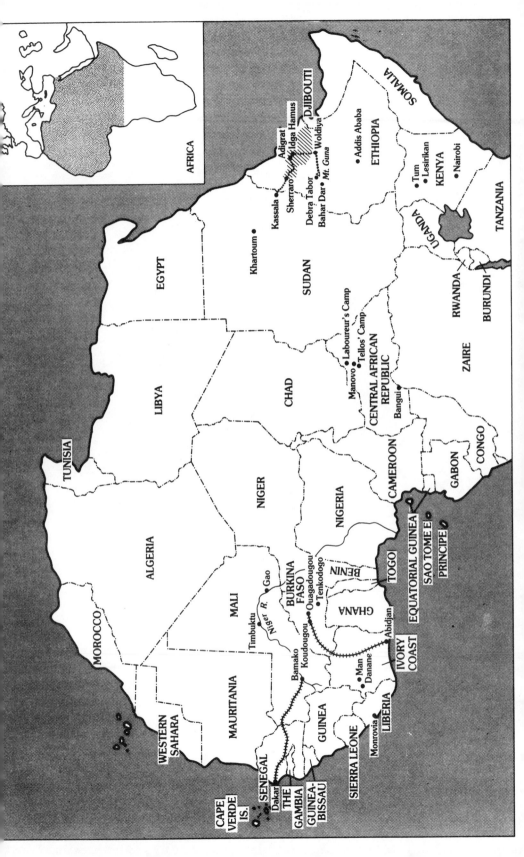

1

Power

Yesterday I went to a dinner party. I ate pâté, duck and crème brûlée served by waiters in white gloves. The men sucked on their cigars and talked with instinctive restraint of the man who was accelerating Kenya's economic decline, President Daniel arap Moi. The women sat in soft armchairs and asked about my forthcoming assignment in New York for *The Sunday Times* magazine. Yesterday my present was luminous and my future was secure.

Last night, when I packed my bag, a hyena whooped at an inky sky. The breeze stirred a palm tree while I slept, and its leaves made a papery rustle. The dawn that ended the night that was yesterday lit a V-shaped flock of egrets on their way to a waterhole.

Today I am under the ground. I cannot see the sky. In fact, I can hardly see at all. My world is small, confined, dark, hopeless. No, not hopeless. To despair is to set in motion a slow suicide of the spirit. All of us down here have been stripped of our possessions, our rights and our freedom. They must not rob our inner core of defiance as well. To think, even for one second, that there is no hope is to let them win. Fatal.

I am frightened because I am in jail. I fear because I am powerless.

Joyce, who tells me she is innocent, is failing. Unlike most of the others in the cell, she has not been beaten but she refuses to eat and is spectrally thin. She would rather die, she says, than stay here. I like Joyce, and her dejection worries me. She ought not to complain. She has only been inside for a month. Her hearing has been set for two months' time.

Joyce has been accused of stealing a sewing machine and has no lawyer to defend her. She faces a possible sentence of up to three years. I have been charged with currency smuggling and could be here for ten years. Both eventualities are so horrific they are inconceivable.

Joyce's brother was an army general, she says, and tells me his name. I recall it well. According to the official version, he was knocked down one night by a hit-and-run driver while relieving himself beside his car. His death prompted much unsubstantiated speculation about a coup plot. His son and daughter, Joyce's niece and nephew, have not raised her bail. She sent them a message, but perhaps they never received it. Joyce's other brother is the general manager of Kenya Railways. Perhaps he did not get a message either. Joyce cannot prove ownership of the sewing machine because there is no one to bring the receipt of sale to court. And she cannot go and fetch it herself because no one will bail her out.

It was an all too familiar situation in Kenya in 1987 when there was a crackdown on Mwakenya, a socialist underground movement that wanted to overthrow Moi. Suspects were regularly denied their statutory phone call, bail or legal representation, according to lawyers. There were to be more than a hundred trials and convictions of alleged Mwakenya supporters. None was allowed to see a lawyer. Only three pleaded not guilty, and two of these men changed their minds after being returned to custody. The detention of three lawyers had also raised concern amongst the legal profession that they could no longer act on behalf of their clients without fear of government reprisal. The police liked it that way because it cut down on paperwork and increased the chances of getting a conviction. Police prosecutors preferred signed confessions because they were notoriously bad at making their case. Beatings and other forms of torture were so blatantly condoned that statements made under duress were routinely admitted as evidence in court.

That was the year that Kenya's reputation for observing civil rights began to acquire a bad smell. The *cause célèbre* at the time of my arrest was Peter Karanja, a businessman and suspected dissident whose death while in police custody had turned him into Kenya's Steve Biko. Post mortem evidence given in court said he died of pneumonia and gangrene caused by two ruptures in his intestines. The inquest was held after his family filed suit against the government. In his testimony, Senior Superintendent James Opiyo admitted that he regularly ignored *habeas corpus* when dealing with prisoners suspected of anti-government activities. Investigations were 'complex' and took more than the twenty-four hours, he explained. No charges were brought against the responsible police officers.

This dungeon runs the length of the law courts, which were constructed by the British in the 1940s. There are twelve cells at each end, containing some 300 prisoners in all. The no man's land in the middle is marked by two huge green metal doors fitted flush with the wall, probably to make them soundproof. They make your flesh crawl when you stand outside them in the dank passageway. No one knows what happens behind them, but perhaps this moral wasteland comes into its own after 4.30 in the afternoon when the law court cells have been emptied.

The political prisoners are brought in after five o'clock for perfunctory, five-minute trials in vacated courtrooms. They have no lawyer. There is no evidence save a confession extracted after physical or psychological torture. For those convicted of possession of a 'seditious' publication, the evidence is invisible. Mwakenya pamphlets are deemed 'prejudicial to state security' so cannot be produced in court.

Round about 3.30 the warders begin to herd prisoners out of the cells. They make them squat down in pairs in the corridor. Soon there is a long line of men and women beside the open drain that runs along the wall. The warders are big, in green pullovers and khaki shorts: they look like Maasai bulls. Some are, in fact, Maasai. Their ear lobes have been cut and stretched into loops the length of mug handles. As government employees they can no longer decorate them with beads so they have hooked them over the tops of their ears. This is the nomad style when walking in the bush. Dangling ear lobes are easily ripped by thorny branches. The warders must be well bribed for they have the affluent bellies and wide shoulders of the meat eater. The prisoners, who are fed a watery gruel, are scrawny. The warders use whips and guns to herd them into the black marias that will take them back to remand. It seems unnecessary. The prisoners have been handcuffed together, which makes it difficult to run away.

Not all the prisoners are kept in remand. The special ones, who are alleged to have committed a serious political offence, are taken to Nyayo House, one of Nairobi's few high-rises. Its basement and three top floors are gazetted as a protected area. There, on the twenty-fourth floor, they are stripped naked, beaten, kicked and whipped during interrogation. All this is referred to in court by testifying police inspectors as 'normal investigations'. If they are still recalcitrant, they are taken to the basement where they are burnt with cigarettes, slashed with razors, hung upside down for long periods and threatened with execution. Often they are left for days without food or water in flooded cells. Their skin starts to rot. They are forced to drink the urine- and faeces-infected water in which they are standing. When I read about this not very long before in an Amnesty International report, I had thought of the torture in a clinical way, calling it human rights abuse. Now those same phrases convey pain and make me uneasy. I do not think I will be beaten, but I cannot be sure.

Nyayo House is near the Intercontinental Hotel on the edge of Uhuru Highway. It presents an innocuous façade. The broken lifts remind visitors of the lethargic pace at which bureaucracy conducts it business, but there is nothing about the grimy interior to warn you of the humiliations of the twenty-fourth floor. I have been there to renew my work permit at the immigration department. They are depressing offices, tainted by the power of petty officials to decide other men's futures.

You can tell a person's attitude to bribery by his behaviour in the waiting room. The refugees from neighbouring countries are dispirited and obedient. They sit slouched on the wooden benches, weighed down by hopelessness, for they are poor and have nothing to offer. The Indian businessmen bristle with bonhomie and call the officials *rafiki* (friend) with feigned familiarity. Unlike the rest of us, they never wait long before the secretary nods at the Big One's door and says, 'He is free.' They are practised in the art of giving just enough to make a man feel important without being lavish. They don't like to give more than 20,000 shillings – US $800. Too handsome a bribe is a mistake. It signals anxiety, which leaves you vulnerable to demands for even more money. The *wazungu*, who are white and so must be rich, make it clear they do not give presents. The ones who have lived in the country a long time display a self-righteous patience that declares their honesty. The stupid ones drum their fingers and pace between window and door. They speak brusquely to the secretary as if it is her fault that paltry government salaries encourage this system of mutual favours. They are the ones whose files are 'lost' and who return week after week until their arrogance has been flattened into polite servility. I have never bribed, but now that I am in a cell, I wonder how long it will be before I abandon my moral high ground.

At first everyone is as dark as soot, their shapes less tangible than their smell. My nose takes in the faintly sour odour of maizemeal gruel and the thick, feline essence of African sweat. The gritty smell of smoke-impregnated clothes is missing. Wood and charcoal fires are ubiquitous in Africa, whether the hearths are in mud huts, cardboard shacks or cement-block rooms. Here there are no reassuring flames to chase back the darkness and make a home for us.

The light beyond the locked wooden door appears brighter than it really is. It casts a shadow on the fetid liquid in the open drain outside. It also seeps through an open square in the door where the space between each of the three iron bars is wide enough to accommodate an out-stretched hand. Three people can look through the bars at the same time if they stand tightly packed together. When my turn comes, I turn slightly sideways and grip the warm metal with clenched fists. The wood on the sill is concave, worn down by days, years, generations of pleading to be set free. But to plead is to show weakness. And that, too, is fatal.

Taking a cue from the habitués, I peer out silently, stony-faced. The posture is timeless. It has been adopted by witches, hags, whores, thieves and murderers through the ages. The wrinkling of the nose is all my own, however. The plump, black-skinned girl on my right reeks. She is fourteen and a thief. On my left is an older, brown-skinned woman wearing a badly torn salmon pink dress. She is a prostitute, booked for stealing $2,000 out of a client's trousers.

The view is a privileged one, as views go down here. Across the corridor and slightly to the right is another wooden door with bars, but the space is bigger, almost the width of the door itself. This is where relatives congregate, plunging from the fresh air down the stone steps and along a dim corridor to plead a prisoner's case with the turnkey. They cannot smell us, but they can smell urine so stale that it must have seeped into the very foundations of the building decades ago. We must be a disturbing sight because the relatives look very gloomy.

Cells stretch down the corridor as far as they can see, which is not very far. The other prisoners are men, characters from a Dickensian madhouse with wild eyes framed by haloes of long, matted hair. Some wear handcuffs even though they are locked away. There is a certain familiarity to their fingers thrusting through the bars. I have seen these men before in the Chamber of Horrors at Madame Tussaud's.

'*Pole, mamma,*' (sorry, mother) they called out when I walked past. I am the only white person amongst the hundreds of people who are crowded in here. The solidarity generated by our circumstances means I am neither favoured nor ignored. Impotence is a great leveller.

Spirits are high in Cell 4 where the women are kept. The dozen or so inmates ebb and flow through the door for reasons that only become clear later. There are greetings but few complaints amongst the chatter. The fortnightly appearance before a magistrate is considered something of an outing by these members of the underworld who have fallen foul of the law while going about their business. It means a day out of remand where conditions are even more wretched.

Whispered conversation with Joyce paints portraits of the others in the cell. The fat woman in the flowered dress and matching headcloth has been done for smuggling goods across the Somali border. Arrest is a professional hazard. She sits on the one narrow bench, hunched forward with her elbows on her knees, waiting for a friend to raise bail. She looks as if she is waiting for a bus.

The prostitute in the salmon-pink dress is arranging her departure as well. Her pimp has been instructed to slip $200 to the court clerk. The simple economics of paying a tithe on the take contradicts the old maxim that crime doesn't pay. Another woman bought her way out before I arrived, Joyce tells me. It was her first arrest in seven years of forging cheques. Her unhindered performance is an encouraging example to us all. It would appear that to be arrested more frequently smacks of carelessness.

The door opens and slams shut again as a barefoot young girl skips into our midst. She giggles and greets several of us with the excitement of a schoolgirl reunited with her mates after the holidays. Indeed, that is pretty much the way it is. She escaped from Langata Women's Prison, she boasts, and was caught after several days of freedom. She is a member of a six-man gang that burgles houses. She is proud of the fact that she carries a revolver when she works, forgetting perhaps that armed robbery carries a death sentence.

She turns to the initiate. 'Have they beaten you?' I shake my head. 'They will. They beat everyone. When they do, deny everything. They asked if I had a gun and I said "No." So they hit me and I still said "No." So they hit me again and my revolver fell on the floor. They said "Is this is your gun?", and I said "No. I don't know what this is and I don't know where it came from." '. Her tip on survival makes me smile. It is the classic criminal protestation of ignorance.

In the corner where the bench meets the wall sits Mary. She has flat, cantilevered cheeks and tip-tilted eyes. She has been writing a letter on lined blue paper of the type that is sold for one cent a sheet in upcountry *dukkas* (shops). I have seen the same paper covered with laborious essays in one-room wooden schools. I have seen it filed in Idi Amin's notorious State Research Bureau, bearing witness to the anonymous betrayals of suspected spies who were battered to death with sledgehammers in the cellar below.

Mary is combing her hair with fierce concentration, pulling and patting it into a flat crest that stands straight up from her head. Without her prettiness, she would be in danger of looking like a startled baboon. Her toilet is reflected in the small green plastic mirror in her palm. As all possessions are automatically confiscated, her activity earns my admiration. Mary has been in remand for over a year and is an old hand at working the system. I find her aloofness alluring and go to sit beside her. I ask her why she is in prison.

Mary cleaned lavatories at the Jomo Kenyatta International Airport until jealousy overrode reason. It was a good job. She lived in a nearby slum and only had to walk a few miles to work. She has been accused of strangling her lover's girlfriend with a rope. Everyone is expecting her to go to the gallows once her case is heard next year. Joyce has already told me she boasts of her crime at night when they are lying on the cement floor. But Mary shrugs into the mirror and says, 'These policemen have made a mistake. I didn't do it.'

Joyce doesn't approve of Mary. After leaving the body on the rubbish dump, she went home, cooked a good meal then slept soundly through the night, Joyce explains. 'I couldn't have eaten,' she says, shaking her head and clicking her tongue against her cheek.

'I can't stand it. I can't stand it. You don't know what these people are like. They are animals. They brag in the darkness. There are women who have killed their children. One woman threw her baby into the Nairobi Dam. She doesn't regret anything. She said she would do it again. The conditions are awful. Our smocks are so torn we have to put our hands in front of our women's places to cover them. They treat us like pigs. We eat out of a bucket and we shit into a bucket. Sixty of us for one bucket.' Joyce looks at me sideways, realising something. 'You will have to empty it tomorrow morning. It's the newcomer's job.'

Yes, I am a newcomer.

My friend and officemate, Kathy Eldon, a restaurant critic, brought me here by official request from the police station at the airport. The police had no car. She transported two prisoners, myself and a silent Ugandan charged with entering the country illegally. The policemen made friendly conversation as we drove into town. Their chief had been going to drop the charges, they said. Then he received a call from State House and changed his mind. Phone calls from the presidential residence can be very persuasive.

When we reached the law courts, I walked through the porticoed main entrance between Kathy and a policeman. We were heading, I thought, for the courtroom. A few paces further on, the policeman took my wrist and led me towards the staircase on the left. 'We will just go down here,' he said cheerily, like a nurse leading her patient to the chemotherapy room. Kathy is somewhere upstairs with my lawyer, Anthony Gross. I have yet to see him.

I am frightened because I am in jail and I fear because I am powerless. They didn't tell me about this when they said I was being taken to court. They didn't tell me about going into the cells or about the dirt and the squalor. Above all, they didn't warn me of the panic that gripped my guts when the turnkey in his blue sweater with leather epaulettes and his surely unnecessary blue cap framing his distended earlobes, *turned the key* in the lock with a well defined clunk and left me in a room ten feet by six feet with criminals and prostitutes, *unable to get out*. And so let it be said of me that I keep company with murderers and thieves. There comes a time, if you live long enough, when every hackneyed phrase takes on fresh meaning.

But this is not a story about being locked up. It is a story about power. African power shifts like sand, changing as suddenly and as subtly as the winds that mould the desert. It is not governed by the Western notion, forged in classrooms and at scout outings, that authority is earned and must be used wisely. It is shadowed by the memory of chiefs whose word was law and who dispensed a justice that was never questioned.

Now, with poverty all around, power is sought after in a naked, unabashed way. It presents the opportunity for enrichment, even if only by a dollar. African ambition contorts Andy Warhol's aphorism. Everyone is powerful for fifteen minutes. Longer, if possible. Anyone who doesn't grab his share is a fool.

I had been foolish, too, though I would not admit it to myself until much later. I pursued the truth, exposing the unpalatable parts of a rotting system, in the belief that it was the proper thing to do. This worried and perplexed my friends. Chivalry, as it has trickled down to us from Richard the Lionheart, is unknown in Africa. A Kenyan friend told me later everyone thought I was playing Russian roulette, slotting more and more bullets into the barrel. No one was surprised when I blew my brains out.

The outcome of the crusade was to break the cardinal rule of survival. I made an enemy of President Daniel arap Moi, leader of the nation, head of the armed forces and a Chief of the Golden Heart. He is Kenya's chief of chiefs who, in an earlier time, might have sat on an ornately carved wooden throne, creased with fat and encased in omnipotence. But Moi lacked the insouciant ruthlessness of those who went before him.

In the nineteenth century, chiefs were responsible for tens of thousands of human sacrifices to appease the ancestral spirits. The King of Dahomey, now Benin, once celebrated a battle victory by lining his palace walls with the skulls of the enemy. On finding himself short, he had the remaining stretch of wall measured up and, after some calculations had been made, ordered the requisite number of prisoners to be executed.

Then, as now, subjects grovelled before the raw and awesome energy of someone who could crush the future, turning it to dust, with one brief directive.

In colonial Kenya, when a handful of British administered areas the size of Scotland, every one, from district officer to white hunter to farmer's wife, dispensed justice, medicine and advice. The Africans, who were punished, dosed and scolded, acquiesced not because the writ of His Majesty's government extended into their villages, but because they acknowledged the prerogative of the powerful to do exactly what they wanted. It was a mistake to think that anything had changed.

The school of African political management advocated personal advantage as the sole guiding principle. Moi, like the majority of his peers, manipulated the law to avenge slights and silence opposition. He used his name to acquire large chunks of the economy: real estate, factories, banks, wholesale and retail enterprises. The elite, the bureaucrats and politicians, followed his example. The powerful used their power to become more powerful. The system worked so well that everyone accepted it without giving it a second thought.

Moi was an African and therefore not to be judged by Western standards. He eschewed the down-home style cultivated by American politicians. Instead, presidential omnipotence hovered near sanctity as befitted a chieftain. His picture was everywhere – on the currency, the TV news, the front pages of the papers and framed in a black wooden rectangle in every office and shop. The media depicted him as a sort of renaissance man who gave tips to football teams, built gabions with farmers and advised leaders in industry. He was an often stern, sometimes smiling father figure in his sixties who professed to act in the interests of the *wananchi* (the common people). Moi had wrapped his tarnished authority in feigned omniscience and, despite frequent tours about the country, was a stranger to us all. His watchful but remote presence was about as cosy as a mollusc.

In reality, Moi was a backwoods boy. Like most African leaders of his generation, he had been born in a mud hut in what was then a remote and undeveloped area in the Rift Valley. He walked to school every day and tended the family goats. Later he became a teacher. In his nostalgic moments at State House, no doubt he would have liked to swap the brisk aroma of furniture polish and the scent of the rose garden for the comfortable, porridgy smell of wood smoke, cow dung and curdled milk that permeated his childhood.

Instead he was obliged to give state dinners for Queen Elizabeth, Prince Charles and Margaret Thatcher when she was prime minister. The guests of honour found themselves placed nearly two feet away from their host, where they were left to fend for themselves. Moi didn't like small talk and tackled his food in silence. State dinners were strictly 'in at eight, out at 9:30' affairs.

On these occasions three tables were set at right angles to the head table like the tines of a fork. Waiters served heaping platters of *tilapia* from the Rift lakes, watery stew and huge chunks of goat and beef. Guests were left to help themselves to the bottles of warm beer, Fanta, Coke and whisky arrayed along the spine of the tables. On the verandah the police band played a vigorous rendition of 'The March over the River Kwai'. By the time the bowls of fruit salad arrived, larded with banana slices already turning brown and dashed with orange cordial, most of the Kenyans, though never Moi, were well and truly inebriated. Moi had dined at Buckingham Palace so he must have been aware that his Kalenjin thrashes weren't quite up to scratch. And he probably knew, as Mobutu realised when he was turned down by the membership committee of Annabel's, that social standing on the international circuit can't be bought.

It was Moi's blandness that attracted the colonial administration. The British singled him out as a 'manageable' Kenyan who could be relied upon to toe the line. In 1955, he was appointed as one of the first African members of the colonial Legislative Council. His allegiance amongst the Kalenjin, the ethnic group to which his tiny Tugen tribe belonged, was derived from a fear that the politically and economically dominant Kikuyu would rob the Kalenjin of their land. Jomo Kenyatta, a Kikuyu, recognised Moi's plodding qualities as an asset and in due course made him vice president. He was unlikely to foment trouble as pretender to the throne. For twelve years Moi was an African version of Spiro Agnew: none too bright with a talent for earning money on the side. He was also given the portfolio of Home Affairs Minister in charge of the police, immigration, intelligence, prisons and licensing. His familiarity with this aspect of the administration came in handy later on. The various departments became tools for coercion.

After Kenyatta's death in 1978, Moi made the quantum leap from number two to the Big One with surprising ease. He wore pinstripe suits and acquired a certain continental stature by brokering peace settlements between the guerrillas and governments of other black African countries. Some of the visitors to State House were struck by his charm and poise. 'He's shrewd and has a native wit, but he doesn't find debate on a rational basis very easy', was how a British diplomat described him.

During the initial years of his reign, Moi shuffled the cabinet frequently enough to engender sycophancy amongst those who should have been his policy makers and set adrift his *éminence grise*, the anglophile Charles Njonjo, on the chimera of a coup plot. Soon the government, trimmed of debate, was as compliant to his direction as the prow of a racing yacht.

By 1988 he had amended the constitution to abolish all political parties except KANU, the Kenya African National Union (a 20-minute session before a submissive parliament); the secret ballot in primary elections (later restored) and life tenure for the auditor general, attorney general and judges (also restored). He extended the period of lawful detention without charge to two weeks for alleged capital offenders. The strange thing was, at that time, opposition barely existed. The military had been purged and appeased after a coup attempt in 1982. Mwakenya was ineffectual. Kikuyu loyalties were sharded. Kenyatta's nephew, Ngengi Mwigai, lost his seat in the 1988 elections which, it was commonly accepted, were rigged. Mwigai was turned away from the ballot counting by a man brandishing a revolver. In the past he had always enjoyed landslide victories. It was probably this needless oppression that fomented the disaffection which was to surface in 1990. By bolting the stable door, Moi encouraged the *wananchi* to kick it down.

This was the autocrat whose unwelcome attention had turned on me two years earlier when I wrote an article in the *Financial Times* about the irregularities of a large hydroelectric project on the Turkwel River in the north. It had been awarded to French contractors without the benefit of competitive international bidding. According to a confidential memo written by Mr Achim Kratz, the chief delegate to Kenya of the European Community, the hefty $270 million contract was more than double what the project should have really cost. It was said that Moi had taken a five per cent rake-off in return for ignoring the official development policy of awarding projects to the lowest bidder.

Apart from the unpleasant consequence of possible imprisonment or deportation, depending on whether you are a local or a foreign journalist, there are other reasons that discourage an exposé on corruption. As with documenting cases of torture, so ingrained is the fear of retribution that it is almost impossible to come by hard evidence.

I made no mention of the payoff in the *Financial Times* story, but for the politicians, diplomats and aid personnel who read the article, it clearly alluded to a well-known boudoir secret. The Kenyan leader had become astonishingly venal.

Moi made his feelings towards me clear in a conversation with the Canadian High Commissioner. It was later repeated to me by a worried friend I had nicknamed Deep Throat. 'I'm going to get Mary Anne Fitzgerald,' he had said.

After that my phone was tapped and my mail opened. I was warned by 'friendly' politicians to watch my step or I would be thrown out of the country. A civil servant from the Ministry of Foreign Affairs demanded I justify a story I had written on food shortages. It was nothing serious, the routine muscle-flexing of a one-party state. I continued to cover the news.

Meanwhile the judicial system was crumbling under the weight of mismanagement. Business vendettas, political power struggles and petty cases of revenge were often settled by bending the law to suit the ends of the rich and powerful. People were detained for running red lights and sentenced to imprisonment for stashing a few undeclared dollars in the back of a drawer. Counsel for civil cases were told that their pleas would be heard only if their clerks could locate the relevant files amongst the hundreds that lay dumped on the floor of courtroom antechambers. There were no court stenographers. Judges and magistrates used their handwritten notes as the official court record.

The backlog of civil cases was so great that some creditors bribed the police to take debtors into custody on a Friday evening. By Sunday they had been sufficiently frightened to write cheques for the full amounts owed. The judges and attorneys for the prosecution split the debt collection fees paid by the creditors between them. It was not unusual for these payments for facilitating justice to reach $20,000. It was a practical alternative to a moribund and overloaded legal system, but it lacked the impartiality of the scales and blindfold.

The prisons were in a worse state than the courts. Lawyers reckoned a prison population of about 60,000 was crammed into jails built to hold a maximum of 14,000 inmates. The backlog of cases grew and, because most of the accused couldn't raise bail, they remained in remand. A man who had been held in custody for nine years on murder charges was tried – and found innocent. A man who had died in custody while awaiting trial for violent robbery was sentenced to hang posthumously. 'He should serve the sentence wherever he is since his death certificate and burial permit were not in the court file,' ruled the magistrate.

Each time I wrote an article critical of the government, I anticipated being picked up by Special Branch. These supernumerary policemen were charged with unearthing subversive political activity and reported directly to Moi. They liked to rifle houses for foreign currency, 'seditious' literature, dope and pornography. Illegal possession was an easy way of preferring charges against those who were being a nuisance. If your house was clean, they planted proscribed pamphlets in your desk or even in your coat pocket. But that was reserved for suspected members of Mwakenya.

Whenever I wrote a sensitive story, it became ritual to file from the office, go home and scoop up an assortment of illicit items: bullets acquired while reporting on coups; shiny black pellets of opium which would never be used but for some forgotten reason had found their way into the Fitzgerald memorabilia; odd bits of foreign currency. Even the shiny red Mao Tse Tung badge bought in China was a potential source of conviction. Communism was a bogeyman in staunchly capitalist Kenya.

The whole lot was stuffed into a plastic bag and dropped off at a friend's office on the way to work the following morning. As an additional precaution, I left the home number of a British diplomat with my daughters, Tara and Petra, and told them to ring him if I disappeared. The cleansing of the house became so frequent that eventually I left everything on permanent deposit at a friend's house and drove over to fetch dollars and travellers' cheques whenever I was leaving the country on assignment. It worked so well that I almost forgot there had ever been a problem.

Then one day the International Monetary Fund blew the whistle on a thriving currency smuggling racket. An IMF team examining the national accounts had discovered a large discrepancy between the value of goods exported and the money remitted back to Kenya in payment. It was estimated that about $400 million had been siphoned overseas in the past three years, equivalent to about half the existing foreign reserves. Kenya ranked fourth in Africa for illicit funds abroad, beaten only by Liberia, Nigeria and South Africa. The IMF warned Moi that he had better stem the flow if he wanted any more standby facilities.

In accordance with the time-honoured custom of finding a scapegoat to divert attention from the root cause of a problem, eight Indian coffee traders and bankers, three of them Bank of Credit and Commerce International (BCCI) executives, were arrested. The charges included illegally retaining $63 million of coffee export earnings outside the country.

Indians first came to East Africa at the beginning of the century. They were brought over by the British as cheap labour for the construction of a railway line from Mombasa on the Indian Ocean to Kisumu on Lake Victoria. When it was finished, they stayed on to work for Uganda Railways, as it was called then, and to open small shops in the countryside. After independence in 1963, the fortunes of many Indian families waxed through hard work and shrewd business deals, just as declining privilege led to the wane of the prosperity of many of the British who stayed on. Asians contributed one third of the national gross domestic product.

This was another way in which power had shifted. I sent my daughters to school on bicycles and worried about the fees. The Indian children arrived in chauffeur-driven cars and threw lavish birthday parties in opulent houses. Their fathers presided over the retail trade and some of the banks and financial institutions. The Kenyans claimed to dislike their exploitation of the economy, but in reality they resented the Indians' success. Lambasting the Indians was a cheap political manoeuvre. Unlike the British, who theoretically could count oh the High Commission to keep watch over them, the 70,000-strong Indian community had no political protection. They were fragmented into separate religious communities and essentially leaderless. There was no ultimate spokes-man to barter for their rights, no institution of last resort to extend protection when guns were fired and soldiers strutted the streets. As such, they were fearful of overnight expulsion from the land of their birth, as had happened under Idi Amin in Uganda in 1972. That was why the Indians were partially responsible for the massive haemorrhage of foreign currency holdings. They were planting a hedge against the day the Kenyans no longer found them useful.

Moi had two Indian business partners, Ketan Somaia and Naushad Merali, who acted as front men for buying into multinational corporations such as the Firestone tyre factory, the Eveready battery factory and Bank of America. A few years later, when BCCI was collapsing, Somaia bought that as well. Somaia was chauffeured in a bulletproof Mercedes by a uniformed member of the elite paramilitary General Service Unit. Another member of the GSU travelled with him as a personal bodyguard. The GSU guarded his house as well. This was a privilege that even government ministers didn't enjoy.

It was thoughtful acts of loyalty that made Indians more useful accom-plices than Kenyans. They were well versed in the short cuts to amassing money, while the threat of deportation or imprisonment was a persuasive deterrent against treachery. And, as the coffee trading scandal illustrated, they came in handy as sacrificial lambs.

There was much publicity in the local papers about the overcrowded and insanitary conditions in the prison where the accused Gujarati businessmen were being held. They were forced to sleep on the floor with only one blanket each as protection against the crisp highland night air. Their diet was gruel and water. It was a distinct comedown for men accustomed to a pampered lifestyle. The softening up process had begun.

I duly reported on the cases for *The Sunday Times*, who retained me as regional correspondent, filling in the background with a few details that had been conveniently overlooked by the Kenyan press. Exporters of coffee, tea, vegetables and flowers routinely claimed that the bulk of their shipments had rotted *en route* and could not be sold. The explanation was accepted by customs officials in return for a backhander.

Another method of circumventing regulations was to destroy the Central Bank documents that confirmed the goods had been exported. This could not have been done without the collusion of the officials who handed the documents out. It was possible because the Central Bank was, at that point, not yet computerised. Given that most private and public enterprises in Kenya had computers, it was not inconceivable that the administration had chosen not to modernise its national banking records so that foreign exchange could be shipped out undetected.

I knew the story was close to the bone by the reaction when it was published. A minister who was a personal friend stopped taking my phone calls and cancelled at the last minute on a charity dance I had organised. He had promised to be the guest of honour and his name was on the posters. It was his way of saying 'Stay away from me. You're dangerous to know.'

As if this wasn't enough, I received a lawyer's letter from one of the accused Indians, denying that he owned Mount Credit, a financial institution in Mayfair, London as I had stated in the article, and announcing his intention to sue both me and the paper. I had substantiating evidence on that point so didn't worry. If I hadn't been so cavalier about my safety, things might have turned out very differently.

The furore in the press over the coffee traders and bankers served to make the general public jittery and customs officers overzealous. Stringent foreign exchange regulations made it virtually impossible to travel frequently without contravening the law. Kenyan residents were obliged to cash in all their foreign currency within twenty-four hours of returning home. When you wanted to travel again, you had to apply to Central Bank for an inadequate foreign currency allowance. The procedure took about a week or, at best, several days. If you were employed by an overseas company, you could hold a dollar account in the company name. As a resident freelancer, no such option was open to me. I often had only hours' notice of my trips, for such is the nature of news-collecting. I had the choice of behaving in a criminal manner or losing my job.

Prior to the arrests, there had been a certain elasticity in the relationship between customs officers and departing travellers, who were obliged to declare their foreign currency and furnish proof it had been obtained with Central Bank approval. Now there were friskings that yielded dinars and marks hidden in bras and underpants. A lot of people were being picked up. Several had been arrested and charged. I had just returned from Ethiopia and was unaware of the change of mood.

One sunny Saturday morning I left the house to catch a plane for New York where I planned to interview Ethiopian defectors for *The Sunday Times* magazine. I told the friend who dropped me at the airport not to wait and waved a nonchalant goodbye. By lunchtime I was locked in a cell at the airport police station, frightened, depressed and not, for once, thinking about how I was going to get the story.

The painful lesson in the nature of power had begun. I was discovering the delicate give and take between the petty tyranny of the captor and the inner equilibrium of the victim. So far I was not doing very well. Unlike the movies where police bark out, 'You're under arrest', there had been no definitive statement on my position. I had walked the half mile to the station with three police officers, two men and a woman. No one had offered to carry my suitcase. It was not a good sign, but not unusual in a society where women are expected to shoulder the loads while the men walk with their hands in their pockets.

At the station a policeman took down the details of what had happened, writing in pencil in a large register. I had tried to leave the country with $600 in travellers' cheques and £150 in cash. I had also torn the travellers' cheques in half before handing them over to the customs officer, an offence regarded in a grave light even though it was not against the law. No mention was made of my real mistake. I had lost my temper.

Someone moved to take my suitcase and handbag from me. 'No, no, I'll keep those with me,' I said, a touch imperiously.

'We'll bring you your toothbrush this evening,' he replied. The truth dawned.

I was led down a corridor past riot helmets and batons hanging on the walls to a small room containing two chairs and three wooden tables haphazardly strewn with files. There were bars on the windows. The policewoman produced an ink pad and laboriously pressed my thumbs and fingers on to it, rolling them from side to side then repeating the process on a sheet of paper. She smudged some of the fingerprints on the first attempt and we had to start again. I tried very hard to co-operate, but her firm grip made it difficult. I wanted to please but had no control over what was happening. The membrane of fear that slides over the imprisoned was in place.

The next step was an identification form. There was no camera to take mug shots. So this questionnaire would be circulated if I escaped. We filled it out, the semi-literate leading the abject, as best we could.

'What tribe are you?'

'I don't belong to a tribe.' She frowned at the cheeky reply, and I backtracked. 'Well, I do belong to a tribe, I suppose. But it isn't any of these tribes marked down here. I'm British. The British tribe.'

'What is your complexion? Black . . . dark brown . . . light.'

'Well, I'm not black or dark brown. But I don't think I'm light either. You see, where it says light, I think they're referring to light brown. And that wouldn't be right, would it? Maybe it would be better to put fair.'

Her eyes lay on my face, stony, impervious, secure with authority. 'You are wrinkled.'

Next came the eyes.

'I'm not sure what colour they are. What do you think? Are they green or blue?' I stared at her. Our gaze met in potential combat before I lowered mine to the form.

'Small,' she said.

Eventually I got the hang of it. No opinions. No advice. Just choose one of the answers even if it didn't make sense. We plunged on, hesitating briefly at 'deformities' and 'habits' until I volunteered 'bow legs' and 'smoking'.

I was led back to the cell and waited for the next encounter. This one was crucial. The officer in charge, off duty over the weekend, had been called from his house. He would not be in a good mood, but if I managed to please him during the interview, he might withdraw the charge. Once again down the grey-walled corridor to another room. The policeman bent low and knocked on the door an inch above the rusty doorknob. It was an instinctive, ceremonial obeisance to the authority that lay within.

'Come in!' a voice commanded. The policeman snapped to attention, an invisible plumb line tracing his spine. He opened the door and led me inside.

Superintendent David Wamalwa was squeezed behind a big wooden desk. He took off his hat and placed it on the floor amidst the flies. He was a large man, covered with thick layers of shining black flesh. I was shrinking, sinking, sucked into a whirlpool of conflicting ideas. Should I be assertive, conspiratorial, an equal who shrugs off this rather ridiculous mistake with a dismissive wave of the hand? Should I be deferential, obsequious, eager to do his bidding? Or should I somehow, heavens knew how because I had never done it before, bribe him with the seventeen dollars in notes I had managed to tuck inside my bra? Later, in Cell 4, I realised that what actually happened was inevitable. Superintendent Wamalwa took the lead.

My passports lay in front of him. It was a distressing display. In Africa, to possess two passports is to bear the stigmata of a spy.

'We found another passport hidden in your suitcase. Why do you have two passports?'

'It's because I travel a lot. It means that I can leave one behind to get a visa for one country while I'm visiting another. Lots of us have two passports. It's quite normal. The British know about it. They don't mind.'

Fingers the size of pork sausages slowly turned the pages. 'I see you were born in South Africa.'

Another nail through the hand. 'Yes.'

His eyes narrowed, drawing the skin tighter across his cheekbones, accentuating their voluptuous curve. 'And you are a journalist.'

'Yes.'

'And you are forty-two.'

'Yes.'

Indignation cinched his face shut. 'At your age you ought to know better. Take her back to the cells.'

So here I am on a Monday morning and not at my desk in Room 8 of the Press Centre seven (or is it eight?) blocks away. Who cares? This world is divorced from the rest of the town. I focus on the immediate and the imminent. The bars confine thoughts of the future to one thing – freedom. Sometime today we will be herded into court to appear before Joseph Mango, the chief magistrate. There is also the heartening prospect, for some of us, of bail. The turnkey has passed me a note from Kathy and Anthony saying they are working on it.

He's not a bad chap, this policeman. He has taken one of the twenty-shilling notes I managed to keep and sent out for cigarettes, skimming off the ten shillings in change. I have passed the packet around the girls. We enjoy our smoke while he conveniently turns his back.

One of the women, a prostitute who moonlights as a cat burglar, tells me her mother is upstairs arranging her bail. 'When I'm out, I'll fix it for you. You can meet someone in the 680 (a downtown hotel) and sort it out. It won't cost much. Maybe 2,000 shillings [eighty dollars]. Then when your trial comes up, he'll acquit you.' The price of freedom is ten per cent of a magistrate's monthly salary.

I shake my head. 'Thanks a lot but I wouldn't do it. I don't want to give him the satisfaction of being bought off.' I don't mention that I have been working on a particularly sensitive story on corruption within the judicial system. I can hardly claim to be an objective reporter if I contribute to the rot.

Joyce has told me that remand prisoners are allowed out for one hour a day except on Sundays, when they go to church. The girls have warned me that it can take two days to raise bail. I want to prepare myself for the worst, so I ask again. 'What's it like?'

The cat burglar sees my anxiety and laughs. 'It's like a holiday. You lie around and bask in the sun.' It is a valuable lesson. To survive the unbearable awfulness, you create your own reality.

The reality of the adjoining cell is enviable. The inmates have been receiving a flow of visitors, including a woman and a child. Some bear food and thermoses of hot drinks; others briefcases and sheaves of papers. Muffled conversation and laughter comes through the wall. They must be having a cocktail party in there. The prostitute in the pink dress, whose turn it is to look through the bars, is watching the traffic with interest. She turns her head to address the cell at large and says in a derisive way, 'There are an awful lot of Asians around these days.'

I join her and enquire who is next door. 'The Asians who were done for currency smuggling. You can see they've sorted things out with all that food going in. They'll be let out soon.'

At this point one of the Indians steps into the passageway to stretch his legs. He is thin, but not painfully so, and has a beard. He looks at me with dull disinterest. I wonder if he is the banker who threatened to sue me. Last month I was exposing crime. This month I am committing it. It's weird. Life is imitating my stories. I don't know it yet, but over the next year I am to make more news than I report.

Right now, I am a beacon of opportunity for the less fortunate. Standing in pairs in the dark passageway, waiting to be marched upstairs into the courtroom, the man behind me tries to pickpocket my remaining money. 'Fuck off!' I snarl. The man next to him gives me a 'Yo, sister' smile.

We come up through the hole in the ground two by two and blink at the dazzling light. There is a bewildered cast to our faces and our breath stinks on the fresh air. The courtroom appears much larger than I remembered it. Seated up in the boondocks behind a railing, Mango, the court clerk, Kathy and Anthony seem very far away.

Justice is dealt out like a poker hand. We struggle to catch the chief magistrate's words. Most of us corpse it when our turn comes to stand up. 'Yessir.' 'Nossir.' 'Three years.' 'Six months.' 'Held over without bail. . .'

The old man who looks like a sack of coal is particularly confused. Was he loitering with intent beside a vehicle at 11 p.m. on such and such a night? He doesn't have an inkling what this means. So taking his cue from a turnkey, he shuffles uneasily and nods in assent. Down he goes in sixty seconds flat. One year. He doesn't know what the sentence is for. It doesn't matter. He's off the streets.

The next lot are as trendily coiffed and dressed as Benetton models. They ooze street cred from their insolent stare to their Nike trainers. Like me, they have a lawyer. He pleads guilty on their behalf to the illegal importation of heroin worth $60,000. They get a year each too.

The man on my right nudges my elbow. He has been booked for forging a school-leaving certificate. It's a mistake, of course. The certificate's genuine. Can he borrow a thousand shillings for his bail? 'Sorry. I can't help. I've got problems of my own,' I whisper. Some guys will do anything to get a job.

The face on my left is new. The young woman wears glasses and speaks good English. A definite cut above the regulars. If she sticks around, I can see her teaching the warders to read and write. I ask what she's in for.

She had a quarrel with her husband over his mistress. She wants him to get rid of her. He beat her up then called the police and lodged a complaint. An hour later she was in the slammer on assault. She worries about her two-month-old baby now she's not there to breast-feed it. 'See that woman there?' She points to a nattily dressed figure in the gallery. 'That's her. She's wearing my clothes.'

I warn her that raising bail can be a slow process and say the baby should do fine on a bottle. Then I launch into some marriage counselling. File for divorce as soon as you get out. The guy's no good. But make sure you get a lawyer who can squeeze him. I'm an old-timer already.

But not a jailbird. The cells have coughed up the inmates on to the corridor floor. The warders' whips dangle above a centipede of kinky black hair and manacled wrists that stretches into the darkness. It is 4.15. My mind resists the proposition of remand in no uncertain terms. It is insisting it must be released from my body. I won't stay with you for this one, it tells me. I'm off. You can go it alone. Is this the onset of madness?

'Melly En! Over here!'

A warder seizes my hand and drags me along in the shadow of his beefy shoulders. Now my body is rebelling too. A tidal wave of fear crashes against my stomach. 'No! There's been a mistake. I'm not going to remand. I'm getting bail,' says a voice.

Then I remember the bucket. '*Nataka kwenda choo.*' We stop beside a door that is falling off its hinges and no longer shuts. The warder takes my handbag, which has been returned, and waits, whip in one hand, handbag in the other. I step over the prisoners and squat amidst the excrement and urine. There is no shame in returning the stare of the men crouched three feet away. I know when I'm on to a good thing. This, after all, is the Ritz powder room compared to what lies ahead.

'Melly En! Over here!' The aggression has been replaced with heartiness. The power has shifted. 'You won't be with us tonight. Your bail has come.'

At the door leading to the staircase, a turnkey smiles in a conspiratorial way, showing me a receipt pad. It has printed on it, 'Being contribution to the aid of medical expenses for Mrs Isabella K. Mosongo who was involved in a road accident sustaining serious spinal injuries.' The extraction of benefits from the public is ingenious and manifold. State medical services, like primary schools, are free but shockingly inadequate. So Kenyans who want to be healthy and literate resort to whip-arounds. I hand over the equivalent of a bottle of aspirin, a bargain price for freedom.

The door creaks open. I breathe in the clean air. Mike Eldon, Kathy's husband, enfolds me in his arms. 'Let's get out of here. This stench is indescribable,' he says.

It was six weeks before the hearing came up. During this time officialdom turned its back on Kenya's latest pariah. I couldn't file stories. The Kenya Union of Journalists and the Immigration Department were waiting for the outcome of the trial before they renewed my work permit. I couldn't leave the country. My passports had been confiscated. I no longer had entrée to government offices. My politician friends refused to acknowledge me. I was infamous.

The European and Indian communities, on the other hand, who thought they recognised their own vulnerability in my misfortune, rallied round. They all infringed the currency regulations in a minor way, tucking a few pounds or dollars into their luggage when they travelled. There but for the grace of God . . . , they thought. They were on the wrong track. These offences were remote from the real black market traffic, which was conducted in millions. They should have referred back to colonial times when the precedent for discipline was set by British District Commissioners. I was being whipped because I had been cheeky.

People I knew only vaguely rang up and offered to do my shopping. I came home one day to find a note in the living room. 'My house in Spain is waiting for you. Take a holiday in it when all this is over. Love, Stewart.' When had I last seen Stewart? Five or six years ago. A longtime friend, who had once spent ten days in the cells, took me to lunch. When the coffee was served, he regarded me with concentrated energy. 'Darling, you've got to get out of here. If you get six months, it will take you years to recover. If you spend longer inside, you'll never be the same again. Get a fishing boat and escape to Tanzania. It's your only chance.'

But I couldn't. I was terrified. Yet there was no option but to see the trial through. My arrest differed from the customary administration harassment of the helpless only in that it had received a lot of media coverage. If I turned tail and ran, it would be a petty but well publicised victory for the government bullies.

Instead I returned to the law courts to bail out Joyce, overcoming my horror of the dungeon to befriend the women warders. Most of them were unmarried and struggling to raise their children on about fifty dollars a month. We discussed in Swahili the rigours of single motherhood. Pauline's son attended a school that had trained several Olympic athletes. He was a budding, but handicapped, sprinter. He ran barefoot. I gave Pauline the money to buy her son a pair of track shoes and contributed to the St Patrick's High School Parent-Teacher Association for which she duly furnished a receipt. I also dished out enough cooked chickens and chips to feed the warders and the girls in the cells. I left with Joyce. On Christmas morning Pauline rang the house and invited me over to the jail to share the warders' Christmas lunch. I was touched but refused.

Early in the new year Joyce was acquitted, having raised the money for a lawyer. I pleaded guilty and was given the option of a fine or a six-month prison sentence. Some weeks later, a few paragraphs on the inside pages noted that a *nolle prosequi* had been entered for the case concerning the Indian bankers and coffee traders. I was told by a Gujarati businessman that all the funds had been brought back with a large chunk falling through the interstices of State House. 'Have you ever seen a Kenyan looking at a Mercedes boot stacked with money? They melt like butter,' he grinned.

With the case resolved, I was out of Coventry. My passports were returned and so was my money. 'Tell me which day you're travelling, and I'll make sure you're not bothered,' the chief customs officer at the airport told me. So when I did finally leave for New York on assignment, I repeated the crime I'd been sentenced for – with official sanction.

I understood this perfectly. I had been punished for insulting the Big One. Francis Bacon, in one of his essays, called revenge 'a kind of wild justice'.

My contacts at the Kenya Union of Journalists and the Immigration Department rang the office. 'We're glad you're all right, Mary Anne. Come down so we can sort your permit out. We're sorry about what happened.' Normally they would have spoken in English, but they said this in Swahili. I took it to mean, 'You have been blooded despite your white skin. You are one of us.'

Yes, I had changed. I knew what it was like to be a small person in Africa who walked without protection. The Europeans had made a big thing out of the trial, for they recoiled at the thought of whites in black jails. They treated justice as if God had revealed it to Moses on a tablet. Africans, on the other hand, knew it was a privilege. In a way, I was ashamed such a fuss had been made over the episode. There had been nothing special about it. Millions of Africans suffered at the hands of corrupt and incompetent leaders.

Measured against a continental yardstick, Kenya's human rights record was still somewhere in the top third. This was hardly an accolade when you saw what had happened elsewhere. Mutinous Ethiopian troops forced into a ditch, covered with petrol and burnt alive. One eighth of the population of Equatorial Guinea murdered on the orders of Life-President Macia Nguema. University professors dying of dehydration in the Mauritanian desert. An information ministry employee in Malawi tortured to death for claiming the economy was in a slump. The omnivorous jaws of authority crushed opinion hungrily. It was happening right under our noses in Kenya.

Things had begun to stir earlier in the year when Blaine Harden, the *Washington Post* correspondent, wrote a carefully substantiated piece on police torture. He was the first Western reporter based in Nairobi to do so. Purely by chance, the story coincided with Moi's state visit to the United States. It prompted questions in Congress and a rebuke from the State Department which called on the Kenyan government to investigate the allegations. Moi was so angry he left Washington two days ahead of schedule. The arrows found their mark, though. Nine detainees were released, and for a while the arrests and allegations of torture were less frequent. Moi recognised the hand that fed him.

British reaction, by contrast, was limp-wristed. Margaret Thatcher, then prime minister, remained silent on the subject of human rights while Moi signed a new fifty million pounds aid agreement on his way home from Washington. Kenya is the largest recipient of British aid in Africa and the fourth largest in the world after India, Bangladesh and Pakistan. Most of it is tied to British exports. British investment in Kenya stands at over $2.3 billion, making Britain the single largest foreign investor in the country. Kenya remains a major outlet for British exports, too. In the light of Thatcher's praise of one-party states during an official visit to Kenya in January 1988, it appeared that these commercial considerations overshadowed humanitarian ones.

British diplomats privately compared Kenya's underground opposition to the IRA when discussions arose on the morality of imprisoning alleged dissenters without the benefit of due legal process. 'Kenya's stable and it works. If some people are sentenced with undue haste, that's the price you have to pay for peace. A few must suffer for the good of the many,' they said. The theory was in those Cold-War days that it was better to have a president you knew than a jumped-up junior army officer bankrolled by the Soviets. Kenya narrowly missed having one in 1982 when Sergeant Hezekiah Ochuka, using Moscow money, led a two-day rebellion and almost became head of state.

Kenya's human rights record began to deteriorate again in 1990. On hearing that the Berlin Wall had been torn down and that Ceaucescu had been shot, all because thousands of Germans and Romanians had demonstrated in the streets, calls for multiparty democracy began to sweep the African continent. The power of the people to change their destiny was an innovative and exciting concept that emboldened Kenyans to join the chorus.

Moi didn't need the events in Eastern Europe to remind him that he was on to a good but perhaps temporary deal. Beneath the guise of divine plutocrat was a man acutely aware of his vulnerability. He rarely read newspapers and was shielded from popular opinion by his coterie of advisers. Even so, he knew that Africa's record for the long-term survival of its leaders was not in his favour. Over the preceding three decades, all but six out of more than 150 African heads of state had either been assassinated or deposed in coups. Few had died in office of natural causes and none had been voted out. Over the next two years another fifteen were either overthrown or stepped down as a result of democracy. In his heart of hearts, Moi must have known that public dismissal could happen to him too. This was the cloven image of African dictators: public power and secret fear.

Kenya had been a *de facto* one-party state since independence in 1963 and a *de jure* one since 1982 when the constitution was changed to proscribe formal opposition to the ruling party of KANU. The Kenyans were restrained in their demands. No riots accompanied public debate on political choice. Even so, the government moved quickly to muzzle independent thought. Sometimes repression assumed farcical proportions. In June 1990, Wilson Leitich, the party boss for Nakuru district, told KANU youth-wingers that if they saw anyone making the two-fingered salute that symbolised multipartyism, they were to amputate the offending fingers with a knife and bring them to his office. Lietich immediately received a reprimand from KANU headquarters.

In July, six government critics were detained without charge. They included two leading proponents of the multiparty system, Kenneth Matiba and Charles Rubia. Moi had branded them 'hyenas' and 'traitors'. Both were former government ministers of some stature. They had become a focus for discontent by articulating grassroots complaints about such problems as the disarray of the educational system and the high unemployment rate.

It was difficult for Kenyans to find places in secondary schools and almost impossible to get jobs afterwards. In Nairobi, only one in every four primary-school leavers found a place in secondary school. So skewed was the educational system that Peter Lekerian, my Maasai foster son, graduated with a D+ and was still placed in the top quarter of the nation's school graduates.

Kamau Kuria, the lawyer who had leaked the torture affidavits to Blaine Harden, the *Washington Post* reporter, sought refuge in the American Embassy. He had been detained in 1987 immediately after filing a suit against the government alleging police torture and had no wish to repeat the experience. Yielding to pressure from the plain spoken ambassador, Smith Hempstone, Moi allowed Kuria to leave Kenya for the United States, where he became a visiting scholar at the Harvard Law School. Rubia's lawyer, John Khaminwa, was held without charge for three weeks. Paul Muite, Matiba's lawyer, went underground for several days, a decision that was accompanied by so much publicity, Moi deemed it wise to leave him be.

Another lawyer, Gitobu Imanyara, was picked up and charged with seditious publication. The offending issue of Imanyara's magazine, *The Nairobi Law Monthly*, carried a cover story that aired both sides of the debate on constitutional amendment to allow the registration of political parties other than KANU. Unlike communist governments in Eastern Europe, KANU was not based on an ideological monopoly. It prevailed because first Kenya's founding president, Jomo Kenyatta, and then his successor, Moi, were the party's chairmen.

A few weeks prior to the arrests, a gang of about fifteen armed men broke into Matiba's home. They fractured his wife Edith's skull and injured his nineteen-year-old daughter, Ivy. Matiba wasn't home at the time. Large *panga* (machete) wielding gangs of thieves were the scourge of home-owners, but the men addressed one another as 'corporal' and 'captain' and carried out the raid with military precision. They stole nothing of value. Kenneth Matiba claimed it was government intimidation.

A rally scheduled for the Saturday following the arrests turned into a confrontation between the crowds and security officials. The government admitted to twenty deaths, but at least a hundred demonstrators were killed, according to 'Taking Liberties', a well documented report on Kenyan civil rights published by the human rights organisation Africa Watch. Over a thousand others were arrested for disturbing the peace. The offences ranged from calling for the release of Matiba and Rubia to flashing the two-fingered democracy salute and driving in daylight with headlights on.

It was a disquieting moment in modern Kenya's history. Kenyans grumbled in bars, but never before had they gone to the barricades. It was not known what proportion of the rioters were genuine advocates of political pluralism. Many were frustrated youngsters who, in another culture, might have gone hotting or wilding. One thing was clear though. Everyone wanted change. Most of the demonstrators were landless unemployed who had nothing to lose and, so they hoped, something to gain. What they wanted above all was reassurance that they wouldn't have to live in cardboard shacks for the rest of their lives.

For the first two decades of independence, Kenya was rightly lauded for its prosperity and tranquillity. Economic growth outstripped a population explosion that was the highest in the world. Kenyans just had to look around them at the massacre and torture sponsored by Idi Amin and Milton Obote in Uganda, the economic collapse caused by Julius Nyerere's socialist programme in Tanzania and the mix of poverty and ideological terror under Mengistu Haile Mariam in Ethiopia, to realise how lucky they were.

Then a combination of circumstances such as global recession, a slump in coffee and tea prices, oil price hikes and an onerous debt burden, conspired to slow expansion to a crawl. Despite this, the Kenyan economy might have maintained impetus if it had not been for a factor that doesn't appear in the national statistics: corruption.

Moi's foreign bank accounts were estimated to hold several billion dollars, classing his avarice alongside that of Mobutu Sese Seko of Zaire, considered to be one of the richest men in the world. World Bank officials reckoned Moi was taking as much as a quarter of Western concessionary funds committed to development projects. He was alleged to have received twenty million dollars in bribes when Kenya bought two Airbus planes, millions more by selling on discounted wheat received under the Saudi aid programme, millions more again through the takeover of gambling casinos. The list of dubious transactions was very long.

Greed is one of the invisible trappings of leadership. It starts at the top and splashes down over ministers, politicians and party officials. It diverts national resources into subsidising a *nouveau riche* lifestyle and leaches once profitable businesses dry. Men who cannot afford to buy large cars and houses on their salaries drive Mercedes Benzes and live in suburban villas strewn with velvet plush furniture. They are called the *Wabenzi* (the Mercedes Benz people).

Greed is necessary because wealth is a statement of power. Kenyans in high places had become masters at expressing their superiority, some-times with a dash of imagination. General Lekerde Lenges, the army chief and a member of the pastoral Samburu tribe, used money acquired through state military purchases to expand his ranch. He also called on the army's resources to run it. Military helicopters searched out grazing for his thousands of head of cattle. Military bowsers ferried water to watering points. Soldiers from the Samburu tribe were assigned the task of herding his cattle.

While Lenges' expenditure was productive, there were those who preferred unadulterated profligacy. Take, for instance, Hezekiah 'Duke' Oyugi, a civil servant in charge of internal security. Once a school teacher like Moi, he was the president's right-hand man, a fixer. He had risen through the ranks to become a prime mover in Kenya's political and financial circles. In the summer of 1991, when the world's press was focussed on the amount of money being lavished on Elizabeth Taylor's wedding to Larry Fortensky, preparations were underway for another wedding that equalled Taylor's for extravagance. Oyugi's daughter was to be married and he wanted to make sure it was an occasion that no one would forget.

The bride was to be dressed by Lindka Cierach, better known for designing the Duchess of York's bridal gown. Oyugi went one better than the British royal. He ordered two wedding dresses in case the bride, in a fit of nerves, spilled something down her front before she reached the altar. Then there were his and hers saloon cars to get the young couple to the church plus a few more for the rest of the family. Oyugi left this purchase a bit late so he had to fly the cars in from Europe on a special Lufthansa charter. The bill came to $150,000. Because the marriage was to take place in Kisumu in western Kenya, and most of the guests lived in Nairobi, Oyugi laid on a DC3 shuttle that made the 150-mile trip every half hour. Those who were lucky enough to be invited sat amidst $36,000-worth of orchids during the ceremony then consumed a banquet brought in by train from Nairobi. The rest of the town partied in Kisumu's bars from three in the afternoon to midnight. The drinks were on the house, courtesy of Oyugi. To round off the celebrations, each member of the bridal party was given a ticket to the United States. It was a memorable fling. And so it should have been. According to those I spoke to, the bill was over a million dollars. Oyugi had made it quite clear he was one of the most powerful men in the country.

Corruption was also Moi's way of winning political fealty. He sanctioned corruption when he wanted to reward just as he allowed public accountability to come to the fore when he wished to discredit. The Oyugi wedding, which took place one year after security forces had shot into the crowd at the prodemocracy rally, was bad timing. Donors had finally lost patience with the blatant profligacy of some of the higher placed members of the administration. They were tired of watching aid flows being diverted into ministerial pockets.

Moi's track record was already dodgy. First there had been human rights abuse. Then his refusal to introduce genuine democracy. It was time to give the president another nudge in the direction of responsible governance.

The United States had reacted to the 1990 arrests of government critics by suspending a delivery of military equipment worth eleven million dollars. Six million dollars were reinstated some months later, ostensibly because of a marginal improvement in human rights performance. In reality, it was because Moi had offered a helping hand during two crises. He had allowed Kenya to be used as a staging post for rescuing Westerners from the heavy fighting that had surrounded the ousting of former president Siad Barre in Somalia. He had also bailed out a CIA covert operation. A Libyan-backed coup in Chad had left 600 Libyan dissidents who were based there in limbo. The United States had been arming and training them to subvert Gaddafi, but since their 'outing' they had become an embarrassment. Moi said he would take the fighters.

Proof that donors were in a position to hobble the administration's strong-arm tactics came during the first half of 1991. While Congress was debating the conditions for aid to Kenya in fiscal 1992, Matiba and Rubia were released from detention. That October, Muite, by then chairman of the Kenyan Law Society, and six other lawyers from the society's executive committee were fined for breaking a court injunction on making political statements. Things were looking up. A year earlier, they probably would have received jail sentences.

Led by the United States, donors were establishing a linkage between good behaviour and Kenya's heavy dependence on aid. The bottom line was: if you don't clean up your act, you don't get the money. According to the *Economist Intelligence Unit*, in 1979 concessionary funding accounted for thirty-five per cent of the development budget. In 1990, aid underwrote nearly ninety per cent. But by 1991, concessionary assistance, which had been running at around one billion dollars a year, had shrunk by nearly a fifth. Donors were angry because so much of it was disappearing into private bank accounts. The World Bank suspended negotiations for a hundred and fifty million dollar loan to the energy sector. The Danish government, one of Kenya's largest donors, terminated its rural development programme after an audit showed that almost all of its forty million dollars in aid had disappeared without trace. Norway stopped its aid programme of thirty million dollars a year following arguments over human rights.

The consequences of unstinting corruption were far from obvious to those Kenyans who abused the system. They viewed state contracts as a source of personal enrichment rather than a way to improve the country. If money for development projects couldn't be skimmed off, it no longer served a purpose. Politicians failed to comprehend that unbridled greed might one day spell an end to their careers. The lesson was brought home to them with the downfall of Nicholas Biwott.

If Hezekiah Oyugi was Moi's lieutenant, then Biwott was his alter ego. He had been the president's business partner for over fifteen years and was his closest friend. Oyugi, a Luo from Western Kenya, was a newcomer whom Moi had only appointed to head internal security in 1988. Biwott had been around for years and, like Moi, was Kalenjin. He was family.

As energy minister, Biwott was in charge of a high-spending sector of the economy. He controlled oil purchases, oil exploration, the construction of hydroelectric dams and the installation of electricity grids. He had also supervised the award of the Turkwel hydroelectric contract which I had written about in the *Financial Times*. Biwott was a shrewd businessman so he turned his position to his advantage in numerous ways. He invested in petroleum distribution, banks and finance houses, insurance, construction, aviation and property. Cover for the Turkwel dam was moved over to his own insurance company. Cheap crude imported through the state-owned National Oil Corporation was sold almost exclusively to his two oil marketing companies, Kenol and Kobil. And so it went. Official and private interests became vertically integrated.

Biwott also took kickbacks on the projects that landed on his desk. They were reputed to be upwards of ten per cent. Biwott's monthly salary was $750. According to the British High Commission, he had hundreds of millions of dollars in foreign bank accounts. He was known as the Godfather.

Biwott had the right attributes for a political heavyweight. He was ruthless, greedy and feared. He was also Moi's longtime ally. During the 1970s, when Moi was vice president and home affairs minister, Biwott was an undersecretary and his personal assistant. As members of the minority Kalenjin tribe, both men were subjected to petty discrimination from the predominantly Kikuyu administration. One way in which this was practised was that the Kikuyu civil servants refused to prepare Moi's speeches. In those days, Moi penned a rough-cut version of English that wasn't up to speech writing. So Biwott used to burn the midnight oil in his office doing it for him.

Biwott was rewarded for his friendship. As soon as Moi became president, he gave him an uncontested seat in parliament. Biwott soon became the most influential member of the kitchen cabinet. He prospered on it. He also looked out for Moi and made sure he got his percentage too.

The International Monetary Fund and donors were keen to see his excesses curbed. The World Bank had cancelled their proposed energy programme because they were convinced that with Biwott in charge the accounts would be fiddled. For years the political machinery had been greased with nepotism (in the form of tribalism), bribes, election-rigging and heavy-handed (and often unconstitutional) discipline. Now unwanted outside interference was making it judder.

The United States had particular reason to be riled by Biwott because of the way he manhandled US commercial interests. In fact, embassy personnel were so angry that in October they leaked a story about Biwott's thuggish practices to *The New York Times*. It ran on the front page. The previous June, Biwott had brought a high court injunction against Citibank to prevent their collection of fourteen million dollars in loans owed by the minister's companies. Most of the loans were secured against his Swiss deposits. When the US Embassy lodged an official complaint over this behaviour, the injunction was lifted. Five years earlier, ministers intimidated the business community with impunity. Now the donors were using their influence to curb the chicanery of the KANU elite. It was an encouraging sign. Still, it was a chilling episode. Citibank's managing director Terry Davidson left the country after he received a death threat from one of Biwott's employees.

The real political scandal, however, was being played out in the Kisumu Town Hall on the shores of Lake Victoria. In February of the previous year, Robert Ouko, the foreign minister, had been abducted and brutally murdered. Scotland Yard had been called in to investigate following suggestions of government involvement in the minister's death. The report was never made public but in the subsequent judicial commission of enquiry, Ouko's sister, Dorothy Randiak, implicated Biwott. She alleged he had received a bribe of over three million dollars from Asea Brown Bovery. The Italian company was hoping to supply electrical equipment to a molasses plant in Ouko's constituency. Randiak quoted her brother as having said before his death, 'Talking about corruption is like talking against Biwott.'

Ouko had a reputation for being a nice guy. A stint at the United Nations as Kenya's ambassador had sharpened up his sartorial image and boosted his self confidence. He looked good and had a charming manner. He made a superb envoy, which was not always the case with Moi's men. Many of them had beer in their bellies and hayseeds in their hair.

Ouko was a popular man respected by the public and adulated by his constituents. His death had shocked Kenyans. As the enquiry dragged on, he emerged in the press as a knight in shining armour whose crusade against corruption had ended tragically. Not so. Ouko, too, was greedy for power and money. But he wasn't ruthless enough. He might have survived if it had not been for his soft underbelly of decency and for a chance series of events.

According to club rules, ministers took kickbacks from commercial deals and development projects that fell within the sphere of their ministry or their constituency. It was all right to be seen to be associated with contractors and suppliers because Kenyan officials were allowed to engage in private business. It was thought this would help to broaden the middle class. There was little foraging to be done in the foreign ministry, however, where Ouko's work consisted mainly of diplomacy. So he was delighted when a two hundred million dollar deal to resuscitate a molasses factory and construct a cement factory, both in his constituency, was offered.

The only problem was, Biwott wanted the deal for himself so he tried to obstruct Ouko. The contracts were supposed to be financed by Italian concessionary funds. Biwott pointed out that the sum involved was more than the entire Italian aid programme for the previous three years. It couldn't be done, he said. The subject was brought up at a cabinet meeting where Moi overruled Biwott. Let Bob have his share, he said. Ouko had won the first round, but the battle for commercial turf turned the two men into sworn enemies.

This was to be Ouko's nemesis in the scenario that then unfolded. Moi had been suffering from an undisclosed illness for several years and regularly went abroad for check-ups. Towards the end of 1989, he visited his favourite German clinic for some routine tests. By mistake, the medical report was sent to Moi via the Kenyan foreign office instead of through Biwott. It landed on Ouko's desk. He had no choice but to hand it over personally to the president.

In the paranoid world of Kenyan politics, the state of Moi's health was considered highly confidential information. To attempt to get access to it smacked of treason. Ouko now had an inside track on the presidential longevity. Biwott was chagrined that his foe should be privy to the succession timetable. Moi's antennae were up too. What was Ouko scheming? Was he a pretender to the throne?

Next on the agenda was a private trip to the United States that included Moi, Biwott and Ouko. When in Washington, Moi made an eleventh hour request to see George Bush and was refused. Ouko, however, was called over the weekend to see Secretary of State James Baker. When he got there, Baker rang the White House. 'Hello, George, guess who I've got with me. Your old pal Bob.' Ouko and Bush were friends from the days when Bush was US Ambassador to the United Nations. Bush expressed a desire to see his old buddy again, so Ouko was whisked across to the White House. That did it. Moi was furious that Bush had given him the cold shoulder but rolled out the red carpet for his foreign minister. On his arrival in Nairobi, Ouko's passport was seized. It was now patently obvious to Moi that Ouko had ambitious and dangerous aspirations.

Ouko, who knew that he was in serious trouble, managed to get an audience with the president. When he turned up, he found Biwott was there and Hezekiah Oyugi, the head of security. It was to be an inquisition by the three most powerful men in the land. Ouko was an extremely worried man. He knew that events could go very badly for him indeed. There was a certain ritual surrounding presidential pardons. Ouko had seen them before and knew what to do – grovel. He dropped to his hands and knees and crawled across the floor. Then he prostrated himself in front of his chief, stammering his loyalty and begging forgiveness. At one point he broke down completely and wept. If Moi had wanted to exonerate him, he would have put a hand on his head and told him to rise. But instead he left the room. Some days later Ouko's body was found in a field by a herdsboy, charred almost beyond recognition and with a bullet wound in the head.

Bear with me as we penetrate further into the Byzantine maze of political thought for the story didn't end there, as Moi's other trusted confidant, Oyugi had been orchestrating the commission of enquiry into Ouko's murder. His brief was to drag it out for as long as possible, so that justice was seen to be done, without actually nailing anyone. Things went according to plan until witnesses (by the end of the first year there had been 168) started giving evidence concerning Biwott's miscreancy with aid money. Was Oyugi trying to set up Moi's friend as the fall guy? After all, the two competed for the commercial deals that delivered their kickbacks and bribes. They distrusted each other.

The economic recession had made competition particularly vicious of late. There weren't as many spoils to go round now that the IMF had imposed a hundred million dollar ceiling on commercial borrowings for 1991. As a result, two juicy deals had fallen by the wayside. One concerned the lease of four new Boeing 757s from the Australian airline Ansett to modernise the Kenya Airways fleet. The forty million dollar contract had been brokered by the British business tycoon Tiny Rowland. The second was a multi-million dollar scheme to supply ID cards to all Kenyan adults. Rowland had been working on this with Oyugi. Rowland had holdings worth $2.7 billion in Africa through his Lonrho conglomerate and was accustomed to favoured status. He was disappointed when both deals were axed while the molasses plant (slashed to fifty-seven million dollars) went ahead. The molasses contract, won by Arkell of Baton Rouge, Louisiana, was fronted by the Indian businessman Ketan Somaia. This was rubbing salt into the wound because Somaia had formerly been Oyugi's business partner on commercial contracts.

Oyugi sat tight while Biwott's name surfaced in an increasingly controversial manner in the Ouko enquiry. Was Oyugi manoeuvring Biwott's demise as well? Worse, did he, too, have unseemly aspirations just as Ouko had? Moi had heard rumours that Oyugi was planning to retire from the civil service and run for election. He also knew he had his eyes on the vice presidency. He could trust Biwott, the donors' *bête noire*, but could he trust anyone else? With all the bad blood flowing, the night of the long knives was inevitable.

In October, Moi suddenly shuffled some of the key administration posts. Biwott was taken out of energy and given the far less lucrative industry portfolio. Oyugi was sacked from the civil service and made chairman of General Motors, a car assembly venture in which the government held majority equity. Biwott had had his wings clipped. Oyugi had been put in a cage. The former security chief was merely a convenience, but it must have hurt Moi to demote his good friend Nick, whose tinder-dry career was about to be consumed in flames. Observers said that Biwott and Oyugi had been demoted as punishment for embezzling state money. But that wasn't really it at all. It had much more to do with the paranoia to which African leaders so often succumb and the fact that the donors had begun to twist Moi's balls. Biwott's ruin took a month. At the beginning of November a letter was read at the Ouko inquiry in which Biwott was quoted as demanding a ten per cent commission for Moi from the molasses factory rehabilitation 'since I take care of the President's affairs'. The letter, from the Swiss consultants BAK, also accused ministers of demanding nearly a third of the project cost in bribes in return for contracts. The public knew this sort of thing happened, but they were surprised by the extent of the greed.

That was one of the weeks when John Troon was on the stand. Troon was retired but had led the Ouko murder investigation when he was still a detective with Scotland Yard. During his testimony he named Biwott and Oyugi as principal suspects in the murder of Ouko. It is most probable that Troon had Whitehall approval before he said this. If so, it meant that the British, too, were squeezing Moi. The following day Biwott was sacked. A week later he and Oyugi were arrested along with Jonah Anguka, a senior civil servant. Ouko had last been seen alive when he was collected from his home by Anguka and three others. Biwott and Oyugi were later released. Anguka, the fall guy, was charged with Ouko's murder.

Moi disbanded the enquiry to allow criminal investigations to proceed. The timing was tardy, however. Donors were meeting that same day in Paris to discuss Kenya. They announced they would suspend Kenya's 1992 aid allocation pending political and economic reform.

The following week, bemused KANU delegates summoned to a special congress were cut short in their ritual excoriation of political pluralism and told to extol it instead. Moi had decided to lift the ban on formal political opposition. Four days later the first opposition party was registered. It was called FORD (Forum for the Restoration of Democracy). Its members included Matiba and Rubia and the lawyer Paula Muite, who had emerged as a high-profile activist. A month earlier, Moi had stated categorically that he did not envisage the introduction of multiparty democracy until the turn of the century.

A year and a half had elapsed since the detentions of Matiba and Rubia. Now the two former ministers were legally recognised opposition and potential future government leaders. The Kenyans who risked their lives for democracy could not have achieved their ends without some help from their friends. Moral coercion from the donors, it seemed, worked.

The local media covered events in salacious detail. They were accustomed to glorifying their leaders, not exposing corruption. Times had certainly changed from the period, four years earlier, when I had stood trial for currency smuggling. Before the democracy debate, state coercion and abuse of power had always been reported in shorthand. It was a survival mechanism that distanced readers from the truth and kept reporters out of jail.

Working as a reporter in Africa is arguably more hazardous than a lot of other places in the world because of the tendency to shoot the bearer of bad tidings. At least forty-eight journalists in black Africa were either killed, arrested, sentenced to jail terms or physically attacked during a six-month period in 1991 as a result of what they had written, according to International PEN. Another twenty-one were already in detention. On top of this, seven newspapers were closed by the government. The majority of newspapers are owned by the state or the ruling party. Only fifteen black African states, Kenya amongst them, allow independent newspapers.

Meanwhile, the foreign press, with its mixture of cynicism, dedication, idealism and disillusionment, bears the brunt of the fourth estate's responsibility to forestall the demise of reason by exposing its abuses. If we adhere to the maxim that today's news wraps tomorrow's fish and chips, then the pain involved in being a purveyor of the truth is pointless. But if, as I believe, the exposure of corruption and tyranny brings hope to those who have been tortured and victimised and to those who stand in danger of receiving the same kind of treatment, then it is worthwhile.

Having witnessed the distortion of justice first hand, I was well placed to write about it. It was the classic foreign correspondent's dilemma. Where do you draw the line between fulfilling your job as a reporter and heeding your own safety? If you come across a sensitive political story, do you ignore it or follow it up? When you challenge the party line, as I am doing yet again by writing this, is the brief moment of public enlightenment equal to the protracted sadness of being parted from home and friends? The personal stakes were high. I knew that if I wrote the story, it would jeopardise my future in Kenya, which had been my home for twenty-two years. On the other hand, I had a thick address book of contacts, and I cared what happened to Kenyans. So one morning I slipped a sheet of paper into the typewriter and wrote. I guess I thought I could talk my way out of trouble if necessary, as I usually did.

The article appeared in *The Sunday Times* in May 1988, when I was in London. It charged that executive manipulation of the judiciary was at the heart of the human rights crisis. The judicial system had been corrupted to curb government opposition (as well as the rising crime rate) and to flesh out paltry salaries. The appointment of Cecil Miller, a West Indian, as chief justice had amputated the judiciary's independence and sutured what remained to Moi's executive powers.

Miller, in his seventies, was an eccentric alcoholic who died of liver failure some months afterwards. He was known as Biggles for his habit of weaving references to his RAF wartime experiences into his judgments. It was commonly known that he liked to sing in chambers and make love to his secretary between hearings. Once he began to strip off his clothes in the law courts car park and had to be forcibly restrained. He was an unusual chief justice in many ways.

There was one other vital inclusion, as far as my future was concerned at any rate. I quoted a lawyer who compared Moi's rule unfavourably with that of his predecessor, Jomo Kenyatta. He said Moi was the weaker man.

All this was well known to Kenyans, but it had never before been presented in print, and in a major British newspaper at that. This banal story, as far as Sunday readers in Britain were concerned, was read with relish in Kenya. That particular issue of *The Sunday Times* was confiscated on arrival at the airport, a routine method of dealing with contentious articles. In an equally routine manner, copies were smuggled off the planes by airport cleaners, xeroxed and sold clandestinely in town.

The story did nothing to halt the demise of justice, of course. In 1988, yet another constraint was placed on the legal profession when lawyers were required to obtain an annual licence under the Trade Licensing Act before they could practise. That year, security of tenure for judges was withdrawn in a constitutional amendment. The public outcry was such that it was reinstated in 1990. My nemesis, Joseph Mango, the chief magistrate, was appointed to sit in the high court. Sensitive cases, which included debt cases against state-owned enterprises, continued to be heard by compliant judges and magistrates who could be relied upon to make a ruling in accordance with the administration's expectations.

Even the expatriate British judges, whose local salaries were supplemented by the Overseas Development Administration, were excoriated for their biased performance. Critics said they were just as susceptible to outside influence as Kenyan judges because they had neither security of tenure nor allegiance to the country they served.

Dereck Schofield, a High Court judge, refused to renew his contract after Cecil Miller, still the chief justice, removed him from a case where he had ordered a prisoner to be brought to court following a *habeas corpus* suit filed by the detainee's wife. 'I cannot operate in a system where the law is so blatantly contravened by those who are supposed to be its supreme guardians,' he explained.

The April 1990 issue of the *New Law Journal*, a British publication, said, '. . . two British judges in Kenya, Justices Dugdale and Porter, have played a major role in facilitating censorship and human rights abuses. Dugdale, in particular, will always be remembered by Kenyan human rights lawyers for audaciously ruling in July 1989 that the courts in Kenya have no power to enforce the Kenyan Bill of Rights.'

The Sunday Times story proved to be a watershed in my life. When Salman Rushdie's ill-starred *Satanic Verses* later caused an international furore, I saw a parallel in our situations. Although the consequences of my actions in no way approximated to Rushdie's, I think he would not have responded very differently to the question, 'Did you know what you were doing?'

Sort of. I knew that writing about the judiciary would make Moi angry. But if I could have foreseen the damage, I would have negotiated the minefield of presidential sensitivity with far more care. As it was, discretion was abandoned for boldness or, as most would have it, stupidity eclipsed reason. It wasn't long before the government broadside reached London.

It was a crisp spring day. The bus rolled past banks of daffodils and the Albert Memorial, which sparkled in the sunshine. I sat on the upper deck, idly flicking through the latest issue of the *Weekly Review*, Kenya's brave imitation of *Time* magazine. Then I saw the centre-page spread. 'Fitzgerald is in the news again . . .'. What did these two pages of dense print have to do with me? That Fitzgerald, depicted as a 'convicted criminal', had nothing to do with this dull creature who was heading back to the flat to do the ironing.

Soon afterwards a sheaf of newspaper cuttings arrived through the post. There was no accompanying letter. Even my European friends were wary of being associated with me now. I learnt that I had been vilified in parliament by the then vice president, Josephat Karanja, a man I used to joke with at parties. I was a convicted criminal who had launched a scathing and unwarranted attack on Kenya, he declared. Burudi Nabwera, a minister of state in the office of the president, put in his penny's worth as well. Kenya would have to reconsider its relationship with Britain unless her press stopped denouncing Kenya, he said. Robert Ouko, at that time still the foreign minister, had appeared on television and implied I had been writing subversive speeches for government opponents.

It fell to Sally Kosgei, Kenya's charming High Commissioner, to voice official indignation in London. 'You're giving me an awful lot of headaches, Mary Anne,' the letters editor said one day when I was down at the *Sunday Times* office. 'This woman has been bombarding me with correspondence. She says we shouldn't believe what you report because you have a criminal record.'

It was customary in Kenya to discredit bothersome individuals by calling them 'rumour-mongers' (who wanted to destabilise the regime) or 'puppets in the pay of foreign masters' (who wanted to overthrow it) or implying they were of unsound moral character. This sort of rhetoric, however, was comic rather than compelling when aired before hardnosed British journalists. My colleagues simply thought I was a brave but unprofessional operator.

'It's okay, everyone,' quipped Peter Godwin, the paper's South Africa correspondent, as I stood up to leave that evening. 'Your wallets are safe now. She's going.'

It wasn't a laughing matter, though. The uproar meant I couldn't go home. Sometimes I stayed awake at night thinking about Moi, a man I had never met. Had he lain in a mahogany bed, his fingers on the counterpane, plotting his revenge? No one likes to be ridiculed. Particularly, if you are an African male, by a woman reporter. Had vindictive thoughts gathered like fly specks in those minutes when sleep evaded him? Or was his a swift and impersonal rancour learnt from ancient tribal chiefs who exercised royal privilege through the murder of hundreds of slaves?

I decided to test the water that December. A discreet enquiry had established my name wasn't amongst those posted at the airport as 'prohibited immigrants'. So Tara, Petra and I flew into Nairobi twelve days before Christmas. The potholes in the roads seemed larger and violent crime dominated the news more than it had done. Otherwise nothing had changed.

I left my suitcase at the house and got straight back into the car. The most unsettling aspect of being away had been the separation from friends. I needed to be amongst 'the family' to know I had truly returned. Over the years I had formed close friendships with Kenyans in a number of communities – the slums, the military, Maasai and Samburu nomads struggling to come to terms with the amorphous society of post-independent Kenya. My life gradually became inextricably entwined with theirs. I gave them support and friendship. They gave me much more. They taught me how to survive with grace and fortitude. Count your blessings in the small, momentary victories that bring you to another day. Next week is in the lap of the gods.

It was the season after the short rains. The sky danced with colour and enamel clouds towered above the Ngong Hills as I drove towards the lip of the Rift Valley. Because she had no telephone, she did not know I was coming. But she was there, standing outside her new stone house. Her earrings tinkled as she shook her head from side to side. 'Merienna. Merienna.' We kissed on the lips, as was her manner of greeting, mingling arms wordlessly, holding tight. '*Umerudi.*' You are back. Women do not show their tears, so for a long time we held hands and watched the giraffe browsing the thorn bushes on the plain below. Then we hefted plastic *debes* on to our backs and set off to collect water. There was work to be done.

Kipenget. Maasai matriarch, my sister, my friend. She is an ordinary Kenyan, one of millions who, according to United Nations figures, can expect to live to sixty and be valued in terms of gross national product at $370 a year. But the figures don't tally with the facts.

I first met her on a dark evening in her tiny mud hut on the slopes of a bald hill. She stoked the fire that was brewing sweet, milky tea and we talked in the easy, age-old morse code of women. Most of her thirteen children lived in this tiny hovel with her, enfolded in poverty, but it was a welcoming place.

Fifteen miles away the lights of Nairobi lit up the sky but an unbridgeable chasm existed between the capital and her *shamba*. There was no electricity to defy the dusk, no medicine to soothe her children's bronchial coughs, no legal recourse to ease life's many injustices.

Every Tuesday Kipenget caught a dilapidated taxi to sell the bead bracelets she made for a meagre two dollars each to curio shops. Then she came to visit me, her approach down the corridor heralded by the jingle of tin discs and arrow-heads. Most weekends I would sit with her outside her hut, sharing jokes and sorrows as hawks wheeled overhead. Over the years she aired a litany of woes, many of them engineered by her tyrannical husband Kili.

She met each drama with fortitude and humour – the days when she or her daughters were savagely beaten by Kili; his marriage to a second, younger wife; the droughts and hunger; the advent of yet more unplanned children; Miriape's traumatic encounter with sodomy; my fruitless attempts to seek recourse through the police; the night thieves used boulders to break into the house and she chased them off with a *panga*, running through the darkness like a frenzied banshee.

I gave Kipenget money for food and school fees; financed the purchase of cows after a drought; bought her fencing material so she could protect her crops from wild animals. For years a battle had raged over the twenty acres of waterless hillside, which Kili wanted to sell. Kipenget bribed the chiefs with goats and beer, and I sought the advice of a lawyer. We both learned that a woman had little standing in the eyes of Kenyan authority. The test of wills had yet to be resolved, but Kipenget was winning, for she was still on her land.

Kipenget will never be lifted out of her trough of poverty, a fact she came to terms with long before I did. I loved her then, for her frailty and courage, and love her still. But I never saw her again because they came for me a few days later.

The phone rang in the office. It was Petra. 'Hello, Petal, how're you doing?'

The determined brightness of her voice triggered the alarm before the words registered. 'Mummy, there are some men in the driveway. They've been asking for you. I'm next door at the Glenns'. Do you want to ring me back on another phone?'

When the girls were still children, I enjoined them to note what they saw. 'Don't look at the obvious. Observe the details,' I said as we drove to town to go shopping. They learnt to recognise the battalion of an army truck from the licence plates; the location of Special Branch above a Persian carpet shop by the cluster of antennae on the roof. It was a lesson in urban awareness just as

Maasai herdboys were taught to decipher the presence of lion from the warning bark of a zebra. As they were never tested by crisis, I sometimes wondered if my pseudo-CIA rantings were an eccentric waste of time.

Petra, now fifteen, knew the home and office phones were tapped and was signalling in code. I phoned her back ten minutes later. She filled me in on what had taken place. 'There were five men in the car. It had ordinary licence plates. They wore suits and ties. I didn't see their socks. (Special Branch had a penchant for brown or red.) One of them had a walkie talkie. They wouldn't give me their names. I said you might have gone to town, but I didn't know when you'd be back. They're parked at the end of the road.'

A+ Petra, I thought with pride. Top marks, too, for Tara, seventeen, who took the news in her stride when I telephoned her at a friend's house. 'Stay where you are tonight. I'm not going home. I'll keep in touch on the phone.'

Peter, my Maasai foster son, was with me. He had entered our lives when the headmaster of the primary school below Kipenget's *shamba* pushed forward a knobbly-kneed little boy and said with Dickensian primness, 'This boy is an orphan. Can you look after him?'

Peter was fired with gallantry. It was the time when he was writing a detective novel of the Sam Spade genre in a school notebook. 'I'll save you. I know a cave in the plains where you can hide. I'll bring you food and we'll all have Christmas together. You can stay there for months. No one will find you.' Cells. Caves. I liked the womblike comfort of my own bed. What was happening to my life?

We spent the night at a friend's house. The next day the excitement reached a new pitch. Plainclothesmen were combing my haunts and frightening the neighbours with their persistent questions as to my whereabouts. They had tried to search my office and had been turned away by Jim Malone, the Voice of America correspondent. Frank Kwinga, the chief immigration officer, had phoned Mike Eldon on his unlisted number to ask where I was. I was rebuffed by the British High Commission, who told me not to fuss and go home. It was only a routine enquiry, they said. As we drove around town, Peter read his book to me. His descriptions of cops, guns and car chases provided an eerie parallel to our own circumstances.

Wherever we went, I was conscious of being as welcome as a leopard in a goat pen. The European community had shown support during my criminal peccadillo, but political delinquency was a different matter. Witch-hunts unnerved them.

Worst of all, Petra was still being harassed as plainclothesmen tailed her around the neighbourhood, asking her again and again where her mother was. Kind friends had moved her to three different houses, hiding her on the floor of the car as they drove past the unmarked vehicles staked out on the road. Thoughts of escaping to Tanzania in a dhow or *matatu* (local taxi) evaporated. I asked the High Commission to pass on a message to Kwinga: expect a visitor.

He had a reputation for brusqueness before supplicants. That afternoon, however, he sailed across his spacious office with pin-striped arms outstretched as if to embrace me. With expulsion a foregone conclusion, I was dispassionate. There was nothing I could do to alter my situation. It was Kwinga, still enmeshed in the system, who displayed anxiety. For a moment, I thought he was going to plant a kiss on my cheek, so great was his relief to see me. His future had been reprieved.

'Where have you been? We've been looking all over for you,' he said somewhat peevishly as if I was his errant wife. He indicated I should be seated in one of the government-issue wooden armchairs and, balancing an open file on his upturned palms, gave me a stern stare over the neatly pinned turban of Mr Sehmi, his Indian deputy. My file was as thick as the New York telephone directory. I wondered what they could have found to put in it.

'Do you know who wrote the story that appeared in *The Sunday Times* last May?' Kwinga intoned.

'I wrote it.'

The confession extracted, Kwinga sat down. The rest of the interview transpired in an atmosphere of such friendly informality we might have been seated round the kitchen table mulling over a family problem. It was the first time I had conducted business with government officials as an equal.

'You will be driven from here straight to the airport where we will put you on the next flight to London.'

'That's not fair. You've got to give me a day to sort out things at the house.' The two men nodded in agreement. 'Also, I know you're accustomed to deporting people to England, but I don't want to go there.'

They looked surprised. 'Why don't you go to South Africa then? You've got family there,' Kwinga offered. It was my turn to be taken aback. The land of apartheid had yet to emerge from the diplomatic wilderness. Kenyan residents were forbidden to travel there. Of course, I no longer resided in Kenya.

Where *did* I live? Adopting a new country on the spur of the moment was a challenge. 'No. Not South Africa. I don't like it there either. I think I'll go to West Africa.'

'Why West Africa?' exclaimed Sehmi. More than twenty years after independence had blossomed across the continent, transport still travelled a north-south axis, adhering to routes established in colonial times. Kenyans were more familiar with anglophone South Africa than francophone West Africa, which was most easily reached via Paris.

Suddenly West Africa appeared foreign and distant to me, too. 'I tell you what. I'll drive to Tanzania. But first I want your assurance that no harm will come to my daughters and that you'll allow my possessions to be shipped out of the country once I've found somewhere to live.' Kwinga gave me his word and shook my hand warmly as I left.

The girls received the news of my imminent departure with impressive stoicism. Tara said she would stay behind to pack up the house. Petra decided to come with me. For Peter and the other children I looked after – Chege, his little sister Peris, Godfrey – there was no choice. They would have to stay behind.

Having lost everything, I had no immediate worries. There was nothing left to lose. So the next twenty-four hours were contained in a pocket of sharply etched calm. I saw no point in cancelling the friends I had invited for that evening. Jengo the cook served the meal just as he had done for over a decade. We talked of the guests' news, not mine.

After they had departed and the girls had gone to bed, I began sorting books, letters, photos and ornaments into piles for Tara to pack, give away or toss out. There were a lot of possessions to rummage through after seventeen years. My husband Anthony and I had come to this place on the edge of the Rift Valley soon after we were married. We had cut down the virgin bush and built a breathtakingly beautiful A-frame house that stood on the shoulder of a ridge. The view from the verandah swept for 130 miles across the Athi Plains. On a clear day you could see the silvery peak of Mount Kilimanjaro in Tanzania. But if I was to look back on the morrow from the foot of this mountain, I knew I would not be able to discern the house's steeply angled roof jutting up through the eucalyptus trees.

By three o'clock I was exhausted. I went downstairs and looked in on the girls. Tara was sleeping peacefully in the cluttered bedroom that had been hers since she was a baby. The task demanded of her was an adult one, but I knew she would manage it, cheerfully trotting her common sense to the fore. Petra had already packed for the journey, a brave gesture. She lay tidily in bed with her old school satchel and a sleeping bag neatly arranged at her feet. In the past they had accepted the vagaries of my Bohemian life with equanimity. But what effect would this sudden upheaval have on them? My heart contracted under the burden of other people's lacerated lives. Were principles worth uprooting the children like this? There was no point in addressing that question yet. There would be time enough for torment.

I sat by my bedside telephone and dialled the number of Mirella Ricciardi, a Kenyan-born photographer whose own adventurous life had generated a kinship between us. Mirella was like a big sister.

'Mirells, they've got me. I have to leave tomorrow.'

There was an intake of breath at the other end of the line. 'Well, darling, you know, life's a safari. One day you're cruising over the plains.

The next you're bogged down in a river in flood and covered with mud.' She gave a rich chuckle. 'We're survivors, you and I. You'll be scaling mountains again soon.'

The next morning I returned to immigration. The widely disliked Sehmi handed me my deportation order. 'It is my duty to inform you that as a prohibited immigrant, it is a criminal offence to enter Kenya. We still have a treaty with Uganda and Tanzania which means you are *persona non grata* in those countries as well. I'll be phoning Namanga [the border post] to check you've left. Once you get to Tanzania, that's your lookout.' A scant movement made the sheet of pink paper, which he still held between thumb and forefinger, tremble. 'You know, sometimes we are instructed to do things we don't want to do. I'm sorry.'

In the privacy of his office, Kwinga briefly removed his mask of officialdom, too. 'Mary Anne, there are many ways of saying things. Why did you do it this way?' I sensed genuine concern.

'It had to be said,' I replied and later regretted my pomposity.

I ate lunch with Angela and Carol, longtime friends and neighbours whom I had not seen since my return. When I told them Petra and I didn't know where we would be sleeping that night, Angela insisted we stay at her husband's safari headquarters on a coffee farm about fifty miles from the border. She drew a few lines and two Xs on a piece of paper and handed it to me. 'Go down the Arusha road until you come to a Total petrol station (little X). Turn right and follow the road a few miles until you see the sign (big X) in the coffee bushes.'

By the time I returned to the house, most of the family had gathered. They had come for Christmas, to celebrate our return, not to mourn our departure. Having learnt what had happened, their faces were slack with dismay. Miriape, Kipenget's eldest son, was there, talking to Peter. So was Chege, the slum child of a prostitute and alcoholic thief who, for as long as he could remember, had parented his younger brothers and sister Peris. Godfrey had come on the train from Kisumu. Gabriel had driven down from Samburu District. He had foreseen this scene the previous night, dreaming the house stood empty. Gabriel possessed a great strength that made us feel safe in his presence, but for once he was helpless. Frustration darkened his face.

Afterwards, they stayed on to comfort Tara. Gabriel packed her possessions into two boxes and labelled them 'Tara's World'. Esta, the gardener, washed the car until she could no longer pretend it was an ordinary day and proceeded to get monumentally drunk. Peter, who was inconsolable, went for a bicycle ride and returned covered in mud. 'My mind went blank and I fell into a puddle. I feel awful,' he said.

In the evening Sintahui, the *askari* (nightguard), joined everyone in the living room to eat *posho* (the maizemeal that is the Kenyan's staple food) and stew by candlelight. When Tara lit a cigarette, Jengo and Sintahui rounded on her. 'You're not to smoke just because you're upset!' they scolded.

'I was very happy then,' Tara said later. 'I felt strong because there wasn't time to be self-indulgent. It made me look at my priorities, and I learned who and what was important to me. I felt really responsible for lots of people.'

But this was yet to come. Right now the neighbourhood wives were emptying drawers into suitcases which one day would join us somewhere. My airline bag, sleeping bag and typewriter stood in the hall. I judiciously added a bottle of whisky to the travelling gear.

'Shall I pack these, M.A.?'

'What about this?'

'Just throw everything in. I don't care.' When you must leave a place you love deeply, it is best to make the farewell a quick one. I had left already for it had become too painful to stay.

Julian Ozanne walked through the front door. He had moved to Nairobi a few months earlier to work as regional correspondent for the *Financial Times*. That had once been my job. Just as this house had once been my home. We had met for the first time two days earlier in the office that had once been my office. He was the only person who had offered to drive us across the border. 'It's three o'clock. We've got to get going,' he said.

They lined up outside the front door, standing in the dust beneath the kai apple hedge. Miriape, Gabriel, Peter, Chege, Godfrey, Jengo. My sister Esta. Sintahui who had carried his spear round the periphery of the garden for thousands of nights. Russi, his plump, contented wife. My family. The neighbours. Their servants. My friends.

'Take care, M.A.'

'My heart is heavy. My mother is leaving.'

'*Kwaheri*, memsahib.'

'What will we do when you are gone?'

'*Safiri salama.*'

'*Kwaheri.*'

'Goodbye.'

'I love you.'

'Can someone please ask Mr. Patel to cancel the Christmas turkey?'

The cinnamon-cheeked bee-eaters looked down from the telephone wire as the car passed the cactuses in the rock garden, nudged round the bush where wild roses bloomed, distanced itself from the tadpole pond where the children used to wade, slipped through the shadow cast by the casuarina at the end of the driveway and grunted into third gear on the tarmac road. I didn't look back.

2

The Nomads

Mara Itolimu etalaki amu Itoningo. (There are always those who give advice. The problem is finding anyone to listen to it.)

Samburu proverb

'Don't put sheets on the bed. He'll get ochre all over them,' was Michael's parting shot. James Leadismo was spending the night.

The guest ignored this remark. He had a knack for editing life around him to conform with his own vision of reality, which was a Samburu adaptation of *Raiders of the Lost Ark*. He sat carelessly on the sofa, smiling with confident pleasure. Placed on a cushion beside him was his travelling gear, a pink sock that was securely knotted above a bulge the size of a cricket ball. It was a European thing that had been adapted to another purpose. Warriors used socks to carry their money in.

'What time will we start tomorrow? We should leave early. It will be a long safari,' he said. When he spoke, it was with small tosses of the chin to emphasise the luxurious length of his hair. It slithered down his back to the beaded belt at his waist, confined in hundreds of delicate braids. They were coated in fat and mirrored the bright swords of sunlight that fell through the window.

Leadismo took greedy delight in his decorations – the slivers of ivory that arced from his ears, the beads heaped on to his naked limbs and torso. It would take him longer to assemble this finery when he got up tomorrow morning than it would for me to get dressed.

The tin ornaments on his arms and legs set off a carillon of thin tinkling as he leant forward to take the mug of tea offered. Delicate designs of blue

43

highlighted his cheekbones. This particular embellishment endowed our trip with a sense of occasion. Usually he painted his dusky brown skin with ochre, a red mineral ground to powder and mixed with animal fat.

I forget how Leadismo came into my life. He simply started being there, just as, some years later, he vanished again, embarked on another opportunistic scheme for bettering his lot. Invariably, the interest and money of a *mzungu* were intrinsic to his 'projects'. At some earlier stage he had gravitated to the tourist hotels at the coast where his exotic appearance and bold manner had endeared him to a string of German women on holiday. They had given Leadismo a lot of things my other Samburu friends didn't have: the chance to shed his naïveté, a Land Rover that was constantly in need of repair, several pairs of silk underpants and a French tickler. These latter acquisitions were discovered in the airline bag in which he kept his possessions by Kipenget's son Miriape. They did far more to elevate Leadismo's status in the eyes of the other boys than his broken-down vehicle ever did. The term had yet to be coined in those days of the mid-80s, but Leadismo was a toy boy.

Once he dropped by the office to announce that he was leaving that evening for Europe. He was, he said, going to a tourism fair with a Kenyan tour operator. When pressed for details, he became alarmingly vague. He couldn't remember the man's name. He had met him in a bar. He wasn't sure of the pay, but it would be good money. Neither was he clear about what the job entailed. As far as I could ascertain, it consisted simply of hanging around and looking wonderfully virile. I had to admit, he epitomised the foreigner's idea of a warrior. His scanty clothing – plastic sandals and cotton *shuka* wrapped about the waist – was eclipsed by the abundance of beads, ivory and chains. I asked if this man had supplied him with a warm overcoat. It was, after all, November. Leadismo said no and dismissed the idea that he might be cold. We spent the next hour buying him some blankets in the market. Leadismo thought I was being needlessly fussy.

Another time he flew to Germany to work for a baker. Again, he was as short on details of his terms of employment as he was long on conviction that this was the path to wealth. He wrote to say that he had a German girlfriend and that the baker had made him shave off his ochre-red locks.

The following morning we collected Lepias Lenairoshi. He, too, had forsaken his traditional environment in search of a better life, but it lacked the glamour and uncertainty on which Leadismo thrived. The security suited Lepias, however. He worked at Bomas of Kenya, a job he had held for about ten years. Bomas, set in the forest near my house, had been created by the government to preserve the art forms of the different tribes. Lepias' contribution to Kenyan culture was to take up his spear every afternoon and dance the hypnotic leaping dance of the Samburu.

Usually the huge amphitheatre was more or less empty. On the weekends, however, it was packed with families who had come to see their vanishing heritage brought to life. Bomas had been intended to attract the tourists with its coastal drummers, Luo drinking songs, and Wakamba acrobats. For some reason, the tour operators, who were still primarily European, shunned the place. I think it was too 'African' for them. They preferred to send their clients to a rival establishment at the foot of the Rift Valley. The view on the way down was stunning and the owners, a settler family originally from England, served up delicious teas.

Perhaps because commercial success eluded Bomas, I was its steadfast champion. At one point I had been responsible for its public relations. In 1975 I took thirty-five of the dancers on a tour of England. None of them had been outside Kenya before. The manager's mistaken faith in my ability to shepherd them safely around stemmed from my British origins and white skin. However, I was a stranger to England, too. I hardly knew London. On previous visits I had travelled like a mole, disappearing into the underground at one destination and popping up into the open air at another. I had no idea that Piccadilly Circus was next to Trafalgar Square. I had never walked from one to the other. I only knew how to travel on the underground. I was hardly better off than the dancers.

Somehow we muddled through. Lepias and his colleagues must have presented an unusual sight to the the officials at Heathrow, but they behaved as if our group, dazed by the novelty of everything they saw, were ordinary passengers. I soon came to recognise that this extreme politeness was their way of dealing with the unfamiliar. The English hid their shyness behind deference.

The men in the party had been given blue blazers and grey slacks to wear. It seemed they were to be detribalised and westernised while on the road. So Lepias did his best. He tucked his long braids into a shower cap and took the ivory plugs out of his ear-lobes so that he could loop them neatly over the tops of his ears. He dismantled his spear and packed it into an airline bag.

There were moments, of course, when modern technology confused us. When our bus delivered us to the BBC studios in Birmingham, the dancers tried to storm the glass entrance doors. We were rescued by the porter. 'You don't need to touch them, madam. They open automatically.' Such was the relief at having finally negotiated this hurdle that everyone was deaf to further assistance. Attempts to point the disoriented troupe in the direction of the cloakrooms went unheeded. They changed into their costumes behind the grand piano in reception while the porter calmly greeted the passing traffic: a comedian, a magician and a singer. 'Good morning, sir. How are we today, sir? This way, madam.'

I was by then consumed with anxiety, wondering if the spears would break the klieg lights. I needn't have worried. The dancers' performance was invariably a *tour de force*. 'Look at those tits, willya,' said one of the engineers with a loose grin.

For the most part, the dancers were treated with unction and a polite disregard for their flamboyant dress. There were exceptions though. I had arranged a photo opportunity for the press with the Samburu posing beside the Beefeaters at the Tower of London. I had no idea how to get there. Taxis seemed the only way. The first two I flagged down refused to take us. 'I'm not 'aving those bleedin' spears in 'ere. They'll go through the roof,' said one. The other eyed the men's glistening ochre bodies. 'Wot's all that red stuff for, then? It'll get all over my seats.'

The media appearances were a warm-up for the grand climax at the Royal Show, where the dancers had a daily slot in the arena in between the livestock classes. I had written a commentary for the announcer. 'This is extremely interesting. The way each dance has a different meaning. But I think I won't go into too much detail on this one. The, em, circumcision,' he told me.

Lepias behaved as he would at home. He drank a lot of milk and disappeared for hours in the cattle pens to admire the bulls. He had never seen such large ones. They made a far greater impression on him than Prince Charles, who visited the Kenyan stand.

Our last day in London was free for shopping. We went to a department store to buy green sheets. Lepias said he needed some new *shukas* to wear. The trip forged a friendship between us. We had learnt from our experiences in England. And we were both secretly relieved to be going home.

At Bomas, Lepias lived in the dancers' quarters, which were hidden from view from the amphitheatre. They consisted of two long concrete dormitory blocks. The walls were smudged with the soot of charcoal fires and fingerprints made by dirty hands. In the middle was a dirt courtyard that had turned to mud around the communal waterpoints. We stepped into the gloom of the passageway and called Lepias' name. He put his head round a door. '*Sopa! Kuja kula chai.*' (Hello! Come and drink tea.)

The room was a jumble of possessions. They were stacked in the corner, under the two beds, on top of the two beds. Cloths hanging from the ceiling partitioned the already small room into minuscule cubicles that afforded some privacy at night. During the day, they were thrown to one side. Priscilla was brewing milky tea on a small charcoal stove on the floor while breast-feeding a baby. I had mixed feelings towards Lepias' town wife. My objections to Priscilla were financial rather than moral. His first wife Nolotimy, who lived the year round in the family *manyatta* in Samburu District, was a good friend of mine. Lepias' Nairobi set-up ate up most of his monthly salary of thirty dollars. Nolotimy had four children to look after. Each time I visited her, she had sunk further into apathy while the children looked increasingly ragged.

I tackled the subject once again as we sucked on our tea. It was early in the morning for such weighty matters and indelicate to air them in front of wife number two. However, I felt that the smiling, compliant Priscilla should be made aware of Lepias' full obligations as a family man. His eyes slid towards me and away again, carrying with them the lie. 'I send her money. I don't know why she is complaining.'

Lepias was going home for his annual month's leave. 'Well, I hope you're bringing a lot of money and clothes and presents for Nolotimy and Goodman and Tipilet. They'll be very happy to see you.' The memory of Tipilet's bony body hugging my leg and Nolotimy's dull eyes made me reckless.

We talked in Swahili for, unlike Leadismo, Lepias knew no English. 'I bought them food and clothes at Ongata,' he said.

Lepias wore slacks and shirt and blazer and had cropped hair. Some time ago he had cut off his locks for his Lkishili age set were no longer warriors. He wore a wig when dancing. Lepias had left the countryside to become a man about town, albeit one of slender means.

Leadismo's ego, on the other hand, relied on his Samburu-ness. He saw himself as a cultural cicerone of his tribe, taking outsiders on a tour of nomadic ways. The fact that he also traded on his self-appointed role as ambassador to achieve his own ends didn't diminish him. He was too charming for that. Besides, Leadismo had a good heart. He was living behind the Ngong Hills on Kipenget's property with Michael, an Irish aid worker. Michael had taken him on to the payroll to help him distribute food to needy Maasai.

These two men, Leadismo and Lepias, both came from a pastoral community that lived on the threshold of survival. It was in danger either of being smothered by the imprecise dynamics of modern Kenya or, more likely, of being left to wither and die through neglect. The colonial British mistrusted the nomads but attributed romantic qualities to them. Their strictures on the size of herds and where they could graze were resented by the Samburu, but they preserved the environment. African governments, on the other hand, believed nomads had no valuable contribution to make to nation-building as long as they adhered to their traditional ways. They regarded nomads much as the Romans must have viewed the Saxons when they first settled Britain: an armed horde of unruly, uncontrolled and untaxed subjects.

Leadismo and Lepias had coped with their ambivalent position in society differently. One by shedding his tribal identity and putting it back on like a mask to earn a living. The other by pretending to have retained his tribal ways while in many instances he behaved more like an urban man. Both were, by African standards, successful in what they had set out to achieve.

The journey north from Nairobi to Lesirikan in Samburu District was as scenically diverse as travelling from Rome to Amsterdam. And as long. Although it was less than 250 miles, it took ten hours, allowing for a tea stop or two. We invariably dawdled along the way so it would be night before we arrived.

The Land Rover climbed over the Kikuyu escarpment, cradled between steep banks surmounted by eucalyptus trees. The earth was as red as lobster roe and coursed with the wormlike footpaths used by villagers to bring their produce to the road. In the season, you could buy carrots, beans, potatoes, plums and small, bitter pears. On this day, boys tried to flag us down to sell us the rabbits they held up by their ears.

We reached the edge of the Rift Valley and stood on its lip looking down on to Lake Naivasha. Volcanic mountains sat on the valley floor beneath us, waiting in the wings for the theatre of the day. Each jagged ridge, clearly etched in the chiaroscuro of the early morning, would be tamed as the sun rose higher, rendering them soft as velvet. But at that moment, they seemed sharp enough to pierce the clouds and meet the sky.

Standing in a mulched field of red earth, we saw flamingos gliding in the thermals. They turned from black to white as they caught the sun, like mobiles. I felt as if we could reach out and grasp them between thumb and finger. But surely they would crumble to dust like a moth's wing if we did.

We passed on, turning right at Gilgil to bounce over the hills and valleys of the former settler country that was known as the White Highlands. It was hard to say where the road to Samburu truly began. Perhaps here, simply because we had been driving for some hours and the main road to Uganda had fallen away in the distance. But the slow and gentle pace of the nomad had yet to make itself felt. Here, in the small market towns, echoes of Nairobi still reverberated. Men and women jostled for places on buses and in the enclosed pick-up taxis called *matatus*. Others gathered to drink beer at the Prowling Lion Bar or to flirt with prostitutes at the Pray to God Day and Night Club.

We stopped at Nyahururu for tea and *mandazis*, triangular packets of deep-fried dough that were greasy and delicious. I filled the car and the *debes* on the roof. There were some 125 miles to go, and it was unlikely there would be another chance to refuel. A young spiv loitered on the petrol station forecourt. His trousers were tucked into his socks above platform boots so they wouldn't get splashed with mud. At his neck was a cravat that would have suited a retired colonel if it had not been so stained and shiny from constant use. On his head sat an orange and green crocheted tea cosy whose loops of wool made it look like a stickleback fish. His eyes, yellowed from ganja, flickered over us, recognising some small affinity in Leadismo's peacock splendour rather than Lepias' temperate imitation of the country squire. He said something in Kikuyu to the man filling the car and laughed, showing teeth made brown by the volcanic water. Then he picked up his blaring ghetto-blaster, covered with another crocheted creation, this time in pink and purple, and sauntered down a refuse-strewn street. The jaunty angle of his head, the cocksure way in which he walked, reiterated the words I hadn't understood. 'Those boys are country bumpkins.'

We passed through Rumuruti Forest and reached the flat table of grasslands beyond. This sere landscape, reticent with its secrets, was at last Samburu country even though it had been divided up into large ranches, many of them still owned by Europeans. I enjoyed this road, beset by deep corrugations and potholes in the dry season and a quagmire of mud during the rains. It was strewn with memories. I had been bogged down along this stretch and had dug the car out with a shovel. It was here at this bend that I had emerged from the bush at the head of a camel train and dreamily wondered, unaware that a coup attempt was in progress, why F5 fighter jets were flying overhead. Down that road lived the drunken *mzungu* who drank his whisky with Coca Cola in the mistaken belief no one would notice his alcoholic intake. At the foot of this hill I once braked to a halt to avoid a trumpeting elephant that was crossing the road. This was the police barrier where an administration policeman in a Second World War overcoat had taken me and two friends into custody. We were on a hunting trip, but I had carelessly left the licences in Nairobi.

Lepias' train of thought was also rambling happily over a variety of subjects. Have you brought any *shukas* for the *wazee* (old men)? Have you ever ridden a horse? Have you bought any camels up north? This latter inquiry referred to my predilection for walking in the bush. For a couple of years I had been playing with the idea of buying some camels to use as pack animals. The answer to Lepias' question, alas, was no. Camels were expensive – thousands of shillings – and extremely challenging to break in. I had decided to give them a miss.

Leadismo, spurred on perhaps by the familiar dryness of the country-side, offered up a wealth of information. The juice of a certain spindly succulent is used to cure malaria. Trees with knotted branches are good for making a *rungu* (the club that every Samburu warrior carries). Samburu women wear a black and white string of beads hanging from one earring to denote that one of her sons is a warrior. (They can also be blue and white. A woman wears two strings for each warrior son.) A black squirrel can kill a buffalo by catching its tongue and holding on to it until it suffocates. The squirrel places a foot behind the buffalo's eye for leverage, he explained, slamming his foot on to the floor and throwing his head backwards in demonstration. I raised a sceptical eyebrow.

Undeterred, he continued. Did I know that eagles like to eat the flying ants that come with the rains? There was silence after this remark for the subject of rain was a poignant one. Kenya was suffering its worst drought in half a century. Nomadic herders, whose survival was precarious and quickly influenced by the caprices of the weather, were the most affected. The milk on which they subsisted had dried up. Most nomads refused to slaughter their cattle for money even in good years. However, government statistics illustrated the extent to which grazing had vanished. In a normal year, the state slaughterhouses butchered 6,000 cattle a month. That year, 1984, the monthly average had so far been 16,000 as ranchers sought to convert their livestock into money before they died of thirst. The warriors had resorted to driving herds of cattle hundreds of miles across sun-scorched land in search of pasturage. Their routes were marked by skeletons picked clean by vultures as tens of thousands of animals collapsed along the way. The Samburus' resilience was being pushed to the limit.

This was evident when we arrived at Lepias' *manyatta* on the Kisima Plains. Kisima was a small roadside trading post eleven miles south of Maralal, which was the administrative centre for the district. It had grown up beside the only lake in the area. The lake was fed by a natural spring, and the soil contained salts, which were an essential part of the cattle's diet. It was more than just a watering point, however. Centuries ago, Ngai, the Samburu god, had introduced the first livestock by sending some down to Lake Kisima on a ladder that descended from the sky.

When the Lkimaniki age set were warriors in the 1950s, 6,000 head of cattle came to drink each day. Now there was only a handful of herds lowing fretfully at the plovers that strutted across the lake's dry bed. Beyond Kisima were miles and miles of flat grassland. Lepias' *manyatta* was on the far side at the foot of some hills.

The women appeared first from behind the thorn barrier that encircled the huts. Then came the children, scampering delightedly and pressing against the doors of the Land Rover. They knew from past experience that sooner or later they would be given sweets.

An air of lethargy and disrepair hung over the *boma*. It saddened me. Lepias' wife, Nolotimy, confided she had run out of sugar and had hardly any tea or *posho* left. Neither was there any milk to give to the children. The animals were dying from lack of grazing and their udders were dry, she said. Tipilet soon found her way to my side. She was much taller than when I had last seen her, neatly fitting in beneath my armpit, but she was painfully thin. Tipilet would have liked to go to school if there had been the money for books and a uniform.

My other special friend was Tipilet's grandmother. Gogo allowed that she was somewhere between fifty and a hundred. Whatever her age, she was determined not to let it interfere with her routine. She appeared out of the bushes, dragging firewood behind her at a tortoiselike pace. Her face was a wonder of tectonic activity. Her clouded eyes lived in craters that had retreated from the landmass of her brow. The cheeks, too, had shifted and sunk as if at the urging of some subterranean volcanic movement. Only her nose had resisted subsidence, thrusting outwards in a sturdy hillock of flesh. She stopped before me and touched my face for confirmation. Then she kissed me on the lips and offered the traditional Samburu greeting. *'Ajalo? Ajangwa?'* (Where have you come from? Where are you going to?). When I told her of what I hoped to do, she shuffled inside her hut and emerged with a walking stick burnished by use. The knobbed handle perfectly fitted the palm of my hand. Gogo sent a jet of spit through the gap in her front teeth and invoked Ngai to bless my journey. 'Watch out for the sun,' she warned. Of all the things that I have left behind in Kenya, Gogo's walking stick is one of the few possessions I truly miss.

It was Goodman who worried me most. He had lost his cheeky strut. I soon saw why. There was a palm-sized carunculated scar behind his knee. He had fallen into the fire, Nolotimy explained. She hadn't taken him to the hospital at Maralal, but the wound had eventually healed by itself. 'Why not?' I asked. Her shrug held many answers. It was too far to walk. She didn't know if she needed money at the hospital, but she had none. Goodman cried at first but stopped after a while. She was weary. In fact, she was almost beyond caring.

Leadismo, who had been exposed to primary health care at the clinic on Kipenget's property, clicked his tongue in disapproval. I fought to dilute my response. This was, after all, Lepias' homecoming. Besides, would I have acted differently in her position? Probably not. 'Nolotimy, you must watch the children closely around the fire. If another one gets burnt, you must take him at once to the doctor. You see how Goodman limps? He can't run properly. This is not good for a boy who must herd the animals.'

Ten years earlier, Kisima had been a place of beauty with a vibrant, lively society. I had visited for circumcisions, weddings and other of the ceremonies that provided the maypole around which Samburu life rotated. I remembered the carpets of green clotted with flowers; the zebra grazing near herds of plump cattle; the moiréed surface of the lake. Those were the days when life was celebrated with dance. Spears twirled under the sky above a snorting, yelling throng of warriors. Bead collars rose and fell as girls stuck their necks out, heads up and eyes shut, reaching for their own personal ecstasy.

Now Kisima was a dusty, parched plain barely distinguishable from the cracked lake bed. This was due to poor rains and overgrazing. But there was more to it than that. An erratic climate was the normal condition here. Most ecologists agree that overgrazing doesn't damage grasslands permanently. However, animals die of hunger if left to search for food in the depleted areas. Pastoralists' survival relies on a flexible response to limited resources, which means rotating pasturage or seeking it further afield in times of drought.

The crisis had been compounded by a change in the population dynamics. In those days, Kenya had the highest population growth rate in the world: four per cent. (At the time of writing, it was down to 3.6 per cent, which was still high.) So the competition for land for the cattle had increased. Where there had been fifteen families fifty years ago, there were now 300. Moreover, as part of a national policy, the land, which had once been shared amongst the eight clans, had been adjudicated to group owners. Turning nomads into sedentary cattle herders, without developing an alternative lifestyle, was destroying the environment.

On top of this, the lure of modern Kenya had robbed Kisima of its men. They had left for Nairobi where they worked as nightguards, returning only occasionally to drink milk and sit in the sun. The momentum of urban drift in sub-Saharan Africa was tremendous. The population of Nairobi grew by seven per cent a year. Most of the migrants failed to find jobs so they joined the forty per cent of the population that lived in shanty towns and squatter camps. It was the young men's responsibility to drive the cattle to distant pastures when those nearby were exhausted and needed time to recover. Without them, there was no one to maintain the fragile balance of the ecosystem. Digging for fool's gold was undermining a time-tested way of life.

To the outsider, the life of a warrior seemed to be an idyllic, random affair, embalmed in custom and shielded by distance from central government edicts forbidding lion hunts and cattle rustling. In fact, traditional Samburu society revolved around a rigid hierarchy compartmented into age groups and age sets. Boys entered an age set in their teens when they were circumcised and became warriors. This grouping provided a special bond that endured for the rest of their lives as they graduated from one age group to the next: *murran* (warrior), junior elder, firestick elder and, finally, senior elder. Ceremonies were the watersheds for each change in status. The current age set of warriors, initiated in 1976, were the Lkiroro. The name meant 'those who dare'.

This system whereby the men were ratcheted upward from boy to warrior to elder was intrinsic to the dynamics of the tribe. Circumcision allowed the warriors of the preceding age set to shave off their long hair and settle down to married life while the junior elders graduated to the more senior status of firestick elders.

It was the task of the firestick elders to act as surrogate fathers to the *murrani*. They disciplined them and instilled *nkanyit*, a sense of honour. As they were two age sets removed from the warriors, they were sufficiently senior to command respect yet close enough in age that real father-son relationships almost never cropped up. In this way, no vested interests existed between the two age sets. A collective group temperament was believed to connect alternate age sets. Thus if firestick elders were remembered as being fiery in their youth, it was accepted that the warriors they supervised would inherit their bold spirit.

I saw parallels in Western society to the men's passage from youth to senility. As youngsters tending the cattle and goats, they were schoolboys. Then they left herding to prepare for circumcision, an initiation rite that in the West has become the subliminal drinking ordeal or even A levels. As with teenage graduates who take a year off to travel or work before entering university, it was a period of transition to manhood. The boys donned sheepskin cloaks, blackened with charcoal and fat, and wandered from *manyatta* to *manyatta* singing *lebarta*, a low-toned invocation directed towards the firestick elders that begged the hastening of their ordeal. At that time it was common to see them walking in twos and threes, dark triangles stamped on to the grass, their bodies bent slightly forward to meet an oncoming wind, like monks hurrying to chapel.

As the year turned and the time drew close, the boys descended to the dry camel country in search of *silalei*, a pungent gum from a species of Commiphora tree, which they would use in their initiation. Boys from the Leroghi plateau around Maralal used to trek north-east, skirting the foot of the Mathews Range, to Marsabit, a volcanic mountain squatting in the Kaisut desert. The 130-mile trip tested their courage and endurance, qualities expected of a *murran*. But many of the Lkiroro hadn't ventured as far afield, settling instead for a fifty-mile walk to Baragoi.

Then came the university of warriorhood, a period of learning, wild escapades and flirtatious romance. After that it was time to settle down, raise a family and build up herds of livestock. Rather like acquiring houses, cars, videos and tape decks. Each age set of elders was like a club. Members did each other favours and pulled strings when necessary. It was not much different from a Rotary or Lions Club. Retirement was spent sitting in the sun watching the grandchildren grow up and passing down oral tradition through riddles, tales and songs.

Age sets moved into a new age group every fourteen years or so when all the youths of the district between fourteen and twenty-five were circumcised *en masse*. As warriors were not allowed to marry, junior and even senior elders did their best to delay the initiation of a new age set to restrict the competition for eligible young girls. But as the years passed and the younger boys' chests deepened and their shoulders grew wide, so they yearned to flex their muscles as warriors. They encouraged the elders of their fathers' age set to press for circumcision. The elders, if they had been careful and wise, now had large enough herds to form nucleus herds for those *murran* sons who would be freed to marry. So the elders, too, on behalf of sons circumcised and uncircumcised, took up the cause.

At this time it was as if a stick had been poked into a beehive. The entire tribe was in a state of agitation. Boys wanted to become men. Some of the older warriors had already begun casting around for suitable wives. The senior elders wanted to see their sons advance through the tribal hierarchy while strong opposition to the formation of a new age set came from those elders who had not yet finalised negotiations for their second, third or fourth wives.

This marriage market was like a stock exchange. And because Samburu society is polygamous, it was inevitably a bull market. The capital was livestock instead of money. It was used to trade in brides instead of stocks and shares. The sale of a daughter to another household resulted in a larger herd. The acquisition of a wife was an investment in future generations who would either look after the cattle or be given in marriage for more cattle, depending on their sex.

We left Lepias' *boma* and resumed our trip, driving through Maralal and climbing upwards amongst the juniper trees. Already, we were anticipating the excitement of arriving, but there was plenty of time for that. There was still a long way to go. Leadismo had taken on a new lease of life and was looking about him with the appreciation of a man returning home. He was aglow with memories.

Whenever we passed a young girl walking along the road, he pushed his head forward and a bullish roar escaped through his puffed out cheeks. His eyes had grown lusty. 'Look!' he cried, pointing to a pencil-thin figure with a thick ruff of necklaces around her neck. 'She is beaded!'

When a girl reached puberty she was eligible for courtship and marriage although one was not the natural consequence of the other. Thick layers of bead necklaces, known as *saen*, were the sign that she had been chosen by a warrior. It was the same as wearing a school ring to show you were going steady. The couple made love but practised *coitus interruptus*. A pregnancy out of wedlock was a grave taboo and brought shame on both the girl and boy and their families. The liaisons were serious, nonetheless. If a warrior tried to steal someone else's girlfriend, he was fought off with every weapon to hand: spear, *simi* (broad-bladed stabbing sword), *rungu*, even stones. Sometimes the fights ended in the death of one of the young men and escalated into a vendetta between clans. These love affairs seldom ended in marriage, though. The fathers preferred to wed their daughters to elders as second, third, even fourth wives. These men had had the time to acquire sizeable herds. They were rich enough to pay the bride price, which was around seven cows.

Sometimes a warrior was bonded to his lover by such deep affection that he felt compelled to make her his wife even though her marriage had been arranged with someone else. As with everything in Samburu culture, there was a safety valve for steamy emotions. In this instance, if the warrior managed to kidnap the girl in the interval between her circumcision and her marriage, she was considered to be rightfully his. It was for this reason that girls were circumcised either the day before or the morning of their wedding. It was a practice that gave no consideration to the girl as her marriage was consummated on the wedding night. Sintahui, my night watchman, thought it a barbaric custom. He was a Maasai, which made him an ethnic cousin of the Samburu. 'We give them two weeks to recover before we make love,' he said.

Leadismo pointed out the warriors he knew with an enthusiasm that rose to fever pitch when he spied one particular young man walking down the road towards us. 'I have been stealing with him!' he cried with delight.

He was referring to cattle rustling. It was a time-honoured practice in northern Kenya that had been unintentionally reinforced by the colonial administration. When the British arrived in the area in 1900, they encountered fierce resistance from the raven-skinned Turkana, nomads who lived to the north of Samburu District. During a punitive expedition against the Turkana in 1915, over 400 tribesmen were killed. But their fighting strength was soon resuscitated. Over the next three years they put together a military force of 25,000 spearmen and a thousand riflemen. The guns, bought from Ethiopians, cost seventy sheep, a donkey mare and a bullock each. (Thanks to regional unrest and arms dealers, an AK47 automatic now costs about twenty dollars.) The British enlisted the assistance of the Samburu to pacify the Turkana. It took twenty years to subdue them, during which time the administration confiscated over a quarter of a million head of cattle. As far as the local communities were concerned, this merely institutionalised stock theft.

The Samburu, like the other nomads in the region, continued to invade enemy territory to plunder the livestock of other tribes with the result that some 6,000 people were killed by cattle raiders between 1975 and 1990, according to the human rights organisation Africa Watch. The warriors who stole cattle were not unlike the youths who went 'joy riding' in stolen cars. Both needed to let off excess energy and prove their manhood. Neither activity was condoned by their elders, which gave the adventure an extra fillip.

It was a handy way of building up herds. It also sounded like good fun. A few years earlier, before the camel phase, I had been casting around for someone to take me on a raid. If only I had known, I would have asked Leadismo. I was surprised that he had participated in such a dangerous pastime. There was more to the man than I had given him credit for.

The warriors armed themselves with spears, shields, arrows and *simis*. They entered a *boma* at about four o'clock in the morning, the dead hour before dawn exploited so often by generals. The raiding parties were always large, sometimes one hundred or more. Two warriors stood guard outside the entrance to each hut while the rest prodded the cattle on to their feet and, having dismantled the thorn-branch gate to the *boma*, drove them out of the enclosure as quietly as they could. If no one woke up, all well and good.

'But what if they did? The cows are bound to moo and make squelching noises in all that mud and dung.'

'If someone comes out of their hut, we kill them,' Leadismo said gravely.

'I don't see why it's necessary to kill anyone. You all hate it when the *ngorokos* (bandits) raid your *bomas* and murder people. It's the same thing.'

'We have to kill them because otherwise they will kill us. We steal from the Turkana and Borana and they often have guns. We never carry guns, but we aren't afraid to die. When they discover what has happened, they chase us and try to shoot us. But we run too fast for them because the Borana are the ones who cut off a man's special parts.'

'But what if you're caught?'

'If a Samburu boy is killed, we take him into the bushes and cover him with leaves. We lie him on his side. If we don't, it means another boy will be killed.'

'Have you ever killed anyone?'

'No.'

'Good. You can stay in the car then. I was considering making you walk.'

This was not the season for raiding, however. That took place after the rains when the plains were lush with good pasturage and there was time for recreation. Now the warriors were bent on the serious mission of saving the family herds. We stopped to ask one his news. He had driven his cattle from Marsabit, 130 miles to the northeast. The camels in the north were only drinking once a month. Their owners drove them to Lake Turkana. As Africa's fifth largest lake, (covering an area of nearly 2,500 square miles, it is a bit bigger than Norfolk or Delaware), it never dried up. He hoped to find water and grazing at Maralal, he said.

Like the other herders, the warrior carried two spears instead of one. 'Twin spears' denoted a long and arduous journey where added protection was needed. There were lions about, and they were hungry. And, of course, *ngorokos* lay in wait in the valleys. Many of these bandits had AK47s that had filtered across the border from northern Uganda, military hardware that had been stolen during the chaos of that country's several coups.

The cattle were pathetically thin and walked slowly for they had no strength. The road was littered with the skeletons of those that had died along the way. We got out to inspect a carcass. Beside it were the still warm ashes of a cooking fire. The warriors had cut out the animal's liver and eaten it. Lunch on the go. Leadismo fingered the dead cow's ear. 'It belonged to the Lpisikishu clan.' He could tell by the number of slits.

Further on we stopped the Land Rover at the top of a deep valley. 'Look, I'll hit the black rocks down there.' Leadismo picked up a stone and hurled it expertly. There was a sharp chunk as it found its mark several hundred feet further down.

The valley debouched on to a plain that seemed to march on to the end of the world. On a clear day, I reckoned you could see the best part of a hundred miles. The eastern perimeter was rimmed by volcanic mountains that were 500 million years old. They stretched out in front of us, so distant and hazy that only the cognoscenti could say for sure those were the Kirisia Hills, those the Mathews Range and those, still far away, the Ndoto Mountains. My heart quickened. This, for me, was where the road to Lesirikan truly began. It was impossible to discern on the horizon, but I could sense its unobtrusive presence beneath the knuckle-sized greyness of the Ndotos.

We descended several thousand feet, slowly negotiating the precipitous twists and turns of the road. Once we were on the flat, I put my foot down, and the needle hovered over the forty-five on the speedometer. Although the road had a dirt surface, it was in reasonable condition as not much traffic passed this way. If you drove fast enough, the car skimmed over the corrugations.

The Rendille encampment was still there – a few huts to the left of the road and some more in a depression on the right. They looked like fragile birds' nests turned upside down. The Rendille came every year in search of pasture. I no longer remember why they were tolerated so deep in the heart of Samburu country. The tribe was nomadic, like the Samburu, and had a similar lifestyle. Sometimes the two intermarried. They were less sophisticated than the Samburu and only rarely ventured into towns such as Maralal.

These country cousins were the butt of Samburu humour. The tale I liked best was of the Rendille man who went to visit his brother in Nairobi.

He strode through the traffic from the bus depot to the Industrial Area where his brother worked as a night watchman at a garage. 'There must have been good rains here,' said the visitor, eyeing the cars. 'The trucks have had a lot of babies.' The two talked long into the night then fell into a heavy sleep. The visitor was the first to wake the following morning. He went outside to relieve himself. 'Why do the babies take off their shoes when they go to sleep?' he asked on his return. Thieves had stolen the wheels off all the cars during the night. I didn't know if the story was true, but it easily could have been.

In time we came to the outskirts of Baragoi, no longer than the length of its main street and not much wider. As the only town between Maralal and South Horr, a distance of a hundred miles, Baragoi was the hub for an area of hundreds of square miles. We passed the boys' secondary school on our left and soon afterwards, on the right, the Catholic mission with its primary school. Then we were in town. Turkana women with their hair shaved into a mohican crest sat on the verandahs of the *dukkas*. Men passed beneath the drooping pepper trees with *shukas* thrown about them like cloaks. There was no need to stop and buy provisions from the Kikuyu store and no time to take tea and *mandazis* at the teahouse run by the fat Somali woman. We pressed on and turned right at the end of the town. We passed the government-run medical clinic, the police post and the District Officer's headquarters where a flagpole was set amidst a circle of whitewashed stones.

This was the final stretch. It took four hours on foot and half an hour by car. In due course, if your eyes were sharp, you could just make out Lesirikan. It was no more than a barely perceptible change of colour, paler than the fawn of the surrounding grasslands and about the size of a pinhead. At night there was no comforting yellow light to encourage you on because Lesirikan had no electricity, just as it had neither telephones nor running water. Kenya's gross domestic product and Western con-cessionary funds for development came to this remote area in a trickle, a drop at a time.

I loved arriving in the darkness. Flying over that empty plain beneath the stars was like travelling through a galactic emptiness. But if you arrived in daylight, you could catch the sparkle of the sun reflected off a corrugated iron roof, no more than that. It was not until you were right on top of Lesirikan that you could discern the dusty street that had attracted a few buildings. It never failed to surprise me how such a place could be the wellspring of so much activity. Yet it was so. This was Africa's Wild West, a frontier land where tradition was being nudged by change. I knew the place well for I had helped to establish a dispensary there. Lesirikan felt like home.

The primary school, church and trading stores made it a focal point for all the Samburu who lived within a radius of forty miles. However, the town, for its few hundred residents called it that, was small by any standards. Six wooden buildings, a rainbow of blues, reds and greens, straggled down the sloping street. On the one side was Chief Thomas Lekisaat's house. The slatted wooden door stood padlocked when he was away, which was often. He was a dedicated capitalist and spent much time trading goods and tending to his shop in Baragoi. Further up was the *dukka* where the old man worked. The place was stacked with bags of *posho*. Where sunlight stabbed the gloom, heavenly motes of white powder swirled in the air. The old man busied himself sweeping the dust into small piles that exploded once again as soon as someone entered. When there were no customers, he squatted on the shaded porch and answered the greetings of passers-by with his stock phrase. As the occasion arose, it meant 'yes', 'I'm well', 'I agree', 'goodbye'. Through constant usage it had become his name too. He was called Mungu Saidia (God help you). Across the way from Mungu Saidia's duosyllabic presence was the hotel, a small and dirty room with one rickety table and two stools. The hotel sold tea when there was enough water to make it. The square-faced man who worked there smiled often and talked little. Lekerde's words were like a rasp attacking metal. He was deaf.

There were three other shops, but only one counted – Kattra's. Its well stocked shelves of packets of *posho* and flaked soap, torch batteries, beads, *shukas*, cigarettes and sometimes a blanket or two made it the Sainsbury's of Lesirikan. Every few months, Kattra even managed to get in a consignment of sodas. The soft drinks were a fast-moving line and only lasted a couple of days. The *dukka* stood at the top of the hill, as befitted the establishment of the doyenne of the community.

Kattra Ismail was a Somali, a merchant of the bush. Like the rest of her kinsfolk, she made money where others still rubbed pennies together. Kattra was a survivor. She lived as a single woman, rare amongst this strict Muslim community, and brought up her seven children single-handed. Her husband, who visited her from time to time, was mad. She was one of eight married sisters who lived all over Kenya. She visited her sisters in Baragoi when she could. This was about once a fortnight as she had no car. The only vehicle in town, apart from the one at the clinic, belonged to Chief Lekisaat. Her beauty still had a potent alchemy although her once dainty, elongated figure, which all Somali women are initially blessed with, had thickened into a pillowy pyramid that was swathed in layers of filmy material. She patronised our clinic with a bountiful supply of eggs and sweet pancakes. In due course, when the clinic's activity quickened, she housed some of the staff in the rooms in her compound. When I managed to repay some of this generosity by helping out with school fees, Kattra wrote me a letter: 'Thanx an elephant! We are very happy about it.' I always visited Kattra as soon as I could to catch up on the news over a mug of spiced tea.

It was too late now for that, however. Instead, we headed for the clinic, a lozenge of darkness at the foot of the town. The side door creaked open, and the boys crowded round us. Mark the Saint, as we called him behind his back, kissed me on the cheek. He was a young New Zealand doctor who had been travelling through Africa when the appeal of working in a bush dispensary sidetracked him. The others were more reticent, unsure of Western greetings, which were more physical than their own. Sometimes they kissed me on the cheeks, not knowing when to stop. We never shook hands, which would have struck a formal note in our relationship that didn't exist. They stood there shaking their heads and smiling. 'How are you for quite few weeks past?'

There was Sammy Lentano, the nurse who had been seconded from the Ministry of Health; Chopiro Lolorurua whom Mark was training as a dresser; Semeji Leseran the cleaner (whose name meant 'cousin') and Muturu, a factotum whom Michael the aid worker had dumped on us. He had been expelled from the Catholic seminary in Nairobi with a virulent case of gonorrhoea. All except Muturu were local Samburu.

The clinic had been constructed by the townspeople in 1969 on a promise from the government that if they provided the building, the Ministry of Health would send nurses to staff it. No one had materialised, though. It had stood empty until I negotiated with the County Council to take it over. It had been operational only a few months and was still in its informal stage.

The long, low building, built with juniper off-cuts, was divided into three barely furnished rooms. In the centre was the dispensary where Sammy, Mark and Chopiro treated a score or so of patients each day without benefit of running water, electricity or refrigeration. The most common complaints were malaria, chest and eye infections, diarrhoea (amongst the children) and venereal disease. The three men were surrounded by pain but no one cried, hunger but no one starved, hardship and illness but no one was unhappy in the angst-ridden way of Westerners.

The feckless Semeji, in his torn cap and tattered shirt sewn with red thread, slept off his drinking bouts in the room to the left amidst sacks of emergency relief grain. He was a soothsayer given to visions in his dreams. No one doubted his prophecies. Once he announced there were snakes around the clinic that would bite people. Sure enough, within a few days, two children from nearby *manyattas* came in for snakebite treatment.

The rest of us stayed in the room on the right. It was large and empty and so engrained with dirt that it was never clean despite regular sweeping. Like everyone else, we had to make do with a few pints of water a day. Washing surfaces other than in the treatment room would have been a scandalous waste of a valuable commodity. The boys slept on mattresses on the floor. I was given the rickety iron bed. In the corner by the door was a charcoal stove the diameter of a football. Next to it stood shelves holding a cabbage, *posho*, tea, sugar and a few tin mugs and bowls. A leg of goat hung from a string. The place needed a woman's domestic touch, but I hadn't come to play housewife.

Lesirikan's needs were basic but mostly unfulfilled. The cutting edge of change had been blunted by ignorance, bureaucracy and central government apathy. It was for this reason that I had become involved in the dispensary, which was badly needed. Kenya spends 1.7% of its gross domestic product on health services compared to 11.2% in the United States. There is only one doctor for every 10,000 people. Over the years, through the dedication of others, it was to expand into a highly esteemed aid organisation. SAIDIA (the Swahili word for 'help' and an acronym for Samburu Aid in Africa) introduced water supplies, fuel-efficient stoves, hide-marketing schemes, tree planting and an education fund as well as building a second dispensary. Although it remained small, it was considered a worthy model for future aid projects by the World Bank, UNICEF, Britain's Overseas Development Administration and the United States Agency for International Development. Unlike the majority of its predecessors, who imposed progress on the recipients of their assistance, the organisation encouraged the communities to make their own decisions and fostered a sense of community ownership. It co-opted members on to committees and consulted the people on how they would like to solve their problems. All but one of the staff were locals. We wanted to banish the old axiom that remote peoples were too backward to plan their own future. We treated them as adults. After all, it wasn't our organisation. It was theirs. One day, we hoped, they would be running it entirely on their own, including the finances.

At the beginning, however, these common-sense theories of self-reliance were still being formulated. Our first steps were faltering as we searched for guidance. None of us had any experience in aid work. Only Mark and Sammy had medical qualifications. I contributed what I could in between my full-time job as a journalist. In those days, we were of the trial-and-error school. There were plenty of opportunities to put this method into practice.

For instance, the water. The only source of water was a well one mile behind the town. And this had dried to a puddle during the drought. Every night women balancing containers on their heads glided silently across the pale sand of the river bed beneath a star-splashed sky. There were also a few men, stripped to the waist and carrying their containers as Westerners do, by the hand. Each by turn clambered down a narrow, thirty-foot cleft and vanished into its depths. The hole required a chain of six people to pass up the tinfuls of brackish liquid scooped up from the sand.

It was a laborious task that lasted from midnight until noon the next day. When the women took their few pints home, it was used for cooking and making tea, but not for washing. There was not enough water for that.

Over eighty per cent of all illnesses in Africa are directly or indirectly caused by a poor water supply and lack of sanitation. Whereas in Europe ninety-five out of every hundred people turn on a tap when they want water, in Africa ninety out of a hundred people dig for it in the ground. In Kenya, only one quarter of the rural population has access to unpolluted water. Water-borne diseases such as typhoid, dysentery, polio, hepatitis, cholera and diphtheria are common. Children under five become malnourished from frequent bouts of diarrhoea and die of diseases that healthy children fight off. Much of this could be prevented by using clean water for washing and drinking. It seemed so simple. Yet it wasn't, as Lesirikan's experience showed.

In 1969 Father Tallone from the Baragoi mission sank a borehole and installed a diesel pump. It was in use for three years. Then a new priest, Father Cornelio, came to town and said the people must pay for the diesel. If the priest had first consulted the people and obtained their agreement to the plan, things might have turned out differently. As it was, the new system didn't work. Some paid for the water while others didn't which led to arguments. Eventually, Father Cornelio confiscated the pump. Angered by these priests who both gave and took away without explanation, some of the warriors vandalised what remained, making holes in the corrugated iron storage tanks with their spears. It was the old story of assistance being thrust upon people who hadn't asked for it. Only fourteen of the fifty-four boreholes drilled in Kenya from 1969 onwards were still working in 1979. But it took two decades before the moral became clear. If you want to help Africans, you must live amongst them and see the problems through their eyes to find workable solutions. I agreed with the elder who said, 'People don't plan sometimes. They just bring planned things.'

Many years after that, SAIDIA raised money through a British church group for a pump that could utilise the wind that swept off the mountain. But there were problems. The Italian government had dumped a consignment of solar pumps on to the Kenyan government. So it was decided they would be installed throughout the district. The wind pump would have to be discarded. Chief Lekisaat's letters as to the whereabouts of the solar pump allocated to Lesirikan had gone unanswered. He had been vested with the responsibility of the people's welfare but he lacked the authority of the pen-wielding civil servants who worked in far-off offices. I, too, had made enquiries at the County Council headquarters in Maralal. The pump, it seemed, had vanished into thin air. I was advised to do nothing until the situation had been clarified, an answer that came too easily to bureaucratic lips.

Eventually, a pump did arrive and was installed on the plains below the town next to the carcass of Father Tallone's ill-fated venture. The water was brackish and used only for the herds. The sorest irony of all was that the solar panels were sited in a rain shadow. Every morning, the traditional time to water cattle, clouds filled the sky. This would not have mattered if there had been storage tanks, but the water engineer from Maralal absconded with the money allotted for their construction. Eventually the people of Lesirikan built a storage tank on their own. The laws of physics dictated it wouldn't work. But it did. Meanwhile, they continued to use the river bed for their drinking water. And they still weren't washing their hands.

One day a friend and I suggested to Chief Lekisaat there might be an easier way to collect this water. Why not, we suggested, draw it up with a rope? Lekisaat shooed away the children and goats and silence descended on the attendant cluster of onlookers for the introduction of new technology was a weighty matter. The container dropped into dark, hidden depths and reappeared filled to the brim. My friend, who had a watch, timed the operation. It was quicker than the old way, he said. After much discussion, a decision was reached. Lekisaat announced he would buy a length of sisal twine from the hardware store on his next trip to Maralal. He never did and the people continued to pass the water up in a human chain.

Years later I discovered the real reason for the broken promise. Water collection is a social activity which, like going to the pub, entails more than quenching your thirst. Waterholes are a gathering point where gossip and news can be exchanged and relayed back to the *manyattas*. The introduction of a system that could be operated by just two people might have disrupted the secondary function of disseminating information. Lekisaat, who realised this, had agreed to our proposal in our presence and ignored it in our absence. He had not wanted to offend the well-intentioned foreigners.

There was also another motive. The British had institutionalised chieftaincy and imposed it on tribes such as the Samburu, where it had not existed before. This unpopular system was perpetuated by the Kenyans after independence. As a government appointee, Lekisaat had no local legitimacy. He didn't want his own infrequent efforts to help the community overshadowed by our innovations. SAIDIA was a threat to his status as a leader. It was something I failed to realise until it was too late.

Even though the benefits of introducing different practices were glaringly obvious to us, conversion was gradual. The Samburu were empiricists whose enlightenment came via experience rather than explanation. Rabies, for instance. Initially, it was difficult to impress upon people the urgency of starting a course of anti-rabies injections within a day or two of being bitten by a rabid dog. Parents didn't see the need to take infected children to a hospital because, at first, there were no obvious symptoms. So children were left at home until they began to behave strangely and foam at the mouth. By then it was too late. I came across two children who died in this painful manner despite our futile, last-minute attempts to save their lives. There must have been many more cases like this before people accepted they could save their children by a visit to one of the clinics. Rabies was widespread.

One of the first concrete achievements at the clinic was to launch a child immunisation programme. In 1984, five million African children died before the age of five, the majority from easily preventable illness. It was comparable to a city the size of Philadelphia being wiped off the map. Immunisation against polio, whooping cough, measles, tuberculosis and the other childhood diseases cost as little as five dollars. Mothers were quick to realise the advantage of vaccination. They were diligent and enthusiastic about turning up at prearranged locations in the Ndotos to get their babies jabbed. Soon thousands had been immunised.

While the immunisation programme was an almost immediate success, the concept of preventing future illnesses through present habits was not so easily understood in other areas. For instance, it was to be five years before mothers began to make the connection between dirty water and dysentery and hepatitis. During that time, the dispensaries became increasingly popular as word spread of their efficiency. By 1991, over 5,000 people were paying a nine dollar 'insurance premium' that gave them unlimited access to medical treatment. Those who didn't pay the annual subscription were asked for a small fee on each visit. SAIDIA was reaching 20,000 people. It was so popular that some patients walked sixty miles to be treated at the dispensaries.

Curbing sexually transmitted disease was another uphill task. It was one of the most common ailments, a fact that didn't bode well for containing the spread of the HIV virus. Warriors slept around just as much as young men in Western cultures. For the most part, they were unaware of the danger of AIDS. It caused us great concern.

The AIDS epidemic, which now blights all of Africa, originally centred on the central and eastern countries of Zaire, the Central African Republic, Burundi, Rwanda, Tanzania, Kenya, Uganda, Malawi, Zimbabwe and Zambia. Its spread could be charted along the trucking routes that pass through these countries. For instance, the Kenyan port of Mombasa is the point of entry for goods destined for Uganda, Rwanda, Burundi and parts of Zaire. Researchers now believe that the epidemic may have fanned out from the heart of Africa towards its coastline. The fact that there is a particularly high incidence of AIDS in the towns that truckers drive through supports this theory. It is believed that truckers carrying the HIV virus spread it through communities via the local prostitutes. In these areas, AIDS is more prevalent than in the worst-hit cities in the United States. A survey carried out in Busia, a Kenyan border town on the main road to Uganda, showed that every trucker and prostitute screened was HIV positive. A random survey of the general adult population in the town revealed a sixty per cent seropositivity.

Tradition, superstition and complacency contributed to the scourge. And scourge it certainly was. By the end of 1992, nearly nine million of the 500 million people living in sub-Saharan Africa were HIV positive. More than one million of these were children. About three quarters of the people who have already died from AIDS lived in Africa. The World Health Organization estimated the global total of carriers to be up to thirteen million.

Some people who fell ill with the disease thought they had been bewitched and sought the services of witch doctors and herbal healers. John Kubai, a Kenyan witch doctor, told me he was confident he could cure AIDS patients with a greyish powder ground from tree roots. Like his fellow practitioners, Kubai often applied his medicines by inserting them into an incision made under the skin. The unsterilised knife would then be used on other patients.

In the Rwandan capital of Kigali, where at least a quarter of the sexually active population was seropositive, misconceptions existed despite a government education programme. One of these was that adultery among married couples was safe. 'Young girls are after married men like me. No one goes after unmarried people because it's too dangerous,' Abdulla Issa, a married taxi driver, told me. Issa eyeing me hopefully expressed surprise that I was faithful to my partner when I travelled.

It was in Kigali, too, that I got another insight into local attitudes towards AIDS. 'People are not so frightened because we are used to illnesses that kill. In Europe you are not used to seeing people dying. One says it's AIDS, but it could also be dysentery or cholera or malaria,' explained Habimana Nyirasafali, who headed Rwanda's National Office of Population.

With AIDS data collected from surveys in black Africa auguring the worst plague in modern history, governments were concerned by the shadow the illness cast across their international image. In particular, they were sensitive to the implied slur of promiscuity. Officials resented the suggestion that the virus may have originated in Africa and refused to grant interviews to Western reporters. The subject was so touchy that when I spent three weeks in 1987 travelling around to research a series of articles, I was unable to interview a single medical researcher, Western or African, who was working in Africa.

Eventually some governments, such as those of Uganda and the Central African Republic, introduced carefully thought out education programmes that contained the increase of seropositivity. Others, such as the Kenyan government, reacted with angry denial. Kenyan officialdom was particularly secretive on the subject for fear of damaging the lucrative tourist industry. Not without reason. In 1988 the international press highlighted Kenya as one of the countries in the African AIDS belt. Tourism earnings dropped thirty per cent as a result. By the end of the decade the AIDS problem had come into the open and there were cautionary posters everywhere. As a result, public awareness increased considerably but caution relaxed again with the news that the Kenya Medical Research Institute had found a cure for AIDS, which they called Kemron. Western researchers I spoke to said the drug was an interferon and could not cure AIDS. It was never endorsed by the World Health Organization.

Officialdom's refusal to acknowledge the epidemic made the aid workers' efforts to enlighten much more difficult. Those who attempted to inform people of the risks of sex with several partners were Cassandras crying in the wilderness.

By this time we had a superb Samburu field administrator called Gabriel Lochgen. Gabriel and I had started SAIDIA with Kate Macintyre, a friend from England who stopped over in Kenya on a round-the-world tour and stayed for years. At the time of its conception, when we sat in coffee shops or lay in front of the fire in my house and endlessly discussed the idea of initiating community development, Gabriel was chauffeur to the military attaché at the United States Embassy. Gabriel came from Lesirikan and was keen to return there and get things started. Kate and I were more cautious. If he resigned his job to run SAIDIA, would we find the money for his salary? Would anyone have enough faith in three untried amateurs actually to commit funds to the project? Gabriel had no such doubts and in due course left Nairobi to return to his roots. It was the first of many instances when he was to prove us wrong. Even during the initial, financially shaky months, we somehow managed to scrape enough shillings together to keep him going.

Gabriel was a steadfast and determined man whose principles were never distorted by the transition from bush to city or city back to bush. It was a rare achievement that earned my love and admiration. This un-swerving honesty was the source of his strength. It soon gained the confidence and respect of the Samburu he worked among as well. This trust made him an ideal candidate for discussing the sensitive issue of AIDS.

In 1988, Gabriel started an education campaign amongst the warriors and their girlfriends. He talked to them as no *mzungu* could, giving an explicit explanation of the consequences of having numerous sexual partners. Many had never heard of the HIV virus. They belonged to an oral society and had taken no notice of the few AIDS posters hanging in the government offices in Baragoi. Those who knew of its existence, had given it no thought. Awareness of Aibu Ingia Duniani Sasa (Swahili for 'Shame has fallen on the earth now') was as slow in reaching Samburu District as every other aspect of development.

At Gabriel's urging, the warriors began to use condoms, which they called socks. They were handed out on the mobile clinics that immunised children and treated the sick. Boxes of them were put on a table in both the Lesirikan and Ngilai dispensaries. The warriors were told they could just walk in and help themselves. Many did. But how many others didn't? The Samburu were spread over an area the size of Israel. SAIDIA's mobile clinics covered only a small portion of the district.

There was no means of gauging the prevalence of seropositivity and therefore of knowing how effective Gabriel's lectures were in curbing its spread. Of the three hospitals in the district, only the one at Maralal had the equipment to test for HIV antibodies, but there had been no random screening amongst the general population. By 1990, there were only three or four verified cases of Samburus dying of AIDS. However, this statistic almost certainly bore no relation to the extent of the epidemic. It was inevitable that warriors such as Leadismo, who were sexually active in the coastal holiday resorts where AIDS was prevalent, would introduce the HIV virus to remote areas that otherwise might have escaped infection.

There was the very real possibility that circumcision was contributing to the spread of AIDS as well. In 1990, a new age set was introduced. This meant that 10,000 initiates were circumcised with knives that cut one foreskin after another without being sterilised. Gabriel tried to persuade the elders to require the circumcisors to alternate knives so that they could be dropped into a pot of boiling water after each circumcison. But he had limited success.

As with everywhere else in Africa, and the rest of the world, the most effective teacher of safe sexual practices was likely to be death itself. As and when AIDS began to scythe through men and women in their prime, so sexual habits would (slowly) change, as has been the case in countries such as Uganda, Rwanda and the Central African Republic.

Then there was education, which was the true catalyst for change. Education revealed to the Samburu why they should use a bank, build water catchments or prevent soil erosion. Even uncomplicated nuggets of knowledge expanded opportunity. For instance, the Samburu used to believe that you died if you ate fish or eggs. Now they know better.

Every Kenyan has the right to free primary schooling. Schooling at secondary level, however, is fee-paying. This sounds good on paper, but the facts are less sanguine. With the population burgeoning, a decline in per capita gross domestic product and social infrastructure stretched to the limit, education remains elusive for many Kenyan children. Each year the gap between expectation and reality widens.

Samburu District is even worse off than most parts of the country. The primary schools are hopelessly ill-equipped. And there are only six secondary schools for an area where roughly 35,000 people are under the age of fifteen. About half the boys in Samburu have some schooling, but only fifteen per cent of the girls ever sit in a classroom. Just over ten per cent of the children who finish primary education are able to find places in a government secondary school.

The alternative to the state system is a self-help school built with money raised by the community. The *harambee* schools (Swahili for 'Let's pull together') are typified by crude wooden benches and mud floors. Teachers consider themselves fortunate if they have a textbook to refer to. Never are there enough copies to go around the class.

The government secondary school at Baragoi decided to ameliorate the shortage by introducing a *harambee* stream of students. This way, the headmaster reckoned, he could double the intake of students. However, fees for the *harambee* students were forty per cent higher than for the government-subsidised boys, so most parents couldn't afford them. SAIDIA helped out by sponsoring needy students.

Lesirikan's primary school was set back from the town in the lee of the mountain. There was a dormitory for the boys, who came from *manyattas* from miles around. But there was nowhere for the girls to sleep, so only a few girls from town were students.

Richard Langat, the headmaster, was a gentle man. He had asked me for textbooks – just one copy for the teacher was the modest demand – and old newspapers no matter how dated. With these few tools, Richard tried to prepare his pupils for the onslaught of the twenty-first century. One of his hardest working pupils was Joffrey. He usually stayed at the school during the holidays, but once a year he made the fifteen-mile journey to his home by crawling on his hands and knees. Joffrey's legs had been wasted by polio.

Joffrey had never travelled further than Baragoi until he came to stay in my house in Nairobi to consult an orthopaedic specialist. We hoped that surgery might make it possible for him to walk. It was the first time Joffrey had seen a tarmac road, buildings more than one storey high, indoor plumbing and rooms blazing with light. It so happened that the day after he arrived, I threw a large buffet dinner for friends from Europe. It was explained to Joffrey what was going to happen. 'I would like you to join us,' I said, 'but if you don't want to, I can bring your food to the bedroom.'

He chose to stay, holding court from an armchair and answering questions with polite gravitas. After dinner, he bade me good night and swung himself on to the floor. Watching him crawl amongst the thicket of legs to the stairs, I was struck by his composure. I couldn't lay claim to knowing him for Joffrey was a young man of few words. But his simple example of dignity amidst our social chatter made the evening seem shallow and sham. In the following days he faced another, more crucial choice. There was the chance of walking on crutches if he underwent a series of operations over two years. Joffrey turned the offer down. It would interfere with his education, he explained.

When Joffrey left to go to the secondary school in Baragoi, Kate Macintyre gave him a wheelchair. He considered the gift so precious, he only used it on Sundays when friends pushed him down the bumpy dirt road to church. Joffrey's quiet pride and his determination to finish school demonstrated there was more than one way to be a warrior.

3

Faith

The beauty and wonder of God's inner things be with you.

Indian blessing

The boys and I sipped tea on the clinic porch and watched the sun break out of an eggshell sky. Baragoi was barely visible as a few white dots in the distance. Otherwise, sitting as we were with our backs to town, there was no sign of buildings in any direction. We chatted, exchanging news.

Sammy, the nurse, had been called secretly at night to a nearby *manyatta* where an unmarried girl, hidden from the prying eyes of neighbours, was dying in obstructed labour. He had saved her life. Chopiro was studying first aid from a book Mark had given him. His hands had a rare gentleness and came into their own when dressing burns. I had often watched him cleaning a child's charred buttocks as it bent stiff legged over its mother's knees. Burns from the open fires inside the small huts were common amongst the younger children and babies. Chopiro was so careful, and they were so brave, that they hardly cried.

Mark had treated a warrior who had been mauled by a lion. The young man had been herding goats out on the plains with two friends. One night two lions leapt over the low thorn enclosure they had built and dragged off some of the animals. The following morning, the warriors tracked the predators to where they were hunched over a carcass, tearing at its flesh. The lioness ran off, but her male companion sprang. The warrior shoved his right arm down its throat and held on to the mane with his left hand. He knew that one bite to his head would finish him. As the lion raked its claws down his body, the warrior slipped his stabbing sword from its

70

sheath and slashed at its throat until it was dead. Mark noted the scars on the warrior's arm, chest and legs and asked when this had happened. Some months ago, he replied. The wounds had healed well. Mark was puzzled as to why the young man had come to the clinic. 'I want you to sew up my ear-lobe. The lion tore it in half. Now I can't wear earrings,' he explained.

The hours wore on against the background noises of the patients' chatter, the scrape of medical utensils in the dispensary, Mark's soothing voice as he talked to Sammy. Young mothers sat in the shadow of the wall, always a baby creeping round from behind their backs to pull, tease and suck on the teat. By the time these children reached five or six, they would be given the adult task of minding a toddler or herding goats.

In the late afternoon the wind talked in rustles and murmurs and chased the dust before it over the brown land. A woman brought a baby that had pneumonia and a hard abscess under its jaw. She had sought help too late, as was often the case, but Mark gave it antibiotics anyway. The realisation clouded her eyes. She put the child down on the cement floor beside me and set up a haunting wail. Tears streamed down her cheeks. Samburu men gathered round, watching helplessly. Someone produced a razor and she shaved the child's head in preparation for burial the following morning as was the custom. She was deaf to our suggestions she take it home. We would have preferred not to spend the night with a corpse in the clinic. As dusk fell, the baby died. We persuaded her to bury it out on the plain. Chopiro helped her dig the grave.

That evening, Mark introduced me to his new friend. Bosco Lekarabi was a dandy in the *beau monde* of warriors. He wore several strands of beads and a golden chain looped from his ears around his chin. What singled out his physical appearance, for he liked to be different, were the tight, springy curls that haloed his blunt features. Bosco had an Afro.

It was difficult, at first, to understand why Mark had been attracted to him, unless it was for his beauty. He was taciturn and responded to my questions in monosyllables. Later, I was to realise that Bosco was followed everywhere by the black dog of melancholy. He was lazy at the best of times, but when it sat upon his shoulder, he retreated into near catatonia. His moods, so different from the sunny nature of other warriors, made me uneasy. Tara and Petra, who were to become his friends too, came up with some useful advice. 'He may be twenty-two, but you must treat him like an eleven-year-old. He just hasn't grown up yet.'

Bosco was soon to grow up resoundingly quickly. The army held regular recruitment drives amongst the Samburu. In the hope of curing his indolent ways, we persuaded him to enlist. A year or so later he arrived at my house on his annual leave. He was different. His flesh had taken on a confident thickness. He was still given to silences, but the petulance had gone. He spoke of month-long manoeuvres on the Ethiopian frontier and of becoming a parachutist. I asked how long he had trained for that. He grinned. 'We don't train. They took me up in an airplane and pushed me out.'

He wanted me to take him to a particular office, I forget where, to collect a photograph. The story behind this expedition emerged in Bosco telegraphese.

'Why do you want this photo?'

'It is of me.'

'What are you doing in it?'

'I am shaking President Moi's hand.'

'Good heavens, Bosco, how did you get to meet the president?'

'I won a competition.'

'What for?'

'Shooting.'

'Come on, Bosco, what's been going on?'

'I am the best marksman in the country. With a Bren gun at a thousand yards. I came first.'

I whooped with delight. It was my dream that the Lesirikan boys would make good. But who would have thought that the seemingly ineffectual Bosco was a closet Rambo.

We were sitting on mattresses on the floor of the dispensary scraping cabbage, *posho* and goat out of tin bowls with our fingers. A kerosene lamp cast a warm glow but did little to banish the shadows. Our lazy conversation was pensive and filled with pauses as if, in our minds, we had already gone to bed. The wind rattled a shutter. A bat swooped above the rafters. This cosy pocket of night seemed a good time to present my plan.

'Let's go and see Lesepen and find out when the drought's going to end.'

The chatter was sucked into a cave of silence. This was an awesome proposal. Lesepen was the tribe's *laibonok* diviner. The Samburu called him *lepayan lelakir*, the man of the stars. Now in the evening of his years, Lesepen plotted the course of the tribe as he travelled with far-seeing, rheumy eyes along the paths of the constellations. No one knew the exact age of the old man. He was a member of the Masula clan of the Lkileku age set who were circumcised in 1923. By this reckoning, he was probably over eighty. In a land where maturity was hard earned, Lesepen was one of the few in his age set still alive.

From his hut under the heavens on the slopes of Mount Nyiru, Lesepen used his self-taught astrology to guide the Samburu through life into death. By noting the positions of the Pleiades and Venus, he could tell if the following year would be good for camels (drought) or cattle (rain).

Armed with this knowledge, he alone decided when circumcision could begin. It never took place in a camel year, as one of the principal features of this ceremony was the slaughter of thousands of head of cattle.

Lesepen was a legendary figure. No one in the room had ever seen him in the flesh or even a photograph. In fact, no one in Lesirikan had met Lesepen except for George Lepadaasa, the school teacher. It was as if I had suggested an audience with the Pope.

Mark was the first to respond. 'It sounds like a good idea, M.A.' Chopiro, who could be relied upon to follow Mark's example, nodded. The opaque personalities of Sammy and Bosco prevented them from commenting until they had given the matter a night's consideration. Muturu was silent too. His most lovable feature was his vacancy.

'We have to do this in the proper way. We can't go in the Land Rover. It would be too rushed. We'll walk.'

'Eeemaaay!' Mark twanged. 'It's over a hundred miles. We can't walk that far.' Of course we could. The Samburu did.

The next morning, as the pre-dawn gloom filtered through the cracks in the door, Muturu resurrected the journey. 'Mary Anne, have you brought gorookos with you?' he enquired from his bed.

'What Muturu?'

'You will need gorookos.'

Everyone in town was mortally scared of the *ngorokos* (bandits) who stole cattle and murdered their owners. 'What are you talking about? We don't want *ngorokos* around. We'll try to avoid them.'

'He means glucose,' said Chopiro.

There was concern elsewhere, too. By breakfast the word had spread. Kattra worried about the lions and the bandits. The others doubted my ability to walk long distances. People drifted by the clinic on the pretext of saying hello while really they just wanted to confirm the rumour and size up my legs. Sammy said there was a mule and saddle somewhere in town. He suggested I hire it. I turned the offer down, but we did negotiate with the old man who owned two donkeys. We secured their services as pack animals for twenty shillings a day.

By noon the safari was an accepted fact. The plan was to head for Tum, a Lesirikan-sized 'town' at the foot of Mount Nyiru. From there we would seek out Lesepen. Mark went through schedules and drug stocks with Sammy who, as a government employee, was obliged to stay behind. Bosco shrugged off his initial indifference and announced he would join us. Chopiro, like me, could barely contain his excitement and showed visible relief when Mark said he could take some days off. Leadismo would have been good value, but by this time he had departed on some louche escapade of his own. Semeji and Muturu, who weren't actually invited, showed no interest in wandering too far from the clinic.

There was to be one more addition to the party, my friend Robert Loboitoong, Gabriel's lanky elder brother. Robert always added brio to any adventure. His teeth, untouched by an orthodontist, shot forth like buttresses from the broad bulwark of his mouth. Robert had an eclectic curiosity and fine disregard for convention. His children were called Hitler, China and Lazarus.

At that time, Robert was considering becoming a gypsy merchant, wandering the plains and mountains selling soap, sugar and maizemeal from the backs of donkeys. This never materialised as no one, including myself, was willing to provide the seed money for his business. Sound financial practice was not Robert's strong point. He had never managed to build up his herds. When, in due course, he announced he was taking a second wife, it met with strong family opposition, particularly from Gabriel, who was the only member of the family on a salary. Families expected those who had jobs to support those who didn't. They needn't have worried. The nineteen-year-old Saalen ran away soon after the wedding and that was the end of that.

'Tum is fifty miles away. You can walk there in a day. We'll go slowly. We'll take two days,' said Robert. It seemed a good decision.

★

The winners celebrate the past as history, but my Kenyan life was too recent to be relegated to a scrapbook. The losers mourn it as fate yet what had happened had been far from inevitable. My life had turned on a pinhead. There was no regret, however. I hadn't lost. I simply hadn't won. I was still fighting.

Petra and I spent our Christmas holiday on the run. The first indication that we would have to go underground came at Namanga, the border post that marks the frontier between Kenya and Tanzania. Petra was summoned to an office that led off the room where people queued behind a counter to have their passports processed. When she returned, she showed me the page that bore her Kenyan re-entry stamp. Someone had drawn a box around it with a pen. Sticking out at a right angle from the middle of each side of the rectangle was another, shorter line: the universally recognised deportation mark. No matter which country Petra tried to enter with that passport, it would be recognised by the immigration officer. From now on when she travelled, she would be asked to step aside, wait, answer questions. I was furious.

I marched into the office without knocking. The man sitting at the desk looked up, the pen in his hand aslope. He had been writing something. Annoyance clouded his face. 'You can't come in here. Wait outside.'

'No.'

He half rose from his seat, his palms pressed down on the desk's pitted wooden surface. On the wall behind him hung a photograph of Moi. 'Get out! Do you hear?'

'No. Sit down.' My behaviour was unthinkable. The man was accustomed to humility in the presence of his power. He knew this and sensed that for some reason I had the advantage. His aggression fell off him like a cloak as he slipped back into his chair.

'Who are you?'

'Mary Anne Fitzgerald.'

'You're Fitzgerald!'

'You've just put a deportation stamp in my daughter's passport. You know what that means for her. They said no one would touch my daughters. You had no right to do that. And you know it.' The words came out like a tightrope, level and tense. I rapped a forefinger on the wood. 'Now you listen to me. You're not going to put a stamp in *my* passport and neither are those men outside. You're not stupid. You know what I'm getting at. But I'll tell you anyway.' Our faces gravitated towards each other above a pile of papers. If someone had barged in then, they wouldn't have known if we were conspirators in some nefarious plot or mortal enemies about to tear at each other's throats. Neither, at that point, did we.

'If there's something your superiors want more than anything else today, it's to know that I'm safely across that border. That I've left Kenya. Now if you put that stamp in . . .' I paused to allow the logic implicit in this statement to take effect. 'The Tanzanians will send me straight back here. You don't want to lose your job, do you?'

I never thought I would read something akin to friendship in his face, but now his angry eyes softened, as if with gratitude. He pushed his chair back and stood up. 'Come with me.'

We returned to the anterior room where Julian and Petra stood waiting. He took my passport and handed it to an immigration officer. 'Stamp this with an exit stamp. Nothing else,' he said brusquely.

The Tanzanian border post spoke of poverty. It was bedraggled and dimly lit. Julian and I handed our passports across the counter. While the immigration officials scrutinised our arrival forms, I regaled them with the story of a friend of mine who had arrived at the same immigration office carrying his pet python in a sack. Somehow, the python had escaped, causing much alarm. In the ensuing commotion an immigration official had killed it, mistaking it for a wild snake that had slithered on to the premises of its own accord. My friend was devastated. Had any of them been around when this happened? As we talked, I took Petra's passport and shoved it across the counter, holding it open at two blank pages. 'I almost forgot. There's this one too.' It was stamped without hesitation.

We arrived at the coffee farm outside Arusha after nightfall. Some of the hunters had just returned from safari and were having a barbecue. No one had warned them we were coming, but they gave us a warm welcome anyway. I explained our predicament. Their response was to ply us with drink and food.

The following day news of my deportation was on the front pages of the papers. This unwanted publicity was easier to bear than the ostracism it generated. Tanzania's socialist apparatus was oiled by a network of grassroots informers. Everyone was a potential spy for the government: the cook, the office messenger, the shop attendant, the man at the bus stop. Via one channel or another, all the minutiae of daily life – visitors, conversations, transactions – were reported back to local party officials. As a result, the Europeans who lived in Tanzania trod warily.

Petra and I soon discovered no one wanted to be associated with us. I tried to arrange a safari with a tour company which I had publicised in a couple of travel articles. 'Do you know what you've done? I'm afraid we can't help you,' said the manager as he showed us the door. The same evening our hostess at the coffee farm came into the bedroom and asked us, a touch shamefacedly, to leave. Sitting there in the half-light as the dusk crept through the coffee bushes, folding my few clothes into the airline bag, I experienced a deep desolation.

There followed a bus ride through the night to the port of Dar es Salaam. We disembarked at the bus depot in predawn darkness. The flickering light of a few kerosene lamps did nothing to keep despondency at bay. We were truly travellers on the road, taking our chances at each new destination.

Petra and I had been given a map, roughly sketched on a paper napkin, showing the way to the house of a bachelor whom I had known vaguely for over twenty years. We weren't exactly close friends, but he was the only person I could think of who lived in Dar es Salaam. We couldn't check into a hotel because our passports would have been handed in for registration with the police. If the police knew we were in Tanzania, we would be told to the leave the country immediately. I wasn't up to another deportation.

We found a taxi and headed out of town, the dove-grey sky and sea keeping pace with the car. Like us, the napkin map had become somewhat crumpled. It was difficult to decipher where to turn. We rolled down a potholed dirt road towards the beach and came to a stop before a curtained house.

'Is this Bwana Walker's house?' I asked the askari.

'*Ndio.*'

'Is he here?'

'*Ndio*. The *bwana* is asleep.'

We paid off the taxi and settled down to wait in the driveway. I wondered why Cecil was driving a station wagon with a baby seat in the back, but hope springs eternal when you have no options. I dismissed it from my mind. Petra suggested breakfast.

'It's a strange old world,' I said into the moist air and rummaged in the sleeping bag for the vegetables we had bought for the trip. When the woman opened the kitchen door just before seven o'clock, she saw two dishevelled strangers seated on the plastic chairs that should have been in her garage, munching carrots and giggling helplessly.

'Good morning,' she said without missing a beat.

'Good morning. I'm sorry. I think we're at the wrong house. The baby chair. It makes sense. We're a bit dirty. We've been travelling. Do you know Cecil Walker?' I was having difficulty explaining things.

Cecil Walker, who lived next door, was on holiday in Ireland, but a phone call established we could stay in the house. We spent several days closeted in a bedroom, partly because it poured with rain and partly because there was nowhere to go. We talked about all the things we had never had time to talk about before and then some.

Petra told me how she felt when she was three. I told her what I remembered of being four. We lived in our own special world that wasn't interrupted by meals or obligations or encounters with other people. We swam and walked on the beach when it wasn't raining, read Cecil's books, bought roasted corn from the roadside stalls. And talked. Gradually we worked our way into the foothills of the present. For the past two years, Petra had been going through a 'difficult stage'. She had been moody and uncommunicative. Whenever I had asked her, with mounting frustration, what was wrong, she had replied she didn't know. Now, suddenly, she was telling me how she felt and I was telling her how I felt too. It was magic. I had never been so close to her or loved her more.

We took a boat to Zanzibar where I was asked to pay for something in dollars. I only had Tanzanian shillings. I broke down and shouted and cried. It wasn't the request for hard currency that had turned me into a banshee. It was grief. Petra stood by and watched the operatic act unfold, embarrassed but uncomplaining. Afterwards she took my hand and said, 'Are you better now, Mummy?'

And, on our last day, there was a mugging at knife-point on the beach. It frightened Petra and left us bereft of cash and credit cards. Violent crime was rife in Tanzania. It took hours to hitchhike back to Cecil's house. No one wanted to give us a lift in case we held them up at gunpoint once in the car. We enlisted the aid of a policeman, but no one wanted to stop for him either. They were also frightened of the police. That's how bad it was.

Still, being underground had its pluses. Petra was wonderful company. She never once lost her temper or descended into gloom. I was filled with admiration. More important, we had become firm friends.

★

We took very little with us out of a misplaced concern for the sturdy little donkeys. A *debe* filled with four gallons of water for drinking and cooking, a blanket for us, two as presents for Lesepen, two bed rolls, a small kerosene stove, a gas lamp, a torch, a pot, five tin bowls, five tin mugs, tea, sugar, *posho*, four pounds of dried meat (filched from the emergency relief supplies), and some onions.

We hit the road at eight o'clock beneath a sky so brittle it was almost transparent. The boys were carrying spears. I had Gogo's walking stick. The mountains marched beside us. First the gentle Ndotos, then the shark-toothed Lkortikal. Soon Lesirikan was in the distance, swimming in the heat of a mirage.

Robert swept his arm across the drought-sapped plains to Lkortikal. 'We fought the Turkana there in 1980. They brought their cattle this far south,' he said with relish. The two tribes enjoyed an unwavering feud over grazing rights. 'No one was killed, but a *murran* was hit from behind with a spear. It entered to the left of his spine. I pulled it straight through. Blood was pouring down, but he walked back to the *manyatta*. We packed the wound with herbs and it healed. We didn't take him to the hospital because the police would have questioned us.'

'It's amazing that no blood vessels or organs were damaged. In fact, it's a miracle he survived,' observed Mark. Robert laughed, exhilarated by the memory.

I strode beside the boys, my arms slung over the stick laid along the back of my neck Samburu fashion. The undulation of the plains, imperceptible from a vehicle, was noticeable on foot, easing calf muscles on the gentle downward slopes and testing the thigh muscles as a wave of khaki grasses rose towards us. I was infused with the pleasure of walking. In the vastness of the world around me; the rhythm of sandalled feet upon the earth, the silence of the air, the sun and my companions; I sensed that these moments of promiscuous happiness were what we searched for all our lives.

By midday we had reached the dam, which was now a basin of parched earth. We stopped to brew tea and eat *sirikan*, dried meat. 'We've done nothing,' said Chopiro, 'less than fifteen miles.'

I helped Chopiro unload the gear and get the tea going. Mark sat crosslegged beneath a thorn tree, hacking away at the meat with a *simi*. Robert wandered off to inspect the dam and scout the way. Bosco stretched out on the ground, using his right forearm as a head rest. That first break established the allocation of chores for the rest of the trip.

That afternoon Robert left us to show a young woman the way to South Horr. She was walking on her own and planned to do the fifty-mile trip in a day. There were no tracks or trails to follow so Robert said he would escort her round the eastern side of Sartim Mountain. We would skirt round its western flank and join him further on. I marvelled at Robert's confidence in finding us again.

Travelling by foot was the only mode of transport here unless you were lucky enough to hitch a ride. Vehicles came to places like Tum and Lesirikan about once a week. If you weren't a friend of the driver, you needed a good reason, preferably a life-and-death one, before you could climb aboard.

I knew of a blind warrior who had started up a goat trading business, walking between settlements and buying goats to sell in Baragoi or Maralal. To get from one place to the next, he 'hitched a lift' with passing travellers, guided by the sound of their footfalls in the dust. I once met him on the road, walking in the slipstream of another warrior and pulling a goat behind him. I stopped and offered the party a ride. The two men stuffed the billy into a sack, threw it into the back of the car and off we went.

On another occasion, I opened the door of the clinic to the sight of a man crawling across the plains on stumps. His legs had been amputated above the knee. Later on I saw him sitting at Bosco's feet on Kattra's verandah, catching the gossip from passers-by. I was intrigued.

'Where have you come from?'

He offered his chin to the northern horizon. 'Over there.'

'What are you doing here?'

'I'm on my way to Baragoi.'

'Why?'

'To ask my brother for food for the family.'

'Why didn't you send someone else? I could ask him for you when I next go to Baragoi.'

He shook his head. 'I want to see how he is.'

Sweat was dripping down my back. It was very hot. I was thirsty, but we were rationing ourselves to one cup of tea at each stop. Bosco noted this and stopped by a small *Commiphora* tree. He used his *simi* to scrape off some of the silvery gum oozing from its bark and handed it to me. The unpalatable taste of incense was soon replaced by a pleasant camphor flavour. Chewing it brought some saliva into my mouth. I nodded my thanks and grinned back at Bosco.

'If you are tired, we can stop anywhere to sleep the night,' he said.

'I thought we had to find a *boma* for the donkeys because of the lions.'

'There aren't any lions around here.'

'The last time I went to Tum, I saw lion tracks in a *lugga* [river bed].'

'Well,' conceded Bosco, 'there are lions, but they don't like us because we have spears. Do you have a torch? If I shine it in their eyes, they'll run away.'

'Why do you always chase the lions instead of leaving them alone?'

'Mary Anne, we can't ignore them. If we did, they would eat us and our cows, our property. When they bother us, we have to find them and kill them. If fifteen of us go after a lion, he will wound each one of us who fights with him. They are bad.'

'Aren't you afraid?'

Bosco laughed. 'We aren't afraid. We can't be afraid.'

We walked for another two hours, gauging our progress by the hills: Maragot, Lodocheke, Uasoboir and later, Partikwet and Lugasera. Finally we drew close to Kowop with its bald, sprawling peaks. Standing in the grasslands that fell away from these camel-like humps was a red-clad figure, as solitary as an ancient anthill. He was the first man we had seen since leaving Lesirikan. When we were less than a mile away, Bosco and Chopiro veered west in the direction of his cattle herd. They wanted to ask news of the way.

They strode as if springs were fastened to the soles of their tyre sandals, holding their heads high like secretary birds. As they drew near to the herder, they planted their spears in the ground. Then they squatted low on their haunches to show they intended no harm. Courtesies like this were observed in frontier territory. The Turkana still raided. So did the *ngorokos*.

Beyond the dun flag of deserted land before us, some miles still in the distance, was the dirt road that led north to Lake Turkana. None of us had a watch, but we knew by the sun it was about four o'clock. Our pace quickened. As the only road we would meet that day, it was something of a landmark. The place where we would cross was known as 'the injection' because it was the junction where Samburu feet mingled with tyre marks.

To our surprise, for few vehicles passed that way, we saw first one and then another Toyota Landcruiser. They sped by in parcels of dust as we drew near. I waved but neither slowed down. By now we were on the edge of the road. A third car passed us, stopped and reversed. A man leant out of the window and said in unalloyed Sloane, 'I say, Mary Anne, what are you doing here?'

The encounter was so out of context, bringing with it another life that was light years away from this one, that I was stymied. What was I doing? I had an explanation for the Samburu, but I suspected it wouldn't seem rational to this red-faced person and his two female companions. I fumbled for an answer. Eventually something came to mind.

'Walking.'

'Walking?' he echoed. 'Where have you come from?'

I pointed behind me. 'Over there.' I was no longer interested in this conversation. My attention had shifted to the water bag hanging from the wing mirror. A few drops of moisture had bled through the canvas. They were so close I could have collected them on my finger and put them in my mouth.

'Where are you staying? Is there a lodge round here?'

Now I was truly flummoxed. This was a question I had been asking myself for some time. It was close to evening yet there was no sign of a *manyatta* where we could doss down for the night. I could have launched into an explanation of donkeys and lions and bandits and the need to find a *boma*, but I didn't. That was Samburu business. It was Mount Nyiru, hunching like a malignant grey goblin on the horizon thirty miles away, that gave me the cue. I pointed once again. 'There.'

'Gosh, you must be fighting fit,' said one of the girls. She had an open bottle of Sprite in her hand. On the back seat was a cool box.

'We're going camping,' offered the man, 'How long is it to Mount Kulal?'

There was no answer to this one. I could only calculate distances by walking. I shrugged. 'I don't know.'

'Well, must be off then.'

We gazed at the departing spiral of dust. 'Who was that?' asked Mark.

'He lives next door to me in Nairobi.'

We continued in silence, working our way downwards through a ravine embedded with stones and boulders. Some fifteen minutes later, as we reached its floor, Chopiro suggested a tea break. Still silent, we tethered the donkeys, unloaded the gear, lit the stove, brewed up the tea and squatted with mugs in our hands.

Chopiro looked at me. 'I say, Mary Anne, what are you doing here?' We rolled on the ground in adolescent giggles, not caring that we'd spilt our tea.

Soon the cool air currents of night had deposited a tonsure of cloud on Nyiru's summit. In a *lugga* we disturbed a Rendille girl taking her goats back to the *boma*. She gave a cry of dismay and ran behind a rock, her long hide skirt flapping in her wake. We had crossed into the no man's land where tribes ebbed and flowed in search of grazing and spoils and where every stranger was assumed to be a bandit. The *ngorokos* – Turkana and Pokot – raided with impunity. Maralal was the nearest police post, but they never patrolled this far. There were lions, too. And still there was nowhere to sleep.

Uneasiness intersected with contentment, unbalancing the happiness of the day. Bosco related how the *ngorokos* had stolen 10,000 cattle not far from here a few months previously. 'They killed nine people,' he said in low tones. I was conscious of tension, not sure if it was my own or shared. I took over the donkeys, driving them on with my stick and an encouraging '*choi choi*'. The others dropped behind, keeping the same steady pace. Perhaps the uncertainty was mine alone after all.

Robert suddenly joined us, appearing around a bend in the *lugga*. As irrepressibly cheerful as ever, he smiled and shouted, displaying a keyboard of teeth. He hadn't been able to find us so had returned to Sartim and followed our tracks from there. His circuitous journey was a source of amusement for everyone, particularly him.

We walked down the *lugga* for another mile or so. Chopiro reckoned we had covered about thirty miles, perhaps more. Had we not come as the crow flies but wandered an elliptical route instead? Or was Tum further away than we thought? The sky and land were gun-metal grey, darned together with rose threads. I was beginning to feel tired. Perhaps we should sleep outside and take turns as sentry with the torch.

As the last light melted away, Chopiro spotted some white dots on a hillside. 'Those are goats!' he cried, 'There must be a *manyatta* nearby.' Mark and I both scoffed at him. It was quartz. A mile closer and the whisper of bells sounded on the still air. I could just make out stick legs, pin heads and flat backs. Goats. 'Of course,' Chopiro grinned, 'They were moving so how could they be stones? My eyes never lie.'

Their herder was a young Samburu girl of only twelve or thirteen. She was accompanied by her father, who had brought along a weather-beaten .303 as protection. They were staying in a wretched encampment on a slope above a *lugga*. It had been built by Turkana, but they had abandoned it long ago. The thorn enclosure to protect stock from lions had collapsed. The huts, rudimentary at the best of times, had disintegrated. We found a small, dilapidated one that was still standing. The walls were falling apart, but it had a roof. We unloaded and secured the donkeys. There was no room in the hut for our gear, so we left it outside.

On the hillside above us, far too close for comfort, we saw the fire of a Turkana encampment. They had no animals with them. What were they doing here? Perhaps they were asking the same question about us. The wind growled and snatched up smoke from the cooking fire. I lay there listening to the dry sounds of night, the scrape of spoon against tin pot, the cry of a nightjar, the rattle of vegetation being disturbed and the barely audible murmur of the Turkana. I was conscious of a palpable tension, of man mistrusting man. At that moment I was Samburu, drawn into their collective unease.

Robert pulled bits of the wall off and threw them on to the fire to keep it alight. 'Don't do that,' scolded Mark.

Bosco laughed. 'This is only a Turkana hut and we are the owners now.'

I found it impossible to sleep. The space was so cramped that we had to lie in a circle, each one resting his head on the next person's feet. I crawled out and lay down in a nearby hut. It was no more than a roofless shell. Mark joined me. We lay looking at the sky. There were so many stars it was like a black colander held up to a spotlight.

'It's beautiful, isn't it?'

'Yes. Do you think a lion could jump in here?'

'Eeemaaay! Don't be silly. Anyway, they'd go for a donkey first.'

It *was* beautiful. And they *would* go for the donkeys. But this didn't dispel my anxiety. I was annoyed with myself. And soon fell asleep.

Dawn broke behind an overcast sky and brushed Nyiru's summit. We left soon afterwards. There was only one waterhole between Lesirikan and Tum, Maji Chumvi (salt water). Robert and Chopiro announced they would go there to fill up the *debe*, a detour of some five miles. We followed Bosco, climbing a gradual, rocky slope. He trudged along behind the donkeys, his mood as cloudy as the day. By ten o'clock, as the haze dispersed, he had brightened. He succumbed to melancholy early in the morning and sometimes at night. I was beginning to understand him. He was governed by the sun.

Hours later Robert and Chopiro caught up with us. The *debe* was threaded on to a pole slung between their shoulders. They had walked on to take a look at Uaso Rongai, the place of rushing water. They reported five mud buildings in an acacia grove and two laconic warriors sitting on a barrel staring at a few camels. Civilisation. It sounded awesome.

Mid-afternoon we turned a corner round Nyiru to follow its western flank, which stretched out endlessly, ridge after ridge. By now we had joined the road that led to Tum. Its sandy surface made the going heavy. It was even hotter than the previous day. My feet were sore and my back ached. My pace slowed. I trailed behind. The boys were patient and didn't chide.

Robert dropped back to keep me company. 'This is the best road in the district. It was made by the Lkimaniki when they were warriors. [They were circumcised in 1948.] The British thought they were causing too much trouble so they rounded them up and put them to work making this road. The men were fastened together in a chain by a rope that passed through the holes in their ears.'

'Robert, is that really true about the rope?'

'Of course it is!'

We hit town at dusk. Some miles before arriving, the boys 'broke' their spears in two by sliding the long metal tips free of the wooden shafts and hid them in the luggage along with their *simis* and *rungus*. Walking unarmed illustrated we were coming in peace. Indeed, we could hardly have done otherwise. We were all dog tired.

George the schoolmaster was there to meet us. His family were one of about a dozen who lived on the mountain. He led us to the house of the headmaster of the Tum primary school. I marvelled at its luxury. There were chairs and a table. We were offered as much water as we could drink. The headmaster's wife made us tea and whipped two eggs into an omelette, which we shared.

Afterwards, when I hobbled out the door, she threw me a small smile. 'You'll feel even worse tomorrow.'

George had arranged for us to stay in an empty room behind his sister's shop. There was nothing in it, but it seemed very cosy.

★

'Hello.' I smiled at the family sitting next to me in the airport transit lounge.

'Hello,' said the wife.

'I saw you on the plane. Were you on holiday in Tanzania?'

'Yes,' she nodded and paused. 'Now I remember. You were travelling with . . . your daughter?'

'That's right. Some trip, wasn't it? Twelve hours behind schedule. No food . . .' I lingered on the last word, but to no avail. 'How did you like Tanzania?'

She cocked her head and pursed her lips. 'Magnificent scenery. And all those *animals*. We couldn't get over it. But such *poverty*.'

'I know. It's terrible.' I shook my head in mock commiseration. 'I just don't know how they cope. I guess that's why they have so much crime. It's unbelievable. You can't leave a thing unlocked. Disappears immediately. Such a pity. It really isn't safe any more. My daughter and I were mugged just before getting on to the plane. They took everything. Cash. Credit cards. We're lucky to still have our passports, I guess.' I furrowed my brow as if a thought had just struck me. 'Still, it's a real nuisance. I mean, here I am stuck in the airport for God knows how long. I haven't eaten since yesterday. And I haven't got a penny on me to buy food with.'

Her mothering instincts came rushing to the fore. She rounded on her husband. 'George, did you hear that? This poor woman is starving. Where are those biscuits? Don't we have a banana?'

George rummaged in a carry-all and produced half a packet of biscuits and two bananas. They were passed over.

'Well, I didn't mean to . . . Are you sure? That's very kind,' I said ingenuously. I'd picked well.

This was what it had come to. Scrounging food off strangers at Nairobi airport. We were flying to England. The only problem was, we weren't quite sure when. The plan had been to meet up with Tara in the transit area and catch a connecting flight to London on Sudanair. However, the flight had been delayed indefinitely. I had been told it would arrive sometime that week. Travelling with the Sudanese was more like taking a bush taxi than flying on an international carrier. When I had complained to one of the ground staff, she had retorted, 'That's what you get for using a bucket airline. If you want service, pay more and take British Airways.' She had a point.

Petra had gone home to join Tara who, by this time, had packed up our belongings and stored them in a neighbour's attic. I had cadged a few bob off someone so I could phone them every day from a call box. One evening friends brought them to the airport restaurant and we signalled and smiled at each other through the glass panel that divided the transit passengers from those on the other side of passport control. But it wasn't a prison. I was enjoying myself hugely.

Every few hours another planeload of people streamed through the gates and milled around. It was like a rollover cocktail party. I sized up the transit passengers and chatted to anyone who looked interesting. The days passed in a continuous round of meals – on them, of course. Bankers, businessmen, tourists. They were only too pleased to have someone to idle away the hours with. And an interested audience for their stories. The old axiom that confidences are imparted to strangers in planes extends to airports as well. My notebook was rapidly being filled with everything from corruption scandals to the funding of rebel movements.

I had an airport buddy. His name was Mohamed. He was a student from the tiny Comoros Islands in the Indian Ocean. He was going to the Sudan to study electrical engineering at the University of Khartoum. When I discovered him, he was in bad shape. He didn't have a Sudanese visa so had been prevented from taking the previous Sudanair flight. Neither did he know when his visa would come through. He spoke only Arabic and French so couldn't make himself understood by the Kenyans. When I met him, he hadn't eaten for three days because he had no money. Whenever I was invited to lunch or dinner, Mohamed came with me. At night we spread out our sleeping bags on the floor of an empty room we'd found. It was all very comfortable.

One night we were rudely awakened by Tara, who was standing over us. 'Where the hell have you been? We're going to miss the flight. I've been looking all over for you.'

'Don't get excited. There's plenty of time yet. The alarm's set for just about now. I wasn't going to disappear. By the way, this is Mohamed. My daughter, Tara.'

'Come on. Petra's waiting for us,' Tara harrumphed crossly. I didn't blame her.

At the check-in point I gave Mohamed all the money we had and hugged him. 'Don't worry, your visa will come soon,' I said in French. He started crying. I started crying too. He looked like an abandoned puppy as he watched us depart.

London was predictably cold and wet though apparently it was a temperate winter. Petra had to go back to school. Tara, who was taking a year off before starting university, was returning to a job in an advertising agency.

In a stroke of synchronicity, my Nairobi office-mate, Kathy Eldon, had moved to London already. She offered me a room in her flat. The girls were given the living room to use whenever they wanted, but they now had their own rooms with their father and stepmother, Anthony and Roseanne, in their country home in Hampshire. It had been decided that Petra would take a week off school and stay in Hampshire to give her time to recover from the rigours of being on the run in Tanzania.

That first day, we did everything an ordinary English family does before term starts. We went shopping in the morning. In the afternoon we watched *A Fish Called Wanda* and laughed heartily. That evening we ate out at an Italian restaurant. It was a small, cosy place. We chatted about school and Tara's job. Then Petra said, 'I wonder what Kipenget's doing right now?'

My heart slipped its muzzle. In the disturbing afterglow of an innocent question visions floated in the candlelight. Sandy river beds sparsely fringed with flat-topped thorn trees; people who stared with graceful curiosity; a vast landscape that embraced several mountain ranges; the silky gaze of soft-humped camels; a pastiche of ochre-clad children, a warrior with an ostrich feather in his hair, a euphorbia bush.

I am a scant drinker and have a weak head for alcohol, but that night, after the girls had gone to bed, I decided I needed a stiffening tot. I discovered a bottle of Romanian slivovitz and poured out a few fingers. It had the bouquet of aviation fuel, but after several sips, a certain peasant fruitiness rode roughshod over the palate. Rather comforting to have that warmth in the stomach. I poured some more fingers. And some more. Sense of time and place ebbed away.

Cold black, coal black sky. A shrivelled slice of lemon moon in the window frame. Out on the plains an animal howled. A tormented, wounded, bestial keening. Close. So close. There must be lions about. A hand on my shoulder. 'It's all right, Mummy. Shssss. It's all right.' The hand slid into mine. The donkeys. We must find a *boma*. I followed.

The next morning Tara phoned her stepmother. 'Mummy's taken an overdose. She's just lying there and doesn't move.'

'Don't be stupid. Your mother, of all people, isn't going to commit suicide. The next train's at 10.12. Tell her and Petra to be on it,' Roseanne retorted. I got there in robot mode. It was a truly stupendous hangover.

The initial months in exile, for that is how I regarded it, passed in an orgy of self-pity. I had resigned my strings with *The Sunday Times* and *The Independent.* I couldn't report on East Africa from London, and there was nothing for me on the desk. Besides, I didn't want to be shackled to an office job in London. I was lucky enough to be offered two freelance jobs as soon as I arrived. For several weeks I was kept busy during the day and had some money coming in.

After that, the void. I talked little and cried often because I was safe and wasn't used to it. I spent a lot of time sitting in my room gazing at naked trees outside the window then watching tiny, priapic buds appear on their boughs. I didn't bother to unpack my suitcase. In Africa I was never bored or lonely, but I didn't know what to do with myself in this strange place.

'You're like a zombie who's graced us with her absence,' Tara chided. In fact, I felt like a caged gorilla. I wanted to drum my chest and send the walls catapulting into the grey sky to the echoes of my screams. Looking back on it, I was a monstrous pain in the neck. Only the unstinting encouragement and humour of Tara, Kathy, her daughter Amy and several other friends kept me going. I was so trenchantly miserable that finally I even disgusted myself.

One day Kathy came and sat on the bed. 'You've gone on like this for long enough. Why don't you do something about it? Let's see some anger instead of all this self-pity.' She was right. I had lived one life in Kenya. It was time to start a new one.

★

We agreed that before visiting Lesepen we would loiter, a favourite Samburu occupation. We washed our clothes and ourselves in a mountain stream. We had a look at the school and passed the time of day in the *dukka*, which was owned by a Somali. We inspected the abandoned dispensary. Three years earlier, the Italian priest who ran it had been murdered by *ngorokos*. They had ambushed his truck, shot him and set his body alight. The bandits had also shot and wounded two of the boys who had been with him. One of them had kept the priest's work alive by becoming the town's catechist.

Tum faced on to the Suguta Valley, a badland at the foot of Lake Turkana that was the *ngorokos'* retreat. No one else, apart from some hardy Turkana, ventured into this sweltering, Dantesque depression where temperatures touched 125° F. Looking down from the edge of the escarpment, it seemed as if some malevolent spirit had been at work, slashing the laval terrain into knife-edge scarps and sprinkling some symmetrically perfect volcanic cones into the interstices.

Geologists believed this hostile terrain began to be formed millions of years ago when radioactively generated heat melted rock deep within the earth. The pressure made the earth's crust buckle and subside from the surrounding plateau like a lift disappearing down a shaft. A million years later, titanic subterranean currents cracked the earth's mantle yet again. Treacly molten rock called magma erupted through twenty-mile-deep fissures, showering lava around with the force of a nuclear explosion. This herculean rifting gave the geological formation its name. The fifty-mile-wide Suguta was the meanest stretch of the Rift Valley.

After the priest was murdered, the army sent a punitive expedition against the *ngorokos*. It was lead by General Lekerde Lenges, a Samburu whose family came from Uaso Rongai. They entered the Suguta on foot with camels. The conditions were so terrible that six men deserted. Two of them died of thirst trying to find their way out of the roadless valley. Another soldier died of heatstroke. Despite disorientation in the harsh environment, the army had an advantage. Military helicopters flew overhead to scout out the bandits' hiding places. They were discovered behind a hill of laval scree. There was a gun battle. Everyone in the *manyatta* was shot dead, including four women and two children. The army mounted four more expeditions to mop up the remnants of the *ngorokos*, shooting the men and confiscating the cattle. For some time after that the area was relatively peaceful. Then there was a resurgence of bandit activity. But by this time, the priest's murder had been forgotten. The army was busy elsewhere.

Word soon got around that a doctor was in town. Late that afternoon Mark was summoned by the catechist. His wife had just given birth and had stomach pains. Mark set off to treat her. Chopiro and Robert went along too. Bosco and I remained behind, 'loitering' in our room.

There was a knock, a face silhouetted in a pole of light as the door opened. 'Mamma, come, come. You are needed,' it whispered. I followed the man along the dusty street, past barred doors and shuttered windows, up the hill toward the church, hurrying beneath an evening sky that lay upon us like a bruise. The town was ghostly and silent, as if it had been hoovered clean of inhabitants.

He swerved left, gesturing with his hand at a cluster of people already indistinct in the twilight. They parted for me and sighed, as if the wind had soughed through their midst. Squatting at their feet, his back to the wall of a building, was a dark and wild-looking man. The newcomer had none of the things that denote a man's status: bead necklaces, earrings, a blanket or cloth, a stick. He clutched a foul-smelling parcel of meat and was naked. An *ngoroko*.

I sensed anger mixed with fear amongst the onlookers as they stared down at this totem of barbarity. The *ngoroko*, on his part, gazed straight in front of him as if they didn't exist. An implacable atavism sat in his crude, obsidian features. This, I thought to myself, is what cavemen looked like.

'Mamma, he was brought to town by two men. Chief Thomas of Parkati sent him.' The silence returned. Bewildered by this responsibility, they had shifted it on to my shoulders. As a medical representative, I had been called upon to do something.

'Are you hurt?'

This was translated into Turkana. The man said something and pointed to his head. Two pie-shaped wedges of flesh had been excised from his skull. They had the symmetry of tribal scarification, but unlike ritual markings, they were teeming with maggots.

'He says it doesn't hurt.'

'Do you have pain anywhere?'

He leant forward to show a back striped with welts.

'Anywhere else?'

He lifted his right arm. It was grossly swollen. Greenish pus oozed from several gashes. Again he spoke.

'He says his arm hurts.'

'What happened to this man?'

'He was caught stealing in Suguta. He was killing animals just to kill without eating them. He also killed pregnant camels and ate the foetuses. The people beat him with *pangas* and sticks and stones. They wanted to kill him, but a *mzee* stopped them. So they tied him to a bush and left him. He stayed there for three days before he was found. Mamma, you must do something.'

A threadbare blanket was thrown round his shoulders. He rose to his feet and followed me down the hill.

I had with me injectable painkiller in case of bullet wounds or lion attacks, but I didn't know how to administer it. Bosco watched, inscrutable, as I handed the man two aspirin with his biscuits and tea. Bosco had changed. This was a new aspect of his personality. He was neither petulant nor carefree. His indifference to the fortunes of others, his ability to shrug off problems, had vanished. This stranger who sat vulturelike in the shadows was a reminder of the danger that lurked abroad. 'And he came here completely naked.' The bold warrior gave me a desolate look, then lay down and pulled his *shuka* over his head. Bandits frightened Bosco.

The gas lamp sputtered and died. I fumbled for matches. Would I be able to fit a new cylinder in the dark? Was the man going to die? At that moment, suspended in an eternity of waiting for the boys to return, the answers held equal weight.

The bandit didn't flinch while Mark wiped his head wounds clean with salt water. Mark did, though. He said it was the most disgusting task he had ever had to perform. Nevertheless, the worms had saved the patient's life. He had packed cow dung on to his head as a sort of substitute disinfectant. This had attracted the maggots. They had eaten the rotting flesh down to the bone of his skull, preventing gangrene. When it was done, Mark bandaged his head and dosed him with a bottle of pediatric antibiotics. It was all we had. The patient was then delivered to Tum's two administration police. These local men, who would have belonged to the tribal police in colonial times, were armed with old G3 rifles. They had no radio telephone or other means of communication with Maralal. Neither were there any vehicles in Tum.

Since coming to town, the boys had been sharing a cowhide to sleep on, lined up on the polished skin like sardines in a tin. I had chosen to spread a sleeping bag on the other side of the room. That night Chopiro said, 'We mustn't leave Mary Anne to sleep on her own.' The others concurred heartily. I laid the sleeping bag next to them and snuggled close. I was touched by their concern and deeply relieved. Their companionship, the sense of family, was a precious thing.

★

14th January 1989

Dear Mam,

How are you? Are you fine? I am actually very sorry for what happened when we were with you. My country has hated you but I feel that there is no one on this earth valuable to me than you. You are my foster mother but a time comes for one to see that you are not only a foster mother but a real mother. You shed your warm tears during departure time and wept because you cared and loved us. With me I wept physically but internally I wept the most. I had a black out for two days and I couldn't know what caused it. I was very much disturbed in the mind and thought of you staying in uncomfortable place in Tanzania. When I saw you disappearing from your home compound I saw as if I am not going ever to succeed in life. The question is 'Will I ever feel the touch of a lovely and caring mother like you? Will you remember that you have a son in Africa who needs encouragement and wisedom?'

As you know, my Aunt is very old. She is growing weak and weak every day. Right now on January she is very ill. Her age group has all passed away and I don't know her day. She is roughly sixty-five years old now. When her time comes I will actually remain alone and will know what is called loneliness. I don't want you to get moved but that is what I am supposed to tell you.

What I would like you to know is that whenever you are in a sorrowful state I am sharing your sorrowfulness state with you. These days tears just drop off my eyes when I remember you and your loving parental love.

Goodbye my mum but not for a long time. God will give us time to meet.

Yours,

Peter Lekerian

17th January 1989

Dear Mary Anne,

Much and lovely greetings from my family and mostly me. How are you and how are Petra and Tara? Say a very big hello to them and tell them I am highly missing both of them.

I received my present and I appreciate very much. We are really missing you M.A. that every day and night I dream seeing your face in front of me and I do even cry when I remember the joy I used to have when you were around.

Peris is very happy for the uniform you bought her and she has sent a lot of love to Petra plus you. She always tells me about you each day asking when you will return to Kenya and live together. But I know one day the light will shine and we will all be together as it was before.

Mary Anne, since you left I first slept on Tuesday the 2nd. I could not eat not even sleep or drink only crying when I remember that you are gone.

The worst day came when I read the newspaper concluding that you are not coming back. My heart stopped for a second. I couldn't believe this.

I am very happy for the letter you wrote and the good news of paying me the garage course and giving food for my family. M.A., I can't pay for that but only pray to God to give you more and keep you safe. I do always during the day and when sleeping remember you in prayers. We appriciate for you good care, love and tender that you've done to our family.

I do try to remember how happy we were when you lived at Langata. We got everything we wanted love, clothes, money etc. and many other things that really enjoyed us but now we are crying asking where you are and how we can meet each other.

Now for the time being the only worst problem is books for our children because my third born brother is in Standard 8 and the fourth born in Standard 6 and Peris in Standard 4 so they told me that they don't have books so they ask help from you kindly. I hope you will.

Me I am fine and only missing shoes. I would request you to buy me shoes in London. My choise is Hi-Tek for they last long and Plata for football for my hobby is football and I always practise and play for the time been. I hope you will thank you.

On my side dad is fine and drinking as usual. Early at seven o'clock he is drunk and also it so happened that on 24th December my father came home. He started vomiting and it came that he couldn't breath. We celebrated the Xmas eve in Kenyatta [Hospital] with my neighbour.

Mary Anne we miss you physically and in our hearts. You have should love for us which I never received from anyone, neither my family. You have cared for us more than our parents. I really know that God will reward you. There is a verse in the bible which says If you give what you have to the poor (the small you have) God will double it to you. Wish that you will find a job and continue with your love, tender and care. We will never and never forget you, M.A., throughout our lives.

With great love,
Chege and family

9 March 1989

Dearest Mammy,

Much and warm greeting coming flying to you wherever you're. Sure can you rely recognise who is on the line communicating to you? It is non other than your son Meriape. I am her in Kajiado thinking much about you and Tara and Petra. Mary Anne sure it was a very sad day when you left us with tears. When mammy had of what happened she started crying and unfortunately everybody in our home too. I hope you're fine M.A.

Here in Olkejuado it is very hot and I am still pushing on with my academic work. The school is fine and I am seeing that I am working very hard for my future. I am also receiving very many letter from Mark and he sounds okay and alright. I have not visited your house but I think on April I will go and say hello to Jengo and the rest. Peter also wrote me a letter and he sounds alright too. I visited Kate [Macintyre] in the office and she is fine but too much work. It sounds from her that there is a lot of work in Samburu.

Mary Anne receive also greetings from Kipiget and all our family. I am sure they are missing you and they want you back if God wills.

How is Tara and Petra. Say supa to them all and give them each my love. In fact, I stayed in your house and take care of everything until the time you came from Tanzania.

How was Tanzania? I think rely you didn't enjoy much there because you left your present place and went and stay with forigener. But all applies the same because we can't do anything to the Government. But I am sure and beliving that one day we shall see each other mammy. Take care and relax, mammy for we are still on your side.

Lots of love,
Meriape.

22nd May 1989
Dearest Mary Anne,

Receive my warm greetings as we are being separated by seas, lakes and hills. How are you pushing on there? How are Tara and Petra? I hope and pray that all of you are in good health. I am very grateful to you what you are doing for me. I know that you mind about me very much. Inside your heart I know that you feel that I am your son and I will always be.

Thanks for the watch you sent for me. I promise that I'll use it nicely and look nice in it. I will reduce my football playing in order to get more time to study. As a result of that I'll try my best in class and I hope that I'll get on smoothly.

Do you remember what you once told me when we were driving down to your home in Langata? You told me 'Peter! A good duck teaches its young ones to wade through the mud' or 'A good lioness teaches its cubs to hunt.' You told me to find these meanings. It means that a good Mother doesn't give children presents and gifts for ever but instead she teach them the ways of getting presents and gifts themselve when their mother is not present. Right now I know that you are helping me to depend on my own in the days to come and I am very hapy about it.

Mike [Eldon] and Kate are helping me a lot. Kate has contributed during my operation and I am very grateful about it. Mike is paying my school fees, accomodating me and look into all my homely affairs. He has become Mary Anne the second. He is helping me to know my career. He gave advices which are very important.

Mum, now it is your time to look after me but I assure you that another two or three years to come you'll also need something from me. I need to take care of you as well as my people. I know that I'll give you and your family a special dinner of my sweat.

May we meet when Our God wishes. Bye bye for a while but not
for ever.
Peter Lekerian

★

Mount Nyiru is sacred. It is the birthplace of the Samburu god, Ngai. It is
the fountainhead of Samburu tradition. It is where boys from the black
cattle group of the Masula clan slaughter a bull on the stone altar of
Kosikos to initiate circumcision. So revered is this inselberg of faith that
the huts which are prepared for circumcision are built with the doorways
facing its slopes. Even the trees, *ltarakoi*, are holy. *Murrani* cut them down
to fuel fires at ritual ceremonies and pluck handfuls of old man's beard
lichen from the bark to wrap around their bead bracelets. At night ghosts
cry in the silver forest, startling the elephant and greater kudu and the
leopard that hide in the dark silence of the ravines.

We wanted to climb to its 9,000-foot summit. We had been told it
would take eight hours there and back. We had planned to leave early to
escape the heat yet it was eight o'clock by the time we locked the door of
our room. There wasn't even a picnic to show for our dilatory departure.
Our only food was one *chapatti* (an unleavened pancake) folded into
Mark's back pocket. None of us had a very strong concept of time.

There were a few house calls to make first. At the administration police
post, the *ngoroko* sat in the sun, naked except for his bandages. He
reported his head felt fine but his arm still hurt. Mark handed over what
antibiotics we had left, and we moved on.

We climbed up a steep track. When it petered out, we made our way
between rocks and scrub to an isolated *manyatta*. We had been told there
was a young girl there whose baby wasn't feeding properly. She was
fourteen at the most, frightened by her new maternal role. The baby
couldn't have weighed more than three pounds. It looked like a shrunken
monkey and was so tiny Mark could cradle it in the palms of his hands.
Mark tried to show her how to tie it to her breasts with a *shuka* to keep it
warm, but she repeatedly placed it back on the cowhide. As exasperation
mounted on both sides, she flung the baby away from her and, to the
sound of her wails, lay down and covered her head with a *shuka*. Mark
picked the baby up and placed it beside her. 'It's horrible, horrible. She's
completely wild,' said Chopiro, shaking his head.

Mark shrugged. 'We can't do any more. It will die.' We left.

As we discovered on a subsequent visit to Tum some months later, this
was not the case. The girl was standing outside a *dukka* with her chubby,
smiling baby tied to her back. We learned the bandit had also survived and
was serving a prison sentence in the Maralal jail.

There was a third patient in need of treatment, who lived a day's walk away on the other side of the mountain. A man had fallen thirty feet out of a tree while collecting honey. His wife had been despatched to town to seek help. Given the distance and our lack of drugs, we had sent her back with a packet of aspirin. We were to meet him, too, on the next trip. I asked how he was. 'Fine, but when it rains it's a bit sore here,' he said, rubbing the back of his neck.

'They get better regardless. Medicine is a waste of time,' Mark commented.

Perhaps this was why, until they came to learn the wisdom of immediate treatment, people often regarded our dispensary at Lesirikan as a station of last resort. This ignorance of medical practice reminded me of the Dinka herder in southern Sudan who asked for an injection in his arm so it could go straight to his heart. The previous one in his bottom, he said, had fallen out through his feet.

One of the psychological principles of medical application in Africa was revealed to me by a doctor from the Gambia who headed a World Health Organization project to eradicate onchocerciasis. River blindness, as it is more commonly known, is a disease caused by a tiny worm that occurs in riverine areas. Microscopic parasites lodge in body tissues and gradually destroy their hosts' eyesight. It was a scourge that afflicted about one and a half million people. Then in the late 1980s, a drug was introduced that killed the worms. Its application was ninety-five per cent effective in the trials, but it sometimes caused an initial side effect of itching and some pain. Dr Ebrahim Samba cheerfully dismissed the notion that this might be a problem. 'In Africa a drug should be felt. It should shake a bit to be effective. So the side effects are a plus,' he explained.

It was certainly true that the Samburu, accustomed to hardship, demonstrated a resilience unheard of amongst Western patients. Another contributing factor to their survival was their knowledge of herbal medicine. They used a wide range of plants to clean wounds and cure disease, an area neglected by Western medicine with its strong bias towards drugs. Only just over a thousand of the earth's 265,000 plant species have been studied by scientists, yet as many as 40,000 could have medicinal or nutritional properties, according to the New York Botanical Garden's Institute of Economic Botany. The virgin forests of Samburu District were a library of medicinal knowledge waiting to be read.

Chopiro's warning about the heat was justified. It sat on us like a fur pelt as we made our way up a defile. I plodded along slowly, leaning on Gogo's walking stick and entrusting myself to Robert's judicious pace, filling the imprint of his tyre sandal as soon as he had vacated it. Like the others, I had lost several pounds since leaving Lesirikan. To make matters worse, we were running out of food just when we needed an extra intake of calories. My physical reserves were dangerously depleted.

Very soon the incline sharpened. Each step was like climbing two stairs at a time. A papery rustle sliced the stillness. I lifted my head to see a kite soaring into the gentian sky and stopped to admire the freedom of its flight. The rhythm of the ascent broken, I hastened on, grateful for the seconds' respite, still hostage to leaden gravity.

My thoughts, few and simple, kept me going. There was the prospect of a drink from a stream when we reached the top and of a sliver of *chapatti*, although the first was more tantalising than the second. I had reached that stage of malnourishment when eating took too much effort. In fact, food was no longer of any concern. I was preoccupied with pride. It had become a point of honour to match whatever the boys did and to match it with feigned ease.

A laborious four hours later we crested a table of pasture, startlingly green in this drought-stricken land. We did not stop to admire the view as Westerners would have done, but followed the path to a *manyatta*. A few yards from the thorn fence that encircled it, a fallen tree lay on its side. Small tongues of flame danced along the bark. Four women came out to greet us. They chattered like starlings. All was well at the *manyatta*. The men were out with the herds. There was water and grazing so the cattle weren't dying. No one was sick. Lions had tried to get into the *boma* the previous night so they had torched the tree to scare them away. Instead of being frightened, the lions had lurked nearby all morning. They had only left about an hour ago. We made our farewells and continued on our way.

Was it coincidence that we had taken the same direction as the lions? Robert and Bosco were walking with a newfound alertness as we wandered amongst the sepulchral junipers. So was I. The forest's breathtaking beauty was somewhat diminished by my efforts to x-ray every bush.

We stopped to kneel amongst some papyrus and drink from a clear stream. Bosco picked a handful of red berries and gave them to me to eat. Later, Mark divided up the *chapatti* and handed the thin strips of dough around. He and I used the short lunch break to climb a hill. From where we sat on a rock, savouring the *chapatti* crumb by crumb, we had a clear view of Kosikos. Its fissures gleamed in the afternoon sun.

It was when Robert spotted a round pug mark embedded in a patch of moist soil that our exploration of Nyiru was transformed into a hunt. We picked up the spoor of four lions, one male and three females, and followed them some distance before the tracks petered out. Robert cast about like a hunting dog on the scent. 'Look!' he cried, kneeling. We gathered round and stared at a fleck of mud no bigger than a pea. 'It has fallen from the lion's foot. They came this way.'

We moved on at a brisk walk, stopping every now and then as one or the other of the boys pointed to fresh spoor. By now the path was heading downhill. That was one small mercy. At least the lions were taking us in the general direction of home. I trotted along, sandwiched between Bosco and Chopiro. It was a carefully chosen position, one that I customarily took up when passing through snake-infested bush. To be at the head of the procession, I reasoned, was to be too exposed. If a lion sprang and Robert ducked – into the meat grinder. To be at the tail end was out of the question. Lions went for stragglers. Of course, they could always attack the flank, too. I could think of only one deterrent against ambush.

'Don't talk so loudly, Mary Anne. You'll frighten them off.'

'Sorry.'

We climbed over a tree trunk that had fallen across the path. Bosco gave it a playful thwack with his *rungu* as he passed, making me jump. He laughed with delight. 'You're not frightened, are you? You mustn't be frightened when you are with us.' Gone was the little boy who had been overwhelmed by a bandit. He was the ebullient, carefree warrior once more. I vowed never again to be critical of his mercurial changes of mood.

A bird called from a nearby tree, signalling danger. We had drawn in on our prey. The lion were only feet away. I kept walking, fixing my eyes on the ground. If I lifted them, I might catch sight of an unblinking eye as still as a copper coin or the twitch of a khaki ear in the interstices of undergrowth. My mind soared upwards to join the kites floating on the thermals of hot air. The woman walking down below began to sing loudly. The soft crash of vegetation was followed by silence. They had gone. I was not like the warriors. I never would be. But I was safe.

The descent was so steep that it took almost as long to go down the mountain as it did to climb up it. Nevertheless, I tackled it with an enthusiasm born of relief. By the time we reached Tum, skirted in twilight, my disgraceful behaviour had been forgotten.

'You walk like a *murran*,' beamed Chopiro.

'She's like a Land Rover. She keeps going all the time,' said Robert.

★

I wore a pink silk shirt beneath a neatly waisted suit. The earrings were fake pearls and diamanté. My shoes had low, clumpy heels that wouldn't get caught in pavement gratings. I guess I looked like a local until I took off my jacket and rolled up my sleeves. Londoners didn't have silver snakes coiled above their elbows.

How I hated interviews. I had thought to break into the magazine world or perhaps television, but in England, if you were a stranger, you needed to have a friend who was somebody who knew somebody. This left me out in the cold. I had compiled a portfolio which I carted around with me. Only Pierre Salinger of ABC Television looked at it. I was so pleased, I forgave him for never phoning back with a job offer.

The longer I stayed in London, the more I realised I was a foreigner. I thought and reacted as a white African. If that was the case then why not write about what I knew? Africa. There was much to be learnt from Africa. It generated fear, undistilled happiness, peace of mind and loathing. Its siren-like qualities seduced effortlessly, perhaps dashing you against the rocks, invariably shifting your perception of humanity. Yet few in the West understood the continent. Perhaps its most special quality was that it furnished the space to listen to your own inner voice. I couldn't lay claim to truly knowing Africa, but I could do my best to reveal its many aspects. The only way to do that, I decided, was to travel and write a book about what I saw.

I lacked two necessary ingredients for the project. Money and conviction. The latter was to come first – from an unexpected quarter.

Since her arrival in London, Kathy had been searching for spiritual answers to her life. She read avidly and meditated. She sought out people who were in touch with the higher planes of their being. One of her new acquaintances was John Howard, a soft-voiced, unassuming man who owned a video store in Eastbourne. On the face of it, John was just another shop-owner in the south of England whose horizons were limited by his job and geographic location. But there was more to John than that. He was a medium. His body channelled the thoughts and advice of spirits who had been on earth in previous lives and had yet to reincarnate into another body.

Several of these spirits took a special interest in Kathy. There was Grey Owl, the American Indian who spoke in parables and loved nature. Dr Gilbey was a Victorian medic given to prim chastisements. Mr Chan was down-to-earth and practical. He counselled her on money matters and career moves. The one I found most sympathetic was Mahatma Gandhi. He was gentle and wise and fond of philosophising.

At first Kathy used to take the train down to Eastbourne for her sessions with her guardian spirits. In due course, however, she began to communicate with them over the telephone. It was easier. When Kathy felt the need for guidance, she rang up John and asked if she could talk to them. Quarter of an hour later, after he had achieved a trance-like state, his wife Lucy rang back. 'Hello, Kathy. I've got Mr Gandhi on the line.'

Whereas Grey Owl's voice was deep and mellifluous and Dr Gilbey punctuated his acerbic statements with tinderbox coughs, Mr. Gandhi talked in lilting, singsong cadences. 'Hello, Kathy. How are you? You have not been centred this past week. You must look inwards to find your stillness . . .'

It was Kathy's habit to ask Mr Gandhi if he had anything to say about me. Invariably he counselled me to be less serious and to open myself up to the good things that were waiting to flow into my life. I appreciated Kathy's generosity in sharing Mr Gandhi's wisdom, but his pronouncements exasperated me. Maybe I was a bit intense, but I wasn't *that* serious.

Then one day Kathy came into my room. 'Mr Gandhi's on the phone. He wants to talk to you.' I sighed inwardly and left my desk. Usually Kathy passed on his messages. I didn't talk to him directly. I preferred it that way. Kathy chatted away to him as if he was sitting in the room with her. But I experienced an unnecessary compulsion to do some spiritual spring cleaning before coming into contact with those who were not physically amongst us. It was like going into a church where you are reminded that God can read your impure thoughts.

'Hello,' I said, a touch nervously.

'I cannot hear anything. Is the lady there?' he asked Lucy. Mr Gandhi wasn't good with technology.

'Yes, I think Kathy has passed the phone over to her,' Lucy reassured him.

'Hello, Mary Anne. How are you?'

'Fine, thank you,' I said politely, knowing he would read the lie.

'Your life is beginning to open up and there are little pieces of advice I can give you which may be of assistance to you. You are not yet sure how to develop the path that you are at present walking. It is making you very serious. Do you understand me? Hmmm? Hmmm? Can the lady hear me all right?' he asked Lucy.

'Yes. I can hear you,' I said. 'Tell me, Mr Gandhi . . . my book. Do you think it's a good idea?'

'In nine months you will find interest to work on subjects that are abroad. And this will give you the roving commission that will be so fulfilling to your own creative need. Because as you write, you will also be growing within yourself.'

The muscles knotted in my neck. 'Why nine months? I want to do it now. I want to go back to Africa in September.'

'In September?'

'Yes.'

'I am knowing that you will be going abroad within nine months and that will be correct. You should be examining the goal which you should attain. And the goal is in your art as a writer. I am giving you what you call in your Western countries a lot of meat to digest.' He gave a fastidious chuckle. Mr Gandhi enjoyed his *bons mots*. 'Some people are great pianists. Some are great painters. But you have an inspiration with words. You have a mind that can see through the walls that people build up. Therefore you must use that gift. But you must choose that which you are writing so that it doesn't simply become something for tomorrow's newspaper, which will be forgotten, but that which will have impact and make many people aware for a long time after they have read it. Hmm. Hmm. I cannot give you any more than that. I am simply reading from your aura.'

'Thank you.'

'It is a great pleasure. If you wish to come back, I will be most happy.'

'Thank you, Mr Gandhi. Goodbye and thank you.'

How could Mr Gandhi predict when I was going back to Africa? It was up to me to decide. Still, I felt. . . well. . . different. I sat down and wrote a letter to Andrew Neil, editor of *The Sunday Times*. I suggested I be put on retainer as the newspaper's roving correspondent in black Africa. I didn't want an office or a base. I wouldn't necessarily be covering the high-profile countries or the news spots. I knew this was not a strictly conventional suggestion, but, I wrote, this was exactly why he should consider it. I would deliver offbeat and colourful stories from remote parts of the bush, jungle and desert that weren't frequented by journalists.

It was a long shot. Bob Tyrer, then the foreign editor, had already told me there was no longer a place for me at *The Sunday Times*. Still, nothing ventured, no money gained.

Meanwhile, I went for an interview with CARE. They were looking for a press officer. I didn't like the idea of sitting in a London office and being on the receiving end of the fourth estate's histrionics, but there were two things going for the job. The agency had projects in Africa and I would be earning a salary. The interview went well. I liked the people. They seemed to like me. At the end of it I was told, 'This job isn't at the level of your capability, but if you want it, we would love to have you.' I said I would think about it and let them know.

The next stop that morning was an appointment with Owen Potts, a former postal worker turned full-time psychic. Kathy's doing again. He was a pleasant man with greying hair who gave consultations from a simply furnished office on the Embankment.

As I sat down, he said, 'Before I start, there is something I must tell you. You have the aura of a healer about you. It is very strong. It will come out in many ways. You have a powerful voice that's enhanced by an inner strength. You must use this voice. It is very, very powerful. You stimulate people's minds and create awareness. Your ability will become stronger once you have opened up your spiritual side. Now,' he paused and continued, 'you have big doubts about your work. You have a choice to make. You can work for someone else or you can work on your own.'

'Well, which shall I do?'

He smiled and lifted his hands palms upwards as if he was weighing the outcome. 'I can't make your decisions for you. Only you can do that. Your direction will be clear towards the end of the year or early in 1990. Link it with the spirit that is your guiding force. If you work for someone, it will be all right as an interim period. Then you must move on to self-employment. I want you to be free. It has got to be. It will make all the difference to what you want to do. Your confidence has been knocked severely. But you will gain back your positive thought and sense of strength and direction. You will make a decision very shortly and your mind will be clear. I feel a very strong opportunity which leaves you no choice. I must say to you, "Do it on your own." The situation is more firm than you think.

'I see a hospital. You work in the medical field but you are not a doctor. The urge to help people is very strong.' I nodded. He obviously thought I was a social worker of some kind.

He paused for a long moment. 'I see very strong emotions that put you back a lot. Now you are moving out of stress on to a very positive path. Your mind is stronger and will be a catalyst for making change.'

I nodded again. 'Yes, that makes sense to me. Tell me about my home.'

'The home you have now is temporary. You will have a home, but I can't see it at the moment. It may take longer than you think.'

'Do you see me travelling soon?'

'No. No, I don't.' My heart sank. I knew then, above all else, I wanted to write that book.

When I got back to the flat, Kathy was bursting with curiosity. 'What did he say? What happened? What about the interview?'

'Hang on. I'll tell you everything. Just let me make some tea.'

The phone rang. It was on the counter next to the kettle, so I answered it.

'Hello?'

'Hello. Mary Anne? It's Bob. Tyrer. Andrew Neil got your letter. He's passed it on to me.' I didn't even notice I had stopped breathing. At least the letter wasn't in the dustbin. That was something. 'He likes the idea. He wants to go with it . . . Hello? Are you there?'

'Yes, I'm here.'

'You'd better come down and discuss it. Give me a ring next Tuesday when things are quieter.'

'That's great news, Bob. I'll do that.'

'Fine. Bye.'

'Bye.'

'Yahoo!' I let out a joyous war whoop and punched the air.

Buoyed by this success, I wrote part of the first chapter of the book, drew up a synopsis and found an agent whom I liked tremendously. Jane Turnbull set up a string of meetings with publishers. The first meeting was with several directors of a well-known publishing house. We sat round an antique dining-room table in a room that had no office furniture in it at all. I talked for half an hour and, an unprecedented event, they listened with interest. At the end of this discourse the managing director slammed his hands down on the table, 'We must have this book!'

I said he would have to speak to Jane and asked if anyone knew where I could buy some bedsheets. The managing director took me outside and pointed, 'Do you see that blue sign? Turn right there. Take your first left and a block or two along you'll see a big store called Selfridge's. They have sheets.'

I squinted into the distance and nodded slowly. 'Okay, I think I've got it.'

The managing director wasn't fooled. He knew I hadn't understood a word. Suddenly he dropped to the ground, squatting on his haunches. 'Look,' he said, tracing the route on the pavement with his pen, 'You go along like this then right here. Then left. And it's here.' This was how Africans did it. They drew maps in the dirt. Now we both knew I would get there.

Which is what happened six, not nine, months after my phone conversation with Mr Gandhi. Spirits are not very good on dates because they live in timeless eternity. For Mr Gandhi, six or nine months was the same as a second.

★

I cannot remember if I had expected majesty, a heaping of finery upon a sunburst of colours. Samburu chic was, after all, African fashion at its creative best. The warriors' paint and glitter was enough to implant deep envy in David Bowie's heart. As the tribe's spiritual oracle, however, Lesepen eschewed vanity. Coils of copper clamped to his arms, the earrings of a *mzee* in his flapping ear-lobes, some thin strands of beads and a tobacco pouch falling on to his emaciated chest, these were all he wore apart from the strip of cloth about his waist. He dressed as a guru.

If Lesepen had driven back to Nairobi with me, he would have been just another illiterate and bewildered old man from the bush, but here he was a patriarch. His stewardship of Samburu ritual was a weighty burden for his bony shoulders, but he was a patently decent man who obviously took his responsibility of safeguarding the tribe's welfare seriously. The Samburu relied upon his wisdom. I saw this reflected in the faces of the boys. Awe had flattened their exuberance.

Time had shrivelled him, creasing his brow and cheeks, accentuating the skeletal thinness of his arms and legs, curving his body into parenthesis as he shuffled over the bare, rocky hillside. He regarded us with milky eyes. They seemed incapable of discerning a lamp on a moonless light let alone the barely perceptible movements of the heavens. 'So. You have come to see me.' Then to his wife, who stood outside her small hut, 'Make tea for the visitors.'

We sat on the ground some distance from his *manyatta*, which consisted of three low huts thatched with wild sisal from the mountain. Crows called from a tree. Some camels walked past. From our vantage point, we looked down on the Suguta Valley. The *manyatta* was some miles from town and had no protective thorn fence around it. Lesepen was raided often by *ngorokos*. Each time, his herds were replenished by the people of Tum.

'I have no need of material wealth,' he said in a voice as dry as tinder. 'God is the prime mover. He decrees our fate. God wills the things that are both good and bad. The lives of the people are like fingers. Some are short. Some are long. Some are rich. Some are poor.'

Lesepen's wife brought us black, sweet tea and for him a brew of herbs plucked from the mountain. 'My body has become feeble because there is no milk to drink,' he explained. 'You want to ask questions?'

I was encouraged by this friendly reception. Some years earlier, I was told, he had been visited by a bearded American anthropologist. Otherwise Lesepen had never received white people at his *manyatta*. 'What do you read in the heavens?' I said.

'This morning I read there was peace in the world. The stars were in equilibrium. I can predict what will happen according to the position of the planets Venus and Mars. We have had no good rains since 1981. This is because Venus and Mars have been blocked since the coup in 1982. God is punishing us with drought because the people have not been sacrificing goats and sheep for rain. That is why they starve. They used to slaughter for sacrifice every four years, but they have not done so since 1979.'

'What is the ritual way to sacrifice?' asked George.

He spoke in Samburu and translated Lesepen's replies into Swahili so that Mark and I would understand as well. George the schoolteacher, who was more learned than the rest of us, understood Lesepen's antique usage of the language. His interpretation was inadequate, he told us later, because the old man resorted often to parable and proverbs.

'*Sorrio* is no longer observed by the people. You must take a grey and black sheep and anoint it with milk and honey before the sacrifice. After it has been slaughtered, you hang the legs of the lamb from the ceiling of your hut as an oblation. You mix the contents of the stomach with the blood of the lamb and sprinkle it on the roof of the *manyatta*.

'Next year the Lkishili must perform the *lmugit* [ceremony] of the leaves for which they will sacrifice a black or grey ram. They will wash it with milk and honey before the slaughter. The *wazee* will watch closely to see how it behaves. If it shakes itself dry more than four times, it will rain.'

I hesitated to ask the next question, framing as it did the true reason for our safari. I feared the answer would carry the unbearable freight of drought, disease and death.

'Lesepen, when is it going to rain?'

His voice rose in pitch. There was, in its deliberate pace, something of the priest reciting the liturgy. 'It will rain in the tenth month. It will rain bountifully in Wamba district but the people will be sick. The people will enter into battle with the Somalis and will suffer. The people near Turkana will be spared but their cattle will die until only half their herds are left. In the other places, it will rain, but it will not be as plentiful as Wamba district. Half their heifers will remain to be tended.'

The hardship was no worse than we had expected. As for the rest, it was encouraging news.

The following October, I returned to Lesirikan, with the intention of making another safari by foot to Lesepen. That time, I was determined to do it on my own. I felt the need to test my courage. This gave rise to much discussion. The boys were adamant that I shouldn't sleep out on my own. Eventually, I had to admit a certain anxiety at the prospect of spending the night unarmed in bandit country. And so a compromise was reached. I would walk on my own all day. In the evening, Mark would meet me in the Land Rover on the South Horr road at the place that was by then known as the 'Mary Anne, What You Doing Injection' or simply Mary Anne's Injection.

That night we were kept awake by the drumming of rain on the dispensary's corrugated iron roof. My clothes were damp when I put them on in the morning. Even the dried meat hanging from a string above the stove had become soggy. Behind the town, the wind blew streamers of mist along the Ndotos. The rain continued through the morning. The drought had broken, just as Lesepen had predicted.

I walked up to Kattra's for tea. She was brimming with news. 'Someone came to town this morning and said they saw lions at the dam last night. I'm not surprised. Last month a man killed a lion at the same spot. He was bringing his bride back to Lesirikan, and it attacked her.' I sat there rubbing my right leg as I listened. I had had a nagging pain behind the knee for several days. Suddenly it seemed much worse. Perhaps it was the rain.

I found Mark sitting with Sammy in the empty dispensary. The inclement weather had kept the patients away. 'You're right. It was a stupid idea. I don't think I'll walk to Tum.'

He grinned. 'We'll drive there instead. Much more comfortable. We won't get so wet.' The death of that particularly hare-brained scheme was a great relief to everyone, not least myself.

Lesepen showed no surprise when Mark and I staggered out of the shadows, laden down with gifts. We gave him blankets, tea, sugar and *posho*, but the greatest delight was the framed photograph of the old man holding the kudu horn that was sacrosanct to the tribe. It was blown only to announce an *lmugit* ceremony or to summon the *murrani* to war.

After he had examined each item, one by one, we sat with our heads thrown back, looking at a pitch sky sluiced clean by the storms. 'That bright star at the bottom is *lakiradorop*, the short star. The fainter star at the top is called *lakirai*, the traveller. Lakirai must pass to the right of Venus for the year of the cow to arrive. Otherwise, it will be the year of the camel. That top star deals with donkeys, people and monkeys. The lower one is for cattle and other animals, including the wild ones.'

'And that star there that's twinkling more than the others?'

'That is politics. When I look at that, I can see what is happening in parliament.'

As the three of us lay on a cowhide discussing destiny, the moon rose over Nyiru's shoulder and flooded the Suguta Valley with silver.

'And that one?'

'When that top star is too close to the others, it means fighting. That is how it was on 2 August [the day of the coup attempt against Daniel arap Moi] and during Mau Mau [the rebellion that hastened independence from the British]. I can tell when the powerful ones are going to die. I read [Mzee Jomo] Kenyatta's death four months before it happened. The day the *mzungu* was shot by *shifta* [Somali bandits] at Loiyengelani [a settlement forty miles miles to the north on the shores of Lake Turkana], I read it in the evening star. Moi has many enemies but he will live for a long time.'

It was all gripping stuff. I had just written a political risk assessment of Kenya. Lesepen's forecast for Moi's tenure coincided with mine. I decided I would visit him again before I wrote the next one.

'The last time we came to see you, you told us the people at Wamba would fight with the Somalis. Did you know that *shifta* carrying automatics have been raiding *bomas* along the Milgis?'

'Yes, it is so.' He nodded his grizzled head. 'Do you have any questions to ask about your daughters?'

Tara was in her O-level year and struggling with the physics syllabus. 'My daughter is working very hard at school for exams next year. They are very important exams. There is one that worries her. It is about how electricity works and why trees don't fall off the mountains. Will she pass?'

Lesepen readjusted his blanket about his shoulders and filled the night with his silence. Then he spoke. 'Yes, the exam will go well for her.'

And it did.

4

War and Famine

The cost of one jet fighter = 40,000 village health clinics.
From a poster hanging in the Idga Hamus clinic

Yemani Gebre stared up at Sister Bernadette with bulging, angry eyes. He was too weak to cry, but he did not like this woman who was feeding drops of liquid into the back of his mouth. The skin was so tightly stretched over his skull it was translucent, but it lay in folds along his pencil-thin arms and legs, robbed of its flesh. He was miniature compared to other seven-month infants, a bonsai baby you could cup in the palm of one hand. When Bernadette had retrieved him from under his mother's shawl, he had lain still, looking like a very old man on his deathbed. Now he was resisting this invitation to live with the only strength he had left.

Gebre had arrived at the clinic hidden from view, strapped under layers of clothing on his sick mother's back, a tiny bundle of rags that was there because there was nowhere else to put it. No one had announced his tentative existence. Gebre's father was only concerned with the recovery of his thirty-five-year-old wife. If she died, he would have six children to look after on his own.

If you sized up Ethiopia with statistics, it was right on the edge of the humanity charts. The World Bank had ranked it as the poorest country in the world. The annual *per capita* income of $120 was a quarter of the average for the rest of sub-Saharan Africa. The fifty million population was made up largely of illiterate or semi-literate peasants caught on a treadmill of suffering. Those who survived childhood couldn't expect to live beyond forty-five. There was only one doctor for every 60,000 people, though even this figure is misleading, as most doctors lived in the towns, while the countryside had only crudely equipped dispensaries where virtually no drugs were available.

It took more than bad luck to come bottom of the global development class. Ethiopia hadn't arrived there without some effort on the part of its leadership. For over seventy years its destiny has been dominated by just two men.

The first was Emperor Haile Selassie. He was a sparrow of a man, five feet four inches tall, who finally shrank to 110 lbs. He ruled with a dazzling pomp and panopoly that blinded his court to the misery lurking beyond the palace gates. In 1953 he was befriended by the United States. Washington ran communications and intelligence-gathering facilities in return for military assistance and $2 million to buy a yacht. The West considered Ethiopia a 'good guy', part of its sphere of capitalist influence.

In 1974, when he was eighty-two, Selassie was overthrown by junior army officers who called themselves the *Derg*, Amharic for 'committee'. One man emerged from the group as having the essential qualities needed for leadership amongst disorder – cunning, determination and ruthless-ness. He maintained power by imposing a gridlock of controls on the nation. His name was Mengistu Haile Mariam. Like all true despots, he lived in imperial splendour, impervious to the miasma of fear and poverty that seeped through the dirt alleys like a fog.

Mengistu switched his allegiance to the Soviets in 1977 when the Carter administration refused to supply arms to quell an invasion from Somalia. In return for adopting Marxist orthodoxy, his regime received almost nothing for national economic development but it gained access to a steady supply of arms worth $8 billion.

Once Ethiopia had moved into the communist arena, it stopped being a good guy. To the average Ethiopian, however, the terms communist and capitalist were semantics. They were still herded around with callous indifference, and life was still a battle for survival.

As with all impoverished states, many of the people who were frustrated by the lack of economic development and the absence of free expression had joined rebel movements. Given the chance of installing an admin-istration charged with their own ideals, they thought, everyone would be much better off. Some of these guerrilla groups just ticked over year after year, making sorties on police posts from the protective cover of the mountains or the bush country in the lowlands. But there was one whose recent military successes made it a front runner for overthrowing the government. It was called the Tigrayan People's Liberation Front, and its fighters were baying for Mengistu's blood.

Famine was biting at the heels of the rebels because the northern provinces of Eritrea and Tigray as well as pockets of Wollo had been blighted by what Western relief officials considered the worst drought in living memory. With hunger, disease and even locust plagues endemic, hyperbole was unnecessary. The prognosis was tragedy. There was the fear that very soon millions of peasants would shrivel to that bicycle-chain thinness that had become Ethiopia's hallmark.

During the great drought of 1984 and 1985, when the rains failed for two years in a row and crops withered on the stalk, hundreds of thousands died before Mengistu reluctantly gave the aid agencies permission to mount a massive relief operation. This time round everyone expected the toll of human lives to be even greater, because two long-standing wars in the afflicted areas made transport a logistical nightmare.

Most of the northernmost province of Eritrea was in the hands of the Eritrean People's Liberation Front who had been fighting for the right of self-determination since 1961. At the beginning of 1989 the TPLF had chased the army out of Tigray, the adjoining province to the south. The Tigrayans had marched on into Wollo Province, walking into unresisting towns and villages. As they swept southwards into the territory of their ethnic cousins, the Amharas, thousands more dissidents swelled their ranks. The 40,000-strong coalition of Tigrayans and Amharas was called the Ethiopian People's Revolutionary Democratic Front.

The EPRDF were soon making sorties into Shoa Province, Ethiopia's geographic and cultural heartland and the administrative seat of the nation. They were prepared for a final assault on the capital of Addis Ababa. In a country where medieval practices lingered on, everyone secretly wondered if Mengistu's head would soon be paraded through the streets on a pike.

When Mengistu addressed the masses in Revolution Square, he depicted the rebels as barbarians who would rape their mothers and daughters. I presumed this was government propaganda to stoke the fires of nationalism, but no one knew for sure. No journalist had ever travelled with the EPRDF to see first hand what they were really like. Thus it was that I chose a trip with the rebels as my first assignment with *The Sunday Times* in my new position as roving correspondent. It was January 1990 when I arrived in Tigray.

Famines present difficult decisions as to who survives. When donated emergency rations are not enough to save the whole family, who gets fed? When people are debilitated with hunger but relief supplies are a four-day walk away, who goes? Some 2.2 million people were being faced with these Sophie's choices in Tigray. In some areas, ninety per cent of the harvest had been destroyed by drought, and the people were suffering.

The babies and very young children were the first to go, more dispensable because the least effort had been invested in them. Then it was the older children and the very old, whose time was almost over anyway. This focus on keeping the strong alive appeared callous to Western aid workers, but it was born of necessity in a land where there was no margin for sentimentality. The family household was the centrifugal force for this ancient farming society. Parents loved their children and wept silent tears when the tide of starvation swept them away. But they also accepted the hierarchy of death. Survival was crucial for the adult males whose seed could be sown when the rains fell and the child-bearing women whose milk would nurture a new generation. The future of the community, of an entire tribe, lay in their ability to endure catastrophe.

'There have been quite a few deaths. Because they have to walk so far, they wait until they are too far gone for these arduous journeys. By the time they get here, they are in a state of collapse,' said Sister Teresa, blinking behind her glasses.

'We haven't got the food to give them. That's our problem. The rice is almost finished. If the food doesn't come, it will be as bad as 1984,' added Sister Bernadette.

The two Irish nuns were smiling, good-natured women, well into their fifties, possibly older. They ran a clinic in the small market town of Idga Hamus. It straddled the road that joined Addis Ababa to Asmara, 125 miles to the north in Eritrea. With the help of Ethiopian nurses, they attended to the medical needs of some 10,000 people. They were the only foreigners in the area.

The clinic was a U-shaped building of dressed stone. It had a few treatment rooms used for dispensing basic drugs and treating suppurating wounds. It was a cheerful oasis of calm. The sisters warmed the small transactions of nursing with a smile and a joke for the mothers, a gentle caress on the heads of the children. Transposed to Europe or the United States, the clinic would not have passed muster. That hospital smell of disinfectant and ether that implies perfect cleanliness was absent. But neither was there the customary acrid odour of smoke mixed with *wat*, the traditional curry. This was probably because no one had anything to cook.

On Mondays and Thursdays the clinic treated the malnourished babies, whose numbers had doubled over the past six weeks. The courtyard was filled with geraniums and marigolds and barefoot women whose braided hair fanned out at the nape of the neck like peacock plumage. There was a time when their throats, ear lobes and wrists had been bright with silver jewellery. But it had all been sold in other famines to buy precious food. They sat in rows on the two benches or on the floor of the open passageways, silent children and folded sunshades by their sides.

A large white tent stood next door, donated by the European Community to prevent emergency food supplies going mouldy from the rain. It was supposed to house supplementary feeding rations for the children – soya beans, maize, fats, powdered milk, sugar and salt. The irony of it was, there were no sacks of food to put in it. And it hadn't rained for months. The interior was filled with a ghostly emptiness. A film of white *fafa* (soya bean) dust powdered the flagged stone floor. Wispy grass had pushed up between the cracks. The last of the dwindling supplies, a few sacks of rice, were stacked in a corner. It was the remnants of a consignment delivered by the World Food Programme two years previously. It was sufficient for a week but could last a month if eked out. The rice was teeming with weevils.

Bernadette and Teresa had no vehicle or telephone and therefore no contact with the outside world. There was no means of knowing if and when food would arrive. They were hostage to the hunger as much as the people they served.

The Bishop of Adigrat, Monsignor Kidane-Mariam Teklehaimanot, and some Catholic sisters and fathers were twenty-five miles away by road. But the walk was only two hours if you headed as the crow flies directly across the mountains. At Adigrat there was also a hospital of sorts where the two nuns referred the patients they couldn't treat themselves. The catch-22 was that if the patients were too ill to be looked after at the clinic, it meant they were also too weak to walk to the hospital. The sisters had that problem now.

A pregnant woman in her fifth day of an obstructed labour had been brought in that morning on a stretcher. In better times, assistance would have been sought sooner. But the journey involved carrying her for four hours over steep mountain tracks. When you are malnourished, it is a trip that sucks all the strength out of you. Her husband had at first been reluctant to ask his friends to embark on it. But when he saw there was only a whisper of life left in his wife, he had decided it was time to go.

The nuns were looking for a car to take her to Adigrat. They hadn't told the woman that she would die if she didn't have a Caesarean section in the next few hours. Nor did they tell her that the baby lay stillborn in her womb. She was too far gone to take it in. Anyway, there is only so much grief that a human being can bear.

Over the past year the government's Soviet-made fighter jets had added another hazard to the difficult task of existing. Ever since the TPLF (Tigrayan People's Liberation Front) had swept the province clean of the Ethiopian army, there had been the menace of planes looking for targets to destroy. Mengistu's tentacles could no longer stretch overland, but the skies were still his domain.

On this day, everyone had been lulled into a false sense of security. The sky was overcast, sandwiching a strip of gentian blue between cloud and the russet mesas that rimmed the horizon. It was difficult weather for

MiGs flying low on reconnaissance. The sort of day, in other words, that tempted people to walk outside, going about their business as they used to twenty years ago when there was no war.

At first glance, the countryside beyond the clinic appeared as a wasteland. Closer inspection showed otherwise. The fields were strewn with rocks to seal in what little moisture was left in the soil. They had been tilled ahead of time this year while the farmers still had the strength to wield their wooden hand ploughs. The fields that lay on flat land were encircled by low stone walls. The ones that descended down the precipitous mountainsides were carefully terraced. Prickly pear grew outside the stone houses. They had been fenced off from marauding donkeys because later the people would eat the fruit. The juicy leaves were sliced up as fodder for the cattle.

Small groups of men strode along tracks that hooves had turned to dust, wrapped in brown rags and anxiety. From afar they looked like pilgrims, cast adrift from biblical times, as they glided across the windless plain. Some drove donkeys before them, urging them on with wooden staves. The empty sacks slung across the animals' narrow backs were covered with eucalyptus branches. It was pitiful camouflage against the MiGs that regularly bombed the villages and towns. Sometimes the pilots even dropped bombs on men as they stood in their fields. But if you were a farmer who had never travelled in a car, let alone a plane, you were not to know that these sprigs of greenery carefully spread across the burlap were useless.

The travellers had covered thirty miles and more in their tattered *gabbis* (shawls) and plastic sandals, marching across the flat-topped mountains. They had been entrusted with a weighty mission on which depended the survival of those family members who had not already died. Their destination was a warehouse in Idga Hamus where, in the shelter of darkness, sacks of grain were to be handed out by members of the Tigrayan rebels' relief organisation. It was called REST, the acronym for Relief Society of Tigray. The men walked in silence to conserve their energy. Even so, the promise of food for the first time in three months put a spring into their long strides.

The nuns lived in a square compound of bedrooms, kitchen and living/dining room that faced on to a courtyard. The exterior was severe, a stone-walled fortress where no one could enter until a key had been turned in the metal front door. Once inside, you stepped into a hodge-podge of flowers and vegetables. There were climbing morning glories, geraniums, petunias and marigolds. Ragged rows of tomatoes, beetroot, potatoes and parsley were trying to grow in the lumpy soil.

Teresa described it with a sweep of the hand, 'This is where we vent our anger and frustration, but we don't have time to work in it now.' In fact, the garden did more than assuage the hopelessness of caring for patients with too few drugs and not enough equipment. It provided virtually the only food the sisters had.

A thin woman was tilling the soil. She had offered to plant some beetroot seeds for the sisters. It was a laborious job, for the pick was crudely made and the iron head shifted back and forth as she lifted it to her shoulder and let it fall towards the hard, rocky earth. She was debilitated by dysentery and light-headed from lack of food. Every minute or so she had to stop to recoup her strength.

As she sat on a stone, catching her breath, two MiGs screamed overhead. They circled once and then again, tipping their wings so the pilots could take a closer look at what lay below. It was a bad sign. From experience she knew that a second circuit was often a prelude to an aerial bombardment. She tried to control her fear but couldn't, knowing it was useless to hide. The MiGs were the ushers of arbitrary death. The victims were helpless against their attacks.

The woman had been bombed before and seen the devastation it caused. She didn't want to witness the howling void that was to come. Her fear was a monstrous thing, an icy clash of cymbals in her body. By standing there she was a sacrifice to futility, but there was nowhere to go and she could not move. Sister Bernadette appeared beside her. She was a stocky, short woman who did not reach much higher than her shoulder. Involuntarily she clasped the nun's hand as they gazed upwards.

'They're going to drop something,' said Bernadette in a matter-of-fact way.

Bernadette led the woman across the courtyard. 'Let's sit in my bedroom.' She produced a set of keys on a ring tied to her waist and fumbled at the lock. 'Wouldn't you know it,' she said in a slow, quiet voice. 'When you're in a hurry, you always get the wrong one.' Then the door opened and they sat side by side on the nun's bed. The woman was trembling. There were tears in her eyes.

Bernadette squeezed her hand. 'It really affects you, doesn't it?'

'Yes,' I said.

'Here, take this. It will calm your nerves.' She handed me a small, white pill and a glass of water. 'I feel that way when somone knocks at our compound door at night. I can't explain it to the other nuns, but there's always that fear that I'll be taken away again. I've been a nun for thirty years. I joined because I thought the order only worked in Dublin. Well, I was wrong. I've been in Italy, France, Tonga and New Zealand. I was here in Idga Hamus for two years without leaving once.

'They took me on February 18th. Two years ago this month. I had to go in the red dressing gown I was wearing when I went to answer the door, but I was lucky because I had some walking shoes. I had just got them because I thought I had better practise walking in case I had to walk to Mekelle if I needed to get out. I had just started that afternoon and walked for half an hour so they were by the door where I had left them.

'I walked for two days before anyone who spoke English arrived. Of course, they were TPLF, but I didn't know that at first. There were six of us, some MSF [Médecins sans Frontières] doctors and some other nuns. They were using us as an example to show how difficult it was for the people to walk to get food from distribution centres. They had to rent a donkey to carry the sack and pay for it with grain. Then they had to stay in people's houses on the way there and on the way back and pay for that too. So by the time they arrived home, they only had a quarter of a sackful of grain left. They treated me kindly but I knew my life meant nothing to them. After two days I said I couldn't walk any more. So they found me a mule. I tried to ride it, but it was so tiring that I walked again. Then I said I didn't care if they killed me, but unless they found me a car, I couldn't go on. Somehow they found me one.'

Sister Teresa tried not to let on, but you could tell the strain was getting to her. Her bright manner was not always spontaneous. Sometimes there was a tightness about her mouth when she was talking to patients. Sister Bernadette, on the other hand, seemed to be reconciled to her long exile from Dublin where her sister and brother lived with their families. She had photos of them on the walls of her bedroom. There were few other mementoes, a shell-shaped dish holding some pearls of soap and two treasured glass swans, a present from a niece. There was also a blanket spread out on the floor where she did yoga.

Bernadette pointed out each possession to me, explaining where it came from. She wanted me to forget the MiGs whose low roar was fading into the distance. They had disappeared, leaving us to come to terms yet again with our vulnerability. We never knew when they would return. Her conversation, too, was meant as a kindly distraction. She understood only too well the unbearable feeling of your bones melting inside you.

This woman had tremendous faith. Perhaps the dirt and disease and danger were a testimony to God. If there was evil, it meant there must be goodness too. As with the Tao symbols of Yin and Yang, how could there be one without the other? The balance of the two complementary principles of dark and bright created harmony. I couldn't figure it all out, but I knew one thing. Sister Bernadette was a real star.

She continued with her account of life in Idga Hamus. 'I was sick last April and had to go home. They wanted me to stay longer in Ireland and rest, but I insisted on coming back. I arrived in Addis the last day my visa was valid. I was smuggled across enemy lines and managed to get to Mekelle. I was there for the evacuation. The Derg mined the town and destroyed the generator for the electricity. In the two days before the

TPLF moved in, there was anarchy. People were raiding the grain stores and carrying away locust powder because they thought it was washing powder. It burnt their hands.

'They were so pleased to see me back at the clinic. They see people abandoning them all the time. When I returned they brought me eggs and baskets they had woven. They were dirty by the time they got to me, but that didn't matter. I'm here without a visa but I haven't thought about that. I don't leave for another two years and who knows what might happen by then? With all these MiGs about, every day is a bonus.'

These two courageous nuns and Tigray Province were in the grip of a pernicious war and a silent famine. The outside world neither understood nor cared very much about either of these phenomena. Unlike the other two droughts that had afflicted Ethiopia in the past six years, the players had been left to enact this particular tragedy on their own. The retreat of communism in Europe had heralded a second spring for US–Soviet relations. With the animosity thawing, Africa had lost its usefulness as a pitch for their power play. When Ethiopia had been the Soviets' most important African satrapy, the Americans had no doubt enjoyed the fact that they donated far more relief food than the Russians did. Now global attention and emergency aid had been diverted to Eastern Europe leaving Africa where it belonged, in the dust.

Besides, the public had become inured to the spectre of mass starvation. There was a misconception that much of the blame for Ethiopia's misfortune should be placed at the calloused feet of its peasants, sixty-five per cent of whom lived below the poverty line. It was felt, by those who had never been there, that they had been derelict in their obligation to Western charity. Why hadn't they rallied from the previous droughts? Why hadn't they brought in sufficient surplus harvest to tide them through this one?

Before, when Tigray was under the writ of Mengistu, journalists who covered the famine were accompanied by government officials. The officials acted as watchdogs as well as interpreters. What the journalists saw and were told they were seeing was sometimes deliberate fabrication, sometimes the partial truth. In fact, there was a lot more going on than we had been allowed to know. A scorching of the earth by government troops. The forced resettlement of the families who had migrated to feeding camps. The conscription at gunpoint of men who trekked to distribution centres. Mengistu had used the famines as an excuse to tear apart a complex peasant economy that had evolved over thousands of years.

A mix of desperation and hope fuelled the Tigrayans' determination to cast off their damnation. Their gracious, unswerving fortitude was both seductive and fascinating. Curiosity had lured me there, but it was their courage and courteous manners that made me want to stay. I also felt a great affinity for the turreted mountains and rugged plains. The harsh countryside endowed each bird and flower with singular beauty. I travelled with the TPLF and REST for over a month and, despite the hardship, was sad when I had to say goodbye. It was a journey that swept me along on currents of fear, depositing me briefly in serene pools of happiness. Tigray was a powerful place.

Naturally, visitors couldn't get to Tigray from Addis Ababa unless they wanted to walk through a battle or two along the way. So they went in from the Sudan, the country that runs along Ethiopia's western border. The trip began as all trips do, with a lot of running around buying supplies and putting the paperwork in order. First we had to get papers to allow us to stay in Khartoum then we had to get papers to allow us to leave.

Officially, we weren't going anywhere, but in reality the authorities had to sanction our travel. The Sudanese hated, feared and tolerated Mengistu because of his large army. He was the regional bully, and they didn't want his troops spilling over into their territory. As it was, the MiGs sometimes flew worryingly close to the Roseires hydroelectric dam next to the border. It would have been all too easy to put it out of action with a bomb or two. So the Sudanese aided and abetted subversion by turning a blind eye to the vehicles filled with arms, food, aid workers and journalists that trundled towards Tigray along the dusty roads.

My companion was a man called James Hamilton. He worked for the *Village Voice*. I had been looking for a photographer and a mutual friend had suggested James. I had met him twice during visits to New York. When we agreed to go on assignment together, the sum total of our acquaintance was less than an hour. He was easy to get along with and good at his job, both crucial factors. He was a bachelor in his early forties who wasn't given to talking a lot. Apart from that, I knew very little about him. I had forgotten to ask if I could see his portfolio.

After meeting up in Khartoum, we discovered we would be travelling with two other media people, a crew from the British Independent Television News. Nigel Thomson, the cameraman, was tall and thin with closely shaved black hair. He was the quintessential war junkie, the reporters' wives' nightmare come true. If your husband was teamed up with Nigel, you knew for certain he would be in the thick of things. Nigel's idea of bliss was to stand outside the trenches filming non-stop carnage and destruction. Once he had been shoved up against the wall of a basement garage in Beirut for a reprisal execution by one of the militias. Dispassionate to the last, he didn't flinch even then. He didn't do it for the adrenalin rush. For Nigel, war was art. I don't think he knew what adrenalin was.

Peter Sharp, the correspondent, was a blond teddy bear, a bit overweight and cuddly. We knew people in common, and we struck up an instant friendship. Peter was a magnificent fixer. He had got hold of two white Toyota Landcruisers and a driver called Ramadan, a burly, black-skinned Sudanese who was fazed by nothing. In fact, he was so relaxed throughout the trip, you would have thought he was motoring through the south of France.

James and I, working on a newspaper budget, were the poor cousins. The other two were travelling in style. They had tins of instant paella and creamed seafood with prawns. Their state-of-the-art camping equipment had been bought at the Survival Shop at Euston Station. We had kapok mattresses bought in the market and baskets of grapefruit, dates and groundnuts. The cars had been hired at a premium rate of $11,000 in case they didn't come back, which was a very real possibility. Peter established the pecking order early on. He said James and I could ride in one of the vehicles with the baggage, but if either car broke down, we would be the ones to stay behind.

Hagos was our minder from the TPLF. He had a round, pock-marked face finished off with a wispy moustache and glasses. He was short and exceptionally slender but worked with the energy of a demon. He drove all night and walked miles under the hot sun to fetch something to eat from the nearest village. 'Here Mary Anne, I've brought you some food,' he would say, holding out a tin bowl. It was invariably a stringy chicken leg and some bones floating in a thin red gravy. I ate to please him.

Hagos was thirty-five and a bachelor. As with many Tigrayans, the war had disrupted his plans for marriage and a career. He had wanted to take a degree in philosophy but joined the TPLF instead soon after its inception in 1975. I had asked him what it was like to be in a battle. 'At first you feel the purr of bullets coming past your head and you're frightened. After that, it's like normal, everyday life.'

There was also the gentle Abebe, deputed by REST to look after us. He was young, in his twenties, and had a beard. This was his first encounter with the foreign press and our schizophrenic (in his eyes) behaviour confused him. We were pleasant and polite to him during the lulls and rudely ignored his pleading 'You mustn't go there!' when the action erupted. Abebe tended to fuss, but he meant well.

While in Khartoum I also made the rounds of the aid agencies to size up the extent of the famine and whether there was enough food going into Tigray to avert disaster. REST was trying to minimise the consequences of the war, which they claimed was directly responsible for nearly two thirds of the crop deficit. Their objective was to bring the food to the people so that they could stay on their land. They wanted to avert a repeat of the mass migration that occurred in 1985. That led to disease, family members scattered like chaff thrown into the wind and fields that stood abandoned when it was time to plant. It was an overwhelmingly ambitious task.

The distance from Port Sudan where the food docked to the heart of Tigray is about 650 miles. Inside Tigray the commitment, desperation and routine hard slog, integral components of any rescue programme, were sharply etched. The route snaked over a desolate landscape of dusty plains and precipitous mountains. Every evening a line of decrepit ten-ton trucks departed from the Sudanese border town of Kassala to bump and grind over rutted paths and deep river beds, circumventing the potholes and blown up bridges. The drivers' punishing schedule called for a round trip of six nights to offload the sacks of grain and return across the border. After one day's rest, the cycle started all over again. They drove for eleven-hour stretches, stopping only to check that no one had broken down and that the caravan was still intact. Many had volunteered their services free as their contribution to the war effort. The others were paid what REST could afford, eighty-three dollars a month.

The spartan offices of the aid agencies inundated me with statistics. What I learned there underlined the frustratingly quirky pace of emergency assistance. REST had warned of the impending crisis six months ago, but the response had been achingly slow. So far 16,000 tonnes of food from the West had docked at Port Sudan while another 76,000 tonnes had been pledged by donors. In all, at least 340,000 tonnes were needed. REST reckoned their fleet of 222 vehicles had the capacity to transport 13,000 tonnes of food a month in the dry season. If the rains fell, as hopefully they would between July and September, the flow would be cut to 5,000 tonnes. Water would turn the dirt roads to mud and wheels would churn the mud into a quagmire. 'We have captured some Russian trucks from the Derg. They have four-wheel drive, and they will tow the other trucks behind them. It may take two or three weeks, but we have to do it,' said Hagos bravely.

I was told there were 50,000 tonnes of grain lying piled up in western and southern Tigray, a day's drive from distribution centres. In one of those ironies that often emerge out of confusion, REST was having trouble getting at it. The famine had thrown up an arcane question. When is hunger political and when is it humanitarian? Donor governments such as Britain and the United States were reluctant to give REST the cash to purchase the surplus harvests. They presumed it would be misappropriated and used to buy arms. This was also the excuse the Ethiopian government gave for its regular bombing attacks on the food convoys. Ethiopian officials claimed that weapons were secreted beneath the sacks of food. It was an accusation that was impossible to prove or disprove. The aid officials who worked with REST praised their efficiency and honesty. However, this was outweighed by another factor. The Americans and British recognised Mengistu as the head of state and the rebels were trying to overthrow him. It wouldn't look good if they appeared to be hand in glove with REST.

The relief officials in Khartoum had a different perspective. They could smell the suffering from their air-conditioned offices. When needs loom large, diplomacy fades into the distance. 'If we are ever asked by Mengistu if we are supplying the rebels with food, we would say, first of all, it's going to the needy. Then we would refer him to the UN charter's definition of humanitarian assistance. The rules change when it's an emergency situation,' said the European Community delegate defiantly.

Despite the brouhaha, REST was valiantly trying to distribute minimum rations of 500 grams a day to three quarters of a million people. They had fed 680,000 in December. By January, as death stalked the land, this had dropped to 500,000 because there hadn't been enough food. They were hoping to do better next month. Most of it came from the cross-border operation and some from the surplus harvest. They were buying the Tigrayan grain with money supplied by aid agencies such as Oxfam and Save the Children. Even so, this reached only two thirds of those who were hungry and it was only supplementary feeding. The rest of the Tigrayans' diet was grass seeds and the bitter, unpalatable leaves of bushes. It wasn't enough and many people had already died.

There had been talk of allowing safe passage through the lines for donor food to be trucked north from the government side. The Joint Relief Programme, as it had been named, was to be run by a consortium of five Ethiopian churches. This had REST's approval because the church was supposed to be impartial even if it did come under government jurisdiction. But the discussions had been dragging on since August of the previous year and nothing had happened yet. Besides, the government's image as a saviour was badly tarnished. When the Ethiopian authorities got their hands on relief food, they often gave it to army conscripts in lieu of salaries or sold it in the marketplace. REST wasn't counting on the Derg to keep its word.

If you totted up the food that had already docked at Port Sudan, the food that had been promised and the extra food that had been harvested in Tigray, it came to just over one third of what was needed. It was difficult to compute tragedy and I was no mathematician, but the prognosis looked gloomy. I could see my thoughts reflected in the worried faces of the aid workers.

'It's a very precarious position. If REST can't stop people from migrating, they won't be able to produce for next year and they will be trapped in a cycle of poverty. And if the food comes too late, the people will die. Looking at it from this end, it's really depressing. I remember 84 and 85. My God, it was terrible. We don't want to go through that again,' said an Oxfam employee who asked not to be quoted by name. He didn't want to jeopardise the position of his colleagues in the Oxfam office in Addis Ababa. It seemed that politics were clouding everyone's vision.

I had been taken to see him by Diop, a Tigrayan from Vancouver, Canada who was on a consultancy with Oxfam. As we drove, he lectured me, trying to make a coherent picture out of all the numbers. I had lost track of what he was saying because I was engrossed by Diop's appearance. His face was webbed with deep scars that wandered from cheekbone to chin and ear to nose like river beds. One eye was a different size and shape to the other eye. Half an arm had disappeared. What was left ended in a puckered stump. He looked as if he had been detonated, then glued back together again. I was hundreds of miles from Tigray in a supposedly neutral country, but the devastation seemed very close.

And, indeed, it was. Only a few days away, in fact. The following week we spent a day and a night and a day at Kassala waiting to 'go in'. Journalists 'go' to press conferences but 'go in' to Soweto to cover ANC funerals. They ask each other if they were 'in' the 1985 Uganda coup. I suppose the word 'in' subconsciously connotes danger. There was plenty of that around, a whole military dictionary of it.

Hagos revealed it to us in an enigmatic, roundabout way. The truck drivers were very brave. They fought for the honour of driving the lead truck. (The roads were stitched with land mines.) We would be travelling separately, each one in a truck. Hagos would drive one of the cars; Ramadan the other. (The convoys were sometimes ambushed with rocket-propelled grenades by government infiltrators or perhaps rival or breakaway rebel factions. I never discovered which. Whoever the authors were, they targeted the cars not the trucks because they were seeking out the TPLF leadership.) We would travel by night and rest up by day. (Ah yes, let us not forget the deadly, cat's paw attacks from the MiGs.)

There wasn't much to do in Kassala. The TPLF didn't like us walking around town. Besides, it was very, very hot. I lay on a bed, staring at the ceiling, delirious with happiness. This wasn't home but it was home. I was too happy to bother sorting it all out. All I knew was, I was where I wanted to be.

The TPLF compound was a sprawling affair with interconnected rooms and buildings. Everywhere there were men and women stretched out in a cocoon of exhausted sleep. They emerged in the evenings to eat lentils and *injera*, the flat, sour pancake made from *tef*, a cereal endemic to Ethiopia. They congregated at the communal water tap to wash and sat under the stars chatting quietly. News from the front crackled out of transistors.

The TPLF radio said there had been heavy fighting for the past three days. There were 9,062 enemy soldiers killed or wounded. Another 300 had been captured. There had been another battle nine days before that had swirled around Kutaber and Hayk near Dessie. Over four days it had left 2,637 enemy dead, 4,274 wounded and 207 captured. These cyclones of megadeath were reeled off like weather reports.

I had been told the TPLF were meticulous with their body counts, that they were not given to exaggeration. Still, I wondered. . . . The numbers were suspiciously exact. Did they despatch men with notebooks to wander over the killing fields? The army mortality rate was so enormous that there weren't enough uniforms to hand out to the conscripts, who were scooped up from schools and the marketplaces. They marched to the front in the clothes they were wearing when they had stepped out of the house in the morning. Many of the farmers who had been caught in the dragnet fought barefoot. In this war where cousin killed cousin, how could they tell who was who?

'We usually kill in the thousands and take prisoners in the tens of thousands. Our fighters know what they are fighting for, so they are more determined than the Derg's army. We shoot to kill. Their recruits are from the countryside, and they don't come voluntarily. They come in waves in their hundreds. When the soldiers are ordered to make an assault on a hill, if they don't go immediately, there are people behind them who shoot them with machine guns. It's a terrible war,' Tsadkan Gebre Tensai, commander of the Debre Tabor western front, said later.

Armed uprisings had been crackling and sizzling in the provinces like popcorn in a frying pan for years. There were at least nine armed guerrilla movements as well as several political opposition groups in exile. They covered a broad spectrum of ideologies, but Marxism was a hot favourite. As far as the guerrilla leaders were concerned, it engendered the sort of discipline that was needed in the administrative vacuum of rebel-won territory. The peasants liked it because it held out the promise of equal reward for equal labour. Perhaps they had forgotten that Mengistu was Marxist too. He had cast the net of a centralised economy over the countryside, but it hadn't given them any return on their productivity. If you stopped to think about it, it didn't make much sense.

Even measured against the African yardstick for mayhem, which was pretty long, the unrest was excessive. As a result, over the years, the stripling military force Mengistu had inherited from Haile Selassie had proliferated like a virus to become the largest standing army in black Africa. In Selassie's day one per cent of the budget was handed over to the army. Under Mengistu, somewhere between half and two thirds of the budget was consumed by defence.

Until the TPLF had come on to the boil, the military had focussed its attention on the Eritrean rebels in the north, who were seeking secession from Ethiopia. The army had been waging First-World-War-style trench warfare against the Eritrean People's Liberation Front for twenty-eight years. Some of the soldiers had literally sat in fox-holes for a decade without leave. The only way they got to quit the combat zone alive was with a leg blown off. There were untold amputees hobbling around Addis

Ababa. Once they organised a protest march to seek state assistance for disabled veterans. Mengistu's reaction was typically brutal and swift. As the crowd set off on its crutches, the police opened fire and killed sixty. There were no records of the mortality rate in the battlefield, but it certainly exceeded half a million. Hyenas were so used to eating corpses they had developed a taste for human flesh and sometimes attacked herdsmen. 'It's like a goddamned meat grinder out there,' an American diplomat in Addis Ababa had said. It was easy to see why the TPLF, armed only with captured weapons, so they claimed, were beating the hell out of the demoralised army.

Meanwhile, the people were trapped in a no man's land while the two sides blasted away at each other with every modern weapon they could lay their hands on. A sinister war machine was steamrolling back and forth across the carcass of a ravaged land.

On the second evening in Kassala the boys and I had been stretching our legs after sunset and, by chance, saw a wedding reception through open doors. We had wandered in and mixed with the guests when Abebe stood on the doorsill, excitement making his eyes several apertures wider than usual. 'Come quickly! We're leaving!' The convoy consisted of three fuel tankers and eleven trucks carrying lentils. James and I were put into the cab of one tanker, Nigel and Peter into another. The trucks went first. 'We'd rather lose lentils than diesel,' said Hagos.

The vehicles trundled into the desert beneath a cavernous black sky. On our right stood Jebel Sidiq Hassan, a pillar of stone that pointed upwards like a giant penis. It marked the border checkpoint where the drivers showed their papers to short-tempered Sudanese officials. Half a mile further on we passed a dim shape in the looming darkness.

'What's that?' asked James.

'An old container,' I said. For corpses. A week or two earlier, an Oxfam consultant, a Swede, had abandoned caution to race the last few miles home across the dusty flats. He had hit a land mine. After that, everyone made sure they kept to the tracks.

By 2 a.m. we were 'stacked up' in a wadi of straggly trees and bushes. Cover for the trucks was infrequent, but each staging post was well known by the drivers. Word had come back, I don't know how, that another convoy had staked out the next wadi. So we packed it in for the night and struck camp. This consisted of parking the battered trucks under thorn trees and covering them with branches, tattered sacks and torn tarpaulins. We cut more branches, and I helped the men brush away the tyre tracks that swerved off the road in the direction of the wadi. Ramadan and the boys sprinkled the ground with water from a container and smeared mud over the white Toyotas with their hands. The idea was to escape detection from the air, but it all seemed a bit makeshift.

The minutes passed in slow spirals of heat and buzzing flies. We were beneath a canopy of grey thorn bushes so low you could only sit or lie. According to the drivers, the MiGs usually made their sorties before nine o'clock in the morning or after three o'clock in the afternoon. But we were told to stay hidden all day because you never knew, you never knew.

Peter took a sleeping pill and disappeared into a long envelope of canvas he called his bivvy bag. It looked like a body bag but cost more because you got to use it while you were still alive. Nigel had set up his Walkman, and Chris Rea blared through the speakers. I stuck a guinea fowl feather behind my ear and typed on my Tandy laptop word processor. A goat kept nibbling at the mattress I was sitting on. 'I think I'm in the bunker on that one,' said James. He was playing computer golf with Nigel. It was all very homely. A picnic in the wilds. The only thing was, we couldn't drive back to get a Band-Aid out of the bathroom cabinet if someone's finger got cut.

The second twenty-four hours were much like the first. We were still in the lowlands. It was so dry and dusty you couldn't credit that anything ever grew there. But the sorghum had been harvested and the golden stalks lay sighing in the breeze. Somewhere along the way we had discovered there were other *ferenjis* (foreigners) travelling with us. There were a young man and woman in their early twenties. They represented a youth organisation in Britain which had sent them out to make friends with the youth of Tigray. It seemed a bizarre expedition under the circumstances. There was also an Australian water engineer called Peter. He was wiry and tanned and wore shorts and rubber flip-flops. He spent several months each year in Tigray fixing all the pipes the Derg had destroyed so the towns could have running water. He looked very much at home in this environment.

The drivers slept under their trucks. They ate a few bits of bread but nothing else. They were as thin as whispers. We hadn't eaten much either since leaving Kassala. I was beginning to feel dizzy from hunger, so Nigel and I boiled up a few handfuls of macaroni and ate it with sardines out of plastic mugs.

The landscape appeared deserted, but it wasn't. A man in white trotted along the fold of a ridge on a donkey so small it looked like a hyphen between the parenthesis of his legs. A starling rustled in the branches above my head as I stood behind a tree washing in a bowl of water. Two girls robed in red walked past balancing calabashes on their heads. I stood there naked and watched them. In the afternoon two small boys from the nearby village approached, clutching tattered cloth satchels. I asked to look inside. One carefully withdrew a small piece of dark bread that was hard and smooth like a pebble. The other showed me the worn heel of a leather sandal. Lying in the palms of their outstretched hands, it was difficult to tell which was the bread and which was the shoe.

We left that evening at six o'clock, heading for the foothills that rimmed Tigray's high-altitude central plateau. The truck tyres disturbed the powder-fine dust on the road and sent it floating into our eyes and throats. As the night set in, the only way we could tell we were climbing upwards was by the angle of the headlights. We were encased in a murky sarcophagus and could see nothing.

The following day was 29 January, 1990, a day when the first pink rays of dawn poked through the gloom just as they had on other days. We were a bit more worn, yes, because travelling in the cab of the tanker wasn't exactly conducive to sleep. I felt like a sock in a tumble dryer. But our spirits were good for we had crossed from Eritrea into Tigray. And we had just passed the small market town of Sherraro.

The trucks descended into a deep river bed and nosed their way into parking bays that had been dug into the twelve-foot banks. The excavations gave the place a more permanent air than the wadis we had stopped in before. It was easy to see why this particular place was used often. The large trees whose branches met above our heads formed a leafy canopy. From the air, all a pilot would see would be a lazy green snake whose contours fitted those of the dry water course.

No one told us that this place was used for grain storage or that it was one of the principle convoy stops. Nor did they tell us that MiGs flew over six or eight times a day searching for vehicles. We were not aware, either, that so far Sherraro had taken scores of direct hits or that its residents spent the daylight hours holed up in their houses or burrowed under the ground in crudely dug shelters. And perhaps because we were so tired, we did not ask why, on this particular day, we were being driven away from the trucks and across fields of stubble to a cottage built against the side of a small hill.

Instead, Hagos told us the place was called Grat Rada, which meant 'the land of Rada'. It had belonged to a feudal aristocrat in the days when the farmers tilled the fields not for themselves but for baronial landlords. It was so dry that the people who lived there walked from three to eight hours to fetch water. Even so, he continued, here in western Tigray the land was fertile. If we had been here before the harvest, we would have seen a sea of six-foot high sorghum.

The elevation of the house provided a good vantage point that gave an unobstructed view for miles and miles straight ahead and to the right and the left. I looked out and saw tongues of mist that licked at the mountains on the horizon and curled around the stunted trees scattered across the plain. How serene and how beautiful, I thought. How happy I am to be here. Later, when too much time was spent reflecting on these things, I realised that Hagos, gazing out on the same panorama, saw nothing but emptiness and over the emptiness destruction. And that was why he had spoken only of Grat Rada.

Our rest house belonged to a woman called Garges. She and her family lived in two stone rooms. They gave on to a small dirt courtyard that was ringed with a wall made of thin stone slabs. The doorway was framed with solid posts of timber. They must have been old for you no longer found trees of that thickness. Some malnourished children stared at us with solemn faces. It was like stepping back into the Iron Age. There was nothing, except the rags they wore, that spoke of Western civilisation. The harvest was stored in wickerwork bins with conical roofs. Garges's husband, who was somewhere else that day, would have tilled his fields with an iron-tipped stick. Garges fetched water in the long-necked clay pots that stood stacked in a corner. Further on, in the mountains, the huts were made of mud and wattle. Most homesteads were at least one day's walk from the nearest road.

Above this house was another room built in stone that REST had commandeered for travellers. It was joined to a larger area that was a room of sorts because it had a roof and was surrounded by a low wall. We unloaded our baggage and settled down for the day. Nigel and James had clambered to the top of the hill with their cameras. They sat under a tree playing computer golf and waiting. Peter Sharp and I climbed out on to the roof of the house below to bask in the sun. Then at 10.15, while we were chatting, something terrible happened.

The sound was so loud and close, so awful that I can no longer recall what it was like. I only remember the instant certainty that this was it. The MiGs had flown low over the hill, but their wings were tilted to the right giving us their bellies. They arced round, passing across the horizon and heading left. There were some dull crumps and cushions of smoke rose into the sky. Sherraro was under attack again.

We had been transfixed by the raid, but now everyone was moving. Abebe's face was grey with fear. 'Quick! Get the camera cases into the shade. They will see the silver!'

The jets passed over us a second time and a third. Now there were red flashes over Sherraro which meant they were dropping phosphorus bombs. I looked over to where the Toyota was nestled beneath a leafless and distressingly small thorn tree. Its roof was pristine white. Why had we forgotten to cover it with mud? Peter stared as the MiGs circled yet again. He held his hands out in front of him, fingers spread as if he was about to play the piano. 'Go home now. Please go home,' he intoned, but it was half an hour before they headed back towards the mountains. At least they hadn't found the trucks.

That afternoon at 3.15 it started all over again. This time the circles were tighter. Much to Abebe's dismay, Peter the Australian climbed out on to the roof and sat in a thin ribbon of shade with his hands clasped round his knees. We could see only too well what was happening in the arena in front of us, but he gave us a droning commentary in his down-under twang anyway.

'These are MiG 23s. They were 21s this morning. They're coming in from the south-west so they must be stationed at Bahar Dar. They're diving steeply over the target. It's a low pass to take a look. They're looping to the north behind us. Here they come again. Right over our heads. You see those silver footballs? They're dropping them two at a time.'

The carefully camouflaged vehicles were almost invisible, but perhaps a wing mirror had not been bent close enough to the door, giving a telltale glint as it reflected in the sun. Or perhaps one of the government spies the TPLF said infiltrated behind the lines had reported our presence. In the end, the manner of betrayal no longer mattered.

For another half an hour the jets banked and dived, flattening out over the gully to blanket the convoy with high explosive and phosphorus bombs. While we watched the livid flashes and dark grey towers of smoke in horror, Nigel filmed Garges, who stood in the doorway of her house with a small child attached to her left breast. 'What have we done to be given a hard time like this?' she wailed. It was an inferno down there.

'Come on, Nigel. Let's go,' said Peter as soon as it was over.

'No, it's too dangerous. They might come back. You must stay hidden.' Abebe waved his hands and bobbed helplessly around the boys. His eyes had opened up to f.1.4. He didn't know how to cope with this *ferenji* insanity. It made him very uneasy indeed.

Nigel and Peter strode across the sorghum fields that separated us from the gully. James changed into a khaki shirt for protective camouflage and followed in their wake. I had been comforting one of the girls, who was whimpering. It made me feel calm and under control. As a calm, controlled reporter, I should have been at James's side, the indomitable team recording the bedlam. But there was a restraining leash tugging at my brain. It was called survival instinct. I stayed where I was.

By 4.30 I was both restless and curious. I set off across the fields towards the gully with an unhappy Abebe trailing behind me. Peter and Nigel were walking back towards us. We drew close, and I threw my arms wide in greeting. 'How is it down there?' My lips had formed those words, I know, but all we heard was a loud scream. We looked up and saw their silver wings too close, excruciatingly too close, above our heads. We scattered like rabbits beneath a hawk.

'Over here!' cried Peter, making for a spindly tree no bigger than a sapling. I caught sight of an anthill and veered left. There was a pricking sensation in my feet. I looked down and saw I was crossing the stubble shoeless and that, yes, my legs were moving back and forth. So why wasn't the anthill closer? Peter recalled later that he felt like Sebastian Coe. I felt as if I was in one of those bad dreams (and this situation qualified as one) where you're trying to run, but it's like moving through treacle. I threw myself against the anthill, which was about four feet high, and lay there clutching it.

And so we made our way back to the house, running while the MiGs bombed the convoy and throwing ourselves to the ground as they passed overhead. After the initial shock, our attention was focused on the MiGs, anticipating the pilots' intentions through every manoeuvre of the raked back wings. We were too busy to be frightened.

A dozen pairs of solemn eyes turned to watch as we climbed over the wall of the compound and stood gasping for breath. A pretty young girl with a baby tied to her back looked over at Peter and churned her arms and legs up and down like a slow but determined steam engine. We all grinned.

While we were celebrating our survival, James was trapped in the gully, literally running for dear life. Three of the trucks had been badly hit and four tons of stacked grain destroyed. A cook and a driver were injured, but no one was dead. A certain notoriety was attached to this river bed so after parking the vehicles, the drivers had decamped to a clearing a few hundred yards away. James had been taking photos of barefoot men trying to shovel up the mess when he heard the pop of a muzzle loader being fired and a shout. Everyone started running and James ran with them because it seemed the right thing to do. The ground shook and heaved each time a bomb landed. Men were screaming, their mouths torn wide with fear, dodging the explosions and cannon fire that ripped along the banks.

I was anxious for James's safety. It seemed a pointless place to die, not to mention inconvenient. On the other hand, if someone from the TPLF had to turn round and drive his body back to Khartoum, they could take my story back with them. I wondered if they would know how to file it to the newspaper. Peter was thinking along the same lines. If James gets killed, Mary Anne will have to go back with the body so we can ship our film out with her. Perhaps we would have been less cavalier if we had known James better, but there was more to it than that. Death is so monstrous that to live alongside it, you must reduce it to a rational denominator. By endowing James's putative corpse with the function of courier, we were trying to inject a few ccs of normality into an imponderable struggle that didn't involve us at all.

The following day, when we came across an Australian aid worker who was returning to Khartoum and from there to Europe, we gave him not only our stories and film but also letters for our families. I penned what I considered a reassuring update to Tara, who was at university, and Petra, who was at boarding school. It had been a good trip so far. We had been bombed a few times but everything was fine. Peter wrote in a similar vein to his wife Sue. A very basic precept had been shattered and we were subconsciously pasting it back together. Unlike the Ethiopians, who were lucky if they were still around when others were having a mid-life crisis, we had expected to live out a full lifespan. The leitmotif of the MiGs was an unnerving reminder that we weren't masters of our survival after all. Africans had a saner attitude towards death than we did. What outsiders construed as fatalism was an acceptance of reality. Our conception of normality, the unequivocal right to health and happiness, was all skewed up.

When the planes wheeled away towards the mountains, we crossed the fields once again. As we approached the tree line, I saw James walking away from the gully. He had his shirt off and was carrying it in his hand but his blue bandanna was still tied around his neck. Reassured, Nigel and Peter turned back. I went on, my attention drawn to a knot of people.

A man lay on the ground. His stomach had been torn apart by flying shrapnel. An older man crouched beside him holding a silver Coptic cross and swatting the flies off the wound. I knelt. This thin man with white and staring eyes was leaving us without benefit of first aid or benediction. The least I could do was offer him human contact. I circled my fingers around his storklike wrist. 'We are here,' I said.

A fly landed on his eye. 'He will die soon,' said the man with the cross. 'He is dead already.' Weldegerima was thirty-seven and had four children. His life had ended because he ran to save his cattle when he saw the planes coming. I stood up and shed a tear but no more. You need your energy for helping those who have survived.

Down in the gully the smoke was so thick it made your eyes water, but already men were swarming over the toppled mountain of sacks, trying to restore order to chaos. They were local villagers who were paid with food handouts to load and unload the grain. Abebe said he was sad when I told him about Weldegerima, but his eyes spoke otherwise. The herder was a particle of dust in the whirlwind that was crossing their paths. He had never been a player in the game. He was dispensable.

The Tigrayans' indomitable commitment had been tempered by the discrimination and systematic genocide that had been visited upon them for generations. The Tigrayan and Amharic kingdoms had been sparring for a long time. The ancient Tigrayan civilisation, once the epicentre of Ethiopian culture, was subdued when Emperor Menelik, an Amhara, united the country at the end of the nineteenth century. Haile Selassie, another Amhara, continued the domination through a mix of oppression and calculated neglect. He punished the Tigrayans for a 1943 uprising by closing all but seven of the schools in the towns. Five years later he responded to further unrest by bombing the provincial capital of Mekelle. At that time there were only seven doctors in the province. The population was 2.5 million.

Things got worse under Mengistu, who considered himself an Amhara as well. Soldiers roamed the countryside butchering plough oxen and destroying farm tools. They set fire to fields of ripening sorghum and torched the grain stored in huts. The troops were plundering an agricultural treasure trove. The Tigrayans had been practising terraced farming for over 2,000 years. The province had been an important genetic reservoir for durum wheat, barley, sorghum, linseed, finger millet and chick peas. California farmers benefit from a barley variety originally collected in Tigray which has a gene that protects their $160 million annual barley crop from the yellow dwarf virus.

As if this wasn't bad enough, Mengistu laid waste to the people too. In 1988 Legesse Asfaw, the governor of Tigray, summoned everyone in Mekelle to the town hall and issued a dire threat. 'If you want to catch a fish, you must drain the sea,' he warned.

This was the year before the TPLF gained control of the province. Parts of the terrain were in rebel hands, but most of Tigray was still under government writ. In those days, markets in rebel territory were held at night to avoid MiG bombardments. People traded grain, salt and coffee by candlelight and bumped into each other in the dark.

However, the market in Hawzen convened every Wednesday as was the custom. Hawzen could be approached by only two roads, for it was nestled at the bottom of a slim valley. It was a small town, but the market was renowned for its variety and was the biggest in the region. Peasants trekked there from Eritrea and even Wollo, a hundred miles to the south. Sometimes 10,000 people thronged the open square where traders had spread out a pastiche of food, cloths, soaps, candles, farming tools and radio batteries. There were goats, cattle and donkeys, too, that milled around in the old school compound.

During the first six months of 1988 Hawzen was attacked eight times, but the market was still held in daylight. The town had not yet been liberated, so no one thought it was under serious threat.

You can imagine the scene on the Wednesday of 22 June. Farmers have walked all night to get there in good time. They are inspecting the merchandise carefully, wondering what bargains they can get after they have sold the chickens that hang head down from their hands like a bunch of bananas. They are thirsty and hungry, too, so the houses are packed with people drinking *sewa* beer and eating *injera* and *wat*.

Then at ten o'clock there is a terrible droning in the distance. As it gets louder, it becomes a clattering, chattering noise. A sea of faces are turned to the sky to look at the two helicopter gunships that are hovering above them. The helicopters stay there for an hour, circling overhead. Everyone is very relieved when they finally depart for the surveillance has made them nervous. But the helicopters return. This time they are accompanied by two MiGs.

For nearly six hours the aircraft pound the town with high explosive and cluster bombs, rockets, machine gun fire and either napalm or phosphorus bombs.

Blata Aragabi, a fifty-seven-year-old farmer, was there so I will let him take up the tale: 'The MiGs concentrated on the markets. No one could have stayed alive in those areas. Meanwhile the two helicopters circled round trapping people as they tried to escape, cutting them down like leaves. Each time the MiGs and the helicopters had finished bombing they went away, and more kept coming, two by two. I don't know how many times new planes came. Because of all the dust it was dark and people were crying all around me. It seemed to be about every half hour or so that they would leave, and there would be a few minutes' interval. People would come out of where they were trying to shelter and pick up the bodies thinking it was all over. Then the planes would return. Most of the people and cattle were being burned by something that seemed like rubber. It burned as it dropped off the sky and didn't cut like metal does.'

No one knew how many were killed before night fell. As Blata said, 'You can't count grains of sand.' Besides, it was difficult to figure out who was who when you found a head here, a hand or foot there, and squashed water melons of flesh mixed with the coffee and salt and sorghum. The priests who helped to bury this mess said they thought 1,800 or perhaps 2,000 died. Of course, that didn't include the thousand or so who were badly wounded and may have died later. Or the bodies that were taken by kinsfolk to be buried in their own villages.

Those who survived were left with permanent scars of another sort. Nightmares and panic attacks mostly. Some of the babies had constant nervous tics. From then on the children froze in terror at the sound of an approaching plane. The government never explained the atrocity, and the people knew better than to ask. It followed a small wave of military successes by the TPLF, so perhaps it was *'pour encourager les autres'*.

That year another 900 Tigrayans were either bayoneted to death or burned alive in their houses by soldiers. Mengistu should have known better. Instead of breaking the people's resolve, his viciousness tempered it. 'We don't care how long it takes. We are doing this not for our children but our grandchildren,' they told me.

The tragedy that was being played out on this desolate stage was redolent of the epic Russian sagas of Dostoevsky and Tolstoy, writers understood and appreciated by the Ethiopians for the parallels they contained with their own history. Both countries had emerged from feudal societies ruled by absolute monarchs. Subsequently, both revolutions withered under despotic dictators.

The TPLF blamed Mengistu's inappropriate vision of a centralised economy for their inability to feed themselves. The price of grain was kept deliberately low. The free market was prohibited so that one region starved while the granaries of another overflowed. Over eighty per cent of farmers' cash income disappeared in taxes. During the 1984 drought, a famine tax was levied on the dying, who had to contribute to their own emergency food supplies. There was no incentive to improve the land because ownership was the privilege of the state.

When Stalin collectivised farms and requisitioned grain to export in return for industrial machinery, it resulted in widespread starvation amongst forty million peasants in the Ukraine. The famine was so severe that up to seven million died and fathers were driven to eat the flesh of their children.

Like Stalin, Mengistu exacted obedience through terror. He created an African gulag by shovelling the Tigrayans around like coal. There was a plan to resettle 1.5 million, ostensibly to allow the eroded mountainsides to recover. Eight hundred thousand Tigrayans were swept away and dumped in hostile flat jungles and savannahs in the south and west of the country. They were kept in barbed-wire compounds until they had built their huts. The programme was halted after that because of an international outcry over its brutality.

At some sites, thirty per cent of the settlers died of disease. Some of the women who had been separated from their husbands were taken as wives by Anuak and Nuer tribesmen who wore ivory armlets and loincloths. The new agricultural areas never became self-sufficient in food. Thousands of people ran away. Some managed the long trek home to the mountains. Others were bombed by MiGs. The TPLF said the resettlement was an excuse to wipe clean the seat of insurgency.

Then farmers were evicted from their homes and marshalled into villages where they could be more easily controlled. Villagers who resisted the move in Gojjam Province were strafed by helicopter gunships. At least fifteen million people had been forced to dismantle their crumbling huts and rebuild them miles away from their fields. Many farmers had to walk several miles a day to reach their plots, carrying heavy wooden ploughs on their shoulders. Their crops were left unprotected from the nocturnal raids of monkeys and porcupines. In theory they were to have access to water, medicine, education and agricultural inputs. In practice, little of this materialised. Most villages did not even have outdoor latrines.

The strange thing was, having seen their people ground into the dirt in the name of Marx, the TPLF claimed that they, too, were his disciples. During a visit to Britain in 1989, their thirty-four-year-old leader, Meles

Zenawi, said they had modelled their ideology on the hardcore brand of Marxism adhered to in Albania. This rang a very flat note in the corridors of Whitehall. The panelled doors were quietly but firmly shut on his heels. When I visited Tigray, relations with the West were so icy they were glacial. Poor Meles. He was a chain-smoking political *ingénu.*

Meles was good-looking and exuded a certain innocent charm. He had a Castro beard and wore fatigues and plastic sandals. I'm sure he meant well, but he still had straw in his hair. Later things improved when the TPLF wised up. They started chanting the right litany of multi-party democracy, free elections and capitalist investment. It made everyone feel a lot better.

Meanwhile, Mengistu was suffering an estrangement from his former Soviet masters. His refusal to barter for peace with the liberation movements or ease up on his draconian Stalinist vision eventually disillusioned the Soviets. They had made it clear they would not renew their arms agreement, which was due to expire in 1991.

The vacuum had been rapidly filled at the end of 1989 when Mengistu renewed diplomatic relations with Israel after a six-year moratorium. His new friends provided cluster and phosphorus bombs and ammunition and spare parts from Soviet weaponry they had captured in their own wars. Israeli technicians were rehabilitating the old US-made F5 fighter bombers that had been shipped from the United States when Selassie was emperor. The planes had been grounded for years because the US refused to supply spares to Mengistu. Some 200 advisers were helping out on military strategy and training new recruits for the army. The Israelis might also have been supplying the napalm that rained down on rebel towns and villages.

The TPLF insisted they were armed only with captured weapons. My friends in exile told me otherwise. They said they knew from reliable sources that the rebel movement had received hundreds of thousands of dollars for arms from such diverse benefactors as Iraq and the CIA.

The Israelis may not have been sure about the TPLF, but they knew for certain the EPLF enjoyed Arab patronage. The Ethiopian coastline was on the Red Sea, and they wanted to pre-empt a pincer of Muslim influence along their shipping lanes. So they told Mengistu they would help to nudge the war along in his favour in return for his black-skinned Jews. They were called the Falasha, which is Amharic for 'dispossessed'.

Angered by the Israeli intervention, the United States managed to stop the transfer of Israeli-made Kfir fighter planes to the Ethiopian air force. It was just as well. The Kfirs had the capability to bomb at night.

Left alone, Ethiopia's ethnic groups would no doubt have continued to squabble amongst themselves. But the death count would have been contained to a tiny fraction of what it was because they would have been potting at each other with old AK47s. Fanned by foreigners seeking greater regional influence, the war had been ignited by BM21s, Hausers and Stalin Organs into a blazing furnace. All this surrogate power play made you want to knock your head against a wall.

We saw it at first hand down at the front where the TPLF had joined forces with the local Amhara dissidents. They called the coalition the Ethiopian People's Revolutionary Democratic Front. There were, in fact, two fronts. The principal one was near the garrison town of Dessie, which was perched atop an escarpment. If you followed the road south for just over 200 miles, you reached Addis Ababa. For the past five months the EPRDF had floundered on the rocks of Dessie's impregnable fortress and neighbouring Kombolcha's air base. The commanders of the opposing sides sat in mountainside trenches glassing each other with binoculars while their brigades were locked in mortal combat on the plain below. These battles continued from dawn to dusk and lasted for days. Thousands were killed and wounded. But apart from wavering a bit here and pushing a bit there, nothing changed. Distilled into a more manageable image, it was like two perfectly matched arm wrestlers.

Things were going better 130 miles to the west at Mount Guna. The EPRDF were inching their way down the road to Debre Tabor. They had held the town for ten days before being forced to withdraw. Their real objective was the town of Bahar Dar beyond. It was a base for the MiGs.

Mengistu's foot soldiers may have been demoralised, but the military maintained a certain advantage thanks to their fleet of over 130 MiGs. The rebels had no aircraft of their own. Nor did they possess ground-to-air missiles. Their only defence against aerial attack was U23 anti-aircraft guns. They scored the occasional hit, but it was rather like trying to down an eagle with a catapult.

In the most recent two days of fighting, the rebels claimed to have immobilised 4,000 government troops. As a result, they advanced three miles. It seemed an exorbitant price for 5,000 yards of earth.

We headed for the Dessie front first. The plan was to stop over at Woldiya, thirty miles behind the lines, and get a briefing. Then we would head for whichever front promised the most action.

Woldiya was a small, comparatively prosperous town sodden by rain that trickled down the leaves of pawpaw trees and granadilla vines into the mud. It was tucked amongst hills whose tops were encircled with tonsures of mist. I was thankful for weather that made us shiver in our damp clothes. The day before the TPLF radio station had said MiGs had dropped napalm and a cluster bomb on a nearby church. Death toll one hundred. Another thirty wounded.

The inhabitants were Amhara for we had descended to the southern reaches of Wollo Province and were not far from the border with Shoa

Province. They clattered down the main street in dilapidated traps. The men drove, shaking the reins at the ponies' angular haunches. The matronly women sat erect, their voluminous white dresses billowing like schooners in full sail. I watched them pass as we sat in the garden of an inn. We were eating a breakfast of eggs, bread and chillies. We had been eating eggs, bread and chillies and only eggs, bread and chillies for days. The distinguishing aspect to this meal was that it resonated to the booming *basso profundo* of the Stalin Organs.

I had presumed we were staying at the inn, for we had deposited our gear in bedrooms and washed in a proper basin that had a tap. However, after dusk, Hagos shepherded us out the rear entrance and into the house next door. 'You will sleep here,' he said, expansive as ever. The interpretation was: 'The Derg sends out death squads to murder *ferenjis*. If you get killed, it would give us bad face.'

I should mention at this point that we had been appointed two nannies. They followed us everywhere and slept on the ground across our doorsills. James's and my nanny carried an AK47, a belt of ammunition and two hand grenades. He wore khaki shorts and gaiters on legs the size of a Percheron's. Goesh was twenty-four.

The house had not so long ago belonged to the local bank manager, since departed for Addis Ababa. The rooms had been vandalised of most of the furniture, but there were some iron beds in the living room. Mine had an x-ray of someone's lungs tied to it. They had been commandeered from the hospital.

There was nothing much to do except get drunk. So Nigel and Peter unscrewed a bottle of the local whisky and set to it with fierce dedication. A few hours later, with no available lavatory, Nigel peed into the basin. It wouldn't drain, so he scooped it all up in a plastic mug and decanted it out the window on to the mud. Aaah, if our editors could have seen us then. It all seemed perfectly normal at the time. Looking back on it, though, our standards were definitely beginning to slip.

The following night we drove to the foot of Mount Guna. It was godforsaken terrain with a farmhouse signposting the road every five or ten miles. Just before first light we left the main road and veered off on to a track. The Muslims say dawn has arrived when you hold up a black thread next to a white one and can tell the difference. Soon it was bright enough to do needlepoint in pastel yellows and we were still driving. Hagos was lost, stopping in villages and coppices of eucalyptus trees to ask the way. I kept thinking, will we get there, somewhere, anywhere before the first MiG flies over? The tension was getting to me.

Somewhere around eight o'clock we drove into Village 03, so named by the officials who had supervised the programme to regroup farmers into villages. 03 was a gridlock of lopsided huts that had been torn from the sides of mountains and clumsily reassembled on a barren plain. There were gaps between the roof and walls and huge cracks in the plastered mud. It was the most pathetic place I had ever seen. Even Hagos, accustomed to the deprivations of Tigray, was shocked by the primitive living conditions. We spent two days there watching women brew barley beer and nodding hello to old men carrying cow-tail fly whisks, all the while concentrating on the thunderous noise of incoming artillery shells. Thin pats of animal dung were piled up beside the huts. It was the only fuel available. When the MiGs flew overhead, the women and children crouched beside them, seeking shelter from the bombs.

We slept on the mud floor of a hut which we lit with candles. The long dark hours were nudged along by drinking whisky and engaging in puerile chat. I remember standing in the shadows and doing an imitation of a teapot pouring out a cup of tea. James spent much of the time curled up under a blanket in a foetal position coping with a painful attack of sinusitis. Peter pondered on his 'chemical dilemma' of how many tranquillisers and how much whisky he could absorb and still remain conscious if we were suddenly summoned to clamber up the steep slopes of Mount Guna in the middle of the night. Things crawled up the inside of our pant legs but we didn't know what they were for we hadn't removed our clothes for days. Peter was recovering from a poisonous spider bite that had swollen his elbow. I had dysentery. Nigel remained disgustingly healthy.

For want of anything better to do, I penned an entry into Peter's diary: 'Woke up drunk and bad-tempered as usual but managed not to hit that old bat, Mary Anne, when she made me look for a pair of socks. Checked the old torso in a cracked mirror. Reluctantly note that yesterday's effort at suntanning has made me look like a fire hydrant. Will I ever get back to former godlike self? Haven't eaten in three weeks. My trousers are luffing about my legs like a sail looking for a breeze. Mary Anne has been so sweet to me, must give her lunch at Heals. Skin on elbow healing after the black widow. Think it will be fine by London.'

We were trying to adapt to circumstances as best we could. For my part, there were certain areas where I wasn't having great success. The boys' frustration emerged in the drinking sessions. Nigel wanted to spend a month in the trenches and get the best war footage ever filmed. 'It sounds like it'll be the whole theatre of war. We can watch everyone get slaughtered,' he grinned. James wanted to get in and get out and spoke of making up for his absence in Vietnam. Peter said he just wanted to get the job done, but there was a telltale flush of excitement on his cheeks as he spoke. Their enforced immobility aggravated the essential anxiety of every reporter. They worried they were missing the action.

A far more primitive emotion kept slithering over my guts like a sluggish snake. I toyed with the words 'responsibility' and 'perspective'. I imagined my two particularly lovable daughters as orphans. There was no getting round it, though. War scared the shit out of me. The boys took the news that I wouldn't be in the trenches with them reasonably well. James, whom I was abandoning, didn't complain. Peter said he would give me a fill. Nigel said nothing. He didn't need to.

Many days later, when we were reunited in the town of Mekelle, Nigel replayed footage of the fighting that swirled around Mount Guna. His audience was REST officials who were too busy distributing food to visit the front. The film showed MiGs sweeping across the sky. As the planes made this initial flyover, people from the village of Debre Tema ran for the only cover, a storm drain that passed beneath the tarmac road. The next shot traced the jets' return as they dropped their load of little silver footballs. They were trying to sever the EPRDF's supply route. Black skyscrapers of smoke rose upwards. Then we saw a mammoth crater where the storm drain had been. 'At least sixty feet wide and twenty feet deep,' explained Peter. It all seemed far removed and impersonal. But the next images to appear were such a harrowing depiction of the peasants' crucifixion that I had to blink back the tears. Barefoot men in sheepskin capes were trying to shovel mangled bodies out of the earth. Women encased in grief danced a mindless jig beside their dead husbands' disembodied feet and hands. The storm drain had taken a direct hit, killing fifteen.

The scenes were a cameo of the political imbroglio, an epitaph for the angst that had forced brother to betray brother and cousin to kill cousin. The Tigrayans watched intently as the carnage unfolded on the tiny video screen.

'It's amazing, isn't it?' prodded Peter.

They were silent and expressionless. Then Teklewoini Assefa, REST's indefatigable field co-ordinator, spoke out. He suddenly looked very tired. 'You are shocked, but we have all seen scenes like this before. They happen all the time,' he said gravely. 'We have all lost friends and family. We may not weep and wail, but that doesn't mean we don't feel anything. If we give vent to our emotions, we will be paralysed.'

We were in the dining room of an inn. Some of the Tigrayans who sat there had come from abroad. One lived in Germany, another in London. Like many of their countrymen in exile, they paid regular visits to Tigray, travelling over the mined roads to visit the front or assist in the rehabilitation of farming communities. Some just came back because they were homesick. I met a man in a bar not far from where we had been bombed who was a taxi driver in Washington DC. He was taking a month's holiday, he told me.

I looked around the table, scanning the faces for a sign of suppressed anger or sorrow – the averted eye, fingers distractedly stroking a beard. There was none. 'Only a drunk man speaks of the things in his heart' is a Tigrayan proverb.

In peacetime, you can absorb scenes such as these, noting the small gestures, the colour of the light, the high-pitched howl of a dog. In war it's like watching the frozen frames of a movie. If it's really heavy, you can only see flickering, nonsensical images as if the film has been loosened in its sprockets. Fear blocks out the details and the interpretation.

There are many images of that trip that still unreel across my brain. For instance: some old men and a woman are staggering towards me across a field. They are literally on their last legs. The crone, hunched over like a question mark, stumbles to a halt at my feet and sits panting. 'When they hear there are *ferenjis*, they come in case you can help,' says Hagos.

That was the day that Peter emerged from a house calling to anyone who would listen. 'There's a dying woman in here! Get Nigel!' We all stepped inside. She lay in dark shadow beneath a row of cow horns. The makeshift hooks were the family's only possessions, apart from farming implements. The dark bundle of rags lifted herself with great effort on to one elbow. She tipped her wizened head forward a fraction. It was the merest suggestion of the courtly bow that was the standard Tigrayan greeting to strangers and friends alike. Nigel filmed and James took photos as she sank back on to the mud shelf that was her bed.

It was so easy to read of scenes like these in the newspapers or to watch them on television, but it was different when you were in the midst of it. Was it worse to watch the gasping, agonising death of the shepherd with the shrapnel in his stomach or to gaze into these eyes that had been numbed by acute hunger? Sister Bernadette had said it took two or three months to succumb to starvation.

The courtyard outside was as quiet as a tomb. A woman sat in the sunlight holding a baby. It suckled listlessly at her empty breast. The shrunken child beside her looked two, at the most three. Abebe said it was five. The father and an older boy stood watching us, saying nothing. The family was silent and very still, a tableau carved in stone.

I asked when they had last had food. Some vegetables. A week ago. Since then they had eaten leaves and grass and *quienti*, a wild seed that blows on to the fields. I had four dates in my pocket and handed them to the mother. She accepted them with grave care and gave one to the baby. I also had a packet of rehydration salts. I handed that to the mother too, explaining through Abebe that she should mix it with boiled water.

I knew that she didn't understand what it was or what to do with it; that she didn't have the strength to boil water; that there probably wasn't any wood to light a fire; that there might not even be any water. I also knew that the baby was going to die whatever I gave it. This charade of the benevolent stranger assuaging her conscience was pointless but I ploughed on anyway. These people were so compliant and so desperate. So different from the TPLF fighters at the front. They were the real victims of the war.

The salacious whirring of Nigel's camera continued in the background. We were a vulgar but necessary intrusion into what was left of this family's life. We could amplify the Tigrayans' cry for help. Journalists were tools in the TPLF's publicity campaign to generate food and money and support for their political ideals. Hagos and Abebe knew that. But this family didn't. They thought I was a *ferenji* nurse who had come all this way to give them four dried up dates and a useless packet of powder.

Another image: we are lying in a *lugga* in the shade of a thorn tree. Two more days and we will be 'out'. Peter and James are sleeping. Nigel has boiled a pot of water and shouldered his canteen and camera. He is set for another day's vigil for MiGs.

'Why do you bother? You've got everything now. Except a bomb landing on us while we sleep.'

He grins at me. 'That's what I'm waiting for.'

My last day in Ethiopia, spent a few miles from the Sudanese border, was unscheduled. The truck I was travelling in had been separated from the convoy when we stopped to help a vehicle irretrievably stuck in a gully. While we yelled and heaved by the dim light of a torch, the others had continued through the night to the border town of Kassala and safety. Our delay meant arriving at the border just after dawn. The Sudanese immigration officials, as vile-tempered as ever, refused to let us cross until after sunset. We drove back a few miles into the desert to wait it out at the collection of thorn-bush huts that was the TPLF's last staging post before the Sudan.

Debre Yohannes, the truck driver, rested his head on the steering wheel and sighed. '*Sono stanco morto*' (I'm dead tired). Like many Eritreans, he knew a smattering of Italian, a leftover from the days when the province was under Mussolini's administration. We clambered out and sat on a boulder smoking cigarettes and exchanging curses directed at Sudanese cussedness. Yohannes saw his family, who lived in Kassala, only one day a week. The refusal to let us cross meant that he would have to turn round and go back into Tigray without a rest. Yohannes wouldn't believe me, but I knew that Peter, James and Nigel would head straight for Khartoum and London without waiting for me. (As it turned out, James did wait for me in Khartoum so that we could fly back to England together.) We succumbed to despondency. I felt like a child who has been told she has to stay on at boarding school when everyone else has gone home for the holidays. The last thing either of us wanted was to spend another day face down in the dirt under the belly of a truck.

In due course, we wandered over to the encampment where about eight men and women fighters in fatigues were lounging around. They didn't have much, but with great good humour and kindness, they offered it all to me, enlarging on their softly spoken Tigrinya with gestures. Would I like to wash, asked a woman, indicating a plastic barrel of water. I shook my head. She seated us on a piece of firewood and brought us tin bowls of goat stew. I knew they had very little to eat and that this was probably everyone's dinner. But to refuse would have been churlish. Afterwards they produced a greasy, well-thumbed and far too slim pack of cards and tried to entice me into a game. I smiled and shook my head again. A young man was strumming a crudely made ukulele. He patted the seat beside him. But I was too angry and restless to settle down.

I decided to alleviate my frustration with an impromptu game of baseball and persuaded some of the fighters to join in. We used a stick of firewood as a bat and marked out the bases with stones. The play was good-natured but clumsy as they tried their hand at pitching and hitting. To my surprise, not one of them, all brawny young men in their twenties, could throw or catch the punctured rubber ball I had found lying in the dust.

After a few faltering attempts, a fighter named Abdel Kadir pointed to the sky and gestured for us to return to the protective covering of the huts. We all knew why he had brought the game to an end, but he felt this was too crude an excuse for spoiling the morning's sport. He summoned up his scant English to explain further. 'We don't know how to play because of the planes,' he said apologetically.

Ethnic antagonism bolstered by arms supplied by foreigners had forced the youth of Tigray to go to school at night and sleep during the day. They didn't know what it was like to run around outdoors in the sunshine. They weren't like other children for they didn't know how to play. When I got back to London, the memory of that topsy-turvy world where children lived in the shadow of war was hard to shed. I had nightmares for three weeks.

At first the dreams were so awful that my subconscious couldn't find images to match the nameless horror. A dark brown amorphous emptiness floated under my eyelids. The murk was as soft as a moth's wing, pulsating and shifting with a life of its own. No words could make sense of this primal, shapeless gloom dredged from the depths of my being. At first I thought I was being overtaken by my own mortality, but it was worse than that. It was a premonition of universal death. The sensation was so chilling that even after I had surged back to wakefulness, it took several minutes of staring at the windowsill with the light on to calm me down.

After a few days, this evil phantasm was replaced by more conventional struggles. I stood beside TPLF fighters firing AK47s, wrestled with faceless figures in brown Derg suits. And inevitably, I was transfixed by a firework display of blistering metal that would annihilate me when it reached the earth.

In my waking hours, I wrote endless stories on the war and the famine for newspapers in England and the United States. I tried to expose the reasons for the Ethiopians' crucifixion but, it seemed from talking to the people who read the pieces, newsprint was inadequate for parsing the grammar of desecration. The story interested its audience for as long as it took to reach the right underground stop.

Zealots are tiresome, and I soon learned to crusade with restraint. Instead of launching into a dirge for the starving millions or a tirade against the purgatory of Marxism, when people asked where I had been, I talked of the need to give money. When their eyes glazed over, I stopped. 'It doesn't matter if you care about Ethiopia as long as you care about something,' I would chant.

I spent some time lobbying Members of Parliament as well. I don't know if I made a difference, but more aid for food relief was, in time, directed to Ethiopia. I also tried to keep track of events inside Tigray. As it turned out, fewer died than expected because the people in the liberated regions bartered goods between surplus and deficit areas, a survival mechanism that had been proscribed under the government's centralised economy. As the TPLF noose tightened around Mengistu's neck, he promised democratic reform but omitted to implement it.

At a press conference I asked a REST official how often food convoys were bombed. 'Not often. But there was an unlucky incident not long ago which you may have read about in *The Sunday Times*,' he said, then looked uncomfortable when a TPLF official leaned over and whispered in his ear. Perhaps he had the right perspective. My personal involvement counted for nothing. I was merely the weatherman reporting the storms. So why did I feel compelled to provide shelter from the downpour?

Having visited Ethiopia for over twenty years, I had come to love the country and its people. Now that I was banned from Kenya, it felt even more like 'home'. Besides, it was all too easy for those of us in the West to regard the famine and war as a tragedy that didn't really concern us. After all, 'they' were at variance with us both ethnically and culturally. They lived so far away and dressed so differently it was difficult to identify with their suffering. My viewpoint had altered because I had seen it first hand. It seemed obvious to make whatever small contribution I could to Ethiopia's future.

The exiles wouldn't be drawn out on the matter, but I detected resentment in their reticence. 'Why is it all right to show us dying in rags on the television, but it's not all right to have pictures of Englishmen suffocating against a fence at Hillsborough? We're all human beings. There should be the same code for all of us,' fumed a friend.

Her brother shrugged and cast a cool, challenging gaze in my direction. 'We think we're unique, but the truth is that no one in the West gives a damn about us. The sooner we realise we're just the same as every other economically depressed and politically backward African country, the better,' he pronounced. It was his way of excusing the absence of compassion. None of us believed what he said.

The indifference that had appeared between the First World and the Third World was in danger of becoming a canyon. It worked both ways for very few Africans were conversant with, let alone cared about, the problems afflicting countries beyond their continent. I knew that whenever I found it in my heart, I had to sluice it away. Unless we all did that, we were on course for moral receivership. It didn't really matter what or who we cared for. What counted was an ability to empathise with others and the knowledge that we could, infinitesimally perhaps, alter the direction of events.

Ethiopia had to be helped because it was in danger of becoming a howling void of disillusion and dust. It seemed to me that if we abandoned compassion, the metaphor would be applicable at another level in Europe and the United States as well. There are many different types of evil and many roads that lead to it. It can lurk anywhere because we, who harbour it in our spirit, are the perpetrators.

5

The Monster

This isn't a real country. It doesn't even have a real name. Central African Republic.
Louis Sarno, a New York sound engineer who lives with pygmies

After Tigray, I needed some light relief. Nothing too taxing, nothing too dangerous. Just a bit of fun. But the contours of the psychological map are misleading. I had experienced happiness in the midst of despondency and was to find melancholy when I expected calm. My next assignment yielded all I was looking for. And more. I didn't know it at the time, but I was about to be served up with a generous dollop of Conradian heart of darkness.

Thanks to John Witherow, the witty and tolerant foreign editor at *The Sunday Times*, I had *carte blanche* in my role as roving reporter. The only proviso was to furnish good copy. Africa is aglow with interesting, offbeat stories. Very few contain any nuggets of political significance for the rest of the world, but they invariably are dusted with savagery, eccentricity and colour. Given my brief, I could easily have just shut my eyes and thrown a dart at a map of the continent. Whichever country it landed on would have provided the goods.

However, that would have smacked of the prosaic. Travel is best savoured when it is a product of that magical alchemy of whimsy, unfulfilled memories and the urge to seek and discover.

I wanted to go somewhere beyond the orbit of the issues that concerned the rest of the world. Somewhere quintessentially African where forces that had nothing to do with Western culture came into play. I recalled a Napoleonic psychopath, resplendent in diamonds and pearls, whose alleged cannibalism had revolted the world. I added to this a documentary

141

I had seen on TV where a tall, dark-haired American pushed aside thick green foliage in search of gorillas. Man's ancient instincts thriving unfettered in a country of virgin rain forest and untamed bush. It sounded a likely formula for adventure. I rang the travel agent.

The Central African Republic is Africa at its best or worst, depending on how you look at it. It is a flat, monotonous savannah hemmed in the south with a broad band of tropical rain forest. Until thirty years ago, it was a French colony. But once you leave the capital of Bangui and head into the bush, life is reminiscent of the pre-colonial days when Arab slave caravans plundered the villages. Lawlessness still prevails, only now the Arabs poach animals instead of people. The country's attraction for outsiders, Arab and European, is its abundant wildlife. It is considered to be the richest repository of game north of the equator.

I had been looking forward to the CAR, as everyone called it. Returning to Africa is like being reunited with your lover. Everything is embalmed in a wonderful, intoxicating familiarity. The intimacy of knowing that it will look like this and smell like that leads you to embrace the virtues blindly and dismiss the faults with affectionate tolerance.

For instance, the torque of friendliness and hostility that propels you through the airport is reassuring. You don't mind that an immigration official has sat with his elbows on the counter, fingering each page of your passport with the careful attention of a seminarian studying the Bible. It doesn't matter that you are despatched to a small room to answer questions about your visa. This is all part of the way it is. You know that ultimately you will be smiled or scowled at by a customs official as he delves into your bag, perhaps get a stern look from a soldier or two, and eventually fall into a sea of cheerful taxi drivers, one of whom will propel you into the unknown familiar and, as sure as the Pope's a Catholic, try to overcharge you because, if he has a meter at all, he will say it isn't working.

Later, you will drink in the smallest details as if they are an elixir. The way the tomatoes and cucumbers have been cut in a bowl of salad stirs excited recognition. So does the staggering richness of the palms and banana and pawpaw trees. Bus shelters leaning at awkward angles because the buses have hit them. Road signs deliberately peppered with holes so they won't be torn down, refashioned into tin trunks and sold for a nice profit. Cars that career straight across the potholes in the road because to avoid them all would take too much effort. It's all wonderful because it's all African.

You stare at women whose bounteous backsides, encased in brightly patterned cloth, gyrate beneath the plates of mangos or cassava they are carrying on their heads. That hypnotic shifting of weight from left buttock to right buttock to left to right is such a triumph of female sexuality that you can't help grinning.

At first, you are so delirious you don't even mind the equivalent public display of masculinity. A hand absent-mindedly placed on the crotch while talking to a friend in the street followed by a blatant squeeze. It is not so much a readjustment of the genitalia as a casual reacquaintance with the axis of power.

Where were we? I meant to describe the Africa I feel comfortable with. And here I am off on a pornographic tangent. There's a reason though. My arrival in Bangui wasn't marked with the expected sense of home-coming. Something was out of sync.

Africans regard sex without inhibition. For them it is a rite of passage to be celebrated as well as the biological means to propagating the tribe. This is why Africa exudes a libidinous sensuality. Here, however, people were so perfunctory about sex it had about as much poetry as ladling food into your mouth. That was the key to Bangui. All the subtlety and allure had been ironed out of it. It was a hard place, starched with fear and aggression. Instead of enfolding you in its arms, it was like a sullen, closed fist, poised for the punch. Even in the extraordinary heat of the day, it was cold and unyielding. It felt as if a dreadful wrath was about to be unleashed.

For outsiders, mention of the Central African Republic evoked one name, that of Jean Bedel Bokassa, who for fourteen years ruled with uninhibited authority, first as president then as life president and finally as emperor, before he departed as he had arrived, in a *coup d'etat*. To look at him, he seemed harmless enough. He was a decidedly short man, stocky and dark with a splayed nose and a small, Brillo-pad beard. But his greed, brutality and delusions of majesty were legend. He regarded the national resources as his personal kitty and his subjects as children whose behaviour called for Draconian discipline. When it came to murder, mutilation and lavish spending, Bokassa's reputation was unequalled amongst African despots.

Bokassa was born to a Mbaka chief in 1921 near a swamp in a forest. When he was six, his father was beaten to death by a French administrator. His mother committed suicide soon afterwards. The young orphan was educated by missionaries but chose to become a soldier, joining the Free French Resistance to fight the Nazis and later serving in the French colonial infantry in Indochina. He was decorated with twelve combat medals and commissioned as a captain. His service to the French was a period in his life of which he was inordinately proud. When the CAR's first armed forces were created two years after independence in 1962, he was made chief of staff. Three years later he ousted his cousin David Dacko, who had been a French protégé. He dissolved parliament and the consti-tution, assumed all legislative, executive and military powers and executed his political opponents. He instituted some development – building roads, a hospital and a slaughterhouse and increasing diamond production – and pocketed most of the profits. So far it was the conventional African tale of the poor boy who had made good.

Then Bokassa's style of government became alarmingly erratic as elements of personal savagery emerged. For a while he shared Hitler's vision of a pure race and swept up deformed beggars from the streets, pushing them out of planes into the river. He had thieves marched out of the prison into the central square where their left ears were cut off before a gaping crowd. He decreed that recidivism would lead to the loss of the right ear, then a hand and finally hanging. In 1972 he celebrated Mothers' Day by executing on the gallows everyone imprisoned for matricide. At the same time, he released all mothers from jail. Most infamous of all, he held kangaroo courts in the gardens of his house, feeding the condemned to lions and crocodiles. It was said that some of the victims also landed up on his dinner table.

Bokassa was spurred on to excesses of revenge, sentimentality and pomp by towering rages and a pathetic desire to be accepted as a person of standing by the rest of the world, particularly the French. When he seized power, his first words were *'Vive la France!'* He idolised General de Gaulle and sobbed *'Papa! Papa!'* at his funeral. He befriended Valéry Giscard d'Estaing, who used to come out every year to hunt elephants. A 200,000-acre reserve was put at his disposal with a few girls thrown in to brighten things up. But Bokassa, heavy-handed as always, overdid it and helped to bring down the French president in a scandal over gifts of diamonds. In 1979 the French satirical newspaper *Le Canard Enchaîné* published a letter signed by Bokassa authorising the presentation of $200,000 of thirty-carat diamonds to Giscard. In his autobiography, published in 1991, Giscard admitted to receiving 173 diamonds from Bokassa over a period of five years but claimed to have sold them all and donated the proceeds to charity. The sum only came to about $22,000 he said. This revelation did little to dampen speculation about the corrupt relationship between the two men. Bokassa was more frank about what was going on. He once explained, 'Everything around here is financed by the French. We ask the French for money, get it and waste it.'

The most shameful example of this happened in 1977 when the French quietly picked up the tab for Bokassa's coronation. What the deranged head of state craved above all was legitimacy. Why not, he thought to himself, emulate another of his heroes, Napoleon Bonaparte, and crown himself emperor? Thus he embarked on a folly that was unsurpassed in Africa. He sat on a fifteen-foot golden throne in the shape of an eagle and placed a crown of diamonds, rubies and emeralds on his balding head. His jacket, a Napoleonic replica, had extra-wide lapels to accommodate all his medals. This bizarre ceremony, attended by hundreds of journalists but not one head of state, unfolded to the strains of Mozart and Beethoven and the incessant beat of tribal drums. It cost twenty-two million dollars, nearly a quarter of the national revenue.

It was hard to imagine that such an extravaganza had ever taken place when you saw the shoddy state of disrepair into which the capital had fallen. The town lay on the Ubangui, a lazy python of a river that coiled alongside the mud shacks and concrete block houses. Some of the buildings were just grey shells that had been partially built then abandoned, waiting for the bush to reclaim them. The roads were made of crumbling tarmac or red dirt, scuffed and pitted like old shoes. The streets were full of people, who appeared to have no sense of purpose. They loitered beside the wooden stalls that sold baguettes and cigarettes and in the doorways of shops. They were still in the same place when you came back an hour later.

Bangui should have been subject to the small stirrings of development and investment that come to even the most out-of-way African capitals – the addition of a new restaurant or a rudimentary soap factory, the construction of roads, the arrival of another aid agency or a fleet of blackmarket Mercedes Benzes. But there was nothing of this. It was as if it had lost the initial, hesitant momentum it had gained after independence and was sliding backwards down the scree of time. There wasn't much in the Lebanese-run shops apart from bolts of cloth, radio batteries, kerosene lamps and cassava sieves. Most of the French shopkeepers had 'gone home' in despair, leaving their premises boarded up. Only 3,000 French residents were left, compared to the affluent Côte d'Ivoire's 35,000. The last optician had long since departed, so if your glasses broke, you sent them to Paris to be fixed. The hospital had run out of X-ray film, so if your arm broke, you took the first UTA flight out. The two longest established hotels had been closed down and stood empty. The inroads of political and economic change that appeared elsewhere on the continent had bypassed Bangui. It was a cul de sac.

From the air the buildings and streets and sun-scorched ground littered with junk and rubbish were reduced to insignificance. The town became a place of corrugated iron roofs and palms that looked like dolls' feather dusters. Antlike people with blobs of bundles on their heads crossed the open places where the junk was so tiny it was nothing. To approach it this way, in a small plane that had been flying for hundreds of miles over savannah or jungle, to see Bangui spread out below, on the bend of the river that marked the boundary with Zaire, was at once exciting and disappointing. It seemed so insubstantial, some tin and concrete splashed on to a giant landscape of green flatness.

It was the colonial architecture, decrepit and decaying, that suggested this was not a temporary collection of dwellings but a place that had been around for a long time. Even these forlorn constructions looked used without being maintained, squatted in for generations by people who had come from the bush or from France, then gone away again. Some of the administrative buildings, such as the police headquarters and the Ministry of Defence, dated back to the 1920s. They were bungalows with sloping tin roofs and shutters that opened from the top as if they were flashing a buck-toothed grin. They were built on high foundations so that you had to climb up steps past pitted, peeling walls to reach their narrow verandahs. The offices themselves contained rickety wooden tables and ancient typewriters. There were tall filing cabinets gathering dust beneath their chains and padlocks. Files were stacked in untidy heaps on the floor and amongst jagged masonry where holes had been knocked in the wall. The government employees who sat there seemed to be steeped in a torpor which the slowly turning ceiling fans could do nothing to dispel.

It was at Kilometre Cinq that Bangui came to life with the leisurely bargaining of the bazaar. The market had the manners of a bush village, not a city, and was therefore more real. Women holding umbrellas over their heads sat on stools guarding small piles of onions, dried fish, peanuts, spices and stock cubes laid out on the ground. There were Muslim traders in dark glasses who wore slippers and *boubous* and spread their goods over crudely made wooden tables. All this food was placed a foot or so from open drains that gave off a rich odour of rot and decomposition. Pigs moved around in the channels of muck, rooting out titbits. There were listless, stubby-legged goats with mango skins and bits of paper hanging from their mouths.

I felt I owed Kathy Arkell, the photographer, an apology for the meanness of the scenes displayed before us. On the few occasions we had talked in London, I had described a different sort of Africa to her. She showed no disappointment, however. When things didn't go our way, which was often, she grinned and said, 'If you can't fix it, fuck it.' I had taken an instant liking to Kathy, who had been introduced by a mutual friend in Fleet Street. Her gutsy and humorous approach to life was reflected in her polished, original photography. She was a sexy, blonde Hungarian who had met her English husband in Budapest, wedded him three days later, and learnt English during the following year. At thirty-eight, she had two delightful sons and a marriage that worked. This enviable clarity of vision when it came to achieving her goals boded well for coming to grips with the vagaries of the CAR. She had brought with her a sheaf of the cheapest type of imitation Rolex watch and used them to hustle with the polished ease of an East European black marketeer. She also exercised her charm with remarkable effect considering she spoke no French. When neither of these approaches worked, she simply retired to her bed and went to sleep.

While I tried to establish contacts, Kathy went on foraging expeditions for food. The restaurants charged extortionate prices that were well beyond the reach of our limited expenses. Nearly all the food and drink was imported, much of it from France. A pizza cost about fifty dollars. A bottle of mineral water was more expensive than a prostitute. So we existed on mangos and baguettes which we ate in the hotel bedroom with a penknife.

Only the foreigners ate in the restaurants. Central African palates were tempted by animals and insects that came from the bush. Bowls of moist grubs and orange caterpillars that crawled over each other like fat worms. Steaks of snake and crocodile. *Viande bucané* – shrivelled and blackened chunks of smoked game meat that looked like dried turds. There were smoked monkeys for sale in the market. They were displayed in their entirety so that the spindly arms and legs would reassure shoppers they were not buying a human baby.

Kathy and I became all too well acquainted with Bangui for my visa had expired and it took a week to sort it out. We also had to obtain permissions from different ministries to work as journalists and to report on the wildlife projects we intended to visit. During this enforced wait, I met a professional hunter called Christian Detudert.

Europeans had two interests in the CAR, both of an exploitative nature. One was in diamonds, which were panned from rivers in the bush by the locals and sold to some half dozen diamond-buying companies. The prospectors brought in everything from the coarse fragments known as boart to the highest quality gemstones and sold them for a price well below the market value. Half the country's foreign exchange earnings came from the export of diamonds. The figure should have been much higher. Perhaps as much again was smuggled out on the black market.

The other enterprise that flourished was big game hunting. This rich enclave of game was popular with sportsmen from Europe and the United States. Sport hunting for elephants had been banned in 1980, but you could still seek out trophies of rare or elusive species such as Derby eland, giant topi, roan antelope and bongo. Professional hunters, most of them French, charged clients from $8,000 to $25,000 a fortnight for a safari. The percentage of this paid in taxes and fees to the central government and local councils was so small that it averaged out at nineteen dollars per square mile of hunting concession. That was equivalent to the market price of a guinea fowl which the villagers, poor as they were, could easily have provided if only they, too, had been allowed to hunt.

Unlike other parts of Africa, where wild animals were crowded out by subsistence agricultural plots, there was no such competition for land between man and beast. The CAR had a population of under three million and was slightly smaller than Texas. On paper it was a ratio of one person for every 1.5 square miles. In reality, most people lived along the rivers or in the towns. The savannah was so sparsely inhabited that in one hunting concession the size of Cyprus, there were just two villages with a total of 1,800 residents between them. Disease had made the women barren and killed off about half the babies that were born.

It was the end of the dry-season hunting which lasted from mid-December to May. Christian, like the other hunters, spent the entire season in the bush, based at a camp of crude huts made in the local manner with mud and sticks. He was in town to wind up his affairs before returning to France to wait out the rains. His name had been given to me by Alain Mosist, a wiry Basque who was one of two hunters who stayed in the CAR year round. Alain had described Christian as handsome and aristocratic. 'He's the gentleman amongst us.' But then Alain's vision was different from mine. On one visit to his home, Alain had asked his servant to bring us coffee in small cups. When the man served the coffee in large ones instead, Alain gave him an annoyed rap on the head with his knuckles. 'The trouble with Africans is that they aren't intelligent,' he had said.

Christian embarked on a courtship which, out of hunger, boredom and a desire to learn what was going on, I allowed to proceed at its quirky pace. We drank sodas by the hotel pool while he related his encounters with poachers. Later, he put me on the back of his mobilette and took me to lunch with his friends Emilie and Michel.

Michel was a French *colon* who owned a garage and a video shop. His wife Emilie was a *métisse* – of mixed race – a pert, olive-skinned beauty with frizzy blonde hair. We sat on green cane chairs covered with chintz cushions sipping champagne and looking out on a yard filled with the bodies of cannibalised cars and trucks. The conversation meandered from civil unrest to corruption and crime, the customary products of a government in political and economic distress.

The university professors hadn't been paid and were on strike. Neither had the police. They resolved the problem of going without a salary for eight months by demanding more money at road blocks. Everyone agreed that driving at night, always an expensive proposition, was becoming too expensive. It was well-trodden terrain, the sort of chat universal to expatriate communities south of the Sahara. In another city on another continent, we would have been discussing bargain shopping or comparing rents and property prices.

Left to Right
Tara, Petra, Mary Anne
Anthony Criffiths

Kipenget (on the left) at her daughter Segenun's
circumcision. Segenun underwent the ceremony against
her will and swore she would be the last of her
generation of Maasai to suffer the indignity.
Miriape Sankaire

The author, photographer Katalin Arkell (on the right)
and a game ranger on the prowl for elephants in the
Central African Republic. *Katalin Arkell*

Lepias' wife Nolotimy in the days when she was still
proud to be a Samburu woman. When Lepias left her
behind to work in Nairobi, she fell prey to a slow
despair. *M. A. Fitzgerald*

The bandit was a dark and wild-looking man who
aroused anger and fear amongst the people of Tum.
Mark, the doctor, treated his wounds with paediatric
antibiotics. It was all we had with us. *M. A. Fitzgerald*

Midday lunch break. Mary Anne cooks camp stew
(cabbage and dried goat) with the help of two Samburu
warriors. *M. A. Fitzgerald*

The boys back from the front line in Ethiopia's civil war.
Left to right: ITN correspondent Peter Sharp, one of the
best fixers in the business; ITN cameraman Nigel
Thomson, the quintessential war junkie; and
photographer James Hamilton who came within an inch
of losing his life but never complained. *M. A. Fitzgerald*

Nigel, Peter and Mary Anne after scrambling for cover
from attacking MiG fighter jets. The bombardment
brought home the meaning of shell-shocked.
M. A. Fitzgerald

Rough justice: game rangers with a captured poacher in the Central African Republic. *Katalin Arkell*

Revolution Liberia-style: stony eyes, carnival dress and
an enemy skull for a fetish. *Daher/FSP*

Paul Settim, the West African fetishist. He wanted to kill
the chief who had laid a curse on Mary Anne.
Alistair Sinclair

Inevitably, the talk moved on to 'the system'. There were no transactions without hustling, no acquisitions without bribery, so it was important to be up-to-date on who was being paid how much and for what. These were the exchanges of money, conducted with oblique conversation and without receipts, which reflected the real cost of living.

'Before, Bokassa was the only one who stole money. Now it's all the ministers as well,' someone complained.

But a *métisse* doctor, who had been the former leader's personal physician, defended him. 'He was extremely intelligent and one of the hardest working men I've ever met. He hardly slept. He did a lot for this country. We were in much better shape then,' he said.

Bokassa was mocked by Westerners for his buffoonish savagery and shunned by other African leaders for giving the continent a bad name. But he still cast a shadow of nostalgia across the CAR. People recalled his reign as a golden time when the economy flourished and everyone had jobs. Many, like the doctor, spoke of him with genuine regard and fondness. A membrane of oblivion had grown over the murders.

When I suggested to a Ministry of Information official that Bokassa's alleged cannibalism had given the country a naff reputation, he bridled. 'What's wrong with cannibalism? You had it in Europe in the thirteenth century.'

Even David Dacko, who had been betrayed by Bokassa, spoke of him without spite. His cousin had kept him in solitary confinement for three and a half years, chained naked to the wall of his cell like a monkey. There was no trace of rancour when he related this.

At our next meeting, in the hotel bar, Christian seized my hand and hoovered his lips up my arm. '*Je veux faire l'amour avec toi*,' he whispered, giving me an earnest stare with faded blue eyes.

'*Oui, ça se voit, mais pas ici.*' I gave what I hoped was a Gallic shrug, and gestured towards the other drinkers. It was an unthinking reply. Flippancy in a foreign tongue tends to be misconstrued.

The following day, Christian turned up at the hotel in the late afternoon wearing a darned checked shirt, khaki shorts and sandals. He had with him his friend Jean Paul who was a vet. They wanted to take Kathy and I for a *promenade*.

We set off past the roadside cigarette stalls, circuited the empty market and reached the banks of the Ubangui. It was a predictably charming scene. Storklike fishermen were paddling narrow wooden dugouts through the khaki water. Egrets as white as an enamel plate strutted on the spits of sand. It would be fun to go for a ride, I commented.

Christian pouted and his thin lips rose in the direction of Zaire. Hiring a boat was dangerous. They were so poor on the other side, he warned, that they kidnapped whites to get money. If you couldn't pay the ransom, they killed you. He had heard of a fisherman who had beached his dugout and never been seen again. They had descended on him like a pack of dogs after a haunch of meat.

We sauntered on beside the river as it turned towards Ndjamena, the capital of Chad, some 600 miles to the north. Ahead of us a witch's cauldron of turbulence roiled around the rocks mid-stream. They marked the end of the river's navigable stretch. Several hundred miles in the other direction, the Ubangui debouched into the Zaire, the artery that took Joseph Conrad's Marlow into the heart of darkness.

We followed the road as it ascended the hill beyond the Sofitel, the air-conditioned high-rise hotel that only the very rich could afford to stay in. 'It was on this road that four thieves pulled me off my moped. It was five o'clock in the afternoon. They yanked off the military belt I was wearing and ran away. I chased them and we hit each other, but I didn't get my belt back,' Christian said.

The grass verges where the sidewalk should have been were littered with discarded paper and old radio batteries that had burst open like overcooked sausages. Christian sighed. 'This was always tidy when Bokassa was here. If he walked along and saw something was untidy, the person responsible would be taken away. Now it's filthy.'

He talked of him in the past tense, but in fact, Bokassa was still there, right above our heads, sitting out a life sentence of incarceration as punishment for murder and crimes against the state. Perched atop the red stone cliff face on our left was Campe Roux, the army headquarters where government opponents were imprisoned. All you could see were a few flamboyant trees and some mouldering rectangular white buildings with long grass licking at their foundations. It was strange to think of him up there, locked in a nine-foot by fifteen-foot cell. He was allowed out once a day into a small courtyard. He had turned to religion and wore a crucifix and read the Bible. It was hard to believe that the ogre had undergone a genuine conversion, but unusual things happen when your fortune changes.

As it turned out, Bokassa had not been invincible after all. His downfall was triggered by a seemingly small event. He decreed that all school children were to wear shirts bearing his portrait. The uniforms, of course, were produced in Bokassa's factory and had to be bought from Bokassa's shop. The announcement came at a time when the economy was declining, and the children protested at this extra expense. Bokassa reacted violently. He was infuriated that children should disobey him. He had them rounded up and stuffed into jail cells. Then he decided to go down to the prison and talk to them himself. When he saw all those cheeky, insubordinate youngsters, wide-eyed with fright and fainting from lack of air, his rage grew. He began to club them with his ebony cane and told the policemen to do likewise. Over eighty died. The massacre reached beyond the pale of French tolerance. Soon afterwards France flew paratroopers into the capital at night and reinstated Dacko.

That was in 1979. Bokassa spent seven years in exile but eventually, so he said, was overcome with homesickness. One day he jumped off a plane from Paris, was recognised by airport officials and immediately taken into custody. After a lengthy and much publicised trial, he was convicted of ordering the murder of at least twenty political opponents and stealing from the treasury. During the last two years of his rule, he had been diverting $64,000 a week from state funds which he shipped out of the country in strong boxes. He was charged with, but not convicted of, cannibalism. It would not have carried a sentence anyway. Under Central African law cannibalism was only a misdemeanour, and an amnesty on past misdemeanours had been declared in 1981. Bokassa was sentenced to death. A few months later, this was commuted to life imprisonment.

I said I wanted to walk on to take a look at the prison down the road. Christian ducked his head into his shoulder blades like an agitated tortoise. His lips were erect with disapproval. That was a very unwise idea. He used to hear the rattle of machine guns at night while the guards tried to shoot down escaping prisoners. If we walked past, there might be trouble. We might be seized.

Riled by this paranoia, I insisted and strode off towards the entrance gates. They were shaded by a leafy mango tree and a flamboyant tree with red flowers. Across the way a man was selling purple bottles of fuel for mobilettes. Little boys skipped down the road pushing cars made from twisted wire. The prison walls were lined with shards of glass, and there were some rudimentary spotlights strung along the perimeter. It looked ordinary, slightly down-at-heel. There was nothing overtly sinister, but the episode had introduced yet another note of discomfort into the afternoon. We turned round and headed back to the hotel before dusk rose up from the river.

Our outing was such a success that Christian and Jean Paul asked us to dinner for the following night, and we accepted. The next morning I bumped into Christian in the corridor of the Ministry of Waters and Forests. He grabbed my arm and leant close. He was behaving like someone who has hidden a fart cushion in the armchair – excited and confidential and talking very quickly. 'It's all fixed. Emilie's aunt has a house outside town in the country and it's empty. We'll have dinner with Jean Paul and Kathy and then we will leave them and spend the night there.'

'Why?' I asked.

'So that we can make love!'

Christian said nothing in reply to my veto, but when I got back to the hotel there was a note expressing regret at cancelling the dinner. Unfortunately, Jean Paul had come down with a stomach ailment and was not at all well.

I grinned and showed it to Kathy, who was waiting for me by the reception desk. She fixed me with a shrewd look. 'You're so naive. Why didn't you turn him down *after* the meal?' That was Kathy for you, practical to the last.

I said I would join her in a second and went to fetch something from our bedroom. I unlocked the door and stepped inside. The curtains were still drawn and the light was dim which was why I bumped into the man standing by the bathroom door. It took several seconds for my eyes to adjust to the gloom and make out the tall, lanky form of the assistant manager. My brain was much slower in focussing. I was more jarred by the change in his attitude than the unexplained intrusion. He had dropped the deferential tone he customarily used with us. Instead he spoke in a chummy, familiar way that inferred we were old friends who did business together. He said there was a man who wanted to see me. I thought I had a clandestine interview on my hands so pressed him for details.

The assistant manager led me to the sliding glass doors that gave on to the swimming pool and pointed. 'There. The Egyptian. He asked especially for you.' He was sitting in a chair in a very brief bathing suit, sunning himself. He had a handsome face and finely proportioned body. I put him at early thirties. Not the type, I would have thought, who needed to pay for sexual services. But then appearances were misleading. He must have thought we had flown out from Europe to turn some expensive tricks. Understandable. What else would two blondes be doing in a dump like this? I turned to the assistant manager and disabused him of this notion. When I told Kathy, she shook her head. 'Won't you ever learn? At least you should have negotiated a price so that I know what you're worth if the going gets really tough.'

Poor Christian, not only was he tight-fisted, he walked with fear in his heart and so, for him, his anxieties were real. Besides, he was not the only one to feel this way. Where other equatorial towns encouraged *cafard*, that listless submission to circumstance, Bangui sweated tension. It was as if people were defenceless against unmentionable, hostile forces that lurked in the dark blue shadows. The Africans were frightened of thieves, the police, the French who had stayed on, crocodile men, sorcerers' spells, mobs and AIDS. The French were frightened of thieves, the police, the Africans, mobs and malaria. All this angst kept you looking over your shoulder in the day while at night you had one ear cocked for the soft slap of a bare foot in the dirt or the rattle of a shutter being pried open.

I heard so many grizzly tales and flabbergasting stories that there had to be something to it. Human flesh had been sold as beef in one of the markets. A thief caught by a mob had been force-fed quick-drying cement. Irate passers by had poured petrol into another thief's ears. The previous month Azande villagers near the Sudanese border had caught some three dozen crocodile men and burnt them at the stake.

Crocodile men were hired assassins who, so people believed, were supernatural. They lived in capsules of air under the water and worked with middle men who demanded about fifteen dollars as hit money to carry out a murder. If you stopped to chat with the fishermen on the Ubangui, they told you that spirits in the shape of men and women clambered on to the bank and squatted there to catch the warmth of the morning sun. Long, damp tendrils of hair fell over their shoulders. They didn't move even when people threw stones at them. When they returned to the river, they assumed the shape of crocodiles and hippos. Sometimes they attacked the fishermen's dugouts.

It was difficult to winnow fact from fiction, but one thing was certain. There was an unusually high crime rate. As with the poachers, who looked upon animals not as something beautiful but as things to be hunted, so in the town men regarded each other as prey. You never walked in the street at night. You never carried anything with you in the day. Kathy and I zipped our belongings into the pockets of our fishing jackets and then zipped the jackets up so they couldn't be torn off our backs. It wasn't the most comfortable outfit in the hundred-degree-plus heat, but it was the safest.

José Tello's story was one of several unnerving tales related to me in the first person. These sagas of injustice always involved either robbery, extortion, physical assaults or wrongful arrest. José was a genial Portuguese who had left his job running Mozambique's game parks to become warden of a remote game conservation area towards the Chad border. Not long before I met him, he had parked his car outside the police station and popped inside on his way back north. During those few minutes, some men had pried out the driver's window, tossed it on the ground, fished out his briefcase from the front seat and vanished. It was a particularly unfortunate theft because the briefcase contained the project's wages, a million of the local francs, which came to about $3,750.

José was a practised Africa hand and knew just what to do. He hired a band of vigilantes who tracked down the thieves in a village twenty miles outside town. The money had disappeared, but the incriminating briefcase was produced. José rounded up the thieves and took them to the police station along with the evidence.

'How did you persuade them to come along?' I interjected.

'There are bandits on all the roads. I always drive with an AK47 under the seat,' he told me. Not that it did him much good on that occasion. The police commander reacted coolly to José's cargo. 'How much is it worth to you if I take these men in and charge them?' he enquired. There's a breaking point even for an old Africa hand. José told the thieves to gethehellouttahere and drove off, muttering in Portuguese.

'You can do anything you want here as long as you share a bit of the profits,' he told me.

It seemed that anger pumped through the Central Africans' veins because they had not yet acclimatised to their newfound poverty. CAR was another of those countries well rooted in the 'poorest in the world' class. It might not have mattered if a *cordon sanitaire* had been thrown up around the country several decades earlier, sealing it off from foreign values. Instead the Central Africans had been invaded. First by the Arabs and then by the French. The French told them they had nothing, which made them feel shabby. Most recently, there had been radio broadcasts from Radio France International. The newscasters spoke of demonstrations for democracy in neighbouring countries, which made the Central Africans feel left out. They had known only dictatorship and dependency. Everything was conspiring to remind them of their 'have-not' status. It was no longer all right to live on $370 a year and die at fifty without casting a vote.

In the previous century, the Central Africans probably thought they were reasonably well off. They lived in the bush in mud huts, hunted game and died young. The only bane of their existence was the Arab traders who were still raiding their villages for slaves as late as 1910. The Arabs were brutal, but they never passed judgment on their lifestyle.

Then at the turn of the century the French superimposed an administrative structure on what was to become known as Ubangui-Shari. The colony was named after the rivers that drained the plateau along its southern and northern borders. It was one of four territories that made up the Federation of French Equatorial Africa. The others were Chad, Gabon and the Congo.

The French harnessed the biddable locals into working for them, mining diamonds, building railroads, growing cotton and tobacco. The conscripted labour force's output was overseen with military precision. The whites often carried arms when supervising the blacks. When they caned, whipped and sometimes murdered their workers for being laggardly or disrespectful, there was no avenue of redress for the victims. Men were robbed of their dignity, families of their providers. Villages and fields stood abandoned. Malnutrition and starvation were widespread.

André Gide visited the colony in 1925 and summed up what he saw as 'a country in ruins for the profit of a few'.

While the Central Africans tilled the soil for their masters' gain, the French sowed seeds of doubt. They invoked everything from the backward education system to evolutionist theories on the size of brain cases to lend substance to their thesis of the Central Africans' inferiority. You could rise to the height of your capability, according to the colonial ethos. However, a conflicting dogma made it clear that those with a dark pigmentation were pretty severely handicapped.

The French exploited the CAR mercilessly and gave little in return. By the time they relinquished formal administration in 1960, the portrait of an independent state was similar to many other countries in the region but painted in more Stygian colours. There was the minimum of infrastructure and very few locals who were at all qualified to govern a patch of bush and forest containing dirt-poor illiterates from eighty different tribes. France did leave behind two enduring legacies though. The first was the example of subjugation through harshness. The second was perhaps more cruel. It was a confused sense of identity. For over half a century, the Central Africans' alleged incompetence had been underlined as the supposedly superior ways of the French had been shoved down their throats. It hadn't done much for their confidence. They had come half to believe the colonial propaganda. '. . . There is no greater suffering for man than to feel his cultural foundations giving way beneath his feet,' Alberto Moravia wrote of Africa.

I met several Central Africans of exceptional charm who were hard working and enthusiastic about their jobs, but the coinage of daily intercourse was a prickly mix of hostility and insecurity. Sometimes, but not often, there was a vein of arrogance as well. It was all a defence mechanism against generations of oppression, under the Arabs, the French and even Bokassa, who was one of theirs. No one had ever praised them for doing well. They had the whipped look of the street dog in their eyes. Like the street dog, they were quick to snarl.

Francophone Africans soon realised that success was linked to a shift in values. The élite took university degrees at the Sorbonne and acquired a coating of French culture. In most of the former colonies a class of *petite bourgeoisie* emerged who wore Parisian clothes and ate *bifteck*. Those in public positions expanded on their former rulers' example and began a vigorous accretion of wealth and power by manipulating official influence for personal gain.

Somehow, though, Central Africans remained stubbornly, well, Central African. This wasn't considered the correct mindset for running a country. So the French continued to make their decisions for them.

Thirty years after independence, France's role as dictator of CAR's political and economic direction was still undisputed.

The French continued to instal the presidents of their choice, not through the electoral process but with *coups d'état* orchestrated by their military. In the last rearrangment of the trappings of power in 1981, General André Kolingba had succeeded Bokassa's old foe, David Dacko. Kolingba was head of the army at the time. As soon as he was made head of state, he suspended the constitution, banned political parties and filled the cabinet with fellow officers. In 1985 he allowed civilians back into the cabinet and the following year introduced a constitution. In 1987 he held elections for what was to prove to be a rubber-stamp national assembly. The people had been given a choice of candidates, but they all belonged to the same party.

Kolingba's coup had been dubbed Operation Barracuda. Rumour had it that his silence in the face of civil unrest was precipitating another one. Until such time, however, he was protected by a round-the-clock guard of French soldiers. They were known as Presidential Security and wore epaulettes depicting a black leopard's head on a crimson field.

Their boss was Jean-Claude Mansion. He was more than Kolingba's *eminence grise*. He had been in CAR since 1979. He ran the country. Nothing happened unless he sanctioned it. If something did occur that was not preordained, it was noted then filed away by his wife, who acted as his personal secretary. Everything, down to the smallest detail, passed across his desk – promotions, demotions, purchases, our applications to work as press. Mansion kept things in the family, it was said, so that no one could put anything on him if things turned sour.

His office was a spacious room in one of the old bungalows at Campe Roux. Every minute or so, conversations were interrupted by a telephone ringing or the two-way radio that crackled at his elbow. '*Patron*, there has been an accident with the fire engine at the airport. We are dealing with it.' or 'Colonel, when would you like to see me? I think I have sorted things out.' He was fiftyish and his greying hair had been shaved into a brush cut. He was obviously in excellent physical nick despite chain smoking. You could see that beneath his khaki uniform his body was as tautly put together as a car spring. When he smiled it was neither an expression of mirth nor a welcome. Barracuda: a predatory tropical marine fish which attacks man. I imagined being sucked into his jaws and devoured.

The rest of Presidential Security had nicknames like Bébé and looked like their chief. They danced with the mirror-lined walls in the *boîtes* so they wouldn't get AIDS, brawled with the locals, played tennis and occasionally lingered by the swimming pool to see if they could catch Kathy's eye. I put it to one of them that it was unusual for a foreign country to feel so responsible for an African president. 'We put him in with a coup. We're making sure he stays there,' he replied.

France's paternalism also extended to underwriting half the national budget and paying for the telephone system and part of the civil service salaries. In return, French troops were garrisoned on Central African soil. Originally the strategic military presence was designed to prevent a Libyan takeover of neighbouring Chad. More recently, it had become a rapid deployment base for the region's increasingly restive francophone countries which were demonstrating for greater political freedom.

Kolingba had hoped his mild reforms would create a sufficiently strong dike to protect him from these waves of multi-party democracy that were washing at the feet of fellow dictators. However, some cracks were beginning to show. An open letter addressed to the president, which charged him with corruption and practising nepotism amongst his Yakoma tribe, was xeroxed and circulated around town. Some months later, Bernard Kowada, Kolingba's juju adviser of several years standing, was found dead in his house. His head had been partially severed and left hanging over his shoulder. There was a message in that brutal murder. It was an even greater affront than if they had killed Mansion. Mansion helped Kolingba out on political matters. Kowada was guardian of the fetishes that protected Kolingba's soul.

While we were in Bangui the university students rioted, not once, but on several occasions. They lived on campus in filthy, four-storey dormitories and were demanding better living conditions. It was an ominous sign. After all, it was student protest that had led to Bokassa's downfall.

I was standing in the muddy forecourt of Radio Centrafrique on one of the mornings the students were busy stoning soldiers down on Avenue des Martyres, formerly known as Avenue Bokassa. The radio station is always the first place insurgents head for in a coup, so I was not surprised when a truck roared up to the gates. Two French military leapt out of the cab and ran inside the compound. They were followed by a dozen or so Central African soldiers flashing the leopard's head on their sleeves and holding their guns with two hands in front of their chests. I presumed the troops would be deployed around the perimeter of the fence. Not so. The two Frenchmen disappeared into the building while the Central Africans congegrated beneath a corrugated iron roof by the gate. A line of old metal beds without mattresses had been laid out in the shade. Soon they had stripped off their shirts and were stretched out on the bedsprings, listening to a radio blaring out the monotonous local music. Their black skins glistened in the heat. *Et voilà.* The Central African army on full alert.

During that week we made friends with Eric Stockenstrum, a quiet-spoken South African. He was the only native English speaker amongst the hunting fraternity. Others had tried to establish concessions and failed. When Kenyatta prohibited hunting in Kenya in 1977, some of the professional hunters based there thought they might be able to resume business in the CAR. They drove west through Zaire, with their trucks and hunting cars and tents and guns, their permissions and licences in their briefcases, filled with the hope of the new frontier like prospectors heading for the gold rush. But they got their fingers burned. When they reached Bangui, things went dreadfully wrong. They were arrested and their vehicles were impounded. My cook had been part of that safari crew. He spent a month in a Bangui jail. The hunters were detained rather than imprisoned, confined to one of the hotels that had since closed down. It was because they hadn't paid enough money to the right people. Kenyan hunters didn't consider the CAR after that.

The code for survival was harsher than in other countries and had a different bias. It had been tainted by spite as well as money. I was told by a Frenchman that he had been thrown in jail for plotting to overthrow Kolingba. It happened shortly after he had devised a method to stop his employees robbing the till. It was their revenge. Another Frenchman, a prison officer, was jailed by Bokassa because he had witnessed the massacre of the schoolchildren. The bottom line was writ large and clear. Europeans could be thrown away and forgotten just like the Africans.

Elsewhere a white skin was like a protective covering. Travelling foreigners linked it to a sort of diplomatic immunity, which, they presumed, spread like an unfolded umbrella over all visitors. 'You can't do this to me, I'm an American!' Threats like this were not why you escaped being manhandled or thrown in jail. They had nothing to do with it. The officials were on the make and they knew that whites were richer than blacks. Whites were easy prey with their heads full of manners and notions of right and wrong and always in a hurry to be somewhere else. You detained them, menaced, threatened. You referred to the regulations, which seemed to have a good effect on whites as if this gave the conversation meaning. You left them alone in a room for a while to reflect on the gravity of the situation, but you didn't lock them up. Once you put a white inside, you had to pay a commission to the police and the warders. It wasn't a good business proposition.

Visitors reacted to harassment with bluster or fright. They resorted to angry or cajoling words, searching for a path of retreat or advance. That wasn't the way. You had to stand your ground and focus, noting every nuance of movement, reading the faces, watching the eyes. Cats did it when cornered by dogs. There was no difference. You might be surrounded by walls, but you were really in the jungle.

If you were a white African like Eric and me, you learnt to fine tune these vibrations. You knew when to speak and when to be silent, withdrawing into

158

blankness to give nothing away. No surprise, no annoyance and, God forbid, never any fear. But this was only the foreplay. The orgasm was the money. If you were practised, you could rob officials of their pleasure, giving only a little or leaving them hanging.

Eric had been doing seasons in the CAR for years and was versed in the local canons. I was glad he was with us when we drove one morning to see Bokassa's house at Kolongo. We left the hotel and headed out of town towards the river, bumping over a potholed dirt road between little heaps of rubbish. The track meandered from left to right to left as if someone had been trying to cross a field in the dark. When we got to the Ubangui, we turned right and headed on past the slaughterhouse.

I had expected remnants of magnificence – an arched gateway, a tree-lined drive, pillars fashioned after the Palais de Justice in the centre of town. There was none of this. It was an ordinary one-storey suburban bungalow set back from a concrete wall. The house was large and had cost money, but it lacked style. I don't know why I was surprised. Bokassa was a village boy who had risen above his circumstances. It was the sort of place that someone might have built if he had won the pools.

The metal gates were closed with a large padlock, so we called for the guard. An old man came shuffling up and let us in. Kathy said she wanted to take some photos of the river and would join us later.

Bokassa had had several official wives and at least fifty-four children whom he recognised. There had also been scores of mistresses and girlfriends. It was his *droit de seigneur*. He had a penchant for blondes and prepubescent nymphets. The parents knew better than to put their daughters beyond his reach, which might have resulted in death or incarceration. They were rewarded for their compliance with cash or perhaps a moped.

Each wife was kept secluded in a separate villa. His number one wife was Catherine, a dazzling beauty whom he had met when she was an air hostess. At his coronation, she was the one who sat beside him as his empress. When Bokassa's fortunes turned, Catherine abandoned him for a jetsetting Arab emir. I had asked a friend of mine, who knew her, if she missed her husband. He had laughed. 'Of course not. I don't think these young women marry old men for love. Do you?'

His second wife was La Roumaine, a hefty blonde cabaret singer from Bucharest. Kolongo was her villa. In the context of La Roumaine, who had been allowed to leave the country after the coup and whose where-abouts were no longer known, the villa's most outstanding feature was the circular revolving bed. La Roumaine had plenty of time to lie on it and contemplate her navel while Bokassa was busy elsewhere, so she fell into the habit of having it off with the security guards. When Bokassa discovered this, three of the guards were killed while a fourth was thrown into the central prison. He was released after the coup and testified against Bokassa at his trial.

This was not the sort of prurient gossip that had drawn me there. More sinister events were supposed to have taken place in the derelict compound overgrown with weeds. It was here that Bokassa had kept the lions and crocodiles that acted as executors of his summary justice. The guard showed us round, talking and gesturing like someone conducting a tour of a stately home. We threaded our way past three-foot-high termite mounds to a drained concrete pit beneath what might have been the dining-room window. This was where the crocodiles had been, but they were gone now, he said. At his trial, Bokassa had claimed the crocodiles were just for decoration. But French soldiers who had dredged the pool on the day of the coup said they had found the gnawed remains of human bones at the bottom.

We crossed to the other side of the compound, moving further away from the house through dappled pools of shade cast by the mango trees. The guard stood in an open space paved with flagstones and pointed to a sort of gazebo, a slightly raised dais beneath a canopy. This is where he sat and talked to the prisoners, who stood where I am standing here, he explained. If he didn't like what you said, you were taken away to the lions or the crocodiles. The guard's monologue was becoming listless with an air of disinterest, but he was still polite.

He was standing in front of two sets of three interlocking cages built into a rock. It was just like a zoo where the keeper can lock the lion in one cage, leave its food in another and then go out again without being mauled. The only difference was that here the lions had been fed people. A well-known story in town related how the lionkeeper incurred Bokassa's wrath when he was discovered putting a few lumps of the lions' meat aside to take home for his supper. Bokassa ordered him to be locked up in the lion cages, but the lions knew him too well and wouldn't touch him. So he was thrown to the crocodiles instead.

We headed towards the back of the villa, where there was a large annexe. There were many stories of Bokassa eating human flesh. I was looking for the cold room where the corpses were supposed to have been kept dangling from meat hooks. There was also supposed to be an abattoir where the bodies were cut up on a table and channels in the concrete floor drained away the runnels of blood. French soldiers, the Barracuda, had found the torso of a mathematics teacher called Massangué hidden in the ceiling of an adjoining room.

When we got to the annexe, we were prevented from going further by two men. They were wearing vests and track-suit trousers and sitting on the steps to the verandah listening to a radio. They had hooded eyes and solid bodies like sacks of grain. A track suit was often a sign of a soldier off-duty.

'*B'jour, patron. On peut entrer?*'

'*Non, c'est défendu.*' The chameleon eyes looked slowly up at us. He blew some cigarette smoke in our direction. There was no point in arguing. We retreated.

To find out if Bokassa had indeed been a cannibal, I needed to get inside his head, not his house. As repeated requests for an interview had been turned down by ministers and even Mansion himself, the best I could do was take a look at Mbaka culture, which is where Bokassa came from. The Mbaka had a reputation for eating people. They even had a special chant to accompany their meals of human flesh, so it was said. A paper written in 1910 by a Dr Poutrin on the ethnography of the Mbaka reinforced this. He stated that when the Mbaka won battles against neighbouring tribes, they ate the defeated. The wounded and dead were brought back to the village and tied to poles so that they could be carved up. The chief was given the first choice of cuts.

The Ugandan dictator Idi Amin was supposed to have devoured his victims, too. He came from the Kakwa tribe who ritually ate human livers. I had spoken to one of Amin's cooks who swore this was true, but then the poor man was desperate for money and you could never prove it. The evidence had been consumed.

There was a widespread belief in central and western Africa that to capture a man's spirit was to render him powerless. You could do this by destroying his *gris gris* (lucky charm) or, in some of the more backward places, by taking a photograph. Bokassa and Amin may have both believed that by consuming other men's vitals, they were absorbing their enemies' power. It may have been their way of capturing the hearts and the minds of the people.

As we made our way back towards the main house, we saw Kathy coming towards us. She was festooned with cameras and lenses and a camera bag. They were hanging over her chest and under her arms and on her hips. She look flustered. They must have been cumbersome in that heat. There was the sound of footsteps, people running. Six young men came through the gate. Some were wearing shirts and trousers. One was naked to the waist. Another was in a mix of civvies and fatigues. He might or might not have been a soldier. Sweat glistened on their skin, which was as dark as eggplant. They had been running for some distance. They had the tight, muscled look of men who do physical work. Fishermen. We confronted each other in the dust midway between the crocodile pit and the lion cages.

One of them threw up his left arm and said, 'She has been taking pictures of these men.'

'What's happened, Kathy?' said Eric.

'I was taking pictures of the river. You know, to get some scenic shots. It's so difficult to take photos here. They always tell you to put your camera away. No one was around, so I was taking the river.'

'She took their pictures!' the man persisted. 'The men were bathing in the river and she took pictures of them naked!' That was the insult, capturing their nudity on film. It was said that many years ago, a priest had taken shots of some bare-assed young girls from his parish in compromising positions. These were later discovered on sale as pornographic postcards in France. This incident had assumed mythical proportions. Every visitor with a camera was regarded as a prospective pimp for black, celluloid flesh. I had heard the story from a Baptist missionary, but I had forgotten to pass it on to Kathy.

'I wasn't taking them. I was taking the river. The opposite bank. I hardly even noticed them.'

'She wasn't taking photos of the men. She was taking photos of the river,' said Eric. It was a three-way conversation because everything Kathy said had to be translated into French. Eric was speaking with a slow, disembodied voice. To hear him, you would have thought his mind was somewhere else, thinking of other things. His body said otherwise. It was relaxed and alert at the same time, the contained equilibrium he used when tracking wounded buffalo. I imagined him scanning the bushes for the telltale quivering leaf that preceded a charge.

'Give us that camera!' demanded the man, pointing to the camera with the long-focus lens.

Kathy unlatched the back and held it up. 'See? It's empty. There's no film in it.'

The man in the fatigues pointed to her other camera. 'It's that one.'

'Yes, it was that one. She was holding it like this and looking at us.' One of the fishermen parodied Kathy's movements.

'No, it's this one. You can see a long way with it. Not where you were washing. Do you want to look through it?' she held the camera out, but kept the strap around her neck.

Eric said, 'She said it was this one.'

'It's that one.'

'It's not. It was this.'

'No, it's that.'

'Give me the camera.'

It was like the old walnut shell trick with the penny underneath. Things were getting confused. When Kathy saw the men clambering up the bank, she must have unloaded her film and pocketed it, but she hadn't had time to unload the other camera as well.

She looked at Eric and puckered her brow like a puppy asking to be let out. A photographer's first instinct is to hang on to the film, but something else was gnawing inside her as well – a warning that we were in a potentially dangerous situation. 'What do they want? I can't give them my camera.'

'*Patron*, she says she is very sorry for making a mistake. She didn't mean to upset you.'

The man without a shirt was doing most of the talking. His eyes were like pingpong balls. His horselike nostrils flared with anger. The men were beginning to shift their weight back and forth on the balls of their feet. Their arms hung by their side. It was the shuffling dance of the mob before the attack. There was a wild violence in their mood that a wrong word or gesture could turn to frenzy. It was important that we stood our ground, because if we moved, they might restrain us. It was important they didn't touch us. If there was physical contact, a shove or a push, we might flinch. Then they would know that white bodies were as easy to kick as black ones.

The man in fatigues said, 'We will have to report you. You must come with us.'

'Let us discuss this, *patron*. We don't want to bother you. What would you like?'

The tension eased momentarily. 'She is not to have our photos. She is to give us the camera.'

Eric turned his head towards Kathy and said evenly, 'Give them your camera.'

'I can't!' she pleaded.

'Well, give them the film.'

Again that puppy look, but she did what he said, opening the back and pulling it out. Bracelets of grey celluloid shone in the sunlight. 'Here you are,' she said with a little grimace. The men looked at them intently as if the coils belonged to a snake. Then the man without a shirt reached out and closed his hand round the film.

'That is not enough,' he announced. 'You must pay these men for the trouble you have caused.'

At last. In East Africa I would have bargained, but Eric simply said, 'How much?'

'Twenty thousand.'

Eric produced a wad of bills from his pocket. His slim fingers peeled off the notes one by one. 'Here you are.'

Seventy-five dollars. What a beautiful, explosive, all-releasing orgasm.

The man without a shirt took them and crushed them into a ball in his hand. He smiled. Then everybody smiled. I can't remember what was said, but suddenly we were chatting together like strangers at a cocktail party.

The men wandered back to the river. We said goodbye to the guard, who reappeared to accept a tip with a polite nod, and walked to the car. When we were inside and the doors were shut, Eric said, 'We were very lucky. They could have killed us.'

Kathy didn't say much about the incident afterwards, but I knew she was as keen as I was to leave town. However, it wasn't that easy. Operating in Africa is really just a game of snakes and ladders. Roll a number that gets you into the right office and you shoot upwards. Roll the wrong one and you're on a bench in the corridor slithering down a serpent's tail. It's an illogical progression that buffets you from one building to the next with hours, sometimes days, between each shake of the dice. Highly placed officials can shove you forward with startling speed or stall you without explanation. The less exalted tend to keep you waiting out of habit, but sometimes they find secret, underground tunnels that bring you out in the sunlight. You're never sure which way they're going to work for you. Like love, it's sort of chemical.

There were two wildlife conservation projects that Kathy and I wanted to visit. One was in the Dzangha-Sangha rainforest to the south, which had a high concentration of elephants, gorillas and chimpanzees. The other covered a vast area the size of Cuba in the northern savannah that abutted on to Chad. It was called the Projet du Développement pour la Région du Nord (the Northern Region Development Project), funded by the European Community and known as the PDRN. Its managers were European – predominantly French but also Belgian and Portuguese. The objective of both projects was to conserve wildlife. Both contained elements of the carrot-and-stick philosophy: poach your way and you will be punished; hunt our way and you will be rewarded.

The projects were at the fledgling, experimental stage. Neither, to my knowledge, had received any press attention. The managers were more than happy to have Kathy and I generate some publicity for them. I had in mind upbeat, positive stories about professionally selfless people dedicated to working with the locals to preserve their environment. There was to be no muck-raking, no scandalous exposures. I had been told the government had been unstinting in its support of the pro-grammes. Under these circumstances, getting there should have been a breeze.

When we were prevented from boarding a timber-company plane to Dzangha-Sangha the day after our arrival, I was disappointed but I understood. My visa, obtained from Paris several months earlier, was about to expire. When the immigration officials fussed and tutted over its renewal, I was patient. When I deliberately slipped mention of this impasse into a conversation with Mansion and ten minutes later my passport was stamped with a six-month visa, I grinned. But why was the Ministry of Forests and Waters moving at such a wilful snail's pace to sanction our trips? After all, whatever I wrote about the projects' endeavours to preserve wildlife would throw reflected glory on to the ministry's officials.

It had been a promising start. I had been given a personal introduction to Mr Doungoube, who was directly responsible for the projects. He genuinely cared about the fate of the wildlife, particularly the elephants. His office door was always open to me, and his round cheeks creased in welcome whenever I walked through it.

Mr Doungoube told me there would be no problem in getting a signed permission, but first I had to see Mr Singha, the *chef de cabinet*. Mr Singha was a difficult man, mummified with surly self-importance. What's more, he was never to be found. One day I managed to corner him in his dusty office. He glared at me, not bothering to introduce himself. 'We don't trust journalists. We have had trouble with a French TV crew. They said they were going to film one thing and they filmed another.'

'English journalists aren't like that,' I retorted.

'That's what they all say,' he sneered. 'You will have to write a request to the minister.'

'Fine. What is the minister's name?'

Another sneer. 'You don't need to know.'

I trailed back downstairs and waited for Mr Doungoube in his office. It was small and had the minimum of furniture. The wall that partitioned it from the corridor was glass from chest-height to the ceiling. The glass had been covered with patterned, mauve wrapping paper to create some privacy. I sat staring at the whorls and blodges and tried to empty my mind, emulating the secretaries next door.

When Mr Doungoube came in, his chipmunk cheeks moved up and down. 'How did you get on?' he enquired. I told him, and he said, 'Good, good. Here, I'll write it for you.' He found some sheets of blank white paper in the drawer of the wooden desk and began to pen a letter in French. After he had finished, he showed it to me. It was two pages long.

'Will the minister think that's okay?' I asked.

'Yes. It will be fine. I'll send it up to Mr Singha and once he has seen it, Mr Singha will send it down to me. I am the one who gives the approval.'

I explained to Mr Doungoube that there was a PDRN plane leaving for the north at nine o'clock the following morning. There were seats on it for Kathy and me. Would we have the permission in time? 'Yes, yes,' he reassured me, 'Come to my office tomorrow morning at 8.15 to collect it.'

The following morning Mr Doungoube's office was empty. I walked into the room where his secretaries sat. That was empty, too, except for a woman with her hair twisted into three nine-inch spikes that ended in fluffy tassels. They stuck out at odd angles and looked like palm trees. She was slumped forward over her desk with her chin propped on her right hand.

'*Où est M. Doungoube?*' I asked her.

'*L'est malade.*'

'*Mais, j'attends un permis. Tu sais où est le permis?*'
She shrugged. '*Sais pas.*'
I went back on to the street where Kathy was sitting in the taxi. This wasn't real. It was make-believe. Nothing made sense. So why not talk in a nonsensical language?

'I haven't got it. Doungoube's sick. Ill. Still asleep. I don't know. The point is, he's not there. We'll have to charm that fucker Singha. I've had it. Why don't you go and chat him up in Hungarian? He won't know the difference.'

Kathy still had time to exercise her wiles. I had lied to Mr Doungoube to allow us a margin for error. We had arranged to meet Michel, the pilot, at the airport at 10.30. It was 8.45. We exchanged places in the back seat of the taxi, and she disappeared into the ministry.

The car was parked under a palm tree in a puddle of shade. I didn't take my bush hat off because it was early enough in the morning for the sun's rays to shine directly into the window. Before leaving London, I had bought a thermometer at the Survival Shop. I stuck my arm out and took a reading. It was only ninety-five degrees. Our driver was slouched down in his seat, eyes shut and with his head tumbled to one side. He looked as if he had been shot dead by a previous passenger. I sat and waited.

Around 10.15 Kathy appeared on the ministry's upper balcony. She brought her fingers up in front of her face and they danced in the air. They were typing the letter. Some time later she reappeared and flashed the fingers of her left hand three times. Fifteen minutes and it would be ready. The mime continued intermittently. She painted circles with her forefinger. The permission was being signed. At 10.50 she showed me ten fingers and pointed to a note that was peeking out of the breast pocket of her fishing jacket. Then she pointed to her watch. With raised eyebrows she spread out both hands then held up a forefinger. The clerk wanted a thousand franc bribe. He would get it if the letter was ready by 11.00. Eleven o'clock slipped by unnoticed by the rest of the town, swallowed by the throbbing beat of the taxi's radio. Kathy continued her mime show with unflagging cheer. It was 11.30. The bribe was down to five hundred francs, less than two dollars.

At 11.45 she emerged from the building with a small man wearing dingy trousers and flip-flops. She bustled along beside him, heading for the street-side xerox machine that stood on the far corner. I guessed they had run out of carbon paper in the ministry. Coming the other way was the hunched form of Christian. He saw me sitting in the taxi and veered in my direction. He leaned down and put his head through the window, right up against my face. Then he did the most extraordinary thing. He stuck his tongue out, clutched his throat and started retching with dry, rasping pants. He looked like a lizard in its death throes.

'Good God, Christian. Are you all right?'

'Jean Paul was so sick. He vomited all night. He couldn't stop vomiting.'

There was a fortuitious slam of the other door. Kathy had leapt in, grinning mischievously and waving a piece of paper.

'*Allez, allez! A l'aéroport. Vite!*' I cried. This had a good effect on the driver. It straightened him up like a spear in the back. He started the engine and accelerated. I leaned out and waved to Christian standing in the dust. 'Sorry! Got to go! See you next year maybe.'

I turned to Kathy. 'How much?'

She touched the note in her breast pocket with her thumb and forefinger. It was so delicate it was almost a caress. 'You're so naive about men. Tease them, but don't reward them.' She laughed, inhaling through her mouth in a breathy way. 'Unless you want to.' And she winked.

When we got to the airport, we told the taxi to wait and rushed to get our passports processed by the police. This was something that had to be done even though we weren't leaving the country. They told us they had seen Michel. They couldn't remember when, but he hadn't taken off yet. We clambered back into the taxi and hurtled over the pitted tarmac road towards the aeroclub where we had arranged to meet him. We were an hour and a half late for the rendezvous.

Our arrival was marked by the same brief flurry of activity as the dust devils that swept across the countryside, tossing the bushes and trees around for a few seconds before everything returned to normal. We burst out of the car, threw our bags and boxes of food on the ground, and paid off the driver without even haggling over the money he was demanding for overtime. He drove away, and we stood there looking around. The aeroclub consisted of an open-sided wooden bar covered with a roof and some chairs and tables set beneath mango trees. Beyond was a hangar. A few light aircraft were parked outside on the apron. Bangui had one, all-purpose airport that accommodated the international passenger jets, small private planes and the French military. There was very little traffic.

My previous visit to the aeroclub was at nine o'clock in the morning when people were drinking gins and tonic as Jaguars roared down the runway. Now the place was almost deserted, suspended in inertia. There was just the bartender and a scruffy man with a blonde, spade-shaped beard. We joined him at his table. Soon Kathy was chatting to him in an incomprehensible language while she gouged out the flesh of a pawpaw and scooped it into her mouth with a penknife.

'This man's Hungarian. He's working on construction or something in the bush. He's had five wives. Picks them up as he travels. Now he's living with a Central African woman. I told him that's nothing. My mother was married five times too. She was widowed twice in her twenties. Once by a football star. He got kicked in the liver. Hungarians like to marry a lot. I must take you to Budapest. They'll all want to marry you. You can have your pick.' She laughed in her breathy way.

Eventually Michel arrived. He wore khaki shorts and a white shirt with his commercial pilot's chevron pinned to the shoulder. His hair was cut *en brosse* like the Barracudas, but there was nothing of the predator in his manner. He was slightly built and seemed much younger than his thirty-odd years. Here was someone who had never experienced the bum's rush of urban life. He had the ingenuous air of the bush man. Michel, who had been born in the French part of Cameroon, had been a hunter before learning to fly. Then, for some reason, he had to close the business and move on. There were a number of people like that who had ended up in the CAR. When someone told you he had taken abrupt leave of his home and career because there had been 'problems', it was shorthand for falling foul of the authorities.

Like so many of us, Michel was colonial jetsam, displaced by the tide of political events. Francophone Africa was his home, but he had neither house nor country to call his own. In the decades following independence the tables had been turned on us. Our ethnic origin, once soaked in privilege, now put us at a disadvantage. Like the herders in the north, who streamed into the game parks from neighbouring countries in search of grazing, we were nomads travelling an uncertain route. We had even less claim on the land we trod than they did. Usually we were tolerated. But when we were evicted, there was no recourse to legislation. We cushioned our passage with money, supposedly investing in the economy but in reality lining the purses of the big and little men who barred our way. We knew where we stood – on eggshells. This vulnerability was particularly exposed in the CAR. It assailed you at every turn. It was exhausting.

Michel loaded us into the PDRN's four-seater Rallye Minerva, an outstanding plane for landing and taking off on handkerchief-sized runways. Fitting in both passengers and cargo was a tight squeeze because all the supplies for the project came from Bangui. I sat in the back so that Kathy could photograph. There was a red bucket partially covering my head. Vegetables were tumbling round my neck. Michel was supervising the fuelling.

'Before you roll the roof over, let's get a picture of the grand departure for the record. Could you take a photo of us with this?' I handed down my camera, and he snapped us.

Right on cue, three policemen emerged from the terminal building and sauntered across the runway. They accosted Michel and a long, low-toned discussion ensued. 'They want the film,' he called across to me.

'I know. I know,' Of course I knew. It was one of the commandments for operating as a journalist. Engraved in stone. Never take photos of bridges, radio installations, prisons, military bases or airports. I must have had a heat-induced brain seizure.

One of the policemen peeled away from the group and approached the plane. He looked up. 'I want a British camera,' he said in French.

I gave him a photo-booth smile. 'You can have a British camera. I will send you one from England. But you must be very nice to me because I am going to give you a present.' Behind him the group had begun to huddle, standing shoulder to shoulder with their heads down, watching something. Michel looked as if he was dealing cards.

'Well, that cost me. You owe me a present for that,' he said later as he carried out the preflight check of the instrument panel. 'It's past 2.30. I have to drop all this stuff off at the different camps on the way. We'd better hurry or we won't get to Manovo before dark.'

'We're doing well. It's still Friday,' I said.

'But the hotel we left eight o'clock,' said Kathy as we taxied down the runway. She sounded puzzled.

People say Africa is big. That is not what they mean. North America is big and Europe, too, if you take it in its entirety. Africa is untrammelled. It is not ensnared by highways or hemmed in by buildings. You can fly for hours and see only savannah or desert or forest, and you will not cast your shadow over a single town. The monotony of the landscape is almost mystical. In the solitude of this sameness, where nothing differs from one mile to the next, you can reach inside yourself and touch that which is essential and good. The restlessness and doubt subside and goals, once more, are attainable.

When you are in a small plane and look down on a ridge of hills or skirt round a grey ball of storm clouds or drink from a bottle of water, there are no distractions. You do that one thing and nothing else. Each act is distilled to a drop of musky contentment. It is this simplicity that is Africa's gift to us. I travelled with it for over two and a half hours. And by the time the plane had tipped its wings at flares of lightning in the darkening sky and mud had clotted the wheels as we taxied down the runway through fresh puddles of rain, the gnarling oppression of Bangui had been washed away. My spirit was no longer depleted. Africa had made me big.

6

The Poachers

Even while they teach, men learn.
Seneca, Letter

Some men poach to feed their families. Others are entrepreneurs who have become the butchers of the bush, killing wholesale and selling retail. Are they capitalists or socialists? They don't own their means of production. Or do they? Do animals belong to the state or the community? In Africa, this is a burning question. Whatever the answer, poaching spells profit for man at the expense of the animals. As such, it is a topic of heated controversy.

The classical solution to preserving the game was a blanket ban on hunting, which meant shoving man's atavistic hunting instinct into a strait-jacket. From what I had learned in Bangui, the PDRN were experimenting with a more equitable solution that benefited both man and animals alike. I was interested to see how they were faring.

Very soon, however, my focus shifted. It seemed that environmental concerns were merely a backdrop for a farrago of moral values in a lawless wilderness. In reality, the conservation issue was a vehicle not for man versus nature but for the dark quarrel that man has with his soul.

Our first stop was at Manovo, one of three administrative posts for the PDRN project, which sprawled over two game parks, four hunting concessions, and some bits in between. In all, it covered about 40,000 square miles of savannah with patches of tropical rainforest here and there. The terrain was remarkably devoid of distinguishing features. I recalled looking down on a ridge of hills as we flew out of Bangui. After that, it was just reams of fuzzy trees, plentiful but loosely packed. From the air, they looked like hair on a balding African scalp.

170

The 300-mile trip overland to Manovo took one or two days if the rivers weren't in flood. Visitors and staff almost always flew because the highway robbers had become so bad. Banditry was on the rise, and the odds were definitely against motorists avoiding an armed ambush. Contact was maintained amongst the camps by radio. When colleagues visited each other, they drove for most of the day over rough tracks cut through the bush. If you weren't used to Africa, you might have called the area isolated.

However, it wasn't the vastness of the physical scale that was daunting. The real challenge was covering the psychological distance between old attitudes and new ones. This included everyone: poachers, villagers, wildlife managers, game rangers and professional hunters. In the old days, conservation was a relatively straightforward job. Game wardens used to be policemen in khaki shorts who loved animals but didn't necessarily understand people. They patrolled their domain and arrested trespassers. It was too late for that now. There were too many people about and too little game, even in the CAR.

These days environment projects called in social anthropologists, who asked penetrating questions such as: Whose wildlife is it, anyway? They said things like: The future of ecosystems is linked to the social needs of the communities who live in them. And: Wildlife has to yield an economic return to the local people or it is finished. The Green Creed proclaimed that people had to be honoured as much as animals. When you looked around the continent at the environmental collapse, it made sense. Trees had been felled to make charcoal. Plains had turned to dust through overgrazing. There were jagged scars of erosion down the mountains. The land had been tortured by poverty.

Still, it was a pretty radical viewpoint for die-hard traditionalists to take on board. And I'm not talking just about the Banda villagers, who killed to eat, or the Chadian and Sudanese poachers, who killed for profit. There was strong resistance everywhere to the PDRN project, which had been going for two years. Even the professional hunters viewed it with suspicion. The PDRN management represented the advent of authority. Everyone had been very happy with anarchy.

The problem was, there was no blueprint to follow. No one had been to this particular place before and talked to these particular people about concepts such as the guardianship of a national heritage or maximising the potential of a natural resource. With good reason. It was a pretty tall order that called for the abilities of an anthropological psychologist, if such a person existed.

The native inhabitants of the region were hunters and gatherers. They were called the Banda. They collected berries and wild honey, fished the rivers and shot out the game. Some of the men hunted with

M16 automatic rifles but most used vintage guns or home-made muskets held together with pieces of string, hide strips and lengths of inner tube salvaged from old truck tyres. They shot anything that breathed.

The Banda had long ago been kicked out of the parks and hunting concessions, so their villages clung to the park peripheries and lined the dirt road that led north to the Chad border, the old slaving route. Those men who had bicycles sometimes pedalled the 150-mile round trip to the Bahr Aouk River. They could fish legally there for it marked the border between the CAR and Chad. But they poached the rivers and streams in the parks as well. They returned from these trips with bulging sacks of fish strapped on to the back wheel. Sometimes the loads weighed as much as eighty pounds. They continued to poach the animals as well, hiding their muskets and game meat from men who wore a uniform or had a white skin. Judging from the size and number of bulky sacks that game wardens unearthed once in a while, some of the villages had been shipping several tons of dried meat to the towns each month.

The Banda lived in mud-brick houses with straw roofs and drank honey beer beneath the star-shaped leaves of the mango tree. The women were sheathed in brightly coloured cloth and hid in their compounds when cars approached, gaping silently over the straw fences. The men were muscled and had splodgy faces that looked like puddles of engine oil. They were solemn, shy people who reacted to the arrival of visitors with a certain reserve.

At the root of this resentment and suspicion was neglect. The villagers' lifestyle provided a pathetic counterpoint to statistics of continental development. Here, where there was neither electricity nor telephones nor running water nor schools nor clinics, there was nothing to thank the government for except a fifty per cent infant mortality rate.

One day I discussed community affairs with George Lazanguere, chief of Idongo village. He was a gentle man whom I guessed to be in his sixties, although he had offered one hundred and then thirty-five when I asked his age. We had been having a polite discussion about the merits of the PDRN. Then I asked if there were any problems in the village. His speech quickened with determination. 'We don't have a hospital. We don't have a school. If someone falls sick, by the time we can get him to Ndele [over fifty miles away], he's dead. This is very serious for us. The trouble is there are too many laws and they don't always help us.'

George was referring to hand-me-down colonial legislation that put hunting permits way beyond the reach of the peasant. It cost the equivalent of thirty dollars to buy a permit for a bushpig; seventy-five dollars for a bushbuck; thirty-seven for a hunting licence. The sums were academic because the villagers operated within a barter economy. They were so poor that they ran into the bush and hid when the collectors came to get the annual head tax of thirteen dollars.

PDRN wanted to revise existing legislation to create village hunting areas, as had been done in Zimbabwe, and reduce the fees to an affordable amount. The idea was to issue the hunting permits on a quota basis that allowed a controlled and reasonable offtake of the different species. That way, the villagers could dry the meat and sell it as *bucané* to the market mammas in the towns. This was happening already, but in a way that was considered illegal. And the offtake was so heavy it couldn't be sustained. The pitfall in the plan was that back in Bangui, the political issue of the day was the repression of multi-party democracy, not of peasants' hunting rights. The proposals had been awaiting approval for nearly two years. No one knew if or when new legislation would be enacted. Until then, all the PDRN managers could do was scold and cajole.

Even their threats to enforce the existing law were chaff in the wind. Poaching carried a custodial sentence of one to six months and a maximum fine of over $1,100. At first, the PDRN wardens had handed over the poachers they caught to the police station at Ndele where there was a courtroom and a jail. Soon they realised there was little point. No one could afford to pay the fines, and the police had no money to feed prisoners. During the previous four months the PDRN had delivered about a hundred poachers to the authorities. None of them had been charged. The police had simply confiscated their arms and set them free.

Mbangui Michel, a Central African and the project's assistant ecologist, told me, 'There were a lot of animals in the 60s, but they're vanishing. If we are here, they will increase after five or ten years. Otherwise the poachers will kill them all. Very often the men get angry because they can't hunt and fish any more. I explain to them you can only see a rhino in books now and this could happen to other animals as well. They must trust us.' However, there was no precedent for faith. Was it blindness or optimism that created the impression it could be sown in this barren soil?

There was another, more alarming battle being waged on the same front. Men from the Sudan and Chad were swarming into the area and systematically slaughtering the game, herd by herd. The Banda may have been difficult to talk to, but these heavy-duty mass murderers were unapproachable except from behind the barrel of a gun. They were the equivalent of the cattle rustlers of the West or the Medellín cocaine cartel. There was no room for negotiation here. It was all-out war.

Some of the poachers were ex-soldiers, and the massacres were carried out with military efficiency. They travelled in large groups, fanning out and regrouping again as if they were mopping up after an invasion. They rode horses and pulled camel trains behind them to carry their bounty. In the early 1980s, they had come with spears in search of ivory, attacking the elephants from the saddle like matadors. Now that the ivory market had slumped and most of the elephants were dead, they came for meat, shooting zebra, topi, eland, and elephants too, with automatic assault weapons. The wholesale commercial butchery was lucrative because there wasn't much wildlife left in Chad and Sudan. Game meat was much in demand and fetched a good price. The poachers were so organised that they injected their horses against the killer bite of the tsetse fly and carried penicillin to treat wounds.

Christian Detudert's hunting concession was in this area. Like the other professional hunters, he sometimes had the misfortune to stumble across them. 'If we meet poachers, we can't do anything very much. The Sudanese are armed for war with machine guns. It's very serious. Also we have our clients with us. We can't endanger their lives. One time a hunter attacked some mounted poachers in Chad to scare them away. A few nights later four or five of the party were sitting having an aperitif. Two men came into the camp and stopped about fifteen yards from the table and shot two arrows each. One arrow stuck in the table. I don't know where the other went, but it missed its mark. But the other two hit one of the hunters and one of the clients. Both in the back of the neck. The hunter was dead within ten minutes. He had his own hunting organisation. So what are you going to do if you come across poachers? You can meet twenty, thirty, forty at a time. I've even come across a band of about a hundred.'

This was the real issue that concerned the PDRN, to save the wildlife from decimation by these marauding gangs. The animals were being shot out because the hunters lived for today and had no regard for consequence. They probably didn't know they were gobbling up a finite resource. If they did, it meant nothing to them.

My first briefing on the poaching scene was from Jean Marc Froment, the project's chief ecologist. We had mutually close friends in Iain Douglas-Hamilton, the elephant specialist, and his wife Oria. It was through their introduction that Jean Marc had agreed to talk to me and invited us to stay with him and his wife Ingrid at Manovo.

Their camp was like an impressionist painting in reverse. It was the colour of bark and leaves and blended so well with the surroundings that from a distance you didn't notice it at all. It was only when you walked up close through the trees that you discerned man-made things: an out-house, a shower room, a guest hut. There was also an enclosure for their two-year-old daughter Fanny's paddling pool where lions came to drink at night.

The most substantial bungalow was a three-room complex that enclosed the Froments' bedrooms and a place where Jean Marc could work on his computer. Some ten yards away was the thatched living area. One end had been walled in to create a kitchen space behind a counter. Otherwise there were no walls. The cook had his own kitchen closer to the river.

That first night, as we sat at the dining table eating off a table cloth decorated with a frieze of giraffes, the chat was of the 'what have you been doing lately?' genre. Ingrid said, 'One evening last week, Jean Marc was playing with plasticine with Fanny in the living room when he heard a noise. So he went and turned on the car headlights to see what it was. There was a lioness about ten feet away and three others behind. They were crouched down quietly watching us. He called me to come from the kitchen to fetch Fanny while he drove them off with the car. Just before, Fanny had wanted someone to walk with her from the bedroom to the living room. I told her not to be so wet because nothing would harm her. She must have passed right by them.' She laughed softly. She had pretty, slightly pointed features and short, blonde hair. She was calm yet vibrant, sometimes serious and sometimes amused. Africa breeds strong women. Ingrid was one of them.

Not long before that, Fanny's nanny, a local village girl, had been bewitched by the mamiwater spirit that lived in the river. The girl ran off into the bush, tearing off her clothes and digging at her flesh with her fingernails. She took Fanny with her. Ingrid and Jean Marc knew they had to locate them quickly for the girl was possessed. In her demented state, she would be oblivious to the toddler. Worse, Fanny might have decided to wander off on her own. There were a lot of snakes, buffaloes and lions in the area. Fanny did not know she should be wary of them. It was four hours before she was found, standing quietly beside her raving, wild-eyed nanny. That time, Ingrid *had* been worried.

All three of the Froments were African-born Belgians. Jean Marc, who was thirty-two, was a second generation colonial from the Belgian Congo (now Zaire). His maternal grandparents had emigrated there in 1917. He had lived in several other francophone African countries as well before taking a degree in zoology at Liège in Belgium. His first job offer, made by the university, was to carry out a study on pigeons. He chose instead to come to the CAR with Ingrid in 1981 and work for the United Nations Food and Agricultural Organization training game guards. Ingrid often used to accompany him on foot patrols through the bush. The couple were totally at ease with nature. If they had not had to collaborate with other human beings, theirs would have have been an idyllic existence.

In a way, the PDRN was Jean Marc's baby. Without his persistence it might never have been created. It all started in 1985 when Jean Marc went to Bangui to do an ivory study for the FAO. He discovered that up to seven tons of tusks were being shipped every month to France, Belgium and Japan. In the ensuing furore the government banned trade in ivory. But the smuggling continued unabated. Jean Marc realised that international concern would only be maintained if he could generate publicity about the decimation of the elephant herds. He raised funds to finance an elephant survey and called on the services of Iain Douglas-Hamilton. He chose Iain because he was a flamboyant character well versed in attracting the attention of the media.

The aerial grid survey the two men made of the Manovo-Gounda-St Floris Park and its surrounds confirmed Jean Marc's fears. They counted 4,800 live elephants and 7,500 dead ones. As it takes three years for an elephant carcass to disintegrate and its skeleton to be dispersed, this meant that the annual offtake was 2,500 elephants, perhaps more. The case Jean Marc pleaded for immediate assistance in fighting the poachers was sufficiently dramatic to attract the interest of the European Community. Eighteen months later the EC committed twenty-five million ECUS over four years for conservation in the northeastern quarter of the country.

It was impossible not to like Jean Marc. He was so gentle, so sincere in his motives. There was an intangible aspect to his personality that was almost ethereal. It was as if he had placed part of himself beyond the reach of humans and reserved it for the animals. He was passionate about wildlife, particularly the elephants, but it was a tortured love. He felt that he could never do quite enough to protect the game. This made him an embattled man, for it is impossible, even in the wilderness, to remain isolated from the disordered, sometimes violent, actions of other people.

I had my first inkling that all was not well with the PDRN from Jean Marc. When you arrive as a stranger in the midst of drama, particularly if you are a journalist, you tread gently to gain the confidence of the protagonists. Then in due course the mystery unfolds. It took some days to penetrate the intrigue that choked the PDRN like a blinding fog. By the end of our two-week stay, I had marshalled most of the facts. But to be honest, a lot of the nuances escaped me because they were shadowed by hate, jealousy and frustration. This backlog of injury and misunderstanding amongst the people who worked with each other was a very private thing to which no outsider could really be privy.

Jean Marc was eager to tell me about the anti-poaching patrols that had begun six months previously. It had taken that long to start them up because, it must be remembered, the PDRN staff had come to virgin land. First they had to construct camps to live in and cut hundreds of miles of tracks. Then they had to teach the rangers a modified version of anti-guerrilla tactics. This had been done by the warden of the other park, Bamingui-Bangoran. Paul Rossy was ex-military. Naturally, the locals called him Barracuda.

There were a hundred rangers: thirty for each park and thirty for Sangba, the pilot hunting zone. Another ten did ecological work for Jean Marc, tracking and counting the animals to get an idea of the population distribution of the different species. The rangers went on patrol for weeks at a time, carrying thirty pounds of food and water on their backs. They walked up to twenty miles a day and slept on the ground. Jean Marc had just got them bicycles so they could travel greater distances. He was also considering halving the size of the patrols to three men so they could spread out over a wider area.

I made some laborious calculations. Manovo was on the southern edge of Manovo-Gounda-St Floris Park, which was a hefty 6,700 square miles in size. The park was so large that two-thirds of it was closed off to tourists in case they never returned from its far-flung corners. If you averaged it out, each of the rangers run from Manovo was responsible for scouting 225 square miles of bush. Jean Marc told me that in the first three months of the operation, the rangers had sighted the tracks of fifty-four groups of poachers. Groups, not men. Say that they came across a quarter or even half of the intruders. And say that they moved in teams of about ten. This meant there were hundreds and hundreds of them out there, shoving hunks of fly-blown meat into saddle packs.

The poachers tended to hack off the legs and leave the carcasses so they could make a quick getaway. They rode about twenty-five miles to get out of the park, hung the meat up to dry in a base camp and returned the following day. The rangers' chances of stamping out this activity sounded as likely as the possibility of the New York Police Force getting all the muggers off the streets.

When the rangers actually sighted a poaching party, it was called a contact. There had been four so far. During the fourth one they came across the plate-sized imprints of camels' feet in the dirt. The rangers could tell the tracks were fresh, for the pimpled impressions of the camels' spongy pads weren't overlaid with the hoof marks of eland or topi. Neither were they covered by leaves or twigs or wisps of grass that might have been carried there by a breeze.

The rangers fell into single file, following the spoor in silence. They knew the poachers were nearby.

Then one of the men spotted the telltale tawny colour of a camel's belly splashed between the trees. He stiffened and moved his hand an inch or two from his body. It was signal enough. The rangers dropped to the ground, their guns trained on the poachers' camp. Looking through the leaves, they counted four men. At that point a bullet whined over their heads. It came from behind. This worried the rangers. They didn't know how many men had stalked their progress, but they appeared to be surrounded. It was getting dark and the fading light made it difficult to sight their targets. Nevertheless, it was time to take the offensive. They took aim and a volley of shots rang out. Four camels sank to their knees, their long necks lying crumpled in the dirt like discarded rope. Another camel and a horse were wounded. The rangers were lucky on that occasion, for the Sudanese chose not to return fire. Instead they melted quietly into the bush.

The animals that lay felled in the dust were not the result of panicked aim but of politics. The rangers had been instructed to fire on the poachers only in self defence. The murder of another country's nationals could have sparked off a border war, which no one wanted. So instead they resorted to the sort of harassment that diminished the poachers' economic returns. On that occasion, the men had lost hundreds of dollars' worth of pack animals and had to make the 200-mile journey home on foot.

There was also another constraint on the rangers. One that didn't enter into the official version of events. These men from Sudan came from the same tribes that had, not all that long ago, raided Central African villages for slaves. Collective fear runs deep. Some of the rangers believed that if they fired on the Sudanese, their bullets would bounce back at them.

The following morning, Jean Marc introduced me to Francois Lopez, the park warden. We found him in his prefab office. Next to his desk was a gun rack stacked with AK47s. An open metal cupboard had banana clips of ammunition on the shelves. An anti-poaching patrol was in the throes of departure, and Romain Kawa, Francois's deputy, was signing the weapons out. I had seen similar scenes many times in game parks all over the continent. There was one telling difference. Elsewhere, with the recent exception of Kenya, rangers were issued with single-bolt-action rifles. These were automatics that could unload a clipful of bullets in seconds.

'It's remarkable that an African government trusts the PDRN team enough to arm them with Kalashnikovs in a sensitive border area like this,' Francois told me. Then he said, to make sure I understood, 'The first priority here is anti-poaching.'

Francois was tall, attractive and fiftyish. He had the sort of looks the casting office would have gone for to play 'The Glamorous Game Warden'. He also had the constitution of an ox. The previous month a worker, whom he had fired, returned to camp and walked into Francois's office without knocking. He fixed Francois with that blood-shot, unfocused stare of the *ganja* smoker. Then he knocked him unconscious with the hammer he was carrying. Francois had just returned from two weeks in the Bangui hospital where he had been recovering, if I remember correctly, from a fractured skull. He was still getting headaches.

Francois's settler history lay to the north in Chad, a country he had had to leave because 'a problem' had arisen. Somewhere along the way he had parted not only from his adopted home but also from his wife and family. He was living with Sylvie, a dark-haired fawn whom I at first took to be his daughter. Their camp was a few hundred yards along the river from the Froments. It was less Spartan than Ingrid and Jean Marc's place. The Lopez ménage enjoyed whisky and wine, good food and company. Kathy and I were made welcome at the lunch table on several occasions. Jean Marc and Ingrid never came with us.

One day Jean Marc and Michel took us on an aerial patrol over the northernmost reaches of the park where the CAR melted seamlessly into Chad. This particular area was ecologically important as it was the only flood plain in the country. The grazing attracted not only herds of elephant, antelope and buffalo but also the ubiquitous environmental vandals of Africa – cattle. They came every year with their herders and the herders' families, trudging hundreds of miles across dusty, barren scrubland as if on a pilgrimage to a promised land. Indeed, that was pretty much what it was. Both Chad to the north and the Sudan to the northeast were in the grip of civil wars. Traditional grazing grounds had been taken over by rebels who, in the absence of a functioning administration, used AK47s to exact unaffordable fiscal tribute.

The Rallye Minerva made a lazy circle then dive-bombed its target, dropping out of the sky like a hawk on the hunt. Just at the moment when a raptor would have let down its undercarriage of taloned feet, Michel eased back the joystick a fraction. The tiny plane skimmed over the black cotton soil, its belly missing the treetops by a few feet. Kob antelope sprang away from its path, leaping over pools of trampled yellow grass.

Michel's eyes were fixed on three boys running at full tilt, driving their oyster-grey cattle in front of them with sticks. Below the fuselage another boy had sought refuge in the midst of his herd. He was bent low, his back flush with the backs of the cattle. The plane was close enough to take in small details – the smoothness of the gourd tucked under his armpit, the patches on his blue *jallabiya* that had been faded by the sun. His eyes swelled with fright as he swivelled them upwards.

Michel pulled the plane up and banked away from an encampment on the bent knuckle of the river. A black grid of lines and nets covered the bank. Silvery shards of light danced across fish that lay drying in the sun. Two naked men lifted their heads to watch the circuit but did not move. For a moment, the window framed a giant tunnel of black smoke tacked on to a strip of charred ground. It was followed by a tip-tilted horizon where a line of trees stood wrapped in shimmering veils of mirage. If the image had been more than fleeting, it might have reminded us of women in a harem.

The plane bucked through a current of dry, hot air and began another roller-coaster descent. A cluster of flimsy huts made of woven branches swooped into our field of vision. Young girls were walking back from the river where they had fetched water. Michel tipped the left wing, and they scattered. 'There, Kathy. Do you think you can get that?' He said it gently, for by now he was in love.

She shook her head and retched discreetly into a plastic bag. If I wasn't careful, I'd get a reputation for trying to kill off the photographers I worked with.

The girls zigzagged to and fro, habit keeping their hands glued to the gourds on their heads as if they were trying to hold on to their hats in a high wind. They looked like ants who had been prodded by a stick, caught up in a tumult of futile activity.

I was too intrigued by a sense of *déjà vu* to feel airsick. I had been here before, but the balance of power was reassuringly reversed. Last time I had been the victim, darting across a sorghum field in Tigray like a scared rabbit. Now I was the invader, banking and diving just like the Ethiopians who piloted the MiGs. I wasn't *thinking* of the people below us. I was *feeling* with them. I could sense their terror as they scurried for cover. 'It's all right. This is a game. We haven't got bombs,' I whispered at the perspex glass.

These tribespeople migrated in rhythm with the rains to the comparative calm of the park. With luck, today's intrusion would be their last for weeks, perhaps months to come. The plane was overworked and could not be spared. And the nearest park post in possession of a vehicle was 125 miles away over rough tracks.

The herders' desire simply to survive as tradition demanded seemed benign enough, but PDRN officials considered they were wreaking considerable damage as they trampled over the countryside. Worse still, the cattle competed for scarce grazing with the Thomas kob and other herbivores. You could run ten cattle to a square mile here. Elephant needed twice that area.

It looked like a no-win scenario. Either the wild animals or the domesticated ones would survive, but not both. It was a situation that frustrated both Jean Marc and Francois, for they did not have enough game rangers or vehicles to keep the intruders at bay.

The only thing Francois had in abundance was ideas. 'We have tried to think of every possible solution, including some really crazy ones. We could build a fence but it would be far too expensive. We even played with the idea of spraying the cattle with alcohol from a plane. As they are Muslims, they wouldn't be able to touch them after that,' he told me.

There had been talk of negotiation, but nothing had moved on that front. Instead Francois had experimented with intimidation. His orders to the rangers were to shoot a couple of calves in each of the herds (as we were to do later that morning). This didn't faze the nomads. They were reconciled to losing up to half their herds from disease anyway. A few calves was a small price to pay for saving the rest of their cattle from starvation.

Even so, when knuckles are rapped repeatedly, they start to sting. Jean Marc worried that if the butchery continued, it might goad the herders into carrying out a reprisal attack. I had seen and heard enough to realise this wasn't paranoia on his part. The social rubric here was medieval in its simplicity. Honour was satisfied through bloodletting.

That was the way it was here. There was no right and wrong, only injury. Injuries perceived and injuries redressed. Professional hunters shot the cattle which wandered into their concessions. Sometimes the herders or poachers shot the professional hunters. There were no more than a dozen policemen in the area and none had vehicles. Nothing impeded the elliptical path of vendetta. Bangui was very far away and the blood dried quickly in the scorching heat.

I asked Jean Marc if I could accompany the rangers on a patrol. To my surprise, he said yes. I had put the same question to game wardens all over Africa and had always been refused. They told me that it was dangerous (true), beyond my limits of physical endurance (possibly true) and, once, out of the question because I am a woman (ridiculous). However, I had to pass up on Jean Marc's generosity. Kathy said very firmly that she wasn't a walker. We agreed to survey the poaching scene from Jean Marc's open-backed Land Rover instead. The plan was to spend the first night at the rangers' post at Pont Gounda. Then we would head north to Godile, another post. It was near the Chad border.

Even this made Kathy nervous. She didn't like the idea of sleeping in the open. The Froments had regaled us with accounts of their own expeditions when the lions came into camp at night and padded on soft paws past their beds. The stories were not boastful offerings, as can be the case with people who work in the bush, but provided as an incentive. For the Froments, the proximity of the lions illustrated the inherent magic of safari. Not so for Kathy. When it came to danger, she felt more at home with urban riots. She was distinctly nervous. Ingrid teased her gently to put her mind at rest. 'We have lived here for eight years and we are still alive. The lions have never harmed us.'

Kathy screwed up her mouth. 'There's always a first time for everything.' Then she fell silent.

The day of departure had been washed clean by the previous night's heavy rain. Mosquito nets of thin cloud were draped across the sky as we packed up the Land Rover. We waved goodbye to Ingrid and Fanny and set off with Joseph the driver. Storks swirled above our heads, riding the thermals of air. There were so many of them they looked like white smoke rising from a bush fire. Jean Marc said soon they would be heading north to the Sahelian dryness of Chad and Libya. During the wet season they couldn't see their prey in the long grass. Kathy stripped down to her bathing suit and settled down in the back to sunbathe. That, I thought, might be a lot more harmful than lions.

We drove through a tunnel of *Isorbelinia* and *Terminalia* trees. They were about the height of a one-storey house so you couldn't see over them and grew thickly enough so you couldn't see through them. It was the sort of country which, in my hunting days, we called Miles and Miles of Bloody Africa. There was little to interrupt the sameness. Once a duiker with a deep rufus coat and black markings tore across the road, its body stretched as flat as a greyhound racing to the finish. Three bull buffaloes looked at us from beneath the low sweep of their horns, tossed their heads, snorted and lumbered away through the trees. Occasionally hartebeest broke away from our path on stiff, rocking-horse legs. A solitary bull giraffe cantered along the track ahead of the car, all legs and neck and bunched haunches. We saw baboons and eagles and blue rollers. They appeared momentarily as we drove past and then were gone.

Once we met a truck that had broken down. A few women and children were perched in the back atop baskets of chickens. They were very cheerful considering they might have been stranded there for days. The men had swathed their heads in towels and shirts and wore dark glasses. They looked more like brigands than road workers. When we stopped to help them, clots of tiny sweat bees danced over our faces and settled on our eyeballs. While Jean Marc and Joseph inspected the broken petrol lead, I wandered down the road, fanning away the insects with a branchful of leaves. There was fresh eland and lion spoor in the ochre dirt.

This was all we saw for three and a half hours. Only once did we encounter a low ridge, rumbling up it in second gear and easing down the other side in first so that the rocks wouldn't puncture the tyres. By now we were following an old elephant path that had been widened by the machetes of the road workers. Every few hundred yards they had cut away squares of bark from tree trunks to the left and right of the track so that travellers would not lose their way. Kathy was still sprawled in the back. I was driving, listening to Maria Callas singing arias from *La Traviata* on my Walkman. The uniformity of the trees was like a mantra repeated for sixty-six miles. It was a period of peaceful solitude. Precious time that could be used to daydream or meditate. That was why I did not ask Jean Marc about Jean Laboureur until much later.

The ranks of the PDRN's foes included two vigilante conservationists, a father and son called Jean and Mathieu Laboureur who ran two tourist camps in the park.

Before I left for the CAR, Iain Douglas-Hamilton had mentioned Jean Laboureur. 'Try and see him while you're there,' he had told me. When I asked who he was, Iain was uncharacteristically brief in his explanation. 'He's got a huge game concession up north. Been there for years and runs it like a feudal baron. You can ask anyone how to get there. Everyone knows him. I'd be interested to hear what you think of him.'

Iain was unaware that a couple of months earlier Jean Laboureur had confessed to the shooting of a PDRN road-maintenance worker. He claimed it was a case of mistaken identity. He had thought the man was part of a gang of poachers. He had given himself up to the police and was now in Bangui on bail, awaiting trial on charges of manslaughter. Jean Marc was convinced Jean Laboureur would be acquitted. It troubled him deeply.

We spoke of him after we had eaten and were sitting in inky blackness beneath constellations of pearly stars. It was a tale that had the makings of a Wilbur Smith blockbuster – murder, intrigue and ivory poaching set in the darkest heart of Africa.

Here is Jean Marc's story, which I have fleshed out with what I gleaned from others who knew Laboureur. I didn't manage to meet the man myself to get an impression of him first hand.

What is important is to think of him in the context of his surroundings. If Jean Laboureur had stayed in France, most probably he would have remained solidly bourgeois, unremarkable and unnoticed. He wouldn't have sold cars or worked in an insurance company for there was obviously a streak of independence in the man. But he might very well have started his own business, building it up over the years so that it provided a steady, respectable income for his family. Instead, geography had attenuated his links with the mores of middle-class France. In time, these values were stretched to gossamer, becoming so fine they were almost invisible.

Jean Laboureur's reputation reached far beyond the realm of his private game concession within the park. In France he commanded admiration as a saviour of wildlife who fought a lonely battle to protect the game from the depredations of poaching. There had been several articles in the French press about him and his son Mathieu, relating in breathless prose how they patrolled their domain armed with M16 automatic rifles. Jean was depicted as a romantic iconoclast, a Robin Hood with his own Sherwood Forest. His son was even more dashing. With his dark good looks and weight-trainer's body, Mathieu in action conjured up a vision of a comic-book hero defending the world against evil. A French television crew had once filmed Mathieu shooting a herd of cattle and torching the herders' village. The French press had nicknamed him Tarzan.

Many people thought Jean Laboureur an extraordinary man. He had certainly led an unusual life. As a teenager, he had been incarcerated in Dachau. After the war, his wanderings brought him to the CAR, where he took up hunting. Giscard d'Estaing had been his client on several occasions. It was said that he still had good connections in high places in Paris. He was reputed to be an expert marksman although he no longer liked to shoot animals. The other hunters spoke of him with open admiration.

Laboureur had managed to lease a concession from the government in 1964. It was roughly 3,000 square miles of picturesque savannah in what was to become part of the Manovo-Gounda-St Floris Park. In 1975 Bokassa had told him to leave the CAR. No one seemed to know the reason for the expulsion any longer. He was reinstated nine years later after Bokassa's demise. Except for the interregnum of his exile, his authority had gone unchallenged until the arrival of the PDRN. Now there was a clash of wills.

The PDRN management and Laboureur should have joined forces in the anti-poaching war. Instead there was bitter rivalry. Laboureur had refused to allow the PDRN rangers to patrol his concession. On their side, the PDRN managers were very uneasy about his attitude towards the villagers. They felt it was detrimental to their aim of making the locals their environmental allies. They also suspected that Laboureur allowed his clients to hunt illegally in the park. In theory, the PDRN was in charge of anti-poaching activity, but Laboureur didn't see it that way. He had enforced rough justice when ivory poaching was at its height. As far as he was concerned, there was no reason why he should relinquish his power to the newcomers.

The concession was threaded with rivers where elephants and herds of antelope came to drink. Tourists stayed in the two camps he had built, Koumbala and Gounda. They were isolated and not easily accessible, but that was all part of the charm. Once you entered Laboureur's kingdom, there was no communication with the outside world. The only contact was on the field radio which he used to talk to his office in Bangui. Everyone who had visited Gounda and Koumbala agreed they were in paradise.

Laboureur's iron-fisted rule inevitably had its detractors – specifically those who suffered under it. In Laboureur's eyes, all black men were potential poachers. They regarded him as a leviathan who was both feared and hated. Even so, his *droit de seigneur* prevailed. Besides, what could they do? The nearest police post was a hundred-mile walk away. They were just as frightened of Mathieu who, they said, also shot suspected poachers. I had heard similar stories in Bangui. It was difficult to dismiss them entirely.

But let us for the moment put this speculation to one side. And let us strip away the hero myth as well. Now what do we see? Jean is a shortish man of sixty-four with a blunt, peasant's face. He can be charming but also has a mercurial temper. He is married and adores his only son, who is about twenty-five. His life has been shaped by antagonists: the commandants at Dachau, the elephants he hunted, Bokassa, the poachers and, most recently, the PDRN managerial staff. He has confronted them all and survived. Gounda Camp and the surrounding bush is his refuge and his home. This remote corner of Africa means everything to him. In a way, his anti-poaching patrols are an enactment of the most primitive of man's instincts: defence of territory. Imagine how you would feel if burglars broke into your house several times a month. He may not be able to put it into words, but Laboureur probably feels violated every time an animal is shot by a black man. Is he then just an ordinary person like you and me? Perhaps. But unlike you and me, who are part of a community, he has been cast adrift from the strictures of his neighbours. Out here in the wilderness he has created a personal code of right and wrong which, as it turns out, is built on quicksand. Would you or I have behaved as Jean Laboureur did if we had been in his shoes? Perhaps, perhaps.

It was 31 January, the middle of the dry season when visitors liked to fly up to Gounda. The short grass made for good game-viewing. On that particular day, Jean and Mathieu had taken friends on a picnic. As they were driving back to camp, they noticed smoke rising into the sky. A fire sometimes signalled the presence of poachers so they drove towards it to investigate. As they drew close, they saw dark-skinned figures moving about. Their view was partially eclipsed by bushes and trees, but (as everyone who had been there said later) it looked just like a poachers' camp. The Land Rover braked to a quick halt. Jean and Mathieu knew from previous occasions that it was essential to take the men by surprise. They grabbed their guns and ran forward through the trees. Afterwards, Jean said he thought the men were poachers from the Sudan because they wore *jallabiyas* and were speaking Arabic.

In fact, they were PDRN labourers employed to maintain the dirt roads. It was the end of a sweaty day's work and the men were bathing naked in the Goro River. They were chatting amongst themselves in Songo, the national language. When they saw the two white men crashing through the undergrowth, they sensed what was about to happen. So they threw their hands up in the air and cried, 'Don't shoot! We're PDRN workers!'

There was a burst of gunfire and Gilbert Bangandombi-Kotali, who was twenty-two, cried, 'I'm hit!' All the workers scattered except for

Pierre Kongbo, who hid in a bush. Pierre said he saw one white man and two black men walk up to Gilbert and look down at him. One bullet had smashed into his spine, shattering the vertebrae. Another had lodged in his thigh. Pierre heard one of the white men say, 'That's well done.' The men turned on their heels and walked away.

The matter would probably have rested there if the shooting had taken place three years earlier when the PDRN did not exist. The workers were so frightened that they did not even return to look after Gilbert. But they felt they should report what had happened to their employers.

It took a while to do this because the workers had to walk over thirty miles before they encountered some rangers on patrol. The rangers immediately radioed Jean Marc at Manovo. By this time it was 5 p.m. the following day. Jean Marc finished off his work and set off for Goro River at three o'clock in the night. He wanted to consult Francois, who was on patrol near Godile looking for cattle, but he didn't manage to contact him on the radio until early the next morning. Once he had received the message, Francois kept the radio open, waiting for news from Jean Marc. They hoped that Gilbert might still be alive. At three o'clock that afternoon, Jean Marc came on to the radio. He confirmed their worst fears. Gilbert was dead. Francois fetched the police commandant at Godile and reached Goro River just before dark. As they examined the body, Francois later recalled, the Laboureurs' small plane circled overhead. There was no radio at the Godile police post, so it was Francois who radioed the Bangui police the following morning to report the murder. Some rangers were posted to guard the body, then Jean Marc, Francois and his deputy, Romain Kawa, drove back to Manovo. The police landed in a light aircraft just as they reached the camp.

The following morning they returned to Goro River. The police spent two hours examining the spent bullet cases, the tracks and what was left of Gilbert. He had been lying on the ground for five days. His bloated body had begun to decompose in the heat. The tyre marks were those of a Land Rover. The footprints were those of Jean's shoes. Confronted with the evidence at Gounda Camp, Jean Laboureur confessed immediately to what he called 'the tragic accident'. He said he had fired both the revolver and the M16. He was handcuffed, bundled into the police plane and flown to Bangui.

The criminal evidence may not have been in Jean Laboureur's favour, but public opinion certainly was. The French in Bangui drew a protective curtain of silence over the case. I could draw no one out on the subject except Eric Stockenstrum, who said, 'You know what it's like when you're in a bad mood. You don't stop for ten seconds to think before you pull the trigger. It doesn't matter if a few people get killed, but he's gone overboard. There have been too many cover-ups for him, and he became arrogant. He was indiscreet and indiscriminate.'

Two months after his arrest, Laboureur was released on a bail equivalent to about $3,775. Under the conditions of his bail, he was not allowed to leave Bangui. According to police sources, he was to be had up for manslaughter. A conviction carried a maximum sentence of life but extenuating circumstances could reduce it to as little as two or three years. The trial was to be in two months' time.

Kathy had retired to her camp bed early with a mild case of sunstroke. By now it was late, so Jean Marc and I crawled under our mosquito nets and turned in as well. Around midnight a lion roared. At 2.30 it began to rain. The next morning we got up at dawn. Hyena tracks circled the fire, but there was no lion spoor.

Some hours later we set off for Godile. By mid-morning the weather was looking ominous. The sky had darkened to pewter grey. Sheet lightning flashed on and off like a neon sign, and there were riffs of thunder. One moment it was dry; the next a downpour was sluicing over us in great drenching bucketsful. Jean Marc, Joseph and Kathy got out of the Land Rover and tried to lash a tarpaulin over the back. They made funny, wet faces, screwing up their eyes and blowing water off their noses as their fingers struggled with knots and loops. I sat in the car to keep dry.

On the plain beyond two male kobs were fighting in the rain. They ran at each other with heads lowered and met with a crash of horns. Then they shook themselves free, backed off and launched on another collision course like two sparring partners warming up in the boxing ring. A dozen or so females were bunched together a few hundred yards away. They had stopped grazing to watch the combat with huge madonna eyes. Like several of the antelope species, female kobs stayed in a herd under the charge of one male. He stood guard against predators and impregnated the females when they came into oestrus. From time to time, these dominant males had their territory challenged by other, usually younger, males. Whichever kob won the duel that was being played out on the sodden plain would become the breeding male for this herd.

Konrad Lorenz, the founder of ethology (the study of animal behaviour in a natural environment), defined aggression as the instinct in man and animals to fight their rivals. These encounters ensured that it was the strongest who passed on their genes. Animals often ritualised their struggles with displays of fangs, hackles and plumage. When they did enter into combat, they never killed each other. At a given moment the weaker opponent acquiesced in defeat and that was the end of that. Some animals turned their heads to expose their jugular vein. Others, as was happening with one of the kob, simply trotted away. It was like throwing in the towel or raising the white flag. The victors instinctively refrained from actually killing. Man's fatal flaw, according to Lorenz, was to have developed artificial weapons. This had disoriented our instincts and allowed the better armed man to press home his advantage to the death.

The road workers had had no defence against the Laboureurs' guns so they had thrown up their hands and shouted, 'Don't shoot!' They had reacted instinctively, baring their jugular to signal submission. But they were shot at anyway. Jean Laboureur lived with nature but he had transgressed her laws. He had created his own paradigm of behaviour. I understood why Jean Marc considered the killing to be an exceptionally heinous act.

Godile was an old rangers' post in the process of being revamped. At one end were a collection of dilapidated, foul-smelling buildings where the rangers still lived. At the other end were the new buildings they would soon move into. They had whitewashed walls and louvred windows. The doors were locked because they had not yet been handed over by the contractor. We camped outside one of the old buildings. The plan had been to go on patrol with the rangers the following morning, but they had left without us.

Jean Marc and I took the news badly. We were discouraged. It was impossible to tell what Kathy felt. The combination of sunstroke and lions had put her in robot mode. As soon as her camp bed was unfolded for her, she lay down on it and shut her eyes.

We went down to the river to wash, then ate supper. Later that evening Jean Marc and I talked of vanishing elephants, the mystery of the bush and the strange things it did to men's morals. He had changed into a clean shirt and shorts and had combed his hair and beard. He looked undeniably handsome sitting on the food trunk in the veiled light of the full moon. But he was chain-smoking again. My heart went out to him. He was a troubled man.

He turned to me and said, 'I'm beginning to doubt everyone. These plans were so carefully made. How could they have gone wrong? I told the men the day after you arrived, just before they left Manovo, we'd be coming to see them. And I discussed it again this morning on the radio. Maybe they don't want you around after that film on Mathieu. You're the first journalist to come here. But I'm pushing it because I want everything to be told before I leave. Someone has to make a statement about what's going on.'

He looked over my shoulder as another thought struck him. 'Maybe it's Francois. I've been fighting him too. He wants to shoot an entire herd of cattle to teach the herders a lesson. But that will make them hate us which will put the rangers in danger.' The contractor's generator thudded gently nearby. I caught a whiff of rotten fish on the breeze. There was nothing for me to say. We both knew that paranoia was blurring Jean Marc's vision.

A tail of dust clung to the vehicle speeding along the road. It was Mathieu Laboureur. He had responded to the plane that had buzzed Gounda Camp some minutes earlier and was racing to the airstrip to meet it. There would be only one passenger to pick up. Me.

As I couldn't talk to the father, I wanted to meet the son. So we had devised a strategy. Michel had joined us at Godile in the Rallye Minerva. Jean Marc refused to set foot on the Laboureurs' place, but why not, he suggested, drop me at the airstrip and fly off before Mathieu arrived. I could make up some cock-and-bull story about how I got there and spend a few hours quizzing Mathieu. Then Joseph, who had been deputed to drive the Land Rover back to Manovo, could pick me up later in the afternoon. Kathy had opted out of the adventure. The sun and the hot air currents had made her queasy again.

Mathieu took my impromptu appearance in his stride. 'A deserted woman,' he said and bestowed me with a glorious smile.

I grinned back from under my bush hat. 'Yes. Some friends of mine said I must look you up. I was in the neighbourhood so . . .' I embraced the airstrip with outstretched arms and grinned again. 'Here I am!'

God, I thought, what a ridiculous thing to say when we're hundreds of miles from anywhere. However, it seemed good enough for Mathieu. That was African hospitality for you. Unquestioning. He gestured for me to climb into the front seat beside him. This was followed by some first-name introductions. A Central African and a good-looking blonde man of Mathieu's age were in the back. Some rods were stacked beside them.

'You'll stay the night, of course?'

'Well, that's very kind of you, but unfortunately I can't. Somebody's coming by to pick me up a bit later,' I simpered. The shirtless Mathieu was very charming and obviously used to the admiration of women. His deep suntan and dark, five-day stubble fitted the rugged image. I noted the slightly fleshy lips and nose. The peasant stock hadn't yet been bred out of the Laboureur line.

'It's a pity you didn't come sooner. My father was in camp for the night but he left yesterday. You know there's been a problem?'

'Yes, I'd heard. Is it being sorted out?'

'Yes. Well, not completely yet. But it will be okay.' I recognised the smile. Part arrogant; part inviting. I was old enough to be his mother yet there were electric currents of sexuality in the air. I felt distinctly uncomfortable. It was bad enough being there under false pretences. I didn't want to flirt with the boy as well.

The camp was pleasant but unexceptional. Rows of succulents trimmed the flattened earth. The guava-pink guest houses with green roofs were obviously for the guests. We retired to a large, open room that looked on to the river. A poster stuck on a pillar solicited contributions to the Laboureurs' anti-poaching fund. Mathieu, his friend Jean Jacques and I sat at a table in front of the long bar. Two of the staff played a desultory game of pingpong while we talked.

Mathieu said the last party of thirty tourists had left the previous day. They were closing the camp for the rainy season as the family was going to France. That meant there would be no anti-poaching patrols for six months. He looked serious.

I was becoming increasingly uncomfortable as we compared notes on the poaching in the CAR and Kenya. I decided to even the odds. 'I'm a bit out of date with Kenya. I haven't been there for a while. I'm a journalist. I was thrown out for some of the things I wrote.' This had the effect of throwing a knife at his feet. Mathieu's smile was replaced with a distracted look. Don't press the advantage to the death, I thought. 'It was rude of me to arrive unannounced. If there's something you have to do, please go ahead.'

'Well, if you don't mind. Yes, there is. Are you sure you won't stay the night? I'll be back in an hour.' He trotted off with relief to go fishing.

Jean Jacques took up the baton and told me the Laboureur version of the killing. Mathieu's father had taken some guests out on a picnic. There had been mechanical problems with the car, so they had returned by a different, shorter route. They saw smoke and went to see what it was. Mathieu's father was suspicious because he had seen camel tracks in the area. They saw some men in *jallabiyas*, which meant they were poachers from Sudan. Mathieu's father pulled out his gun to fire a warning shot and somehow killed one of the men. Two days later François Lopez came into camp and accused him of manslaughter. Of course, that was not the case. He looked me straight in the eyes and used the same words that Laboureur had uttered at the time of his arrest. 'It was a tragic accident.'

Joseph and I drove for five hours through the sweet-smelling night. The only buildings we saw in the seventy-five-mile trip were the shadowy shapes of Koumbala Camp. But we ran after a pangolin and shone the headlights on to a stork fishing in a puddle with its red and yellow beak. It was oblivious of us even though we could have leant out and touched it. I liked the way its stick legs jerked up and down like a marionette on a string. Joseph must have liked it too, because he smiled at me.

After that, I climbed into the open back to gaze at the stars. I put my head against a donkey saddle confiscated from a poacher and propped my feet up on the tailgate. I held my radio against my ear and listened to a

BBC programme on the development of Birmingham. That was how I liked England: faint and distant and around for only ten minutes. Some time later the car slid to a halt. I peered over the side and saw three lionesses six feet away. We sat and watched each other.

'Are you frightened, madame?'

'No, but I would be if they did this while I was in bed.'

'They are never naughty,' said Joseph reassuringly.

Jean Marc and Ingrid were enfolded in despondency when I arrived after dinner. Jean Marc had been summoned to Bangui. He, Ingrid and Fanny were flying down the next day. The EC officials considered him a troublemaker. Jean Marc thought they would ask for his resignation. 'You're very philosophical,' I said to Ingrid. There was little to offer as consolation.

She shrugged and smiled, 'I try to be. No one likes us here. We have no allies.'

'I want to finish with you so we can tell the story of Laboureur. Then we can go,' said Jean Marc, waving some photos at me. I must have looked as tired as I felt, but he had acquired the doggedness of the condemned. As he talked, he passed the fuzzy images across one by one. They had been taken by one of the rangers. The first picture was of a naked body. The arms and legs were at awkward angles. It seemed to me, through my mist of fatigue, the skin had assumed a greenish hue. The corpse was alarmingly strange. Parts of it were pinched and shrunken and parts were swollen and fat. Next came a shot of some men staring down at it with handkerchiefs clasped to their mouths. 'It smelt a lot,' said Jean Marc. Finally, a shot taken at Gounda Camp. A snowy-haired man in a white shirt was walking away from the camera. A policeman held his arm, which was unnecessary as his wrists were manacled together behind his back. His hunched shoulders made him appear old and vulnerable. I felt sorry for him.

José Tello, the warden of the Sangba hunting concessions, whom I had met in Bangui, was more tolerant towards local custom. In his youth he had been a fanatical ivory hunter in South Africa's Kruger National Park, so he was attuned to the delicate stages of metamorphosis from poacher to gamekeeper. In José's case, conversion came in the form of an accident. His partner was shot dead by an anti-poaching patrol. After that, he joined Mozambique's game department.

When the Froments left for Bangui, Kathy and I went to stay with José and his common-law wife, Theresa. By this time the rains had started in earnest. We awoke to see the trees draped in a blanket of cloud. The Colobus monkeys flew like hang gliders from one branch to another, leaping through shafts of silvery light. They shook large drops of water on to my head as I walked to Francois's office to use the radio.

José was amused when Francois told him Kathy and I were planning on making the drive in the wet. His laughter crackled over the air waves like logs in a fire. I wasn't discouraged. Nothing would ever be accomplished in Africa if you waited for the elements to accommodate you. 'Tell her to bring axes and machetes, because lots of trees have fallen on the road. I'll prepare hot water for them. They will have had plenty of cold water wading through all those rivers. And tell them to start as soon as possible. Over.'

'Mary Anne is here beside me. She is smiling. Over.'

'It would be a good idea if she starts tomorrow morning at three repeat three a.m.' There was another chuckle. 'Mary Anne, we will have coffee ready for you at eight. Over and out.'

'Over and out.' said Francois. He laid the mouthpiece on the top of the radio set and turned towards me. 'Now that you have a spare day, why don't you and Kathy come over for a meal?' I accepted. I wanted to hear Francois's version of the killing.

By chance, Francois had paid a visit to Gounda Camp the day after the road worker had been shot. Of course, he told me as he sipped his whisky, he had no idea at the time of what had happened. He arrived with Romain Kawa, his deputy, at 12.30. Mrs Laboureur invited them to stay to lunch. Around two o'clock Jean Laboureur appeared. He sat at the table but didn't eat. Both men thought he was acting strangely.

'The PDRN has big blind spots. They should have seen to it that the government made radical changes in the law before starting the project. The law has had it. If you kill someone in the park, it's you who gets all the shit,' he told them. Laboureur went on to talk about the time he was wrongly accused of murdering a child. He seemed haunted by the memory.

The police report stated that three shots had been fired, Francois went on to explain. They couldn't tell from the wounds which of the bullets had entered the body, but there had been a clearer range from where Mathieu had stood. Jean's line of fire was obstructed by trees. It was easy to reconstruct what had taken place, he said, by studying the tracks. Two men had leapt from a Land Rover at a run. One of the men had knelt and fired a 5.56 calibre bullet, the type used in M16 rifles. Then he had jumped down a seven-and-a-half-foot bank and run on. It was the action of a fit man. Some five yards to the right, the police had found the casing of a 9 mm Parabellum bullet which must have come from a revolver of the type used by the French army. There were no footprints leading from one casing to the other. The revolver had been fired by a different man. Francois left me to draw my own conclusions. As far as I could see, the evidence pointed to a cover-up.

Kathy and I set off for Sangba at 3.30 the following morning, driven by the gentle Joseph. It was within a cat's whisker of noon when the dirt track we had been following debouched into a delta of human habitation. As far as I could make out, we were on the periphery of a band of rain forest. An insistent, rhythmic smacking of water drums broke through the screen of vegetation at the bottom of the clearing. It was the young girls from the workers' compound flailing their arms in the river.

The clearing was sprinkled with huts, some in disrepair, some obviously in use. We had spent the equivalent of a working day in the Land Rover bumping through the bush. Once or twice we had passed a cluster of huts with their roofs caved in on crumbling mud walls. This place, rudimentary as it was, seemed an oasis.

A woman stepped out of a long thatched bungalow and watched with one hand on her hip as we unloaded our gear. In the other hand was a cigarette which she kept close to her mouth as chain-smokers often do. She had a high forehead and a strong nose. Somehow she reminded me of an eagle resting on a branch. 'You're much later than we expected. Did you have any problems? Good. You never know with these roads. They're terrible, terrible. José's out. He'll be back soon.' She was sensibly, almost severely, dressed in a white shirt and khaki skirt with her hair pulled tightly back from her face in a ponytail. When she spoke it was like a rake passing over gravel.

Theresa led us to the small thatched hut that was our sleeping accommodation. There were two beds, separated by a small table, and a chair. The brick walls were chest high, a compromise, I presumed, between ventilation and privacy. A strip of cloth hung over the entrance, becalmed in the midday heat. There was no door. Theresa left without showing us the bathroom facilities, but I found them easily enough. Behind the hut was a long drop enclosed by a sagging and disintegrating reed screen. A few feet away there was a tree with a nail hammered into its trunk so that you could hang up your towel. Next to it was a bucket. It had no water in it.

The camp looked exactly what it was: a place carved out of the jungle by settlers. When the Tellos had been posted there two years earlier, they had seen only virgin forest tangled with vines. They put up tents by the river and began to build the camp, constructing everything from local materials. They baked red bricks from the earth of termite hills and laid the floors with stone. They felled trees and dragged them through the forest behind their Land Rover so they could use them as beams to support the roofs. These back-breaking tasks had been made even more arduous by daily downpours of rain. One day the river flooded its banks and washed their tents away. They retrieved their possessions by wading into the swiftly flowing water and carrying everything back to land on their heads.

José told us all this over a lunch of hartebeest steaks. He talked as if he was gargling a good wine, pausing frequently to puff on a cigarette and say

'Eerrrr', or to look at one of us over the rim of his glasses. He had a paunch and a grey beard and a nice sense of humour. He was a pirate who had put his swashbuckling days behind him.

The long, open-sided bungalow where we ate was sparsely furnished: a dining-room table and metal chairs, another low table surrounded by wooden chairs with cushions on them. At one end was a bar, dominated by the three-foot horns of a Derby eland. The knickknacks were culled from Sangba: the poaching paraphernalia of crossbow and arrows and a musket with a stock bound together with animal hide; several mounted antelope horns and a nine-foot python skin. The decor was devoid of mementos, as if the Tellos were refugees who had been washed up here by chance. The only homely touches were the fishing rods tucked against the roof and two small dogs.

In a way, the Tellos *were* refugees, fleeing the disintegration of their dreams. José had built up the game parks in Mozambique only to see them wither, first under socialism, then beneath the boots of Renamo guerrillas. The chimeras of politics had touched them personally too. Theresa's brother and mother had been jailed for a period, wrongly implicated in a terrorist attack on an oil refinery. It is wounding to see your labours destroyed for goals that seem senseless. Perhaps that was why they had not laid out the familiar realm of books, pictures and photos. Sometimes the past hurts too much to keep it in your pocket.

I thought of my own circumstances and decided all three of us were wanderers rather than refugees. 'Refugee' spoke of a longing to return while 'wanderer' was a more hopeful word. It suggested an ability to enjoy the present and look forward to the future. But hope is a fickle creature. When it wins out, it is called faith. When it loses, it is merely the forerunner of despair. I didn't trust it.

I travelled unencumbered by anything more personal than my Swiss Army penknife. If I was a wanderer and not a refugee, why did I never carry a point of reference to the people who touched my heart? Why did I look at photos of Kipenget and Gabriel only rarely and always in private? Why did I not daydream about my house in Kenya? I never let my mind linger on the ochre-coloured tiles of the verandah where the parched plains could fly up into my eyes. I never traced the undulating lip of the Rift Valley with my finger. Never lay flung out on my stomach in my bed, listening for the squeak of Sintahui's gumboots in the darkness as he passed by the window.

Of course, I knew why I couldn't do these things. When I saw Kipenget's face, it butted against the back of my throat, which made my eyes moisten with tears. I couldn't pull her out of that place inside me she had crawled into and stand her in front of me so I could hug her as I used to. And, try as I might, the house was unapproachable. It was always the same. I would cross the culvert where the dirt driveway met the tarmac road and pass the casuarina tree with the giraffe rib nailed to its trunk. I would take a few tentative steps towards the seasonal pond that oozed tadpoles during the rains. Then I would look up and see the cinnamon-cheeked bee-eaters perched on the telephone wire. The sight of those little brown birds sitting there like a row of clothes pegs invariably brought me to a standstill. They made me stop and shudder and swoon with self-pity. I was encased in a sarcophagus of unresolved grief, and I didn't know how to claw my way out. So I kept travelling.

I liked Theresa and José for the unreserved welcome they gave us. I felt at home. It was a special gift whose value they, too, appreciated. For months after their arrival, no hospitality was forthcoming from either the professional hunters or, as far as I could gather, the other Europeans in the PDRN. José had been mulling over how to extract more money from the hunting concessions for the development of the villages. One possibility was simply to raise the fees. Another was to award the concessions to the highest bidder in an auction. When the Tellos drove to the hunters' camps to discuss these ideas, they were met with hostility. If the table was set for lunch, they were not invited to sit down at it. No one offered them so much as a glass of water. 'It was terrible, terrible,' said Theresa. Perhaps, said José, it was the French way.

The Tellos were touchingly eager to show us their work: culling the animals, hunting with the villagers, collecting honey and tanning hides. The more we saw, the more I marvelled at their patience and tenacity.

There is no such thing as a blueprint for saving the environment. Like all good conservationists, they realised that each situation had its own truth and several avenues of approach. So they plodded along their *via dolorosa* which was stationed with misunderstanding and disappointment.

'We were forced to come into conflict with the people because the situation was so out of control,' said José, when I questioned him on the rampant poaching. 'People believe that wildlife has no owner. We have to teach them that everything belongs to somebody. It can be the government or the village or the hunter. When you kill an animal, you have to pay somebody.'

Nine days after they first pitched their tents, José and Theresa paid a call on the village of Idongo, seventeen miles away. We are here to help you and to protect the game, José told them. The villagers looked at him in silence, for this was a preposterous statement. What little manioc they grew in the sandy soil was raided by baboons. The animals they shot were the staff of life. If they could not hunt, how could they be helped by this bearded stranger who addressed them through a translator?

'They were very unfriendly. They thought we were more white people come to make their life difficult,' José explained.

The Tellos set out to prove otherwise. José employed twenty men to help build the camp. Theresa, who had trained as a vet, treated their coughs and worms. Whenever the Tellos visited Idongo, the villagers were careful to hide their weapons. 'We never found the smallest piece of skin or meat, not even a tooth. I told them, I want to go out with your hunters and learn your traditional ways. There was a very old hunter there. I wanted to employ him. But every time I went to the village, he was never there. They didn't trust me. They thought I wanted to learn their ways to make it easier to catch them. So I told the chief, 'Okay, you don't believe us, but I know you're hunting illegally. I'm going to catch you.' Five days later I caught a poacher. I called the chief and told him, "Either you start to work with us or we start to make life difficult." I warned him I would confiscate his gun unless he bought a permit for it. If he had a licence, he could hunt. It was the first time someone had told him he could hunt legally. He thought it was the prerogative of the whites. He bought the licence and showed it to me. Then I knew it was time to start the hunting scheme,' José said.

Meanwhile Theresa, as director of wildlife management, started up a small demonstration abattoir and tannery. She also began to teach the Banda low-tech apiculture to increase their honey yields. The Banda's traditional method of honey collecting was simple and destructive. They got at the honey by felling the trees, then smashing the hives open to scoop it out. The result was lots of dead trees and a black mess of honey clotted with bees and crumbled honeycomb. Theresa's pilot scheme demonstrated how to smoke the bees out of the hive without harming the tree and extract a clear honey that could be sold in Bangui for a good price.

I missed much of this activity because I came down with an excruciating bout of malaria. Kathy went on culling trips with José but passed up a morning's hunt with the Banda. She was doing marvellously well given the rough conditions, but she still resisted walking. Meanwhile I lay in bed with red-hot wire coiled around my head and sweated.

My notes, when I felt well enough to write them, took on the tone of an explorer's journal. Tuesday: 'The jungle is alive with singing crickets. At night it literally throbs.' Wednesday: 'The fever has gone. I feel better. Edmond takes me to see the tannery. His wife cost him $375. It took him two years to save up the money from his monthly salary of $75. Stagger back to camp perspiring and weak. The women are playing the water drums again.'

My nights were restless, veering between malarial dreams and hyena insomnia. Sometimes it rained accompanied by concertolike thunder. The trees creaked and swayed overhead. When the lightning flickered, I could make out the gaping doorway, our clothes thrown on the chair and Kathy humped in the bed. Nothing ever disturbed her sleep. I envied her.

Kathy was afraid of lions but unaware of the unpredictable nature of hyenas. The popular image of the hyena is that of a scavenger whose jaws are so strong they can crush diamonds. In fact, they are brave animals who also hunt in packs and make their own kills. They attack people, too, while they are asleep. They go for the face.

There was a mutilated hyena with only three paws that hung around camp at night. I think José and Theresa regarded it as a sort of mascot. Our first night it went to the open kitchen and devoured the remains of our dinner, crushing a saucepan to pulp. Then it wandered off to the workers' compound and gobbled a chicken. Another night it broke into the cook's hut and seized his bowl of manioc. Before we had arrived it had eaten one of the dog's puppies. It had also bitten off the bitch's tail as she tried to defend her offspring. The bitch hated the hyena and trailed behind it, barking incessantly. I would lie awake, marking the hyena's progress from hut to hut as the high-pitched yapping, at first some way off, drew close then receded again. As we had no door to keep it at bay, I placed a lit lamp in the entrance instead. I knew that wild animals were either repelled or attracted by light. I couldn't remember which it was.

By this time I was accustomed to the cavalier attitude our PDRN hosts had towards personal safety. The Tellos, however, were more than nonchalant. They had a stunning disregard for basic precautions.

One night, on a honey-collecting expedition, Theresa called Kathy over to photograph swarming bees. The sting of the African bee, in sufficient numbers, can be deadly. Kathy gave me a wry grin and muttered, 'What's it to be? Suicide by bee or hyena?'

'Ask Theresa,' I said.

Kathy turned to her. 'Theresa, why isn't there a door on our hut? What about the hyena?'

'Hyenas don't harm people,' she scoffed.

'What about that man who was killed?'

'He was drunk. He'd passed out on the path on the way home.'

Kathy persisted. 'What about that woman and the child you told us about who were taken out of their huts?'

'Yes, so why isn't there a door?' I chimed in.

Theresa looked flummoxed. 'Well, I didn't think of it. We don't have one.'

'So it's suicide by hyena,' Kathy announced. We laughed and the honey-collectors, seeing there was a joke, joined in.

'The men like it when we laugh,' said Theresa.

Our last few days were spent back at Manovo. The Froments had returned from Bangui, where it had been mutually agreed they would leave the project within the next couple of months. Instead of easing the tension, the decision had stirred it. One afternoon Ingrid appeared in our bedroom with Fanny. 'Take her,' she said through a pinched mouth and hurried away. She was crying, which was unusual for Ingrid.

I heard a crash and a man shouting. At first I thought a servant had broken something. Then I heard Sylvie calling Francois. There were snatches of angry voices. 'I've never seen anything like it . . . for weeks and months . . . responsiblity . . . you are mad . . .' It was Jean Marc. He was quarrelling with Francois. The dam had burst.

I sat outside the bedroom writing my notes. A soft evening light basted the trees. Six waterbuck filed past on black-stockinged feet. They saw me and hesitated, their tails twitching. Then they walked on, moving with the silence of nuns in a cathedral. The sun fringed their dark hair with gold. Why, in these magical surroundings, had peace eluded everyone?

On our way back to Bangui Kathy fell asleep and awoke with a start at the end of the journey. 'Where are we?' she asked.

'Bangui.'

'Fuck the details. Which country?'

7

The Savages

I'm going to rape you, then kill you and drink your blood from your skull.
A Liberian soldier talking to Michelle Faul, an Associated Press reporter

For the most part he's a stereotype African rebel. T shirt. Jeans. A wild smile that doesn't match the stony eyes. And, of course, the gun. He's a kid from the bush unversed in political dogma. But what the hell. He's been given a weapon, and he's having fun with it. So there he is, squatting on the ground with one foot slightly forward for balance, posing for the photographer in the drizzling rain with his AK47.

But wait a second, what's this Mae West wig curling over his shoulders? Is this a drag show or what? No, it can't be. There he is again, only he's dead, chucked into the back of a truck. The wig must have been a good fit. It's still in place.

That's the cameo of rebellion. Now here's the vignette of revolution. Someone else in T shirt and jeans. He is being questioned by men in civvies, so they must be rebels too, like the kid in the wig. They're talking at him, but these guys don't care what the man answers. The man must know this because he is silent as they paw at his chest and pull up his jeans to inspect his ankles. They're looking for the giveaway indentation on his skin of a military dog-tag which he might have torn from his neck or of army-issue boots that he could have discarded in the bushes.

The rebels are on a witch hunt for soldiers. They must have overrun the town a few days ago because the tokens of battle are no longer fresh. The corpse over there, for instance. The bottom half is a dead man clad in olive drab pants. The top half is a skeleton picked clean by stray dogs. Like the

199

town residents, they're hungry. All the shops have been looted, of course. Empty bottle crates lie in the mud so there's obviously been time enough to finish off all the booze.

Now the rebels have turned the man around. Someone is fumbling in the back pocket of his jeans. He fishes something out and holds it up triumphantly. It's small, about the size of a credit card. Why, you wonder, did he keep his ID? Like everything else here, it's senseless.

The men move quickly. They are jabbering. It is the frenzied, high-pitched baying of hounds. They have torn the man's shirt off and tied his hands behind his back. They are pulling him along by a rope attached to a noose around his neck. The man has fallen to his knees. This brings everyone to a halt for a moment while they stare at him.

Then a young boy breaks up the frieze. He is giggling as he takes some high-kneed dance steps on the balls of his feet toward the group. In his fist is a stiletto knife. It sways rhythmically, level with the bandanna knotted round his head. This guy may idolise Bruce Lee, but he's pure Shaka Zulu.

The man is babbling, his eyes fixed on the kid and his knife. Your stomach turns and the bile rises in your throat. You don't want to watch his guts plop on to the ground in a moist grey heap, but you're mesmerised.

The knife soars above the boy's head and jerks backward. Another rebel has restrained him. They are not finished with this soldier yet. He must be taken away and 'questioned'. They throw him into the back of a hijacked four-wheel-drive. The last you see of him is the image of a condemned man. Head thrown back and twisted sideways so that he can place his drowning, pleading eyes on yours. Fear has made them huge, like an angry bull's. His lips are flapping in a loose, rubbery sort of way. He is trying to tell you something, but you can't hear because the windows are shut. It doesn't matter anyway. He is as good as dead.

Scenes like that cling to you for a long time, like cigarette smoke on a dinner jacket. Afterwards, on holiday in Sweden with Tara and Petra, I felt as if my soul had been rolled around in green slime. I wanted to talk about it, vomit up all that savage filth to throw off my depression. I couldn't. Words were inadequate for the horror of the last days of Liberian President Samuel Doe, another poor boy made good who holed up in his Executive Mansion while tribe massacred tribe outside the porticoed doors.

This was revolution Liberia-style, conducted with the freewheeling whimsy of a children's game and just as cruel. Five months earlier, a man then unknown to the world named Charles Taylor had infiltrated into eastern Liberia with some fifteen followers and attacked a customs post with shot guns. Since then the Gio and Mano tribesmen who formed the backbone of his ragtag army had oozed through the countryside like a mud slide. They were bent on slaughtering Krahns because that was the tribe of the man they intended to oust from power, Samuel Kanyon Doe.

The rebels were so bizarrely dressed that at times they seemed more like a tropical carnival parade than a guerrilla force. The march into battle was made in bathrobes, women's dresses, Halloween masks, underwater goggles, wigs and baseball caps pillaged from the houses of expatriates living on the Firestone rubber estate. Along with the burlesque trappings went a far from laughable hodgepodge of knives, axes, machetes and guns. The carnage inflicted by this makeshift arsenal was astonishing. By the time the civil war had subsided into a grudging stalemate that autumn, at least 13,000 people, mostly civilians, had been killed. About half the population had fled from their homes to escape the fighting. Three quarters of a million children's lives had been affected through severe malnutrition or losing their parents or both.

It was a grotesque parody of war in our time. The fighting was not motivated by ideals or beliefs. There were no echoes of Nelson Mandela's struggle against apartheid or Steve Biko's rallying cry of black conscious-ness. Neither were there traces of the Tigrayans' naive vision of a Marxist Utopia. This was a war fuelled by revenge. At first men, and then women, children and babies, were killed for the crime of belonging to a different tribe. Most were shot or knifed. Others were murdered in more hideous ways. Some boys of thirteen and fourteen stripped a man naked and sliced off his ear. They gave him a glass of water to drink then shot him. Men were dismembered with chainsaws while still alive. Refugees said they had seen the arms, legs and torsos piled in a heap by the side of the road.

Even so, beneath all this hatred and blood lust lay something else. It was politics in its most basic form. The rebel ranks of the National Patriotic Front of Liberia had been swelled by men and boys who wanted to squirm their way up through the dung heap into the fresh air. They saw their chance to shuck off the poverty and rags and years of toil under a blistering sun and they seized it. The soldiers of the Armed Forces of Liberia resisted them because they had been born in a pile of shit too. They didn't want to go back there.

Nothing could have prepared us for what took place. All of us – Liberians, journalists, diplomats, doctors, nurses and relief workers – were not just deeply shaken by what we saw. Much of the time we were mortally scared.

When writing of it for *The Independent* magazine, I referred to Evelyn Waugh's *Black Mischief* at my editor's suggestion. I later regretted this glib allusion. The savagery may occasionally have been buffoonish, but what happened during those months of turmoil was intensely evil. As order dissolved into anarchy, conscience vanished. If exercising moral choice marks the boundary between man and beast, then thousands of arms-bearing Liberians took an evolutionary leap backwards. The barbarity of the soldiers and rebels made me ashamed for Africa. Even if they had wanted it, their conduct provided nothing on which to base an apologia.

In a world free of obligation, I would never have chosen to step into the mayhem, but Lord Copper pulled the strings back at *The Sunday Times*. I can't speak for other foreign correspondents, but when I'm on assignment, I spend a lot of time flying by the seat of my pants. Liberia was no exception.

It was another heat-sodden Tuesday in Bangui bringing with it the usual run of mediocre luck. I set out early in the morning in a malarial trance to make an overseas phone call from the post office. From all the accounts on the BBC World Service, Liberia was brewing up nicely, which I had pointed out to the desk. Should I catch a plane over there? We'll let you know, they said. I'd heard nothing, so I was making last-minute arrangments to fly with Kathy to the Chadian capital of Ndjamena the following day.

It was the fever that made me careless and forget to zip my money into my fishing jacket. Some well-muscled thugs grabbed the plastic bag dangling from my hand as I was walking down the street. I would have run after them, but they leaped down an open manhole that led into the sewers. After an hour of Keystone Cops stuff with the police, Presidential Security and the fire department (they thought they could flush the guys into the fetid Ubangui with a hose), Kathy and I left the scene of the crime empty handed.

A few blocks later, we were besieged by five freelance vigilantes demanding a hefty reward for giving chase to the thieves through the sewers. Things started to get a little rough so we took refuge in the nearest hotel, a small family-run affair. I remember sitting with my head cradled in my hands while half-naked, very smelly bodies swarmed angrily around me. 'Go away. I've got this terrible headache,' I muttered.

Someone yanked me to my feet. 'Run!' he commanded. Kathy and I were clattering up the stairs and racing down a corridor. There was a commotion behind us. The hunters after their prey. The man unlocked a door. We hurtled through. He turned the key in the lock. Kathy sat down in a chair. I sank on to his bed. The noise subsided.

For the next twenty minutes I used the bedside telephone to negotiate with the mob via the manager. They were demanding seventy-five doll-ars in return for everyone's sanity. 'Call the police,' I said. Madame, you don't understand. They wouldn't come. This is an affair that must be settled privately. 'Give them 8,000, [thirty dollars],' I conceded, acknow-ledging that we didn't quite have the upper hand. Madame, the voice was congealed with anxiety, they are not happy with that. They are threatening to tear the place apart. They will wreck the cars outside. 'I think 8,000 is fair, don't you?' I could hear voices flare then the line went dead. Seventy-five dollars later the mob left, tearing off a few wing mirrors as they went.

'Well, we've had the worst of the day,' I observed as we arrived at our hotel in one of the vandalised cars. Not so. The receptionist was waving a telephone receiver in the air.

'*Madame, c'est Londres.*' The start-of-the-week editorial meeting must have just finished. Its function is to establish which stories to assign so that us lackeys in the field can work on them during the run-up to Sunday. I took the phone.

'Hello, Mary Anne. It's Richard here. How are things?'

'Hi, Richard. Just fine. How are you?'

'Fine thanks. How are the milk shakes?'

This was the desk's running joke about Bangui that I still hadn't fathomed. 'Same as ever. They're great.'

The tone at the other end became more businesslike. 'How soon can you get to Liberia?'

'God, Richard, this isn't JFK, you know. We're lucky if there's one flight a day out of here and heavens knows where it will go to. I don't know what the schedules are like. I've got to cross half the continent.' I didn't know if this was true because I had only a vague idea where Liberia was.

'Well, do your best. Do you think you can get in by tomorrow?' They always said that.

'I'll do my best.' I always said that.

'Good. Will you be filing from the rebel or the government side?'

'That depends, Richard. The airport is closed to commercial flights so I'll have to see what gives when I get to Abidjan [the capital of the Côte d'Ivoire]. If I can't hitch in on a plane, it might make more sense to go in with the rebels and march into Monrovia with them. They seem pretty close now.' While I drivelled on, I was trying to figure out which course of action minimised the chances of getting shot at. Neither looked very promising.

'Great. What about your photographer? We'd like some pictures.'

I looked at Kathy, who was standing beside me. You want to come? I mouthed.

'I don't do wars,' she said firmly.

'Kathy's got to get back to England fairly soon. She doesn't want to get tied down in a place where it may be difficult to get out.'

'Okay. We can take agency stuff. Let us know how you're getting on.'

'Sure. I'll ring you when I know what's happening. Bye.' By that token, they'd never hear from me again.

I rang the American embassy for a travel advisory. They thought I was mad. There were some flights still landing at the small, downtown airfield. Foreigners were being evacuated by sea, land and air. The sizeable Lebanese community, which dominated the retail trade, had made an exodus to the relative safety of Beirut. Thousands of Liberians had fled as well, which gave a better idea of how nasty it had become. Traffic was nearly all in one direction, and the embassy's advice was to stay away. As usual, I'd be cruising against the flow.

I imagine that working for a newspaper might be something like the space programme at Cape Kennedy. Blast off – or in our case, the deadline for copy – is an immutable point in time. You can start off in a fairly relaxed manner, but there's an inevitable frenzy towards the end. The story was going into the early, inside pages of the paper so blast off was 8 p.m. Friday. Automatically, I worked backwards, counting off the days, hours or minutes that remained. By the time I got to Abidjan via a twenty-four-hour stopover in the Congo, it was Wednesday night. I had two days to get the story.

Groups of men from Charles Taylor's National Patriotic Front of Liberia were hovering round the outskirts of Monrovia. Some had been sighted as close as twenty miles outside town. It wasn't clear why Taylor was delaying the final offensive. Neither was it known when it would take place, but the tension was mounting. The conflict had attracted quite a few reporters, photographers and cameramen who hoped to be there for the fall of the capital. Some had gone in on the rebel side. Most had chartered small planes to land at the Spriggs Payne airfield in Monrovia. A good fifty per cent of the slog under these conditions calls for being a mix of a logistics officer and some sort of whacko tour operator. You've got to get in, establish a line out for filing copy and, ultimately, get out. This was what I needed to figure out in Abidjan.

I met up with a CBS crew who gave me a fill on how to operate the government side. Charter planes were available at a price. The hotels were open. CBS was shipping in its food and drinking water, but you could buy it there if you wanted. They weren't as sanguine about the rebels. You had to hire a car and go self-contained, taking all your own petrol, food and equipment.

If the mobile office looked too good, there was always the chance the rebels would 'liberate' it. They were short of transport. CBS hadn't travelled with them, but by all accounts the trip sounded one hell of a lot rougher than hanging around Monrovia. A cameraman who had been with them reported seeing skulls stuck on top of sticks along the road. I decided to give both sides a hit and opted for the rebels first.

The wellspring for the rebel insurgency was Nimba County, the seat of the Gio and Mano tribes. You reached it by driving across from northwestern Côte d'Ivoire. I had a lucky break. Early Friday morning there was a commercial domestic flight on Air Ivoire to Man, a town eighty miles from the border. The idea was to make contact with the rebels and file a story from Côte d'Ivoire, as there were no working telephones on the other side. After that I'd wing it. Perhaps I'd go on. Perhaps I'd turn back. Instinctively, I knew it wasn't a good idea to disappear into a no man's land on my own. These guys weren't like the Tigrayans. They were off the wall. Anything could happen and no one would know about it. Don't make decisions yet. Wait and see, I told myself.

It was still dark when I got up. My overnight bag was already packed with the barest essentials, sufficient for one day or three weeks. Pocket French dictionary, notebooks, dressings for wounds, sterile syringes, hat, string, penknife, radio, spare trousers, loo paper, fork and spoon, book, clock. By the time I boarded the plane, I was in countdown mode. Eleven and a half hours to go to deadline. We landed at 9.00 in the midst of a coruscating emerald mosaic of vegetation. Among the boarding passengers walking towards us across the runway was a swarthy man carrying a television camera. I went up to him.

'Have you just been in Nimba County?'

'Yes. How did you know?'

'With that camera? Where else would you have been? Tell me quickly. What was it like?'

He looked drained, and it wasn't a heat-induced exhaustion. 'It was hell. They're crazy. They stopped all the time to rape women and raid the bars. Sometimes they were so drunk we had to drive the cars for them. Never again. I'm not going back there.' He looked at me. 'Are you going in with them?'

'Thinking of it, yes.'

'Are you on your own?'

'Yes.'

He paled visibly. For a second he regarded me with bright concentration. The look was more eloquent than his 'Well, be careful.'

We parted. That was one decision out of the way. The guy was a hardened professional. What was hell for him would be hell for me too. The rebels weren't going to have the benefit of my company.

A party of Red Cross and Médecins sans Frontières workers begrudgingly offered me a lift to Danane, the nearest town to the border crossing. It was a fifty-mile drive. Before setting off, they stopped at a restaurant to eat breakfast with agonising leisure. By the time they dropped me off at the Danane prefecture for the obligatory courtesy call, it was noon. No one had talked to me all morning. They didn't like to be associated with journalists. I didn't blame them. I guess we compromised their neutrality.

So I was surprised when one of the doctors approached me as we stood beneath the slowly turning fan in the prefect's office. She brought her mouth to my ear. 'I've been meaning to tell you since this morning. You have a very large tear in the seat of your pants.' And on that token kindness we parted.

I made my way to a sleepy dosshouse where the rebels' middleman, someone called Everice, hung out. I had rung him the previous evening to inform him I wanted to make contact with Taylor's men. Everice wasn't there. Nor was anyone else except the bartender. He told me Everice was in a meeting somewhere. So far, situation normal. It was like hunting bears mid-winter. There was nothing for it but get a taxi to the border and see what gave.

I walked down to the road. The bag and Tandy laptop were getting pretty heavy in the hundred-plus temperature. Nothing stirred in any direction. Even the flies were riveted to the shadows. I was stranded in a dry white heat. It was one o'clock. Seven hours to go, and I knew no more than when I left Bangui.

There are times, doing this job, when you wonder if you are seriously insane instead of just amusingly mad. Such a proposition isn't constructive, however. Insane, mad or just a bumbling fool, you still have to file the story. So you plod stubbornly on like a mule turning a water wheel. If you will something to happen, eventually it does.

In this case it was the simultaneous appearance of a taxi and a young man who introduced himself as Edouard, the brother of the dosshouse owner. Suddenly I had a guide and wheels. The gloom lifted. We spent some time combing the town for 'them' and pitched up at the house of Charles Taylor's brother. He wasn't there, but his wife was, got up in curlers, T shirt, sarong and flip-flops. We shuffled into the enfolding gloom of the living room. Edouard and Adamas, the taxi driver, flopped into some battered vinyl armchairs. I excused myself to change into my spare trousers, an Afghan number with voluminous legs and deep pockets.

Mr Taylor, Mrs Taylor told me on my return, was in a meeting but would be back soon. That means nothing in Africa, so we got back into the taxi.

'How far is it to the border?' I asked.

Edouard said, 'Thirty miles.'

'Come on, boys, let's go and let's go fast.'

All this while I'd been talking. Well, not talking really. Think of it as a dentist prodding around someone's mouth for cavities.

How's your husband, Mrs Taylor? He must be very busy with all these meetings.

Yes, he is, she said. He works with his brother. They have been waiting to attack Monrovia and now they are going to do it, so they are very busy. They are at a meeting at the frontier right now. (Thanks, kiddo, we'll pass on the tea and split.)

So how's business in the hotel, Edouard? I bet you have Charles Taylor as a customer what with it being the best place in town.

Yes, we do, said Edouard. He drinks at the bar.

He must be a pretty interesting guy, huh?

Yes, he is. The last time he was here he made a phone call to the United States from the bar. He was calling his wife because he needed more money to buy arms. She said she would arrange it and he looked very pleased.

So you had all those weapons coming through town? That must have been pretty exciting to watch.

Yes, but you don't get to see them because they're covered up in trucks.

(Gotcha, Edouard. I'll be toasting you tonight.)

Colonel Gaddafi had given Charles Taylor arms support worth eighteen million dollars and trained some of his men for six months. This had made the Americans pretty twitchy. As Liberia's historical ally, they couldn't ignore what was happening, but they didn't know which way to play it. Five years ago, they might have contemplated military intervention. No longer. There was no winning side to back – no good guys. It was a choice of the devil and the deep blue sea.

In the past, the United States had nourished Samuel Doe's greed and indulged his cruelty. Recently this astonishingly corrupt monster whom it had suckled had become an embarrassment. Doe had seized power in a military coup ten years earlier and enriched himself on state money in the intervening years. The Reagan administration allocated more than $500 million for development and military aid. Liberia became the largest per capita recipient of United States aid in black Africa. A sizeable but undocumented portion of this dropped through the treasury's sievelike coffers into the pockets of Doe and his cronies. Doe was believed to have about seventy million dollars secreted in South Korean and Swiss bank accounts.

In return for this unquestioning financial support that turned a blind eye to an abysmal human rights record, the United States erected strategic telecommunications installations at the cost of about $450 million. Liberia became a US listening post for a good chunk of Africa. The farcical nature of the patron-client relationship was made clear when Doe prevailed as head of state in a shift from military to civilian rule. In 1985, after he was voted president in blatantly rigged elections, then Secretary of State George Schultz chose to praise Doe's democratic instincts. The two countries acted as each other's stooges.

Nevertheless, the Americans were wising up. Fiscal assistance, that fickle measure of political faith, had withered on the bough. Over four years US aid had dropped from $53.5 million in military and economic assistance to $10 million in fiscal 1991 for food and humanitarian needs.

The cutback underscored US dissatisfaction with Doe, who had emerged a loser. The Americans didn't want him around any more.

Unfortunately, the forty-two-year-old Taylor appeared to be no better than the man he had vowed to overthrow. Anyone could see he wanted to grab the spoils for himself as well. 'I would hope that we have a really good marriage and a really good honeymoon,' he said, anticipating not only leadership but an alliance with the United States. This US-educated Baptist sporting designer sunglasses was a thug who had turned his position as head of the General Procurement Agency to his advantage. He fled the country in 1983 following charges of embezzling $900,000 of state shopping money. When he got to the United States, he was jailed, but managed to escape while awaiting extradition.

So the US State Department feigned impartiality to mask its indecision. A naval task force of 2,000 marines was sitting offshore on board six warships. The State Department said they were there to evacuate their nationals if needs be. In reality, they were keeping an eye on their communications facilities. Not only did they beam Voice of America transmissions across the continent, the National Security Agency used them to eavesdrop on Libya and everyone else in the region. There was also a 1,400-foot Omega transmission tower, the tallest structure in Africa, which was a navigational facility for ships and aircraft that guided nuclear submarines.

As for Charles Taylor, it sounded as if he was running short on discipline, money and arms. So he'd sent his wife off to raise more funds to regain impetus. The Libyan largesse must have dried up, which was why he had been hanging back from Monrovia. Edouard's inadvertent admission that arms were being shipped through Côte d'Ivoire bore out a story confided to me by an aid worker. His nurse girlfriend had stumbled on to an overturned civilian truck near Danane. Ivorian police were standing guard over the arms that had spilled on to the road. The Ivorian president, Houphouet Boigny, thought Doe was a gangster, but had sworn blind that his country was not being used as a conduit for the Liberian rebels' weaponry. The Ivorian economy was held up by the French in return for toeing the Western political line. And here were all those guns trundling through into the hands of Libyan-backed rebels. I knew why Houphouet Boigny was being a naughty boy. He disliked Doe intensely because Doe's henchmen had kidnapped and killed his son-in-law. There were all sorts of regional implications. It was all supposition, of course, but it looked as if Taylor's onslaught on the capital was imminent. Things were shaping up nicely.

We rounded a corner and shuddered to a halt to avoid hitting a car coming the other way. The white saloon bristled with excited faces and gesticulating arms. It was my friend Everice with some of Taylor's henchmen. The unbridled excitement of revolution suffused the taxi with adrenalin. We had arrived at the border.

'You must turn round! We are having a meeting. It's forbidden to go further. Go back!' Everice shouted.

I conducted an interview of sorts with the men in the car while parleying an entrée into Liberia. Everice was despatched with my visiting card and returned some minutes later. They were adamant we should go no further. I pointed out we were still under Ivorian jurisdiction and brandished the prefect's *laissez passer*. Everice was intractable. 'I will bring Mr Taylor to see you this evening at the hotel at eight o'clock,' he said.

I glanced at my clock. Just before four. If we pressed on after they had turned round, there was a good chance of being locked up in a room. I had to get to a phone by 7.30. 'Very well,' I said meekly, 'I'll see you back at the hotel.'

Everice's car leaped back and forth between the thick vegetation and headed in the direction of the border. When the dust had settled, I leaned forward. 'Stay here, chaps. I'm just going to do peepee. I'll be back.' I still had to walk into Liberia to get the Nimba County dateline.

Later, on the way back to town, we stopped by a refugee village to troll for stories on army atrocities against the Gio and Mano people. I hated this part. Sitting on a stool, notebook in hand, looking as calm as a traffic warden writing out a ticket. And all the while asking these beaten, bewildered people if they could describe exactly how their families had been mutilated and murdered.

'They took our children and put them in the back of a truck and drove away. Then they poured gasoline on them and burned them because they said they were rebel children,' said Amara Krama. He was soft and gentle with me. I did my best to return the courtesy.

Now all I had to do was find a telephone. The one in the hotel bar was out of bounds because of the owner's friendship with the rebels. By 6.15 I had been turned down by the Red Cross, Médecins sans Frontières and the parish priest. The post office was shut because Cameroon was playing Argentina in the World Cup. I would have to find one in Man.

I turned to Adamas. 'Okay, we're off to Man. You've got to keep your foot flat on the floor the whole way. This is important.'

There was a stop at a garage to fix the spare tyre, then we were hurtling along the tarmac. I kept my head down, putting the story into the Tandy. It was just as well given the way Adamas was negotiating the oncoming traffic to get round all those lumbering trucks.

We fetched up at a hotel as the sun was setting. I paid the boys off and checked in. The place looked deserted so I don't know why the receptionist led me past the swimming pool to an annexe. But the room had a phone in it, so I wasn't complaining. 'Get me London, please. And please hurry,' I told him.

I paced around a bit while I was waiting for the call. I was dishevelled. I was tired. I smelt. I was covered in red dust. I was probably bonkers too. I had to admit it, though, I was damned pleased with myself. Nothing mattered except getting the story in the bag. 7.30. Half an hour for dictating. I was on the nose.

The phone rang. I seized it and sat on the bed.

'Copytakers please. Hello copytakers? This is for foreign. The name's Mary. Anne with an 'e' on the end. Fitzgerald. Catchline Liberia. Open paragraph.' The line went dead.

You become very calm in those moments. I dialled reception. 'I'm sorry to bother you, but I've been cut off. Could you try that London number again, please?'

Five minutes later they were back on the line. 'Hello copytakers, it's Mary Anne Fitzgerald again. Let's go. Open paragraph.' An almighty drumroll of thunder broke overhead to be followed a second later by a sharp, crackling noise that seemed to have come from within the room. 'The electricity's just gone. I'm holding my hand up in front of my face, and I can't see it. I'm going to have to call you back.'

I was a woman obsessed as I felt my way along the wall to the door with the Tandy tucked under my arm. It opened on to pitch blackness and lashing rain. Flashes of lightning illuminated the walkway as I battled through the downpour. I had to get to reception where there would be an oil lamp. But when I found the steps leading to the swimming pool, the way was blocked by a gate of vertical iron railings with pointed tips. It was secured with a padlock. Undeterred, I shoved the Tandy between the bars. Then I climbed over. Rather, I tried to. A horizontal bar fixed across the bottom provided purchase, but the gate was still too high to step over. I threw one leg across then the other. This left me sitting on the spear tips, which was rather painful. I jumped off them very quickly. Something was wrong, though. My feet weren't touching the ground. It was those damn spear tips. They'd skewered the Afghan trousers. What was I doing in this tropical rainstorm dangling from a gate like a rag doll? It wasn't what I had in mind when I said I flew by the seat of my pants. I wriggled and yanked and ripped and suddenly was free.

Afterwards, when I had dictated the story by candlelight and was standing there, soaked, muddy and flashing a lot of bare leg, a woman walked up to the reception desk and dropped her key on the counter. 'Excuse me,' I said, 'We don't know each other yet, but would you like to share a bottle of whisky with me?'

'I'd love to,' she smiled.

Much later, having drunk Edouard's health and eaten a good dinner, I asked the receptionist if he would unlock the gate so I could retire to bed.

'Unlock the gate?' he enquired. 'There isn't a gate on the way to the annexe. I think you must have come the wrong way.'

Standing in the lobby of the Abidjan Hilton the next day, I was approached by a short man with a bristly moustache. 'You must be Mary Anne Fitzgerald.'

'Yeah. How did you know?'

He looked at my clothes and back at my face. 'It's not difficult to pick you out. Rosy said I should look you up. He says you know how to get around Africa. I'm going to Monrovia.'

Rosy was *The Philadelphia Inquirer*'s foreign editor. Ed Hille worked for the paper as a photographer. He had shot stories in Central America and knew about Third World soldiers, who are an unpredictable breed. It was his first time in Africa. Ed was calm, kind and funny. They were the right attributes for relieving the sinister atmosphere. We teamed up and hitched a ride into Monrovia on a charter plane.

Our first stop was at a Lebanese clothes shop to change money on the black market. Then we went to the morgue. Two attendants were bringing the bodies out one by one and working on them in a corridor that gave on to a yard at the back of the John F. Kennedy Memorial Hospital. They were hoping to catch some fresh air, but there wasn't any in that stench-filled heat. Sweat streamed down their faces.

In a back room seven corpses were piled in a heap. They had been collected off the street that morning. Some were so mutilated they were barely recognisable. One was an old woman. Another a child. Ed told me not to look. I did anyway.

'You can take photos, but don't show our faces. Make it snappy. We gotta get outta here before nightfall,' one of the attendants told Ed. They were folding sheets of plastic around a corpse and sealing them down with Scotch tape. One of the dead man's ears was missing and chunks of flesh had been hacked out, probably with axes. He was grossly swollen as if he had head-to-toe elephantiasis.

There had been plenty of time for decomposition to set in and the body gases to bloat him out. After the soldiers had finished with him, they dumped the body in a swamp. That had been Saturday night. This was Monday evening. His name was Butler Freeman, and he had been an auditor in the finance ministry. The mortuary attendant said he was his cousin. Freeman and two friends, a sculptor from the university and a town councillor, had been apprehended and killed by soldiers when they had tried to curtail a looting spree.

The murders had shaken the town, for the men were neither soldiers nor rebels but respected citizens. Until now it had been a tribal thing, rather like inner city gang warfare. These victims were Americo-Liberians. The hatred had begun to taint everyone. Even so, people still traded in hope. The Americans would step in. There would be a ceasefire. The two sides would negotiate beneath the flags of truce.

Liberia's history set the stage for the tragicomedy that was being acted out. Americo-Liberian is the term used for the descendants of slaves from Southern cotton plantations. Their visionary return to their roots was the consequence of the United States decision in the early 1800s to proscribe the slave trade. Under the sponsorship of the American Colonization Society, whose supporters included Daniel Webster and Henry Clay, the freedmen set sail in 1822 from the United States in two small schooners.

The black Pilgrim Fathers landed near the mouth of the Mesurado River where Monrovia now stands. They were accompanied by Robert F. Stockton, a US Navy captain. The local chiefs weren't too happy when everyone pitched ashore. They had a premonition it was the end of their lucrative slave-trading days. They weren't much good at bargaining, though. Pressured by the sharp-eyed Captain Stockton, the chiefs handed over a strip of land in return for a downpayment of six muskets, a small barrel of gunpowder, six iron bars, ten pots, one barrel of beads, two casks of tobacco, twelve knives, forks and spoons, a barrel of nails, a box of pipes, three mirrors, four umbrellas, three walking sticks, a box of soap, a barrel of rum, four hats, three pairs of shoes, six pieces of baft and three pieces of calico. The balance of six iron bars, a dozen guns, three more barrels of powder, a dozen plates, decanters and wine glasses, some barrels of biscuits and forty pairs of boots were on credit. The $300 transaction was out of the same book as that other sharp real estate deal, Peter Stuyvesant's purchase of Manhattan from the Indians.

The Americo-Liberians aspired to transporting the civilising influence of their birthplace to Africa. The laws were codified at Cornell University; the constitution drafted at Harvard Law School. 'The love of liberty brought us here' was enshrined as the national motto. But over the years, like the accented vernacular based on English that was the *lingua franca*, their lofty ideals disintegrated into a pidgin culture.

The settlers set about exploiting the locals with a ruthlessness that far outstripped that of their former masters on the plantations. The first constitution was promulgated in 1847, the year Liberia became a state. 'We the people of the Republic of Liberia were originally the inhabitants of the United States of North America . . .' it began, tidily dismissing ninety-five per cent of the population, who were referred to as Aborigines. It is interesting to note that an article appearing in the *National Geographic* magazine in 1948 also referred to the indigenous people as 'Aborigines'.

It was written by Henry S. Villard, who served as Deputy Director in the State Department's Office of Near Eastern and African Affairs.

In reality, the state consisted of a coastal littoral twenty-five miles wide. No contact was made with the forested hinterland until the 1930s, when President Edwin J. Barclay travelled through the interior in a hammock carried by porters. It was still an unknown place of darkness run by traditional chiefs. During this epoch the League of Nations accused the government of hunting down its citizens and shipping them as slaves to the island of Fernando Po. There is still a place outside Monrovia called Smellnotaste. The hungry villagers chose the name because of the mouthwatering aromas that wafted on the breeze from Americo-Liberian kitchens.

By the time Ed and I got there, Monrovia's veneer of normality was cracking. In the weeks to come the town became an open-air morgue attended by scavenging dogs. The dead were so numerous, they lay where they fell, rotting in the sun. No one was safe once the rebels hit town. But these were the days when the murdered were still buried, despatched to the grave with haunting renditions of Negro spirituals. Martin Luther King's rallying cry, 'We Shall Overcome', was a favourite.

The outdoor funeral of the three town elders was held in their neighbourhood, Clay Ashland. You passed through gleaming green vegetation and bumped over dirt roads to get there. Clay Ashland was the heart of Americo-Liberian respectability. It had some interesting examples of antebellum architecture even though wood rot had long ago attacked the gabled roofs and dormer windows. The men wore chinos, sneakers and alligator shirts. Their wives prayed in church every Sunday beneath tiny hats with tiny veils *à la* Jackie Kennedy thirty years ago. On the day of the funeral, the mourners grouped beneath a louring sky. They were stunned and angry. The violence had shattered their staid suburban life. I think they knew the grisly murders were a foretaste of the anarchy that would soon touch them all. Women dabbed at their eyes and wept on their husbands' shoulders. Handkerchiefs were much in use that month to wipe away the tears and keep out the stench of death.

A young man approached as I watched the proceedings from the shade of a mango tree. 'They speak of peace. No one wants to open their mouth against this oppressive government. Why don't they just run the man [Doe] down? Run him down!' he said savagely.

Others greeted me with an awed 'How you, Miss Elizabeth?' That day was the first of many occasions when I was mistaken for Liz Blunt, the BBC radio's West Africa correspondent.

As a general rule of thumb, the African press is cowed into silence when the government hits adverse times. There were brave exceptions to this in Liberia where editors spoke out despite imprisonment and the closure of their offices. Yet they were unable to travel outside the capital. Liz's first-hand reporting from both sides of the lines had provided immediate coverage of the conflict since its inception. For most people, listening to the BBC news was the only way of finding out what was happening on their doorstep. They tuned in to Big Ben's chimes and the opening strains of 'Lilliburlero' with ritual regularity.

Liz looked like Peter Pan and had the unstinting courage of a warrior. Her listeners included the soldiers whose actions she sometimes reported on. They didn't like it much. When she started receiving death threats, the British ambassador, Michael Gore, hid her in his house. A few days before we arrived, she had been smuggled out of the country on a cargo ship. We all had the same feeling about the soldiers. They snuffed out life as casually as a candle. Liz sat in Abidjan champing to return, which she did less than three weeks later. She was something of a local heroine.

On that particular morning, Bishop George D. Brown spread his arms wide above a wooden coffin and raised his head to the oyster-grey sky. 'In spite of what has happened today, God has not forsaken us,' he intoned.

A chorus of mellifluous voices rose in defiant agreement. 'Oh yeah! Oh yeah!'

Part of the country's high-profile US heritage was a Southern brand of Christianity that formed the moral bedrock of urban society. It provided the only solace for the apprehension that scraped at every heart. The town's numerous Methodist, Episcopalian and Baptist churches became the forum for appeals to end the violence. Services were packed. The previous week one of the newspapers had printed Psalm 23, 'The Lord is my Shepherd', in the editorial column. There seemed nothing else left to say. The frustrated and frightened Monrovia residents had turned to the only one they knew was on their side – God.

You wondered, though, if He really was rooting for them. As the rebels' noose tightened around the town, so the soldiers became increasingly jittery. In response to rebel victories, as many as four-fifths of the army deserted, taking their weapons with them. Their replacements were conscripted youths who had been picked up off the streets. Many of them were petty criminals and pickpockets. I saw one with 'killer' painted on his helmet. Commander-in-Chief General Henry Dubar admitted that once he issued his men with ammunition, he could not trust them to obey orders.

The soldiers were everywhere, roaming the streets and riding in the back of pick-ups with their guns sticking up like antennae. Inevitably, they shook down motorists at road blocks for whatever they had on them – money, cigarettes, watches. My friend Michelle Faul, an Associated Press reporter, addressed them imperiously through tight lips. Ed gave them a lazy grin and enquired, 'How you boys doing?' When it came my turn, things sometimes got sticky. The Ministry of Information had mistyped the name on my press card. It said 'Mary Anne Elizabeth'. That gave rise to remarks I didn't want to hear. 'We don't like what you say 'bout us, Elizabeth. You'd better watch out.'

At night uniformed men clustered into death squads, combing the neighbourhoods of tin shacks and cinder-block houses for alleged rebel sympathisers. They pulled them out into the darkness and shot them. As commuters walked to work, they found bodies on the road, in the swamps and bush and on the beaches. Some had been decapitated, others castrated. Tens of thousands of Gio and Mano who lived in the capital or who had fled there to escape the fighting in the countryside were no longer safe.

Scores had sought refuge at the United Nations compound. Some days before we arrived, government troops had stormed the place and abducted and killed about thirty men. As a direct result of this, the UN closed its offices and evacuated its international staff. Meanwhile, the tally of atrocities mounted daily.

Monrovia straddles mangrove swamps on the western shoulder of the continent, a few degrees north of the equator just above the armpit. Before it became a charnel house, it was a pastiche of *Gone With the Wind* and Papa Doc's Haiti. The suburban bungalows on the beach front collected the breeze off the Atlantic Ocean and had scented frangipani trees in the garden. A few blocks away there were moss-encrusted houses raised off the ground on concrete blocks or boulders. Their sloping tin roofs framed windows where old men watched the world go by while ducks splashed in the drains and palms sagged in the lashing tropical downpours. In downtown Carey Street there were crack dens where men temporarily forgot the war. Outside the musty-smelling Holiday Inn (no connection to the international hotel chain) soldiers gang-raped young girls in the shadows.

The imprint of American culture, distorted by distance and time, was nevertheless much in evidence, just as it is in the Caribbean. The street stalls displayed packets of Marlboro cigarettes and Wrigleys chewing gum. There was Kraft salad dressing on sale in the supermarkets. The police force, which soon vanished off the streets, wore the cast-off summer uniforms of the New York Police Department. You could tell because the navy blue shirts still had the NYPD insignia sewn on to the shoulder.

I pointed out the Rooster Sudden Food Restaurant and the Surprise Electricity Store to Ed. He didn't agree the place was reminiscent of the United States. He was probably harbouring an image of the Partridge family's ordered, clapboard suburbia where nothing untoward ever took place. On that point he was right. That was the disquieting thing about Monrovia. Life's daily routine balanced precariously above a deep abyss. Even in Uganda, in the days when Idi Amin's State Research Bureau thugs tortured and killed at random, there had been a certain order amidst the chaos. Here was different. You sensed bedlam round every corner. You knew that beneath the bright colours lay a Hieronymus Bosch allegory of hell. From the moment you woke up, you wondered what nastiness lay in store for you that day.

Even in peacetime, a disquieting undercurrent flowed beneath the funky, jostling exterior. The faded gentility and religious devotion was counterbalanced by another, darker side of the national psyche that paid fealty to sorcery. Liberia was a crucible for the juju that was exported with the slaves. At first, it may have been a weapon of despair, wielded through secret acts performed around tongues of fire licking at the night. By the time it had been reimported to Africa with the freed slaves generations later, it had become voodoo. The resulting mix with indigenous witchcraft and dashes of Christianity was potent and pervasive. Few people were impervious to the supernatural. Leopard men were supposed to stalk the villages in the bush. As elsewhere in the region, ritual murder was common. Even in peacetime, men floated on the Atlantic swell bound to crosses, their bodies painted with hexes. The assumption can never be tested, but it is possible that political change might have followed a more decent course if its perpetrators had not believed that shadowy forces beyond their ken stalked their souls.

The current protagonists were no different in their beliefs. Both Charles Taylor and Samuel Doe had their own recipes for survival. Protective charms called *gris gris* hung beneath Charles Taylor's shirt. The rebel leader used the services of a *marabout*, a sort of Muslim soothsayer cum witch doctor. Taylor visited the *marabout* before launching his insurgency and paid for protection for himself and a dozen colleagues. Later, when the fighting subsided, Taylor sent an emissary to consult the *marabout* before attending the various rounds of peace talks. As it turned out, I was to ask the advice of the same *marabout* before the year was out. Like Taylor, I was seeking extramural assistance to bend the future in my favour. The *marabout* was a simple man who lived in a mud hut in the bush. I found his beatific presence reassuring. I presume Charles Taylor did too.

Samuel Doe, on the other hand, was believed to have chosen 'proofing'. There were certain witch doctors who could render their clients bulletproof, macheteproof, arrowproof or axeproof. The spells weren't always successful. A police official had shot himself to test his bulletproofing and died. Doe once boasted to reporters, 'No bullet can touch me. No knife can scratch me.'

So far he had been right. Over the course of the years, several plots against his life had been quashed. The most recent involved the former defence minister, Gray D. Allison. He had been found guilty of the ritual killing of a policeman. Allison had intended to use parts of his victim in a voodoo ceremony that would have ensured Doe's demise. The court martial had taken place the previous July. Allison was believed still to be awaiting the execution of his sentence, which was death by firing squad.

He had murdered J. Melvin Pyne, according to the opposing counsel's summation, 'with deadly weapons known as a blunt instrument and knife made of steel and iron, with which said J. Melvin Pyne was knocked on the head, his throat cut and severed, the heart and other vital parts extracted and his blood drained and collected in a container as required for ritualistic purposes through fetish black magic to obtain power, wealth and influence, satanic belief and exercise, and as a result, the deceased J. Melvin Pyne did there and then and in the peace of God die.' It wasn't just the grammar that was horrific.

Despite the recourse to juju, the embattled Samuel Doe, whose ten-year tenure as head of state was drawing to its inevitable close, must have been wondering if he was going to meet the same fate as his predecessor, William R. Tolbert Jr. The pyjama-clad Tolbert was found dead in his bed, disembowelled and with three bullets through his head. An eye had been gouged out for good measure. He was murdered by enlisted soldiers in the 1980 coup that brought Doe to power. At the time, the twenty-eight-year-old Doe was a master-sergeant. Along with his job promotion he and his wife and four children got to move house from an earthen-floored room in the barracks that had neither door nor glass in the windows to the marble-fronted Executive Mansion. It had been built for Tolbert by the Israelis at a cost of six million dollars. The coup ended a 143-year dynasty of decadent, colonial-style rule.

Power had slipped through the Americo-Liberians' fingers, but they still clung to their vanished grandeur. It was said their 'boys' knelt when serving food and crouched by bedroom doors early in the morning, poised to bring coffee at their masters' first stirring. Doe's crowd may have restructured the political hierarchy, but the social one remained intact. The beach front executions of thirteen of Tolbert's cabinet in front of a cheering crowd had been well publicised. Images of men in soiled underpants slumped away from telephone poles had horrified the world. What surprised me, though, was how few reprisals there had been against the Americo-Liberians after a century and a half of oppression. Now the native Liberians were beating the hell out of each other instead. So far, with the exception of the Clay Ashland murders, they had ignored the old guard.

It had happened in Kenya during the Mau Mau rebellion when Kikuyu slaughtered Kikuyu instead of the British. It was happening in South Africa with the township warfare between the Zulus' Inkatha Freedom Party and the Xhosa of the African National Congress. Hatred can be hard to focus. The African propensity for knocking the shit out of your neighbour remained a mystery to me.

The villagers in the bush didn't notice any change in the status quo either. Doe ruled by neglect, just as his predecessors had done. There was a smattering of middle class in the small towns, but for the most part, prosperity eluded the bulk of Liberians, who lived in the countryside in grinding poverty. So great was their mistrust of the government that a European who visited one flyblown village was told by the chief, 'Master, you buy everyone here and we work for you. Then you look after us.'

The strange thing about what was happening to Liberia was that it had been considered a still point on a heaving continent. The United States lauded its political stability and the studied eloquence of its rulers. President William V.S. Tubman's bombast and pompous attire (a frock coat and top hat) were overlooked. So was Tolbert's fiscal sleight of hand when he succeeded Tubman. The ordained Baptist minister and onetime chairman of the Organisation of African Unity was thought to have extracted some $200 million from the treasury and stashed it in US bank accounts.

Samuel Doe was even welcomed into the White House by Ronald Reagan. Reagan must have mislaid his cue card, for he addressed him as Chairman Moe. The social gaffe was less offensive than the US policy towards Liberia, predicated as it was on protecting strategic interests. Doe's record on human rights, democracy and economic management was pretty messy, but by that time (two years after seizing power) he had brushed up on his English and his appearance. He wore three-piece suits and owlish non-prescription spectacles. His hair was fluffed into an Afro every morning by a hairdresser.

Meanwhile, the leaching of the economy proceeded apace. After the 1980 coup, the Americo-Liberians and Lebanese merchants flushed some thirty million dollars out of the country. It was equivalent to about a quarter of the national currency base. Then Doe and his henchman took over. They behaved with aid money and commercial contracts like bears with a honey pot, while acres of worthless 'Doe dollars' were printed and circulated for domestic consumption. In April 1989 the United States warned it would have to invoke the Brooke Amendment and halt economic and military aid if at least seven million of $183 million owed wasn't paid by the following month. Doe responded by calling on private citizens to donate to the arrears fund, which they did. 'In my mind, I think it is America that owe us. We don't owe them,' he claimed with un-swerving arrogance.

The economy was based on rubber, timber, iron ore, diamonds and the registration of internationally owned ships. By the time the rebels invaded, it was collapsing. Loan arrears amounted to about twice the value of annual exports. Liberia was technically bankrupt, having mortgaged nearly all of the 1990 foreign exchange due from exporters in advance. It was hopeless. The IMF had threatened expulsion if repayments on the $310 million it was owed didn't start by August, and the Brooke Amendment still loomed large. By then, of course, Doe was concentrating on saving his skin, not the economy.

He tried to stall reality by issuing a series of meaningless communiqués. He offered to resign and call elections. He'd hold them sooner than he first said. He wouldn't stand again for president. The rebels, by now lurking around the Firestone estate thirty miles away, were impervious to his promises. Then Charles Taylor agreed to talks with the remnants of the Doe government in neighbouring Sierra Leone. The few ministers who had not yet fled the capital clung to the last shreds of hope for a peaceful solution as they listened to the BBC. Foreign press coverage was their only way of finding out how the talks were going. The telephone link between Monrovia and Freetown, the capital of Sierra Leone, was out of order.

In absurd contrast to this, I received a phone call from Washington one evening. The man on the other end introduced himself as Michael Hogan of Van Kloberg and Associates. He said Doe wanted to see me.

My byline was appearing regularly in the *Washington Times*. The stories were faxed to the information ministry (and probably Doe as well) the day they appeared on the streets in Washington. Now Doe wanted to tell me his version of events. He was spending part of his considerable fortune hiring a public relations firm to carry out the hopeless task of improving his image.

Most of the journalists, including Ed and myself, were staying in a vacated US embassy flat, ten minutes from Doe's headquarters. However, the interview was arranged through Washington. On several occasions Hogan phoned me, phoned Doe's office and then phoned me back. This triangular relationship eventually resulted in a summons to the Executive Mansion.

We were to be taken there by William Glay, a congressman who fronted Doe's financial transactions in partnership with Edward Slanger. They were as venal a couple as you could get, known to all as Sugar and Glucose. Glay was the president's cousin. It was said that in the wake of a 1985 coup attempt, he had personally killed some of the conspirators.

Half the national income was thought to be in the hands of five per cent of the population, most of them members of Doe's tribe, the Krahns. As we sat on the back porch of Glay's beach-front bungalow drinking ginger ale, I idly speculated just how much of that fifty per cent Glay could personally lay claim to. These boys knew no modesty when it came to accumulating money.

The lawn was shaded by flowering trees. A man cooked lunch in the garage, stirring something in a large tin bowl placed over a coal-filled oil drum. Ed was discussing the Philly '76ers basketball team with Glay's bodyguards. It was a homely scene except for the guns scattered around like holiday souvenirs.

Glay was sandwiched between Ed and me on his porch swing. He turned to me as we rocked gently back and forth. 'How long you been a journalist?'

'A long time.'

'You don' look dat old.'

'She's a lot older than you think,' joked Ed.

The swing juddered beneath us as Glay rounded on him. 'You rude to her, I hit you on de head,' he glowered, the perfect gentleman.

The conversation fizzled out after that, so we got into Glay's brand-new, navy-blue BMW with smoked windows and made for the mansion. Ed and I were in the back. Glay sat in the passenger seat in front while a bodyguard wearing a baseball cap drove. Ed nudged me and pointed at his feet. They were resting on an Uzi automatic.

Doe's house was guarded by about a thousand Krahn soldiers and members of the Israeli-trained Special Anti-Terrorist Unit. A typo in the last budget had transformed them into the Special Anti-Tourist Unit. On that count, they were doing a spectacularly good job. These presidential watchdogs were thought to be the authors of most of the nocturnal killing.

We were ushered into a marbled hall. It was badly in need of an interior decorator. We passed a statue of Jesus and fetched up by the lifts next to a bronze bust of Tubman on a pedestal. Beside it, in an ornate gold-leaf frame, hung a grainy photograph of the old Executive Mansion used by Tolbert before he built this one. It was pure *Gone With the Wind*. Porches ran around three of the storeys. The fourth and uppermost storey was trimmed with dormer windows. At the entrance, a soldier stood at ease by a sentry box, his gun aslope. Times had changed.

Ed sat down on a mock Louis Quatorze chair and made faces at a soldier dozing on a leather sofa who had a Kalashnikov draped across his knees and a hand grenade pinned to his shirt front. I gazed out on to rain-sodden palms across a balcony stacked with boxes of ammunition. Then I wandered off for a closer inspection of Doe's excruciating taste.

'What's your name?' The man wore camouflage dress and boots.

'Mary Anne Fitzgerald.'

'I seen ya reportin' evyweah.' He looked me up and down, a man eyeing a woman. At Michelle Faul's insistence, I had borrowed one of her dresses.

It was flowery and form-fitting. A bit too pretty, really. I wanted to be back in my dirt-encrusted trousers.

'No, you have not,' I said and turned on my heels.

'Those boys better keep away from you,' growled Ed.

Beneath us, in the basement, there were cells packed with Gios, Manos, lunatics and thieves. The floors were caked with excrement. The Krahn took them on to the beach and slit their throats or beat them senseless with their ammunition belts. The rest starved to death, for they were never fed.

It was a far cry from Doe's living conditions upstairs. He had retreated to his sixth-floor den where he lounged around in tracksuits or a baggy Donald Duck T shirt that came down to his knees. In the weeks to come, when the fighting was street-to-street, he was cut off from his troops and became totally isolated. The media described him as being 'holed up in his fortess-like mansion', but this was not the case. His troops had been whittled down to a force of about 150. A single, tripod-mounted Bren gun guarded the front steps. There weren't even any sandbags for gun emplacements because the soldiers were too lazy to dig up the sand.

Doe spent most of his time playing draughts, watching old movies and chatting on a radio telephone to the BBC or his wife Nancy, who had fled to their house in Wimbledon. Doe had hauled in a British engineer to fix up the communications system, which passed via satellite through Britain's Portishead aeronautical transmitting facility in Somerset.

When he spoke to Nancy for the first time in nearly a month, she couldn't believe it was him.

'Hello!' he shouted.

'Hello?'

'Hello!'

'Who's that?'

'It's me!' The response was a resounding ululation of joy. After that they chatted together daily.

Doe kept the engineer busy restoring his communications. He was in there most days, fixing things up around the mansion. It may sound astonishing that he was still in Monrovia at this late stage, when everyone who could had already fled. But there are always those who like to look over the precipice.

Usually, the businessmen are the buccaneer types who know how to turn a quick buck in times of crisis. Such was the Spaniard who was selling seats on the US-sponsored evacuation flights that were supposedly free. Some had interests to protect like the expatriate couple who remained behind to look after their chimpanzees. I never caught up with what finally happened to that menage, but last heard of the husband and wife were on valium and gin to calm their frayed nerves. They spent much of the time lying in the corridor of their house to escape the crossfire. The chimps, unfortunately, were being eaten by the soldiers. There was also an American woman who was a professor at the university. She remained behind in a blaze of patriotism, saying that Liberia was her country and she wasn't going to abandon it. You always get an oddball thrill-seeker or two as well, such as the couple who had been passing through and stayed on because they wanted to see what civil war was like.

Most of these people eventually left. They all had hazardous journeys out. Back in London, I commented to the engineer that it must have been a pretty frightening time. 'Not really,' he said, 'I get frightened when I'm in debt.'

During this later period, John Weseh Maclean, the Minister for Presidential Affairs, sat at an ancient typewriter taking down Doe's edicts. Maclean slept in the guesthouse in the garden and was the only cabinet member left. He had tried to leave on a chartered Soviet troop carrier bound for Sierra Leone, but was dragged off the aircraft at gunpoint by soldiers and taken back to the mansion. Most of the directives he typed out concerned the hoarding of rice. There were only a few sacks left in the palace. It was not unusual for the soldiers to go two days without eating.

While the loyal remnants of his troops went hungry, Doe dreamed of a genteel, scholarly life in exile. He confided to the British engineer that he hoped to do a master's degree in political science at Oxford or Cambridge. A thirst for learning was a hallmark of his rule. A semiliterate dropout when he became head of state, he diligently studied for a bachelor's degree in political science for three or four hours every afternoon. He liked to cite historical precedent when discussing Liberian politics. It's unlikely that Nero was part of his curriculum.

As it turned out, Doe funked the interview. Perhaps it was because he had been told there was a photographer with me and his Afro wasn't looking good that day. It was just as well. He had liked Ken Noble, the *New York Times* reporter, so much he had invited him to move into the mansion. I didn't fancy dossing down in the executive suite.

One morning we attended the opening session of the court martial of three men accused of the Clay Ashland murders. It was the government's first and only move to restore a semblance of order and justice. We were expectant, for an information ministry official had confided to us, 'You're going to watch some executions.'

The trial was held at the Barclay Training Centre in a spacious wood-panelled room that must have once been the barracks' NAAFI. Rows of freestanding shelves had been shoved into the gloom at the back. They stood empty except for a few sachets of Provençal herbs and some bottles of orange-blossom water. The public consisted solely of the foreign and local press.

Someone evidently thought that age would imbue the proceedings with gravitas. Isaac Nyeplu, the advocate general, was not much younger than the grizzled members of the four-man military tribunal whom he swore in. Colonel E. Doe Gibson, the prosecuting counsel, was so old he had begun to shrivel. The accused sat on straight-backed chairs beneath a ceiling fan that sliced away ineffectually at the thick air. They looked unconcerned and relaxed, as if the whole thing were a charade. One of them read a newspaper while the tribunal stenographer struggled to roll sheets of paper into his typewriter.

It soon emerged that none of the prisoners had lawyers to represent them, which irritated the advocate general. 'This is not a football game where spectators go and cheer,' he barked. When instructed to name his lawyer, one of the accused pointed at Gibson. Everyone, including the prisoners, laughed. 'The prosecutor is not your defence. He's the one who's going to cut you to pieces!' Nyeplu roared.

At this point, an almighty row broke out as Nyeplu castigated the prosecuting counsel for failing to apprise the prisoners of their rights. Gibson defended himself with high-decibelled vigour. The trial rapidly spiralled from farce to slapstick. 'Order!' shouted Nyeplu for the fifth time. He beat a tattoo with his gavel and adjourned for the day.

We rushed over to interview the prisoners, who were still sitting on their chairs. Jeff Bartholet, the *Newsweek* correspondent, leant over Major Henry K. Johnson, pen poised above notebook. 'Are you afraid?' he asked.

Johnson shrugged. 'I'm not afraid. Afraid of what?'

Jeff persisted. 'Do you think you'll be shot tomorrow?'

Johnson gave him an insolent look. 'How do I know?'

The press was barred from attending any further sessions, but as far as I know, the promised executions never took place.

One evening, Ed and I drove to St Peter's Lutheran Church. We wanted to talk to some of the 4,000 Gio and Mano people who had sought refuge behind the compound's rickety metal gates. They were jammed into an area less than an acre in size. There were six toilets. Pastor Allison was concerned there would be an outbreak of cholera. However, it was the spectre of violent death, not disease, that worried the Gio and Mano who washed their babies in plastic paint containers and waited for the darkness to settle. Whenever a truckload of soldiers drove past the Red Cross flags that drooped in the stillness, a frisson of apprehension rippled through the crowd. The walls could easily be scaled and the Geneva Convention meant nothing.

The following Sunday we attended a service at the Providence Baptist Church on Ashmun Street. Hundreds of Americo-Liberians packed the teak pews. It was a hot, sultry day and the besuited men sponged their beaded brows with clean white handkerchiefs. The passion rose as we worked our way through the prayers and hymns to the sermon.

'God is looking for a man. There are men in the Executive Mansion,' cried Reverend Momolue Diggs.

'Yes!' chanted the congregation.

'There are men in the legislature . . .'

'Yes!'

'. . . judiciary . . .'

'Yes!'

'. . . army . . .'

'Yes!'

'. . . but where are the men of God?' The bumble-bee drone of a transport plane could be heard in the ensuing silence.

'Let us join hands and beseech the Lord for peace,' the reverend commanded. Satin and tulle shifted and stirred. The congregation sighed as it rose to its feet. A girl brushed lifeless fingers across my palm, forlorn offerings attached to a thin arm. My other hand disappeared into the meaty grip of the man to my right. He looked at me and a smile passed across his face.

'We can't do this alone, Jesus! We call on you to give us strength!' Beyond the slatted shutters a scream trembled in the air. I wasn't sure if it was a girl or a goat.

'Aaaaaay-aaaaaay-men!' we sang.

The last evacuation flight was scheduled for that afternoon. (As it turned out, the last flight was a month later.) Lord Copper had ordered me back to Abidjan. I wanted to stay. Doe had relented and was talking of an interview for the following day. Besides, I was beginning to enjoy myself. The two army officers who kept Ambassador Michael Gore and his dogs company at the British residence had offered to cook me dinner. Even better, they were tennis players. The plan was to tell the desk there were no seats on the plane, then hitch a ride out on the deck of a cargo ship later in the week.

This quest for entertainment may sound callous in the midst of tragedy, but we needed light relief. Monrovia was a city under siege, and some pretty nasty things were happening outside our US embassy flat. As soon as we opened the front door, we were reminded of it. The embassy had pinned up a notice of glorious sangfroid. It said something like, 'If a man in uniform comes to the door, remain calm and try not to excite him. If at all possible, do not let him into your apartment.'

In the beginning, some of the shops and offices and restaurants remained open as people clung to the vestiges of routine. It was at night that you began to feel jittery. We ate out to let off steam and then hoped to hell we wouldn't be ambushed or shot by soldiers on the way back. Ed had taken a room in a hotel, which was empty except for the military, to use as a dark room. Often he came back around midnight, ducking and dodging the soldiers along back alleys. I was always relieved when he walked through the door unharmed.

Journalists have been known to organise diving contests and whist drives during coups. The alternatives are to drink too much, chain smoke, have an affair with another journalist and quarrel. By comparison, a few sets of tennis and some good cuisine was a pretty harmless way of relieving the tension. And tension there sometimes was.

Numbers fluctuated as reporters and photographers came and went, but on average there were a dozen people dossing down in a flat designed to accommodate a family of four. I was lucky. As the only other woman, Michelle had offered to share her double bed in the master bedroom. Ed had staked out a patch of floor next to the dining-room table. There were two more beds in the second bedroom and three sofas. Everyone else slept on the floor. Considering the circumstances, our lodgings were remarkably sane. There was still water and electricity, albeit sporadic. Sometimes the lights went when we were rushing to meet our deadlines. On these occasions I put a flashlight in my mouth and shone it on to the Tandy. Other people used candles. The cook who worked for the American couple that had been evacuated appeared daily and did our washing. Michelle kept an eye on the housekeeping and made sure we always had a supply of food.

From time to time, however, arguments flared over sharing: the food, the bathroom, the information we had collected during the day, the one telephone line we used to file our stories and Ed's pictures to the papers. All in all, though, we were a pretty harmonious family.

On that last Sunday Michael Gore threw a pizza lunch for some of the few expatriates eccentric enough still to be in town. His philosophy was the same as ours: if you don't do something to take your mind off all this shit, you'll go crazy. I arrived with a bathing suit, towel and tennis racket. Heavens knows where I found them all.

'I've come to play,' I grinned.

'Bad news, I'm afraid,' Michael said. 'Arthur says the boat's off. Some chaps from the French embassy got there before you. There's no room.'

'But I'm very thin. I don't take up much space.'

'I can see that. Question of life jackets, apparently. Not enough to go around.'

At Spriggs Payne the rain pelted down on a press of Liberians frantically waving boarding passes at the pilot. Ed scythed his way through the crowd with me in tow. Then he stepped behind and shoved me on to the plane steps. 'Get your butt up there,' he complained. 'What the hell are you waiting for?'

Back in England, as the weeks went by, I followed the unfolding chaos by any means I could and worried for those left behind.

One day I had an argument with Tara. 'I hate being in London,' she protested.

'Do you think I like it any more than you do?' I shouted back and slammed the door on her disappearing back.

A few seconds later it opened and her face peeked round. 'You should have said that before. It makes it easier for me and Petra to know you hate it too.'

At that moment the phone rang. It was Andy Hill, a friend from Reuters. 'Fitz, they broke into St Peter's Church last night and killed everyone. Women with skulls smashed in by rifle butts. Their babies still tied to their backs. Corpses draped over the altar. The wires are talking about 600.'

The tears were useless but they came anyway while Tara stroked my hair. 'Poor Mummy. Poor Liberians. Our own troubles aren't important, are they?' she whispered.

The massacre happened at the instigation of my erstwhile intermediary, William Glay, according to one of his former girlfriends. By then, Monrovia was a ghetto of horror, scrapped over by three separate forces. Prince Yormie Johnson now led a splinter rebel faction. Johnson claimed he didn't want to be president. He just wanted to get Charles Taylor. A former army captain, he was generally considered to be a nicer guy than Taylor. However, his judgment had been clouded by an overuse of amphetamines. He stayed awake two or three days on the trot in order to command his untutored band of 200 to 400 men personally. At one point, Johnson shot dead one of his own men as he stood before the rebel leader handcuffed to a Catholic Relief Services worker. Johnson had accused them of 'profiteering'. In fact, they were distributing rice to the hungry. Alistair Sinclair, an Associated Press photographer who recorded the murder on film, said afterwards he thought Johnson was drunk. The man obviously needed a rest.

During the two-pronged advance into town, the guerrillas had cut off not only the water and electricity but also the telephone link to the outside world. The shops had been looted and burned. People dug in the dirt in search of water and roots. The front lines looked like crazy paving and changed hourly. You went to sleep with the rebels and woke up with the Armed Forces of Liberia.

One morning the Italian ambassador was scanning the beach with his opera glasses and a decapitated body came into his field of vision. 'The authorities ought to clear it away,' he commented, overlooking the fact there was no authority left. Michael Gore sent someone down to bury the corpse. Soon, even this minimum civility became impossible. About 300 bodies littered the shoreline below the British residence.

Those who could, fled, but several brave diplomats and emergency workers felt it their duty to stay. Gore and other ambassadors used to drive down to St Peter's every evening to boost the morale of the Gio and Mano and 'show the flag' to the soldiers. Short of armed intervention, there was little more they could do. When the massacre eventually occurred, it was like a Greek tragedy. Inevitable and played out before an audience.

By this time, the Red Cross workers had decamped to the flats Ed and I had stayed in. The US embassy, which was a few hundred yards up the street, was guarded by a detachment of marines who stood watch on sandbagged scaffolding. It was in a battle zone between the army and Johnson's men.

Pastor Allison maintained links through a diplomatic walkie-talkie network. One afternoon in late July he came on the air. 'The soldiers have come round and say they want to come in. I'm worried.' The US diplomat to whom he was speaking replied that it was too dangerous to cross town and he would have to do the best he could. At 2 a.m. Allison came on the air again against a background of gun shots. 'The soldiers are climbing over the walls,' he pleaded.

'We are unable to help you right now. Keep your head down and use your own judgment. Stay away from the windows and doors,' came the answer. Horrified listeners stayed glued to their receivers as the night-long slaughter went out on the air. Afterwards, the US embassy tried to play down the incident, putting out a figure of 250 dead. People who had gone there and counted the bodies said it was more like four hundred or even six hundred, most of them women and children. When journalists visited the compound in October, three months later, the corpses were still there.

On that particular night, the British engineer happened to be a patient in the only hospital that was still operational. He was critically ill with malaria. He later recounted to me the scene the following morning.

'They brought all these people in from the Lutheran church. I got up to see if I could help. It was ghastly. There were tiny babies with their hands chopped off and things like that. Just dying on the ground, actually. They went to the church once and picked up what they could with the ambulances and cars they've got. The second time they [the soldiers] fired on them. There were bullet holes in the ambulance. Then the army turned up at the hospital the day after that and said they were going to execute Dr Poto and various other black doctors. [There was a Médecins sans

Frontières team working there as well.] They got them all in the back of the truck and were sitting there with pistols at their heads. They said "Now we're going to drive you down to the beach and finish you." ' Dr Poto and his colleagues were rescued by the Special Anti-Terrorist Unit.

By mid-August the ICRC and Médecins sans Frontières, judging conditions too dangerous to work in, had left. (They returned later.) Several journalists stuck it out, often at considerable personal risk. They were detained, beaten, accused of being spies, caught in firefights and ambushes and, on one final occasion that sent the remnants of the press rushing for the Côte d'Ivoire border, subjected to a mock execution.

My friend Gill Tudor of Reuters was amongst these stayers on. Gill is in her late twenties, practical and meticulous about her reporting. A reliable sort who looks as if she would be good in a crisis. She recounted her month-long stint with the rebels over lunch at an Italian restaurant in Abidjan. It was her second foreign assignment.

'I wanted to go in for my own experience because it was something I had never been exposed to before. It was kind of important for me to push myself, so I stuck with the photographer, pretty far forward. I thought I would get used to the gunfire, but actually I got more and more scared the longer it went on. I don't like adrenalin. I got very tired of feeling scared. The turning point came when I was trapped under fire. I remember lying there thinking what a fucking stupid way to get killed.

'When I got back to the house, I felt almost hysterical that I was relatively safe. I sat on the covered verandah on my own, hearing the rain falling and thinking, "At this particular moment, I do not have to worry about being shot." I didn't know whether to laugh or cry.'

She told me most of the rebels were cowards who preferred looting to fighting. This had worked fine until they reached Monrovia, where they met last-ditch resistance from the Krahn soldiers. Many were teenagers who got some Dutch courage from smoking dope. 'They were terrible fighters, most of them. There were some who were a bit trained. You know, the key guys, the foreign-trained ones. Most of them were just acting out war films, probably modelling themselves on Sylvester Stallone. You had extraordinary scenes like one little guy leaping out into the middle of the road and spraying bullets everywhere, leaping from one foot to the other.

'I only saw one person killed before my eyes. The rebels had found some bullets and part of a soldier's uniform in a hut belonging to this skinny old man. They were interrogating him and knocking him around. He was terrified. Babbling. He let out he was Krahn. It was inevitable that at some stage he would get killed. Suddenly one of the rebels pushed him away and somehow you intuitively knew. This guy raised his gun and shot him. He fell back on to the grass verge, bleeding but not dead. I wasn't sure what the rebel said, but it sounded like "These motherfuckers killed my sister." It would explain why they suddenly snap and kill these guys.

'People who know Liberia say there's always been an edge of lunacy to the place. I know I haven't seen it at its best, but to me it's the arsehole of the world.'

The political stalemate might have dragged on for months if Doe hadn't decided to leave his mansion to negotiate with the enemy. No one knew for sure why he did it. Some said he wanted to hand over power to a caretaker coalition. Others thought the Americans inveigled him into it. This could have been true. The three-week ceasefire agreed between Doe and Prince Johnson expired that day. Meanwhile Taylor was pushing through Monrovia's eastern suburbs towards the city centre. Time was running out. No one, including the Americans, wanted Taylor in the Executive Mansion.

Doe had an obsessive hate for the rebel leader. Taylor had been the only civilian member on Doe's ruling military council in the early days of his rule. Doe felt he had betrayed their friendship. He planned to stand down in favour of an interim government once Taylor had been brought to heel. As far as Doe was concerned, his resignation was still several months away.

Doe's immediate anxieties focussed on his anticipated academic life. 'I'm looking forward to relaxing, but I wouldn't like people to ask me about all this when I get to England,' he confided to the British engineer. Again, contrary to press reports, Doe exercised enormous willpower during this period. He wasn't drinking or smoking *ganja*. He remained lucid, if a little out of touch with reality. Whatever the reason for his precipitate action, Doe was probably getting restless, sitting in his den all on his own. Maybe he just wanted a change of scenery.

It was Sunday, 9 September. An offshore breeze stirred the palms. Slate-grey breakers tormented the shoreline. Down at the port Liz Blunt and Abubakar Sadiq of the BBC Hausa service were waiting to interview General Arnold Quainoo. Quainoo, a Nigerian, headed the West African peacekeeping force that had landed a fortnight earlier. The Economic Community Monitoring Group (ECOMOG), as it was called, consisted of troops from Nigeria, Ghana, Guinea, Gambia and Sierra Leone. The military intervention was a first for post-colonial Africa. So few heads of state could lay just claim to leadership that they were loath to violate the sovereignty of their neighbours. They feared that once the precedent had been set, it could rebound on them. Now here they were despatching their military to Liberia despite their cannier instincts. That was how messy the fighting had become. Suddenly there was a flurry of excitement. Doe had arrived in a motorcade of flashing lights, sirens and dozens of bodyguards. Liz takes up the tale: 'We moved to the foot of the stairs, microphones at the ready. Then, confused shouting – Johnson's men were there. Soon they were striding up and down stairs, loud and threatening. Voices rose, guns were being cocked. We stepped back, ready to duck behind a filing cabinet. Then a Nigerian officer grabbed me. "In there. Lie down. Lie down." Someone pulled Sadiq the other way. Prince Johnson came into the office where I was, shouting and raving, two ECOMOG officers trying to calm him. I saw the hands of one of them shaking as he tried to open a can of beer for Johnson. Then I heard Johnson yelling, "Men, open fire! Open fire!" And that was it. For an hour and a half I lay on the floor in the middle of a deafening gunbattle. I could hear Johnson. "Let's get Doe. We'll get him this time." ECOMOG officers were begging, pleading for sanity. Every time it stopped and I raised my head, the firing started again. Finally there was silence, stunned silence. The survivors crept out. The corridor was pooled with blood. Bodies were everywhere. And President Doe was gone.'

Over sixty presidential bodyguards lay dead. The ECOMOG soldiers hadn't fired a shot.

They took Doe to a suburban bungalow on Bushrod Island that Johnson had converted into his headquarters. Doe's hands were tied tightly behind his back. He had been shot in both legs and was bleeding profusely. Johnson's men were swaggering and squealing with delight. The Anglo-Saxons used to put a price on a man's life as compensation for those he had slain. This 'buying back' was known as wergild. Doe was to pay, too, for the slaughter of the Gio and Mano he had sanctioned. It was the ritual murder that consummates ethnic conflict. But before death there was to be torture. In Africa you sacrifice your flesh.

'His hands were pinioned behind him, a knife was passed through his cheeks, to which his lips were noosed like the figure of eight; one ear was cut off, and carried before him; the other hung to his head by a small bit of skin; there were several gashes in his back, and a knife was thrust under each shoulder blade; he was led with a cord passed through his nose, by men disfigured with immense caps of shaggy black skins, and drums beat before him.'

This scene was witnessed by a man called Bowdich in Kumassi, a town in Ghana which is not so many miles from Monrovia. The human sacrifice was made to appease the shades of those who had departed before. The year was 1817. Nineteenth-century missionaries in West Africa were constantly running into these barbaric displays. One can only surmise that the ritual disfigurement, such as amputating the ears, was passed down from father to son as part of oral history. Did Johnson's men realise they were upholding tradition, that the mutilation of Doe drew upon the essence of a cultural heritage steeped in witchcraft?

Johnson must have felt the stirrings of ceremony, for he ordered his camera crew to record the occasion on film. A month later he replayed what transpired to journalists whom he had invited to his Bushrod Island house. Johnson, a former army captain, sat swigging Budweiser beneath a picture of Christ. Beyond the verandah children played in the rain. Images of rebels flickered across the screen of a colour TV as Johnson's wife fast-forwarded to Doe, stripped down to his underpants and staring up at his tormentors.

There are gashes on his head and face. 'I want to say something if only you will listen to me,' he pleads.

'Cut off his ears.' It is Johnson's voice. He says it softly.

The rebels lie Doe down flat and stand on him. Doe screams as a knife slices through his ear.

The rebels watching the TV screen clapped.

Doe drops his head forward. He is pursing his lips and trying to blow away the blood that is dripping from his head and face on to his chest. He is crying. The rebels despise this show of weakness. One of them shoots him again.

Afterwards, they took him down to the river and questioned him. How much money had he stolen from the Liberian people? What had he done with it? Doe kept protesting his innocence to the last so they made him surrender his forces to 'Field Marshall Johnson' and then left him. Throughout the night he pleaded with his guard to loosen his bonds and give him a drink of water. He cried a lot, too, as he sat there on the bank. Around 3 a.m. the whimpers and the tears stopped. His death was probably caused by massive loss of blood from one of the femoral arteries. Or it might have been heart failure from sheer fright.

The next day they pushed the body through town in a wheelbarrow. A couple of fingers were missing. So were the testicles. People slashed at the corpse with knives. Each thrust of steel was a declaration of independence. They were the powerful ones now. Or so they thought. Their power didn't count for much. The butchery and fighting and starvation continued for over a year.

I suppose it is fruitless to conjecture what would have happened if the United States had followed the French example in the Central African Republic and ousted Doe in an overnight coup. Or even called on the by then deeply unpopular leader to step down. In September, the Assistant Secretary of State for African Affairs, Herman Cohen, visited the region for the first time, three months after Monrovia began to disintegrate. He urged an end to the conflict, to no avail.

Could the 2,000 Marines stationed offshore not have prevented the bloodshed? Why were they never sent in to save civilian lives, not least the 600 who were massacred at St Peter's Church? The invasion of Somalia two years later illustrated the United States could act quickly on military intervention if it wanted to. The deployment of 20,000 troops in a matter of days was ostensibly a humanitarian operation to alleviate a famine. No one mentioned that Somalia guards the Red Sea or that anarchy in the region might disrupt the supply route for much of the West's oil. But Liberia was of no conceivable interest to the Bush administration. With the Cold War over, Africa was no longer regarded by the West as a battleground between Marxism and capitalism. The West's attention had battened on to the Middle East and Eastern Europe instead.

Nevertheless, many of us – journalists, diplomats, emergency workers and certainly the Liberians – considered the United States had been delinquent in its obligations as patron state. The horrors of Liberia's civil war could have been prevented even though the West African peacekeeping force failed in this task. Yet just at the moment when the demand for democracy threatened to spark tribally inspired violence across the continent, Africa was being left increasingly to its own resources. The Liberian tragedy underlined a shift in Western attitudes towards Africa. With the exception of a few countries where there was trade and investment, such as Kenya and the Côte d'Ivoire, the West was losing interest in black Africa. When the shit hit the fan, Africa's former patrons weren't going to clean up the mess. It was a sobering message which African leaders ignored at their peril.

8

Witchcraft

He hath awakened from the dream of life –
'Tis we, who lost in stormy visions, keep
With phantoms an unprofitable strife,
And in mad trance, strike with our spirit's knife
Invulnerable nothings.
From *Adonais* by Percy Bysshe Shelley

A few column inches in the local newspaper catches the eye, 'Beheadings Terrorise Mozambique'. We learn that on 29 June, 1991, the Renamo rebels massacred people in the town of Lalaua and nearby villages. The rebels lined up the severed heads of the dead on the shelves of shops, a witness said. Does this make sense? Of course not. So the Reuters report chooses its words carefully.

'A possible reason' is revenge against a 'quasi-religious cult' called the Naparamas. It is led by a 'Christian mystic' named Manuel Antonio who takes his men into battle using only bows and arrows. Antonio's followers 'believe' his 'medicine' makes them bulletproof. Over the past two years they have inflicted heavy defeats on Renamo. Why have they beaten the rebels, who are armed with guns? Because the rebels are 'superstitious', Reuters says.

There was a time when I would have said, 'How disgusting!' Now I can look beyond the barbarity to read a meaning. The story is about hope, faith, fear, obedience to supernatural powers: the stuff of which religion is made. The Naparamas enlisted the aid of spirits and magic for their battles. It scared the hell out of the Renamo guerrillas because they subscribed to these things too.

233

To understand African beliefs, we must leap beyond the rational to explore a world where truth is intangible and reality displays many aspects. To travel here calls for intuition, not intellect. The supernatural cannot be tested through hypothesis.

Physicists would agree that all matter is energy. It is called the theory of relativity. They would also concur that matter, or atoms, cannot be destroyed. It merely assumes a different form. So there is a kind of cosmic energy dancing through the world, keeping it in flux, changing shape and form through time. This is a phenomenon we can evaluate, but our perceptions are not bound by what we can see and touch or what we can measure.

Dreams and drugs and meditation, even daydreaming, remove the brain's filters to expose other dimensions of the world about us. Belief, too, can unveil a reality that has no scientific explanation. Who is to say what can and cannot happen on these different levels of truth where all is alive and nothing is only itself? In traditional African religion the universe moves by spirit reacting on spirit. Matter is interchangeable. So who can refute with absolute certainty that a man can become a leopard or a leopard can become a man?

And how can I be 'factual' as a Reuters editor would demand? Impossible. I can only tell you what I saw myself and learned from others.

There is a telling difference between the traditional Western and African perceptions of universal order. Africans do not believe in chance or accident. Everything is preordained. Our fate was written when we were born. The only way to alter it is through the intervention of spirits, who bend what we might call cosmic energy to the advantage of their supplicants. Spirits live in trees, bushes, blades of grass, which are their 'resting places'. Each animal has its own spirit. We too have spirits who attach themselves to us. They guide us through life just as guardian angels do.

Many West Africans believe in both good and evil spirits. There are three benevolent forces – genies, ancestors and minor gods. They protect us from the evil forces and act as our intermediaries with a pantheon of supernatural beings who are too exalted to communicate with directly. Traditional religion is nevertheless monotheistic. These thunder, river, snake, chameleon and smallpox gods, or fetishes, in turn pay fealty to a Supreme Being. Professor Seraphin Essané, head of the department of African religions at the Abidjan university in Côte d'Ivoire, compared devotees of the thunder, river and snake cults to the Anglicans, Protestants and Catholics of the Christian faith. 'This religion touches a little on magic. It's what we call in Africa the religion of power. It's useful because it resolves man's problems with nature and on a social level. But it isn't the same as Christianity,' he told me.

All these spirits must be placated and honoured through sacrifice or they might rob us of our health, our sanity, our very breath. The sacrifice is usually a chicken or goat or white bull, but it is consistently said that the right amount of money can buy more potent magic obtained through the sacrifice of babies and young children.

There is historical precedent for this. Along the west coast of Africa nineteenth-century missionaries used to write home with alarming descriptions of human sacrifices. They were particularly prolific during periods of war. It was customary, for instance, for the children of enemy warriors who had been slain in battle to be offered up to the gods. A Gambian chief called Kemmingtan sacrificed a twelve-year-old girl by having her feet planted in the ground. He watched as she was coated with clay until she smothered. This grisly totem was meant to keep intruders at bay.

Reverend Thomas B. Freeman, a Wesleyan missionary, wrote the following account of his visit to the Ghanaian town of Kumassi in 1839. 'Throughout the day I heard the horrid sound of the death drum, and was told in the evening that about twenty-five human victims had been sacrificed, some in the town, and some in the surrounding villages; the heads of those killed in the villages being brought into the town in baskets. I fear there will be more of this awful work tomorrow.'

Most West Africans wear charms, known as *gris gris*, tied to their upper arms or around their waist. Designed to ward off evil spirits, talismans vary. In Togo and Benin, parts of dead animals are sold from stalls in the market place. In Senegal, people wear scraps of paper inscribed by *marabouts*, Muslim holy men, which are encased in red leather pouches.

We all need a recipe for survival or an explanation for why things have gone wrong. Sometimes it is on the trivial level of superstition, which falls into the realm of magic. Why else do we touch wood, skirt round ladders or, in my case, tap on door and window frames? Sometimes it is to see the future when we don't know which way to turn. In the West we resort to psychics and tarot cards. In Africa, it is tribal diviners and monkeys' knuckles.

We also enlist the offices of higher beings to keep an eye out for us, which we call religion. Surely there is a parallel between carrying a St Christopher and wearing an amulet for protection. Or between Abraham's attempt to immolate Isaac to appease Jehovah and sacrificing a goat to a household god.

The injustices of poverty are fertile ground for the seeds of belief, whatever the continent. Hindu beggars and cripples work their way up a ladder of reincarnations to become one with *nirvana*. In the peasant communities of Latin America and southern Europe men and women with furrowed faces believe the drudgery of this world will be rewarded in a Catholic heaven.

Perhaps the simplest way to define the difference between religion and magic is submission and intervention. The religious submit to the will of higher beings while the devotees of magic appeal to spirits or gods actually to alter the course of events.

There is white magic, which claims to heal and protect. And there is black magic with its undertow of envy, greed and fear. If you covet your neighbour's wife, you put a spell on him. If you fall ill, your neighbour is jealous of your material success and has put a spell on you. Black magic can also be a safety valve for community tensions. In the Tanzanian bush, witches are blamed for a variety of misfortunes from cows that don't yield milk to stillbirths and drought. Once the unfortunate women have been identified, they are subjected to a summary trial by the villagers and invariably condemned. Sometimes they are stoned to death. Otherwise they are cast out and left destitute. They end up in towns as beggars and prostitutes.

To the outsider, the notion that incantations and potions can alter fate may sound absurd. Call it sorcery, witchcraft, black magic or juju, in Africa it seems to work. When domestic or commercial crises arise, many Africans – from presidents to beggars – have resorted to the uncharted powers of the supernatural for help. So have I.

While I was living in London, I discovered a schism in my articles of faith. As an African, I believed in fate and magic. As a Westerner, I suspected I willed my own destiny. Only one thing was certain. Someone had made an awful hash of my life. I had been expelled from the only country I wanted to live in. I had uprooted my family without being able to offer them an alternative home. I was unable to be with my friends. I had resigned from my job. My financial security was tenuous. I wasn't particularly happy.

The whole situation was so awful that 'mid-life crisis' was an inadequate description. Who was responsible for all this mess? Surely it wasn't me? I had the fugitive suspicion it was. So I decided I had better come to terms with myself. After all, I didn't want to create any more catastrophe.

The search for self-knowledge and serenity can plunge you into religion, take you on an exploration of the paranormal or start with a physical journey. I was to dabble in the African version of both religion and the paranormal, but I opted to begin with travel.

Blaise Pascal, the seventeenth-century French mathematician and philosopher, said that our restlessness can be defined by the inability to sit quietly in a room. Travel, he reflected, diverts us from our despair. If that is the case, then travellers are the same as alcoholics or workaholics, who deny their own melancholy by creating a surrogate situation – addiction to the bottle or the office. In the case of the traveller, it is addiction to movement and change.

I wasn't sure I agreed entirely with this theory. The Samburu do it because they must. When I walked with them, of course, I was proving my 'Samburu-ness'. Robert, Bosco, Chopiro and the others had nothing to prove. They were being what they were – nomads. Could travellers, I wondered, be obeying a primitive imperative to migrate just as the Samburu do? We have been settled for centuries. Our journeys are not predicated on survival – the search for rain, grazing, food. Without purpose to our trips, we are no longer travellers. We are wanderers. Is this why we mount expeditions, write books, study alien societies and environments? Do we feel obliged to inject a sense of purpose into our escape into the unknown? Are we seeking credibility for our malaise?

One of the greatest travellers of our time, Wilfred Thesiger, had no such doubts. As far as I know, he never examined his wanderlust. He simply did what he liked doing best, which was to live rough in wild places. Thesiger slept in a tent or under the stars until he was in his early seventies. Then he pandered to his reclusive nature and lengthening years by retiring to a tiny wooden cottage outside Maralal. It stands next to the house he built for his Samburu foster son, Lawe Leboyare, who is the town mayor.

I first met Thesiger in 1976 when filming a Samburu circumcision ceremony in the juniper forests above the town. The occasion had begun on an acrimonious note, for when the circumcisor saw the camera, he downed tools and demanded more money. The elders soon put paid to his greed by suggesting none too gently that he shut up and get on with the job. During all this, Thesiger strode across the cow pats and stood before me. Although he had already greeted the men in our party, until then he had treated me as if I was invisible. He thrust his craggy nose forward. 'Bloody women, you always go and mess everything up!' he said crossly. Later, I saw him crouching over the boys, shaking antibiotic powder out of a plastic bottle on to their raw penises as if he was salting a stew. He actually circumcised a few of the boys himself. One of them was Lawe.

When we met again in Maralal, more than ten years had passed. Thesiger was fuming over a telegram from James Wilde, a *Time* correspondent based in Nairobi. Thesiger's autobiography *A Life of My Choice* had recently hit the bestseller list in Britain and Wilde was seeking an interview. The telegram was designed to find a crack in Thesiger's well-known misanthropic exterior. Wilde had addressed it 'To My Lord Explorer'.

'He's a fool if he thinks it pleases one. He's ridiculous,' Thesiger sniffed.

Despite this display of stuffiness, time had mellowed the old man. He was disconsolately nursing a week-old toothache and wondering if he should seek the limited services of the government doctor. He was so grateful for the antibiotics my friend Ursula gave him, he invited us both to join him for lunch.

We chatted as we ate goat stew and *posho* out of small tin bowls. I was keen to discover why a man should spend his adult life roaming the globe. Had he, I wondered to myself, acquired insights on life that would enlighten us all? It soon became apparent Thesiger wasn't long on philosophy. Prompted to name the pinnacles and troughs of his extraordinary existence, he swatted a fly with some plastic netting tied to the end of a stick and pondered.

'Excitement,' he decided, and the shame of accepting a hare's liver from his Bedu companions in the Empty Quarter. 'It was more than my share,' he said with genuine regret.

Thesiger's life amongst far-flung tribes from the Hindu Kush to Marrakesh proved him as fearless an explorer as Livingstone or Stanley. However, he shunned duty to Queen, country and God (which motivated Livingstone) as much as personal glory and reward (which motivated Stanley). He never made a formal study of the peoples he travelled with or the countryside he walked through. He found writing excruciatingly difficult and only committed his wanderings to paper under considerable pressure from friends. He didn't give a damn about sharing his experiences which is why he was my hero. He also hated acclaim, so I prudently kept my feelings to myself.

Even the Samburu admired Thesiger. The young men recalled the excitement of watching him appear over the dusty horizon at the head of a train of camels. He used to give them boxing lessons. Several of the Samburu who had been to school had read his books. In his unwilling role as an adventurer, he transported them beyond the mundane cargo of sick cows and drought.

It was the Samburus' respect for Thesiger, who travelled for the sake of it, that led me to believe that at some point in our lives we should all make journeys that have no apparent purpose. Although it was not the case with Thesiger, impromptu wandering affords the time to embark on a bit of spiritual first aid. Whether the departure is prompted by ennui or crisis, it amounts to the same thing – dissatisfaction with the status quo. At the outset, we probably blame our angst on circumstance. We would not be suffering, we complain, if events had taken another course or those around us had behaved in a different way. Of course, this is a lie. We chart our own course through life.

There is something miraculously therapeutic about moving in solitude through a crowd. As the panic of the Hegira subsides, so the soothing balm of the pilgrimage takes its place. Thus by the end of the trip, if we are lucky, we can cross a space alone, as Thesiger does, without feeling lonely.

As I mulled this over, I took Pascal's theory to what seemed to be a logical conclusion. We travel to discover our internal world and join it seamlessly with the external universe. In that way, we are at peace when we return home. We have exorcised our restlessness and unveiled the serenity that lies within us all.

While I was in London, I had yet to tame this angst. The yearnings of the exile flashed on and off in my brain like the filaments of a neon sign. So in the months that followed my expulsion from Kenya, I became adept at being a gypsy and did a lot of travelling. I wandered through West Africa, East Africa, Central Africa, West Africa again and even visited Mauritius. I was happy as soon as I hit the road.

My first journey began after I had finished an assignment in West Africa for the *International Herald Tribune*. I was in a telephone booth shouting down the line to Will Ellsworth Jones, then editor of the *Sunday Times* travel section. Outside was a harbour in Dakar, the capital of Senegal. The midday heat made the street look as flat as a reflection in a shop window. In a few hours, the beautiful market women would have rearranged their little piles of groundnuts on the kerb; the limbless beggars would be back at their stations; the shops would have reopened; the hustle bustle and colliding colours would have returned. But for now there was only the old tramp who lived in a cardboard lean-to against the harbour wall. In the mornings, while others trooped to work, he dragged out a sheet of cardboard, spread it flat on the pavement and did sit-ups with his arms folded across his chest. At this moment, like the rest of the city, he was asleep.

'I don't understand what you see in Africa. Why don't you come back to London? We don't need the story.'

'London? Are you crazy? It's glorious here! Besides, I've already borrowed four hundred pounds from a nice gentleman. So you've got to send me the money. The paper's honour is at stake.'

The line was very fuzzy, but I thought I heard Will sigh. 'I don't know. It's been done before. How could you make it interesting?' Silly question really.

Fifteen minutes later, I hopped on to the back of a motorbike. 'Well?' said the nice gentleman.

'Sold. You'll get your money back.'

The trip had been inspired by whimsy. Random moments from the past were transmuted into a vague but attainable objective: a scolding nanny threatening banishment to Timbuktu; a description of a heart-of-darkness boat ride as my hostess knelt over an atlas and traced the Niger River's sweeping arc with her forefinger; a day in the school attic reading *Beau Geste* while everyone else was in class. They seemed an excellent reason to head for Mali.

Timbuktu is sandwiched between the foot of the Sahara and the Niger, a smooth brown python of a river that marks that fragile buffer between verdant savannah and sand that is known as the Sahel. Greg Woodsworth, a Canadian who worked for the United Nations' Food and Agriculture Organization, had offered to take me part of the way on the back of his motorbike. Our planned route hugged Senegal's border with Mauritania and Mali, terminating in a small town, Bakel, that marked the end of the 'passable' road. From there I would take a bush taxi to the border town of Kidira, about a five-hour journey, and wait for the train to Bamako, the capital of Mali. Michelin maps scrutinised after a good meal and a bottle of wine can inspire reckless generosity. Greg's offer of a 'lift' meant travelling 900 miles out of his way. My trip was to be much longer. I didn't know where it would end.

Our first stop, at Touba, coincided with the congregation of one million worshippers to celebrate a Muslim holy festival. We stayed with a *marabout*, sharing his courtyard with about fifty pilgrims. The *marabout*'s eldest son, Simbaye, made us a *gris gris* to keep us safe on our journey. It was an age-old practice. Amulets date back to pharaonic times. Last century, Europeans were still wearing anodyne necklaces to prevent whooping cough and as a cure for worms. Simbaye's *gris gris* was the tip of an ox's tongue wrapped in a piece of paper on which the *marabout* had written extracts from the Koran. Simbaye put the spell into a tiny red leather pouch and tied it beneath the front fender of Greg's bike.

The *gris gris* did well as far as accidents and breakdowns were concerned, but it couldn't keep a locust plague at bay. Billions of them, the size of a man's forefinger, were munching their way through the crops. They fluttered and drifted like snowflakes, stretching from horizon to horizon, darkening the sun and silencing the birds. We wrapped ourselves up as best we could, but riding through them was like being pelted with stones. It was exhausting for Greg to drive like this day after day. The roads were a slippery green carpet of crushed insects. They gave off a sickly sweet smell like rotting tropical flowers. There had been several fatal accidents with drivers skidding uncontrollably. After less than 400 miles we turned round and went back to Dakar. I took the train to Bamako instead.

In a symbolic gesture of shedding excess baggage, I was travelling with a small knapsack I could carry easily in one hand. It contained espadrilles, a *kikoi*, suncream, toothbrush, toothpaste, notebook, guidebook and map. I wore tennis shoes and a cotton shirt and skirt I had borrowed from Petra. By the time I reached Bamako, I was beginning to feel a lot better. I drove along the dusty streets in a borrowed moped and slept in a house empty of furniture except for a bed and chair. I trimmed my hair with a penknife and said to the mirror, 'Aaah, you're beginning to let go. Good.'

I met a group of American women who were on a bead-buying expedition. When I told them I had been exiled from Kenya, they sympathised and said how frightening it must be to have neither home nor possessions. 'It's not frightening,' I said and almost meant it.

The next leg of the journey was on a river boat that plied an 800-mile stretch of the Niger. The end of the line was Gao, a once-rich Beau Geste trading town that had become an alluring speck on the horizon for Tuaregs smuggling goods across the Sahara. Beyond Gao were impassable rapids. And 250 miles before it, Timbuktu.

I was still materialistic enough to choose a first-class passage, which meant a shared cabin, communal washing facilities and plenty of deck space. Fourth-class passengers slept on the open deck and performed their ablutions in the river while the boat discharged its cargo. Men squatted at the river's edge to urinate next to women washing their children. A few feet further downstream, people scooped up the same water in their hands and drank it.

Many of the passengers were heading for riverside villages virtually inaccessible by road. But most were sharp-eyed market women touting gigantic baskets of tomatoes, lemons and tangerines. We passed pirogues filled with fishermen, a few snorting hippo and dusty villages tacked on to a flat landscape. The temperature hovered above a hundred degrees. Hours, then days, sliced shapelessly into each other. My notes dried up. I sat on deck and watched the world go by in a state of delicious anticipation, as if it were Christmas Eve.

Timbuktu's reputation as a citadel of magnificent riches dates back to Phoenician and Roman times when it was a crossroad for the blue-hued Berbers. Their camel caravans transported gold and ivory to the Mediterranean and returned laden with a far more important commodity, salt dredged from the desert oases. It needed a dedicated imagination to conjure up the glories of the past, however. Although the town's mystique had endured, the reality was dingy mud houses in an eroded wasteland subject to cyclical famine.

We docked on the outskirts, and I ventured ashore. I accepted an invitation from an Italian aid worker to share his spaghetti lunch and missed the boat. So I stayed for dinner too. 'Don't worry, we'll drive you to your hotel tomorrow,' said my host. That was in Gao, a five-hundred-mile round trip over rough and waterless tracks. It was the sort of hospitality that is borne of isolated places.

In the desert outside Gao I stood by a well and looked at two Tuareg men, one darkly clothed, the other in white, kneeling in prayer on the edge of a vast expanse of sky. Each prostration, forehead drifting down to the sand, then pointing up to the evening stars, was an affirmation of the incontrovertible link between spiritual eternity and the corporeal present. *Allahu akbar.* God is great. Even the infidel was moved.

By this time I was behaving like a tramp, settling down to sleep wherever I happened to be when darkness fell. I looked like one too. Petra's skirt was held up by shoelaces and the tennis shoes were disintegrating. My appearance didn't deter the Tuareg, who asked me to accompany them on a smuggling expedition into Algeria. It was getting close to school holidays, and I wanted to be with Tara and Petra. I declined with regret and began to think of returning to Bamako, Dakar and finally, London.

One day I was summoned to Gao's only proper hotel, which had large, empty bedrooms, a bar where locust-control pilots downed numerous whiskies and a courtyard surrounded by crenellated walls. There, in a high-ceilinged room, a dark and handsome man sat beneath a slowly turning fan. He was encased in a voluminous blue *boubou* (a robe) richly embroidered with gold.

'Madame, please be seated. I have been watching you. You are like the sun. Since your arrival, the town has revolved around you. Everyone seeks you out. I would consider it an honour if I could lend you a robe while my servants wash your dress.' He leaned forward and wagged his finger in my face. 'Because, madame, I know you are a journalist. And if you are to do interviews, you can't walk around with five kilos of sand on you.'

'Thank you for the offer. It's very kind of you, but there's not much point in trying to make me clean. I'll be dirty again tomorrow,' I said.

Despite this refusal, we became firm friends. Mamadou Senogo, who owned the largest private insurance company in the country, embodied the courtesy and wit on which Malians thrive. One day he took me to his farm on the banks of the Niger. A graduate of the French education system and a devout Muslim, he had invoked protection that was neither Western nor Islamic for this latest venture. His fifteen-acre plot of rice fields and banana trees had been subjected to regular nocturnal raids by hippos until one of the farm workers, an old man dressed in rags, planted an anti-hippo fetish of sticks by the river.

I know now that the sticks must have been cut from a tree that harboured the spirit of a god. Then I was ignorant of these things, so I asked Mamadou what the fetish was. He shrugged. 'I don't know, but whatever it is, it works. So I believe in it.'

That afternoon, basking in the contentment of sharing a meal beneath a mango tree with an exceptional friend, I was overcome with a longing to be home. I retreated some distance from Mamadou and the old man, who were scooping rice from a bowl with their fingers. I didn't want them to see the tears in my eyes.

Mamadou walked over and placed his hand on mine. 'You must pull yourself together, Marianne. You don't have your feet on the ground.

Everyone in Africa spends time in exile. I had to live in Dakar for two years after a misunderstanding with the president. He thought I wanted to overthrow him. But, you see, I am back again. You will return to Kenya. You must have patience. You're an African.'

I understood these words better than those of the American women, who had felt sorry for me. It seemed to me that Westerners clung to loss. The African way was to heal with acceptance. During my travels I had seen people weather hardship through faith. Religion or witchcraft, God or gods, it didn't seem to matter. It kept them going in the face of drought, disease, poverty and political turmoil. The more I travelled, the more I would learn, I decided.

All the same, I was using these journeys to play a psychological trick on myself. Zoologists say that an animal's territory is not necessarily where it feeds. Territory constitutes the place that an animal knows intimately: the refuge to which it can retreat and be safe. In lay terms, an animal's territory is its home. As travellers, we aren't surrounded by the familiar views and possessions which define our territory. Therefore while I travelled, I kept reassuring myself that it was normal to sleep in hotels and other people's houses or under the stars. It was normal, I insisted, not to have a home.

Yet all the while I was travelling, as I sat on buses or trains, looked out of windows on to brown landscapes, rode pillion on motorbikes, strode sweating down sleepy streets, all that while that I did these things and saw these new sights, another part of me was reaching down inside to my subconscious. I wanted to find out who this fragile and fragmented person called Mary Anne Fitzgerald really was.

I fumbled blindly, only half aware of what I was doing. The strangers I met read courage in my walk. I did not tell them it was bravado or that a frightened, lost little girl hid in my rib cage for I didn't know it myself. At first, I pretended I was as brave and insouciant as I appeared to be. Yet as I moved across thousands of miles and played the voyeur in hundreds of lives, so I learned as much about myself as the countries and cultures I encountered.

I recognised the wilfulness that emerged to do battle with officials; the intolerance expressed for the blusterers, the bigots and the pompous; the confusion experienced when men tried to invade my territory with sexual overtures. In particular, I confronted the lack of compassion for the self-pitying, for I saw myself reflected in them. Once I had acknowledged the existence of these destructive Mary Annes, they didn't evaporate, but I was able to tone them down and, for the most part, keep them in check. Some of my friends were generous enough to say I had become a nicer person.

Giving myself credit for my positive aspects was more difficult. Unable to praise, I was driven to try harder. I couldn't shake the delusion that if I kept working on it, one day I would achieve near perfection. In this, I thought as a European not as an African, who doesn't struggle against the odds.

African fatalism is misinterpreted by Westerners. If Africans had a truly *laissez-faire* attitude, witchcraft would not exist. Witchcraft attempts to bend the laws of nature. It can make a healthy person die within days. It can turn men into animals or soften stony hearts. But more of that later. Suffice it to say there are lessons to be learned from living with Africans. In many ways they are accepting and tolerant. They don't try to roll back the barbed wire of life as we do. They look for a way over it that won't tear the flesh.

All around me, people were living graciously in the face of misfortune. Somehow I couldn't do the same. The young man who led me to a street tailor by a rubbish dump and chatted while my knapsack was being repaired was a school leaver who would never find employment. The woman who offered me food as I passed her hut had less than enough to feed her own family. The aid worker who gave me shelter for the night in the Sahara was there because his family connections were not good enough to get him a job in the city. These people didn't indulge in recriminations, but I did. There was a compulsion to compensate for the mess I had made of my life. If I wrote three stories, it should have been four. If I walked at night down a street where thieves lurked in the shadows, I scolded myself for being nervous. It took a very long time to admit that I, like everyone else, was vulnerable and weak or that it was okay to expose these aspects to the rest of the world.

That was probably the hardest lesson of all: learning to love all my personae – mother, lover, comic, warrior, iconoclast, eccentric, helper, child. Once that became possible, I felt more whole, more a woman, than ever before. I stopped trying to change those around me and concentrated on changing myself instead. It seemed to me it was the first truly constructive thing I had done. Fear of change is misplaced. It is a blessed gift because it creates an avenue for growth. Handled thoughtfully, change brings strength, serenity and the ability to redefine goals.

Part of me was thankful the house and its contents were beyond my reach. We have too strong a sense of possession, be it people or objects. Fear of loss and failure throttles our desire for change. Once we have lost and emerged intact, our goals are limitless. Surely, I pondered, this is what we admire in the nomad. There is no attachment through permanence. When the grasslands that sweep to the foot of the mountains are parched, they migrate to the valley that provides water and grazing. They are at one with their surroundings, yet apart. Existing in harmony with the world around us is the universal canon of religions. Gautama Buddha put it best: 'You cannot travel on the path before you have become the Path itself.'

This enlightenment, if you can call it that, didn't present itself in the Damascene version. It took me nearly two years or, to be more precise, all the years that I had lived so far, to decipher it. My pain and sorrow acted as levers that gradually prised away most of the sham Mary Annes. The cheering thing was, I quite liked what was exposed as the masks clattered to the floor. And once I had discovered the real me, I was presented with a truth of astonishing clarity and simplicity. Home wasn't a place. I carried it with me wherever I went. Like the nomads, I was free.

Few conversions are absolute, and mine certainly wasn't one of them. I liked who I was. I had peace of mind. Yet it wasn't enough. Self-discovery made it easier to be in exile, but it didn't get me home. Perhaps a little intervention was called for? As the second summer in London unfolded on hot, still air, the doubts and misgivings began to prick.

One morning I left the flat to buy a newspaper from the corner shop. A form squatting by a lamp post caught my eye. A beggar with twisted legs had shuffled down the street on his hands and was taking a rest. It was a natural thing to see until the man, wearing the hard hat of a construction worker, stood up and walked away, wrenching my heart up into my throat as surely as if it had been connected to him by a piece of string. Memory escaped its cocoon and presented unanswerable questions. Why did everyone walk upright in a hurried, deliberate fashion? Why did they smile seldom and without innocence? Why did no one lean against the wall of the grocery store with their feet crossed at the ankle as the Samburu warriors did outside Kattra's *dukka*? Even the tramps of the neighbourhood relaxed in a different way. They sat on benches with both feet planted in front of them like passengers on the underground, clutching bottles and sharing cigarettes. Their loitering had the wrong shape.

I was overcome with nostalgia for familiar sights, smells and sounds. I recalled Kipenget threading beads on to loops of wire, sitting with her legs straight out in front of her as African women sit; Joffrey crawling 15 miles to school, dragging his wasted calves and unused feet behind him. I yearned for an all-encompassing silence shattered by a moth's wing against the glass of a kerosene lamp instead of the continual rattle of passing traffic. I needed the comforting African odour of wood smoke, damp earth and rancid animal fat; the absence of furniture and walls. I fantasised about living outside and keeping my word processor in a crate.

On the better days my feelings twisted and turned like a snake in a sack. That was tolerable, for I knew I was still alive. On other days I felt so numb I wondered if I was dead. I was still homesick. It depressed me. I feared it would never go away.

One night I dreamed I was on a bush path. I offered a drink of water to a passer-by, placing the glass on a wooden stool. 'I'm sorry I can't offer you more,' I said. 'This is all I have at the moment. Please make yourself at home.' Konrad Lorenz said that to offer a gift to a stranger is a way of defining your territory. When you put the kettle on the hob for a visitor, you are making a statement. You are saying, this is my home and you are my guest. With the symbolic offering of a simple glass of water, my subconscious was trying to cauterise the wound of homelessness.

That summer Kate Macintyre passed through London. She had resigned from her job as SAIDIA's project director to do a master's degree in primary health-care administration. We spent an evening together at her brother's flat in Islington. I arrived armed with a bottle of champagne. She had chilled some bottles of white wine. Or perhaps it was vice versa. I no longer remember, and I don't suppose Kate does either.

She talked long into the night about SAIDIA and my extended Kenyan family while I listened. The charity was flourishing. Its projects were so successful, they were being used as blueprints by large aid organisations and even the World Bank. By the time we entered the labyrinth of development philosophy, it was after midnight. We were into our second bottle of wine. The champagne had been polished off long ago.

'SAIDIA's making history, M.A. It's been assimilated into Samburu folklore,' Kate said into the noise of a passing car. 'Gabriel gave a lift to some young boys the other day on his way back from Loikumukum. They sat in the back singing a song they made up about SAIDIA. They had no idea who Gabriel was, so it must have been spontaneous. One of the verses was about Mburu the driver. Gabriel was a bit miffed because there wasn't a verse about him.'

While Kate talked on, slipped down into the chair with her legs stretched out in front of her, I tried to recall what Loikumukum looked like. It was no use. I couldn't even remember where it was.

'Oh, I forgot to tell you. You've been a target of Samburu culture as well. Just before you left, Chief Lekisaat got a witch doctor to put a spell on you. We only found out by chance the other day. So when all the government diatribes against you appeared in the papers, Lekisaat took the credit for it. I guess he thought you were getting too influential around Lesirikan. Challenging his power. The spell restored his credibility though. Everyone in Lesirikan reckons the magic must be pretty deep to get you thrown out of the country. We were wondering what to do about it. We don't want people to think SAIDIA can be influenced by black magic. It might be a good idea to make it known that you've put a really potent counterspell on Lekisaat. Aren't you going to West Africa next? Perhaps you could fix something up.'

West Africa, Benin in particular, is reputed to be the crucible of the most potent juju on the continent. The curse of witchdoctors, who are servants of the devil, destroys the *wa-wé*, the abstract essence that links body to soul. When that happens, the bewitched person responds obediently by dying. My behaviour after being cursed by Lekisaat was not much different. I had allowed my life and my personality to disintegrate. There were ways of lifting spells. I wondered if I should give it a try.

The seed of an idea was there. I could have dismissed it as ridiculous, but I didn't. During the following weeks I played with the proposition endlessly. It was impossible to relate the fear of war unless you had been under fire. You couldn't explain the satisfaction of walking a hundred miles through the bush unless you had done it. How could I describe the mysteries of African magic, how it held sway over millions of people's lives, if I didn't experience it myself? Besides, there was always the chance that a counterspell might work.

Some years ago, Lee Lyon, a beautiful and talented camerawoman, was trampled to death by a young elephant. She had been filming its release from the back of a truck. It was said that she had been having an affair with Adrien de Schryver, the Belgian game warden who was the first person to habituate mountain gorillas to man. It was also said that de Schryver's Zairean wife had put a spell on Lee. Lee had already filmed several elephants being released into the wild during the shoot. They had all been sedated, including the one that killed her. None of the others had demonstrated any aggression. Was her death just an accident?

Geoffrey Gorer, who travelled in West Africa in the 1930s, was initiated as a fetishist of the panther cult. As dawn broke at the end of the ceremonies, he found himself standing in a field. He describes the scene that followed in his book *Africa Dances*.

'After about half an hour, a full-grown panther walked out of the maize and started moving among the people; it was quickly followed by another, and in a short time there were fifteen panthers amongst us. They arrived from every direction. We had been told most earnestly on no account to touch them, for they would only harm wicked men (i.e. sorcerers). When the fetisher stopped singing, they went away again.' Leopards, even more than other cats, are shy of humans and would never have behaved that way in normal circumstances. How had it happened?

By the time I landed in Abidjan once again my mind was made up. I'd let the practitioners of magic have a lick at getting a presidential pardon out of Daniel arap Moi. Compared to the murders some of them were renowned for executing, changing a man's mind should be child's play. I really did want my house back. There was no harm in giving it a try.

There were three types of spirits whose aid I could enlist. First there were the *umyen* (ancestors), the moral guardians of a clan or community. When a man is properly buried by his son, his soul is liberated from its mortal body and returns to earth in a stick or tree or even the body of a grandchild. His departed spirit becomes a family deity that is worshipped and consulted in times of crisis. If a man has no son to bury him, he enters the afterworld in disgrace, the equivalent of limbo, and is unable to preside over the welfare of his lineage. This is one of the reasons for polygamy. The numerous offspring of several wives ensure that at least one son will survive to conduct the burial rites of his father.

Then there were the *asié-usu* (genies), superhuman beings who were despatched to earth by the Supreme Being before mankind existed. They took possession of the lakes, mountains and forests and have remained there ever since. The genies' permission is sought before crops are planted or trees are felled. If there is drought or excessive rain, the weather won't improve until the genies have been mollified. Their provenance was primarily nature, but they sometimes helped out on personal matters as well.

The most intriguing prospect were the *amwi*, who are minor divinities inasmuch as they channel the power of the Supreme Being into men. Each one has a symbol which represents him or her on earth and is the object of cult worship. For instance, the royal totem of the kings of Dahomey was the panther. The cult priests sanctified man-made objects through ritual and used them in the worship of the *amwi*. They were called fetishes. In many areas, the fetishes themselves were treated as if they were divinities in their own right. The men who were the custodians of the fetishes were called fetishists.

Ritual murder was still practised too, but I deemed it wise to give that a miss. In the lexicon of witchcraft, the most powerful spells for easing the path to success in love and career, or for exacting revenge on an enemy, are the dismembered parts of a human corpse – the head, the veins, the heart, the genitals. When I was last in Ghana, 10 people were executed by firing squad for their roles in the particularly gruesome deaths of two women and an eleven-year-old boy. Evidence that emerged during the hearings before the Public Tribunal, the Ghanaian version of a people's court, unveiled the shadow side of the African psyche. The murderers had hacked out their victims' hearts and removed their genital organs, fingers and veins. The body of the boy, Kofi Kyintoh, was found decapitated. Two of those accused of his murder were his uncle and great-uncle. They had planned to sell his head to a sorcerer to raise some cash, they said in their testimony.

The issue of the *People's Daily Graphic* newspaper that carried the executions on the front page also printed reports of two separate arrests: a sorcerer for allegedly possessing human bones and a teacher who attempted to smuggle a human heart in his suitcase when travelling to neighbouring Togo. Both men were probably party to a lucrative line in export earnings – grave robbing.

When you first arrive in Abidjan, this undercurrent of mysticism and sorcery is obscured by the sheer brashness of the city. It is a glitzy, steamy port that is considered the plum West African posting by expatriates, despite the moist, oppressive heat that makes men have wet dreams about Alpine air. Measured against a continental yardstick, Abidjan is affluent. Its palm-lined villas, broad boulevards and glass-fronted skyscrapers are an anomaly for black Africa, most of which is riddled with tin shacks and decay.

The well-heeled Ivorians, of whom there are many, eat vegetables that have been flown in from France and cooked by their chefs from Benin. Their villas are guarded by watchmen whom they call *boy*. They come from Burkina Faso and live in small rooms off the garage known as *boyeries*. Friday nights everyone stays home to watch *Dynasty* dubbed in French.

The aroma of Gauloises and eau de cologne drifts in the stairwells of the marble-faced ministries. Elsewhere, the odour most commonly associated with the corridors of power is an acrid mix of urine and stale beer. There are other sure signs of prosperity. The taxis have meters that work and the handles don't detach themselves when you wind down the windows. And the police training school has floodlit tennis courts, one of a number of municipal extravaganzas. In most countries, the police force is so strapped for cash its officers have to hitch a lift to the scene of the crime.

The key to this deviation from the unrelieved poverty that is rapidly becoming an African hallmark is the indulgence of the Côte d'Ivoire's former colonial master, France. It is the only one of France's former black African possessions that was properly colonised. Before the Second World War thousands of settlers replaced vast tracts of rain forest with bananas, oil-yielding palm trees, cocoa and coffee. The French no longer stride across their plantations in khaki shorts, but their presence is still evident in the form of government advisers, industrial investment and generous dollops of aid. There are some 35,000 French in Côte d'Ivoire. Most live in Abidjan, enjoying the tropical highlife in the shadow of what the Ivorians proudly refer to as their 'Manhattan skyline'.

Amidst all this form there is also substance. Nestling noisily and smellily across the lagoon from the skyscrapers are the slums, which are unabashedly chaotic. Here the pimps, thieves, whores, office messengers, bar girls, taxi drivers, curio dealers, beggars and unemployed know there is no celebration without sacrifice. Here you can buy a man's soul with a bottle of gin and a rooster. I sensed that my quest for exorcism would lead me into these *bidonvilles*. But I didn't know anyone connected to the chimerical world of voodoo. How was I to find them?

There were three categories of practitioners whom I wanted to visit. The healers specialise in curing illness, which is symptomatic of the presence of evil spirits. The fetishists are the mystical priests of fetish cults who channel the energy of the gods through fetish paraphernalia and idols. They deal with those things that worry us all: life and death, romance, revenge and material success. Both the healers and the fetishists are animists who believe there are many gods and many spirits. Then there are the *marabouts*, who practise a syncretistic mix of the occult and Islam. They are Muslim holy men who profess to cure spiritual ailments with amulets and divination.

Those who deal with spirits maintain a masonic-like secrecy, or so it seemed to me. Tracking them down became something of a chore. I felt as if I was entering a forbidden landscape, prohibited to those who did not believe. A friend's tailor knew a good *marabout*, but the tailor wasn't on the phone. We kept missing each other. Another friend, the son of a cabinet minister, said his mother consulted an excellent fetishist at least once a week. He wasn't on the phone either, and my friend kept forgetting to tell his mother I was in need of a bit of juju. So it went. Some promise, but no delivery.

Meanwhile, there were tantalising glimpses of this other world. When President Felix Houphouet-Boigny, who is ninety-ish, falls ill, Ivorian yuppies have been known to clear their desks, go home and lock their doors. Tradition demands that when a Baoulé chief dies, a retinue of warriors, wives and servants be buried with him to tend to his needs in the afterworld. Whether or not the 'Grand Custom' will prevail on Houphouet-Boigny's death, remains to be seen. Chiefs also used to pass on messages to their dead fathers by imparting the news to a bystander and then having him killed immediately.

Houphouet-Boigny regularly consulted a fetishist on his health. I asked if this conflicted in any way with his construction of a basilica some hundred feet taller than St. Peter's, for a reputed $300 million. 'No,' I was told, 'the fetishist keeps him alive. When he dies, the basilica is his ticket to heaven.' The ageing president was a wise man. He was hedging his bets.

In Abidjan I learned that someone had been seen, chicken in hand, shaking blood over the office chair of the president of the African Development Bank. He was seeking promotion. I travelled to the Liberian border to interview refugees and met David Lythgoe, a Danish Red Cross worker. A local girl who had romantic designs on David left a pouch containing amulets on the seat of his car. The idea was this would increase David's desire. David said he wasn't interested. I never wrote to ask whether he eventually succumbed.

On my return to Abidjan, I stopped over at San Pedro for some deep-sea fishing. Charles Perry, the wire man from North Carolina, spliced two fishing lines together in his mouth, a feat which transfixed Harouna the boatman. Harouna's cheeks were scored with tribal scars that looked like cat's whiskers. 'I can't do that,' he said, shaking his head from side to side in admiration. 'I can make people disappear, but it takes a bit longer.'

Everyone, it seemed, had access to magic except me.

Finally, after two weeks of fruitless inquiries, I took a taxi down to the Treichville market where shoppers diced with con men. The stalls were as tightly packed together as beach umbrellas on Coney Island. They were stuffed with cheap clothing, brilliantly coloured native cloth, plastic mirrors and combs, trinkets and lipstick, everything to enhance your looks. In the right-hand corner of the upper floor of this seething arena of commerce were the curio dealers. They had cartons of centuries-old trading beads, boxes of brand new ones, piles of masks, mounds of figurines, mountains of carvings. They also knew, as it turned out, the whereabouts of a healer. She lived in a part of the city where houses were rented by the room and the open drains glistened with still, black ooze. It was the sort of place the expatriates warned you not to visit alone. A hefty young man offered to be my guide.

Young men stripped to the waist watched us in silence as we passed down an alley that had the dark and dusty aspect of a coal mine. They were clustered round a bench where a game of draughts was in progress. I tightened my lips, looking like a memsahib who has been served tea in the wrong pot. My nervousness made me suspicious. Everyone was a potential mugger. But it was more than that. I recalled the words of a World Bank consultant from Cameroon whom I had lunched with that day: 'We believe a lot in gods. We tend to trust them to change things, and it's not good.' Perhaps that was it. I was paying a stranger to put my destiny in the lap of unknown beings. It made me uneasy.

If I had been expecting an ancient and primeval force to reverberate through the healer's household, I was wrong. The women pounding *manioc* for dinner and the dog stretched out on the flattened earth of the courtyard struck an ordinary, homely note. I sat on a bench shoved up against the wall and watched the chickens and the children scrabble in the garbage.

After some minutes, Kouakou Adjo presented a glimpse of herself through the doorway as she crossed the dim passage that bisected her house. She was dressed in a bra and a local *peigne* which she had wrapped about her waist. The cowrie-shell necklaces draped across her chest looked like bandoliers fitted with cartridges. This warrior image was enhanced by the feathers that bobbed in her hair and the clay that streaked her body and face.

Later, I shook her hand, and she stared at me with flat brown eyes. Adjo was a healer of repute, her son Yan Hylaire told me. Over a hundred clients came to see her every weekend. This was also the time when the spirits danced in the corridor and twirled about the courtyard to the beat of drums, he said.

Hylaire had presented himself as translator for the utterances his mother would make while she was in a trance. He looked at me and offered a preliminary diagnosis. 'You are a dreamer. I can see from your eyes. It's no good. When your spirits leave your body, the bad spirits come in. You are not strong enough to resist them.' He had a point. Nobody in my family would refute that I was a dreamer.

I wanted to find out, however, why my protective spirits had abandoned me. It might have been because I had broken a taboo on sex or food, though I wasn't sure that tribal strictures pertained to outsiders. Perhaps it was because I hadn't paid due homage to my ancestors and genies. After all, I had never performed a sacrifice. Or was it, as I suspected, through Chief Lekisaat's black magic? Healers didn't usually have the power to lift sorcerers' spells, but they had the ability to 'see' them on the accursed.

Adjo retired to her bedroom, a nine-foot by four-foot cell. It was dominated by an altar surmounted with four painted wooden idols. One had an egg tied to its stomach. At their feet were an array of bottles and bowls. Several empty gin bottles had been pushed back under the altar. Adjo knelt before it and turned a bowl round and round. She scooped some grey powder up and smeared it on her lips. Hylaire and I sat on chairs in the doorway, informal but attentive as if we were lovers or friends who had paid to watch another couple making love.

'Uh huh. Uh huh.' The breathing was deep and insistent like a woman rising to orgasm. A stream of incomprehensible language poured from Adjo's pale lips. She was possessed.

'Eh heh. Eh heh,' responded Hylaire. 'You are not sick. You are well. Do you understand?'

'Eeh. Eeh,' I nodded.

'Uh huh. Uh huh. Uh huh.'

'Your spirit has wandered from your body. You must bring it back. Do you understand?'

'Eeh. Eeh.'

'You are African. You are part of an African family. Do you understand?'

'Eeh.'

Adjo was banging the bowl on the ground. Her head swayed like a cobra poised to strike. A genie had climbed on to her back and taken possession of her body. Its shouted commands were punctuated with yips and yaps and whistles.

'You will go back to Kenya, but you must do it on a Friday. It is an auspicious day to travel. If you can't do it on a Friday, try Tuesday. Do you understand?'

'Eeh. Eeh.'

'Uh huh. Uh huh.'

When Adjo's trance ended, Hylaire and I retired to another room to discuss the weighty business of sacrifice. Hylaire said it required a white ram and two bottles of gin. Out of the corner of my eye I could see the next client kneeling respectfully in Adjo's doorway. The two talked softly and briefly then a few crumpled notes as soft as chamois leather crossed the sill.

Adjo was a good woman, but she didn't have the right bedside manner for my condition. I lacked the faith for travelling to Kenya on a Friday and taking pot luck. It had been done before and hadn't worked. There must be more to it than that. I wanted Adjo to influence Moi's thoughts. It was as if she had prescribed aspirin for pneumonia. Besides, her speciality was spiritual malaise with physical symptoms. I had no outward manifestation she could treat. I paid and took my leave.

Shortly after this I headed for Burkina Faso to do a couple of assignments. I needed a photographer and Alistair Sinclair, who worked for the Abidjan office of the Associated Press, had agreed to come with me. We had met in Liberia. Now twenty-eight, Alistair still retained the hippy image acquired when he left home at sixteen. He wore a vest and jeans and his hair fell untidily around the nape of his neck. He was slow to start in the mornings. He needed time, tea, a few blasts on his saxophone, and more time. He had his eccentricities. So did I. We got on just fine. At my insistence, we were travelling to Ouagadougou, the capital of Burkina Faso, the punitive way – on the 'Ouagadougou Choochoo'. Alistair was quite happy with that as long as he was fed regularly.

Côte d'Ivoire and Burkina Faso (the locals call it Boor-kee-naah, embalmed in lilting vowels) were once united as a single French colony, but they are like chalk and cheese. If Côte d'Ivoire is the spoilt only child, then Burkina is the struggling orphan. Ouagadougou (Waa-ga) was founded 500 years ago by Naba Oubri, titular head of one of several Mossi kingdoms. It stands on the edge of the Sahel and is an impoverished city even by regional standards. The French neglected Burkina, which had little to offer except its muscles. Then as today the Mossi people are Burkina's best resource. More than half a million Burkinabe men work as migrant labour in Côte d'Ivoire.

Few foreigners choose to travel between the two cities by train, preferring to cover the 600-odd miles by plane or car. For locals, however, the railway line is the artery connecting the Atlantic Ocean to the interior. The passengers are market women laden with produce to sell in the hinterland at a hundred per cent profit; families visiting relations for funerals and weddings; homewardbound workers bearing bicycles, frilly children's clothes and radio-cassette players that will electrify mud-walled villages with the songs of Ivorian pop star Alpha Blondy.

I can't resist trains in Africa. The purchase of a ticket is an excuse to plunge into local life and float with the current of commerce and socialising that sweeps along the corridors and spills on to the platform at each stop. Best of all, the carriages that chug steadily through the rainforest and over the savannahs are a stage for soap opera that gives free rein to the gregarious African spirit. You may not encounter the high drama of Graham Greene's Orient Express, but you are sure to be entertained by an ebony-skinned version of *Neighbours*. Even the most jaded of travellers cannot fail to have their ennui jolted.

Alistair's shoe-string guide book said the Gazelle had two-bunk compartments with wash basin, air-conditioning and a 'decent' dining car. It left every morning at 8.30. The Express left in the afternoons, slept four to a compartment and had neither air-conditioning nor dining car. Despite its name, it took twenty-seven hours instead of the Gazelle's twenty-three.

Our departure seemed to stretch as tantalisingly into the distance as the railway tracks. The train is full. Today it is the Express, not the Gazelle. This train comes from Burkina and would not be good for madame. The forecourt hummed with activity on these dawn excursions with our luggage in tow. Women hawkers sat on the ground exchanging lazy laughs as they rearranged delicate piles of tangerines and dried fish. The penetrating odour of stale urine rose from the station entrance where a wall-eyed beggar with an amputated leg sat on the window sill. *'Bejour,'* he said, winking with his good eye.

A tidal pool of passengers always swirled around the platform gate. The cloth-wrapped baggage on their heads was so enormous that on another continent it might have contained bedside tables and perhaps a small washing machine. Instead they held stools, pots, woven baskets, clothes and food jumbled together into outsized Dick Whittington bundles. Their heads swayed gently to keep their balance like daisies nodding in the breeze.

On the fourth day all seemed in order, almost. 'The sleeping car has not come from Waaga, madame. I am sorry,' said the conductor, bowing us through a door with a theatrical flourish. The unventilated compartment had four bunks with tassels of dirt hanging from the ceiling. I exchanged a shrug with Alistair, and we deposited our bags amongst the dust on the overhead racks.

Watching us from the lower berths were two women encased like mummies in rolls of traditional cloth. Gold cascaded from their throats, wrists and ears. *'Bonjour, mesdames.'* They nodded their heads graciously.

There was a mellow trumpet blast from the front of the train, and we jolted into motion. I dug into my handbag and produced an inch-high wooden doll with a plug in its mouth. Known as the talking telephone, it was the voodoo equivalent of a St Christopher. I took out the plug and said to it, 'Please may we have a safe journey.'

'*Aller retour*,' added Alistair judiciously.

As we pulled out of the station, several bystanders suddenly threw themselves at the steps of the carriage and clambered aboard. The Gazelle (no one ever owned up that it was really the Express) was carrying its fair share of unauthorised traffic.

Abidjan's lagoon curved at our feet as we edged round the side of a hill and sliced through the red earth banks of the suburban slum of Adjamé, a patchwork of shacks that reverberated to the cries of playing children and smithies hammering sheets of tin beneath the eucalyptus trees. Waterfalls of black garbage streamed down the hillside between the houses. The smell was so atrocious it was a wonder the inhabitants put up with it. The answer was simple. As with many intolerable things in Africa, they had no choice.

It was the hour after breakfast and men were defecating behind bushes, modestly shielded from the street life on the other side, but baring their bottoms to the passing train. It was a statement of our voyeur's role in the crudest sense. A man emerged from a bush pulling up his pants. A few feet to his left was an open-air market where butchers hacked up carcasses on rickety wooden tables to the chainsaw buzz of swarming flies.

At Adjamé station the one-legged beggar alighted and hopped up a steep bank with the agility of a mountain goat. Then he shrugged his crude wooden crutches under his armpits and bobbed past a sign that said '*Pas d'uriner et de déféquer.*' This illicit inner-city commuting went apparently unnoticed by the conductor. He was too busy with his own nefarious pursuits.

Clouds of vegetation swept past – palms, forest, a banana plantation. At each stop thin-hipped women strode up and down the platform with tin plates of food on their heads. The merchandise became less opulent as we neared the savannah. Pineapples and avocados gave way to oranges, tangerines and papayas. By the time we had reached the baobabs, transfixed in a sun-bleached landscape of withered grass, there were only yams, parsnips and onions.

At one station there was a general exodus from the first-class carriage to converge on a woman bearing two plates of pink meat swimming in a thin gravy. Our conductor, who never failed to comport himself like a Big Man, bought seven pieces, including a long rubbery tail and a clawed foot. Someone else bought a lump with a row of pearl-sized teeth in it and sucked eagerly at the flesh. It was the local delicacy. Cane rat.

This was merely the retail trade, however. The conductor was buying wholesale, hauling aboard branches of bananas, armfuls of pineapples and avocados and stowing them under the bunks. Mesdames had been busy too. The floor of the compartment was awash with boxes and sacks sprouting greenery.

The two women had taken their shoes off and sat on a lower bunk with their feet tucked under them. Madame in the brown dress fanned herself with a handkerchief, twirling it round and round like a flapper in a cloche hat playing with her string of pearls. Madame in the green dress struck up a conversation. 'You are going to Waaga?'

'Yes. Are you?'

She nodded sweetly and inquired where I was from. Then she leaned forward and stroked the aluminium and silver bracelets I have worn above the elbow for over twenty years. They are my Samson's hair. 'These are Kenyan?' She clicked her tongue in appreciation. 'You are African then.'

'It is very cold in Waaga. It is eighty. You have brought a sweater with you? I am frightened of the cold,' she said and grimaced.

By mid-afternoon the focus of activity had shifted to the *buvette*, a compartment stacked high with crates of beer and orange sodas. Amidst all the jumble the conductor was holding court for several jovial Ivorian policemen who drank their beer from the bottle. Crouched timidly in the corner were two girls from third class. They gazed upon the bacchanalian scene with cow eyes and never uttered a word.

I edged through the press to buy two beers. When the policemen saw my arms, the questions came thick and fast. 'Madame, your bracelets show you have been in Africa a bit. Where do they come from? What are they made of? Are they heavy? Do you ever take them off? How do you wash?' And then the real question. 'Are they magic?'

'Yes, they are my *gris gris*.' Amused laughter was followed by nods and relaxed smiles. This was something they understood. I had been placed as almost one of them, as if I had gone to the right school.

Later, on my way to the lavatory, I squeezed past the fattest of the policemen as he opened a compartment door. I glimpsed the white shirt and braided hair of one of the girls and a police uniform. The two were dipping their fingers into a bowl of greasy stew propped on a box in front of them.

The next morning the carriage had the melancholy, bittersweet air of a party winding to a close. Men sat on the carriage steps, sprucing up their hangovers in the breeze. A muscled young man in jeans and knitted beret languidly paraded his naked torso up and down the corridor. The Ivorians in the *buvette* had been replaced with Burkinabe policemen, for we had crossed the border at midnight. Like the countryside, they were leaner and tougher. They wore dark glasses and boots and had pistols hanging at the waist. The cicatrices on their cheeks looked like a game of noughts and crosses waiting to be played.

The conductor emerged from his compartment to reveal bowls of half-eaten stew (cane rat?) on the floor and a plump woman who sat by the window with her legs drawn up. He padded past us on slothful bare feet. We lay listlessly on our bunks, too hot to stir.

Then, mid-morning, disaster struck. The train had stopped for an unusually long time at Koudougou, the last town before Waaga. I made my way down the strangely silent carriages to find out what had gone wrong. A few passengers dozed with heads flung at awkward angles. Many had climbed down on to the platform and unrolled raffia mats in the train's thin shadow. Those who were still awake stared glumly at their feet. None of the babies was crying.

It was the knot of locals by the last carriage that alerted me. A policeman was standing on tiptoe on the buffer and sticking a long thread of wire down a ventilation pipe in the roof. He withdrew it, flicking a pair of plastic shoes on to the ground. Minutes went by and the pile grew higher and higher. By the time it had become a veritable mountain of footwear, other policemen had boarded our carriage and were barking officiously. 'Take it off! Take it off!' Sweating porters staggered under the weight of boxes and sacks of vegetables and fruit. No wonder there was a general air of downcast detachment. Everyone was implicated for, I now realised, everyone was a smuggler.

Worst of all, the conductor's extensive contraband was issuing forth in an avalanche from the lavatory. Bereft of his swagger, he had sidled up to me in the corridor and stood gazing vacantly out the window. When a policeman shouted 'Whose are these?', he did not even turn his head.

Then they descended on our compartment. Madame in the brown dress had disembarked some hours before, but the eyes of Madame in the green dress were ablaze. 'Guard everything!' she snapped at me and sallied forth with arms akimbo to do battle.

Outside the window the porters were hauling away the plastic shoes on hand carts. 'You'll see those in the market tomorrow,' said Alistair. Fifteen minutes went by before Madame returned, imperious, tight-lipped and victorious. Her groceries were intact.

The train covered the last miles to Waaga with its passengers in a sombre mood. The conductor had retreated to his compartment, where he slumped listlessly with his feet thrust out in front of him. 'Do they catch you often?' I asked.

He lifted his shoulders in a Gallic gesture of resignation. 'About once a week.' The great pineapple smuggling ring had been busted. The party was over. Or until the next departure from Abidjan, at any rate.

At the railway station Alistair and I took a taxi to a hotel. It threaded its way through the mopeds that hurried with antlike determination over the dirt roads. They threw up so much dust that our first sight of the city was through a golden veil. We passed one-storey buildings with hooded, lozenge-shaped windows. At a roundabout a stone peasant shouldered a hoe above the shibboleth, *'L'édification de l'état des droits démocratiques et révolutionaires est la garantie des droits individuelles et collectives.'*

Burkina was another African anomaly. It was a pathetically poor socialist state where neither slums nor corruption existed. The people were charming and the telephones and electricity worked. Expatriates who were not of a materialistic bent loved it.

We had two hours in Waaga in which to wash and change before being driven into the Sahel to visit aid projects. On our return two days later, I was briefed on Oxfam-funded cereal banks by the charity's regional director, Mahamadou Kone. There was a sharp edge of wit to his conversation that the gentle Burkinabe lacked.

'I'm sure we've met before,' he said.

I have the regular sort of face that often elicits this statement. 'I don't think so. As you know, I've only just arrived here.'

'So have I. I arrived four months ago.'

'Where are you from?'

'Mali. Could it have been in Bamako?'

Mali is renowned for its strong magic. 'Maybe. But I'm sure I would have remembered you.' I liked this man. Had there been time for trust and experience to bond us, he might have become family. I acted instinctively. 'Mahamadou, I have a problem back home that I want to sort out. Do you know any good fetishists?'

He answered as calmly as if I were in need of a dentist for a toothache. 'If we were in Bamako, yes, but not here I'm afraid. Let's see if anyone else knows.' He raised his voice. 'Madame!' A thin woman appeared. 'Madame, can you help our visitor? She is looking for a fetishist.'

Her hand flew up to the silver crucifix that hung from her neck and fingered it nervously. 'I don't know these things, M'sieu Kone.'

'Thank you, madame.' He dismissed her with a gracious nod and the hint of a smile passed across his face. 'Don't worry. I'll find out for you.'

I rang Oxfam the following morning. Caution had intervened on both sides during the time that had elapsed. 'Mahamadou, *bonjour*. Um, it's about those things we've been discussing . . .'

'Yes, yes,' he said, 'I don't really believe in it myself, but come over.' I knew he was lying. He had his position as regional director to protect.

When I arrived Mahamadou was in a staff meeting. He gave me a nod and pointed in the direction of the accountant's office. Zabsonre Fatou was pretty and very efficient. She had already phoned her cousin at Tenkodogo, a small town near the Togo border. He was the local correspondent for the government news agency. He was expecting us to arrive that afternoon.

'Do you believe in juju?' I asked her.

'Yes. If you believe in it, it works. It's like reading the Bible and praying. If you believe in that it works, too. Ask for Konda at the kiosk on the corner near the courthouse.'

'Please may we have a safe trip to Tenkodogo and back again,' I said to the talking telephone. I said it in French to make sure it would understand. We were in a hired car. Alistair was driving. He had earlier made it clear that in his opinion I was cracked and juju was mumbo jumbo. When Alistair was uninterested in a situation, he fell asleep. I hoped he would stay awake long enough to take some photos. And that he would keep his opinions to himself. I also made a mental note to feed him a lot. It helped.

The countryside was flat and yellow and dotted with squat trees. The goats and sheep had eaten it into a wasteland, and the sun drowned it in heat. By late morning the animals were huddled into the bars of shade that fell from the roofs of the village houses. The vast landscape shrunk the mud-walled huts to insignificance, yet their conical straw hats struck a cosy note. They reminded me of garden gnomes mislaid in a park. At one point an old man crossed the road on a black horse. The horse had an arched neck and a red bridle. The old man wore a gold-trimmed robe and looked like a prince.

That evening we made plans with Zabsonre's cousin, Tessore Konda. The discussion was held at an outdoor bar where Tina Turner was blaring so loudly I had to lean forward to catch Konda's heavily accented French. Ghanaian whores danced lazily beneath a mane of eucalyptus trees. Konda ordered a Coke. I ordered a beer. Alistair was stalking about looking ominously bad tempered. He needed feeding again.

I told Konda that I had been expelled from Kenya and wanted to return. 'I use a fetishist myself, but a *marabout* would suit you better. I know a good one not far from here. We'll go early tomorrow morning. Charles Taylor uses him. He consulted him before he invaded Liberia.' This sparked my interest. Tenkodogo was the best part of a day's drive from Waaga. I guessed the *marabout* must have star-rating for Taylor to make the trek to his village.

We discussed the merits of *marabouts* and fetishists, then moved on to *bayé-fwé*, who, in the context of juju, are equivalent to Europe's black witches. *Bayé-fwé* are sorcerers, servants of the devil, and deal in fear. They assume the shape of serpents and fly through the night from hut to hut, seizing the sleeping from their beds and making them their slaves. On the shores of Lake Tanganyika, fishermen whose catch is consistently larger than anyone else's are accused of being sorcerers. The other fishermen say they have turned children into zombies who swim beneath the water and chase the *dagaa* into their nets.

Sorcerers are also associated with leopard men, baboon men and crocodile men, hired assassins who assume the shape of an animal before committing murder. 'They say they are eaters of men, but when you die your body is still there. They must be eaters of souls,' said Konda.

Konda didn't mention the poisoners, who are just as evil. These men use *dwuhuré*, a black potion, to bewitch people without actually going near them. The victims eventually die. Their other method for long-distance murder is to stick pins or nails into an image of the victim, a practice that typifies juju for Westerners. Some healers have the power to lift this latter spell by making incisions in the victim's body and sucking out the nails or pins.

Witchcraft is predicated on the proposition that a man's nail clippings or hair shavings, or a doll in his likeness, are to all intents and purposes that man. So anything that is done to a part of someone or something that is in his image is as effective as doing it to the person himself.

Kapoyargo village lay beneath mango trees amidst stubbled fields. The children came to greet us, bowing with bended knee as if we were chiefs. The *marabout* was an ordinary-looking man dressed in brown slacks and shirt. He had just returned from town on his moped. I looked into his eyes, yellowed by dust and sun, and knew he was an old soul who had been through many incarnations. I don't know why I never asked his name. Perhaps I was overwhelmed.

He led Konda and me to a hut and motioned us to be seated on a bench. Alistair wandered about outside. Konda and I were separated from the *marabout* by a narrow table. It was stacked with sheets of paper covered in runic writing. I cast my eye about the small space and saw some calendars, two clocks, a watch without a strap, more papers on the dirt floor and several empty bottles. A huge Indian cloth painting of a tiger hung behind the *marabout*'s head.

He said something to Konda, who translated it into French. 'Tell him your problem.' While I did so, the *marabout* punctuated the explanation with exhaled 'Aaaah haaaas'. They were as soft as a pulse or the tide washing the shoreline.

He wrote down my name and that of Chief Lekisaat and Daniel arap Moi. He asked if anyone else had suffered at Lekisaat's hands. As I talked, he swiftly laced a sheet of paper with Arabic and a strange calligraphy of his own invention. Then he took a fresh sheet and covered it with squares and lines and doodles. He folded the pieces of paper over and over until each one was no bigger than a peanut. Then he bound them with white thread. This one I was to bury beneath my bedroom window in London, pronouncing Moi's name as I did so. The other I was to keep in my handbag until I returned to Nairobi so I could bury it in my garden. He gave me some herbs to throw on to the fire as well.

Then he produced a slim cloth-covered book with tassels attached to the pages. Three times he opened the book with the tassels I had chosen.

Three times he read the script revealed and nodded. It was like throwing coins for an I Ching reading.

Next, the *marabout* selected a broken mirror and reed pen and wrote our names in concentric circles, covering the entire surface. A woman with a baby tied to her back appeared in the doorway and knelt with lowered head. Her pancake breasts flapped above a bowl of water. The *marabout* took the water and rinsed the writing off the mirror, pouring the liquid into a plastic bottle. I was to wash myself in the magic potion every morning for a fortnight, he instructed Konda.

The eighteenth-century explorer Mungo Park encountered a similar incident in West Africa. Often hungry, he would write poetry on a blackboard in return for food. Sometimes his hosts literally drank the words in by washing them off with water and swallowing the mixture.

There followed many more instructions. Konda made sure I wrote them down which was just as well. They were too complicated to remember. 'And don't forget,' said the *marabout*, 'to slaughter a white chicken on a Friday. You must give the chicken and a metre of white cloth to a beggar.' Soon after that we took our leave.

Back in town Konda and I wandered through the narrow alleys doing our shopping. A man produced a strip of white cloth from a trunkful of claws, snakeskins, bones and shells. Another man, who had a wooden stall next to the church, sold me a metal ring for a dollar. We bought six cowrie shells, salt, thirty millet cakes and four white cola nuts. Konda helped me divvy these into two packets to give to beggars.

Several sat in the dust of the main street opposite a bar. I singled out a blind man with a wispy grey beard and placed one of the packets on the ground beside him. He began to croon when I touched his palm and said, 'A present for you, old man.' A young boy, perhaps his grandson, opened the package and inspected the contents one by one as if it was a Christmas stocking. He ran up to the car and stuck his head through the window. '*Merci beaucoup*! *Merci beaucoup*!'

We drove back to Waaga in a benign darkness that was broken only by tentative drops of light from the kerosene lamps that lit the towns. I felt extraordinarily peaceful.

Back at the hotel I tied a strip of cloth round my head and chanted into the bathroom mirror, 'Daniel arap Moi. Daniel arap Moi.'

'You're crazy, Fitzy. But you're okay,' said Alistair.

'I have a problem,' I told him. 'It's this chicken business. I have to sacrifice it on a Friday, right? But I fly back to London next Thursday. You know what that means, don't you?' We became hysterical with laughter. The idea of trying to fob off a dead rooster to a wino in Leicester Square seemed very funny.

Our flight back to Abidjan was preceded by the customary search. A soldier rummaged through my bag and, one by one, withdrew the spells, the magic powder and the bottle of magic water. Each time he asked 'What is this?' And each time he nodded in understanding when I said, '*Gris gris.*'

Having dispensed with the formalities, we went to the restaurant so that Alistair could get something to eat. There was no food, so we ordered something to drink instead. While we were waiting for the sodas, I took a photo of Alistair with my camera. Within minutes I was arrested. I had forgotten, yet again, that it is forbidden to take photos of airports. A soldier marched me off to see some officials. On the way I met Mahamadou Kone.

'Hello, Mary Anne. What are you doing?'

'Hello, Mahamadou. I'm under arrest.'

'Oh yes? I'm here to meet a colleague.' The soldier and I walked on. I managed to extricate myself from the situation with the film intact. Soon afterwards, Alistair and I boarded the plane.

All very African. The French missionaries and administrators had assumed they had instilled faith in God and a sense of Napoleonic justice in the colonies. This wasn't the case at all. What the French regarded as wrong, the Africans considered to be right. In Waaga, senseless arrest and juju charms were perfectly normal. I wondered what the soldiers would have thought of EST therapy and flotation tanks.

Back in Abidjan I was coming down to the wire. With Christmas approaching, there was no leeway on the Thursday departure. So Wednesday was pretty hectic. There were interviews at the university in the morning; a story to write for the paper over lunch. I was also throwing a farewell party that evening. Luckily, Michelle Faul, my friend from Associated Press, had instructed her cook to buy and prepare the food. Alistair said he would arrange the wine. That left me free for the afternoon. I used it to follow up a hunch.

Alistair and I set off down the highway, crossed the bridge over the lagoon and cruised through the industrial area. 'Fitzy, are you sure you know where you're going?'

'Yeah. Yeah. Just drive slowly. I'll tell you where to turn.' Trashed cars, banana trees and wooden shacks replaced the factories. Soon even these petered out. What appeared to be a giant garbage heap loomed in the distance. It wasn't until we drew close that I was sure we were in the right place. It was Zoe Bruno, the meanest of Abidjan's slums.

We parked the car and set off on foot down an alley. Here, where there were no buildings, only shacks patched together from the detritus of the city, everyone lived outdoors. Women sat by rickety tables that offered a few vegetables or peeled oranges. On one, a baby lay asleep next to four tomatoes piled in a pyramid. A group of middle-aged men were hunched over a game of draughts like tramps round a fire. We passed some young men who were tall and muscled and snappily dressed. They eyed us up and down.

Alistair was lagging behind. 'Come on! What are you doing?'

'A guy back there wanted to sell me some smack.'

'Hardly surprising the way you're dressed. Come on. I think it's down here to the left. I'm just trying to remember what this guy's called.' I was looking for a compound that was much larger than the hovels we had seen so far. I had been there before to interview the owner. He was the secretary to Zoe Bruno's chief, but I suspected that wasn't all he did. His name came to me as we arrived at a wooden doorway beside which a large billy goat was tethered. Paul Settim. Framed in the opening were phallic-shaped mounds covered with a congealed mess of candle wax, feathers, food and blood. We crossed the threshold.

A short, sturdy man in T shirt and boxer shorts stepped into the sunlight to greet us. To my surprise, Paul remembered me clearly. 'Mary Anne Fitzgerald. You came here two years ago. You gave money to the school. How are you?'

'It's good to see you again, Paul. I've come because I have a problem . . .' As I talked, I took in the dead hornbill hanging from a rafter and '*Sogbo tout puissant*' (all powerful Sogbo) inscribed on a blue wall. Before these things had been the strange trappings of an alien culture. Now, knowing what I did, they assumed a new meaning. Paul was a votary of Sogbo, the fiery god of thunder.

He swept aside a curtain and led us into his cramped quarters. We stepped over a fat woman asleep on a mat and entered a second room. Paul gestured for me to sit on a stool. The space was so tiny Alistair had to crouch in the doorway.

The place was like a magpie's nest, filled with the pieces of junk that are the fetishist's accoutrements. A sleeping mat and some clothes hung on a nail provided the only oases of recognition. Beyond a jumble of bottles and shells stood an altar draped in white cloth.

Paul got straight down to business. 'This chap, you want me to kill him?'

'No!' I cried. 'Can you kill people?'

A noise like an engine starting up escaped from between his pale teeth. He rang a bell and looked at me with disdain. 'Of course I can kill. I can do whatever you want. You just have to tell me what it is.' My heart lurched. Paul was a poisoner. I hadn't bargained for this.

'Aren't you afraid of the power you have?' I asked.

'No. I do good, so why should I be afraid? The bad ones are the sorcerers. You have to watch out for them. They have eyes on the side of their head and lots of hair.'

Paul thrust a four-inch wooden figure in front of my face, a simulacrum of a man and woman back to back. 'If you want to harm a woman, you speak to her. If you want to harm a man, you speak to him.' He rotated the fetish idol's carved faces before me as if he was fitting a light bulb in slow motion. 'You see, the man has a padlock attached to his stomach. When you put a spell on someone, you unlock it and give him your instructions. Then you spit gin on him three times.' He paused to pour two tots of gin into a glass. 'Like this,' he said, covering the doll in a spray of alcohol.

'You see the bottle attached to the woman? It has a powder in it you must eat when you have a bad dream. If you dream of a dog attacking you, someone is sending you bad spirits. Then you eat this.' He unscrewed the bottle and dabbed the grey powder on to his tongue.

'With the proper sacrifices, this will obey all of your wishes for the rest of your life.' He must have discerned scepticism in my look, for he pressed on. 'I tell you, it works. Two women came from Canada especially to see me. They paid me 350,000 francs. They wrote from Canada to say everything had worked out very well.'

'It would have been cheaper to stay at home and hire a hit man,' Alistair muttered.

Paul ignored him, for he didn't understand English. 'We will sacrifice a rooster now and a goat at midnight.'

The next hour, spent driving against the rush hour traffic, was weird. While I was being propelled into dark, unexplored regions of the soul, everyone else was going home to eat dinner and watch a video.

At the market Alistair and I sat in the car while Paul went shopping. There was a squawk as a chicken was thrown into the boot of Michelle's car. It was soon joined by a bleating goat.

By the time we got back to Paul's place, it was evening. Then things got really wild. Paul was moving about his room, getting bells, shells, bottles and a knife into place, muttering under his breath as if he were a cook pottering in the kitchen. I stood watching, naked from the waist up and holding the trussed cock by its legs. When all was ready, he seized the chicken and swung it like a censer about my head and shoulders. I wondered if he would sever the bird's neck over my upturned face and squeeze its blood into my mouth as if it were a skin of wine. An African National Congress fighter I knew told me that he always drank a rooster's blood and ate its raw heart before running guns across the border into South Africa. The sacrifice protected him, he said.

The chicken did a St Vitus's dance of protest as Paul clamped it to the dirt floor beneath his octopuslike foot and carefully sawed away at its throat. Sacrificial blood is at its most potent when the animal is still alive. For a moment I thought the chicken had flown up into my face to suffocate me with its feathers, but Paul had lifted it there, holding it before him like a priest offering the host at communion. Then he smeared its rust red juices over my body.

Outside, children squealed as their mothers dried them after their evening bath. Paul paid no attention to these noises. He was slapping blood and feathers on to the fetish doll. He folded the idol into a newspaper and handed it to me. 'Carry this in your handbag when you go to London.' I had my misgivings. It was unlikely Heathrow immigration officials would regard sorcery with the same tolerance as the Burkinabe soldiers at Waaga airport. 'And take this powder too. If you eat it, wild panthers won't harm you, and the men who are pretending to be panthers will lift their masks off and run away.'

As I left, Paul was murmuring incantations in front of the altar with his forehead pressed to the ground. 'I can't wait for the goat. I have to be somewhere and it's late. Alistair will bring you the money tomorrow.' I passed through the outer room, trying to button my shirt while clutching the parcel, and stumbled over something soft. It was the fat woman. She didn't move.

I drew a long breath of velvety air and looked around the compound. Alistair was asleep on a bench beneath the inscription to Sogbo. Was the god of thunder now my ally or had I become his victim?

Even if I had known the answer then, I wouldn't have thrown the doll away. The fetish violated my most sacred tenet that we live by exercising our free will. Yet I was frightened this vulgar wooden idol would direct its evil towards me if I discarded it. So it became part of me. Call it superstition, if you will, but at least the chained cur of prejudice had left my side. I was open to all truths. At that moment, if a man had turned into a leopard before my eyes, I would have nodded and, like the Naparamas in Mozambique, said, 'Yes, this is the way it is.'

9

The End

Teneo te Africa.
When Julius Caesar landed at Adrumetum in Africa, he
tripped and fell. It was a bad omen, but with great presence
of mind, he pretended it was intentional and kissed the soil,
exclaiming, 'Thus do I take possession of thee Africa.'

It was a crisp January morning, and I was walking down the street with my
friend Sharon Balas. We had been working out at the gym. Sharon was
wearing a short jacket and sheer tights that made her legs look as if they
started under her armpits. The truck drivers were shifting down to first to
get an eyeful of this saucy bit of body topped with a shock of blonde curls.
Yet another salacious grin was thrown her way as we passed a phone box.
It had a pink 'Maid to Discipline' sticker on one of the panes. 'Come on,
Sharon. One of them's going to hit a lamp-post soon. Stop smiling at
them.'

We were heading for Mr Chivers in Shirland Road, which was in the
down-market part of Maida Vale in North London. There were some
drug dealers, pimps and prostitutes. A smattering of yuppies who'd
picked up on the bargain property prices. Some gypsy Irish squatting in
boarded-up houses. The men were always in fights. Their women wore
white high heels in the middle of winter and stole the clothes from the
Oxfam collection bin by the flower shop. My neighbourhood. I liked it
because of the Sudanese and Rastas who lived there. They gave the place
a sort of familiar feel.

Mr Chivers was my local butcher. He was going bald and wore a striped
apron over a white jacket. He had bought his shop sixteen years ago so he

knew most of his customers pretty well. When Sharon and I walked in, we said hello to him and to Pat, his goodlooking Irish assistant. Pat liked to hand out a few jokes with the meat and was not averse to flirting with the housewives.

Mr Chivers called us 'the young ladies', but Pat said, 'What can I do for you girls?'

MAF: Have you got any live chickens?

PAT: Sure. Come down to the basement after closing time, and I'll show them to you.

MR C: There's no live chickens. They're all dead. Why do you want one, then?

MAF: We're going to sacrifice it.

MR C: How beautiful. Will I do? (*laughing, then serious again.*) I'm just trying to think where you'd get one.

PAT: You want to sacrifice it?

MAF: Yeah.

PAT: What for?

MAF: Because I've got a spell on me, and I want to lift it.

PAT: (*deliberately adopting a tone of extreme reason*) Spell on you for what, love?

MAF: A chief in Kenya put a spell on me. I have to sacrifice a white chicken to get rid of it.

PAT: (*to* SB) Is she for real?

SB: She's for real.

PAT: (*to* MAF) Are you a liar? Are you coming at me alive, now?

MAF: I'm alive.

PAT: It's witchcraft.

MAF: That's right. And I've got to get it sorted out.

MR C: (*nodding in agreement*) Mmmm. These West Indians up the road here, lay down and die they would. If you don't mind my asking, is he just a chief or is he a witch doctor?

MAF: The chief got a witch doctor to do it.

MR C: Oh, I see.

MAF: So I went to a fetishist, a juju man. He said he'd kill the chief for me, but I told him not to bother. You can take revenge too far, can't you? I'm using a *marabout* to get the spell lifted.

MR C: They can do all these things, can't they? They're very powerful.

PAT: It's impossible. All this mumbo jumbo. (*Hands raised and backing towards the cold room.*) She's hypnotising me. I'm hypnotised. How about Kentucky? Try there. I can't help you.'

MR C: (*still very serious and helpful*) You know, I never even thought about it. Years ago you could buy live chickens on a Sunday down Petticoat Lane. The animal rights people stopped 'em selling all dogs and cats and live poultry and that. I'm just trying to think where they do . . . you know, chickens. A Jewish slaughterhouse. That's it. There's halal butchers, but you could explain yourself better to a Jewish butcher.

MAF: Not really. The *marabout* I went to is Muslim.

MR C: Hackney. You've got the best of both worlds there. Plenty of kosher and plenty of halal. Get a number 6 bus.

MAF: I've got a car.

MR C: You've got a car?

MAF: Yeah. Upmarket.

PAT: When you see the chief, tell him I said hello.

MR C: I don't think you should. He's not nice, the chief. Especially if you believe in him. You see these women and things. They get into trances and fall over on to the floor, don't they?

PAT: (*nervous*) Yeah, what if he comes in here and says 'Whoo-ooo, I've put a spell on you.'

MAFF: Would you believe in it?

PAT: (*angry*) I believe in Jesus and that's the end of story, isn't it?

MR C: Well, I wish you luck anyway. Let me know how you get on.

MAF: Yes, I will.

Next we tried St John's Wood. It was only a five-minute drive away, but it reeked of affluence. Going there was like crossing the Mason-Dixon line. We chose Bifulco's Stores Ltd, which had its name written in large black letters above a plate glass window that was shaded by a striped awning. Behind the counter an older man with a creased, lean face stood next to a younger man with black hair. I told them what I wanted. The older man said nothing. He just looked down at the floor through his glasses and walked away. The younger man moved back from the counter and leaned against the wall with his legs and arms crossed. He said he couldn't help us. The atmosphere was decidedly frosty.

'A little toffee-nosed, don't you think?' I said to Sharon when we were back on the street.

She giggled. 'They thought we were a *Candid Camera* team.'

We got back into the car and drove to Sharon's place so she could change. After some cheese and biscuits, the quest for purification resumed.

By the time we got to Hackney, the afternoon was bitter and damp, and the sky looked all mushy. We couldn't find any halal butchers so I dropped into a doner kebab place. The Turk who was tending to the slowly turning column of skewered meat didn't speak English. I was about to walk away when a man sitting on a chair by the counter stopped me. He had a straggly moustache and a thick gold chain around his neck. His hands were thrust deep into the pockets of an old leather jacket. 'They're in Whitechapel. All down the road. None here.'

In Whitechapel the shopkeepers were sweeping up the debris on the pavement and rolling down their store fronts. Lozenges of light from the lamp posts sat in the puddles in the gutter. A bearded man in a striped apron told us, 'You won't be able to do it yourself. It's against the law. No one can be a killer unless they're licensed.' Then he pointed to the only customer in his shop. 'Why don't you slaughter him?'

'Too scrawny. Who would want to eat him?' I could be poker-aced with the best of them. 'Come on, Sharon, let's go home. I'm frozen.'

The following day I had an appointment with my publisher in South Kensington. I had dressed up for the occasion. You know the gear: Sigourney Weaver in *Working Girl*. On the way home I dropped into Boucherie Française in Bute Street where the yuppies take their pheasants to be plucked. One of the butchers was holding a leg of lamb in one hand and a large knife in the the other. The other butcher, who emerged from a back room, was an Algerian. There was a customer, too, a man in a camel-hair coat.

MAF: Where can I get a live chicken?

BRITISH BUTCHER: There's a place in the East End. Do you know where the East End is?

MAF: Sure.

BB: Have you ever heard of Petticoat Lane?

MAF: I have.

BB: Well, they open on Sunday.

MAF: That's no good. I want to kill the chicken on a Friday.

BB: They're Jewish, you see. So they're closed Friday and Saturday.

CAMEL-HAIR COAT: Yes, closed for their religion. It's their . . . er . . .

MAF: Their sabbath.

BB: Why do you want it Friday?

MAF: It's for a sacrifice. I have to do it on a Friday.

C-HC: Just tell me, are you a white witch or a black witch?

MAF: Neither. I'm someone who's had a curse put on them.

C-HC: I understand. Voodoo.

ALGERIAN BUTCHER: (*His eyes are dilated, and he's pumping his elbows up and down. His English is halting. It has taken him this long to catch up with what's going on.*) You want a *live* chicken?

(MAF *smiles at him with raised eyebrows. She nods and draws a finger across her throat.*)

C-HC: You need a halal butcher. North End Road. They'll do it for you. Take the number 74 bus. It'll take you all the way to Fulham.

AB: No. Brixton. Down in the market.

BB: That might be better.

C-HC: They'll know about voodoo. There's lots of blacks down there.

MAF: Well, thanks a lot. You've been very helpful.

BB: Good luck!

I was stepping on to the zebra crossing when a voice called me back. 'Excuse me. You don't know how to get to Brixton. I'll take you there. I can get an hour off work.' It was the Algerian. 'Perhaps you will have dinner with me too.'

'Thanks,' I said in French, 'but no. I'll find my own way.'

He slipped into French as well. 'If you have dinner with me, I will butcher the chicken for you afterwards.'

'No. Really.' He looked crestfallen. I smiled benignly at him. 'Look, you're from Africa. You know about these things. You don't do sacrifices while you're on a date. It's not the right mood. The *marabout* wouldn't like it.'

'*Marabout?*' He looked puzzled.

'Yeah. You know. *Marabout*. Holy man. You must have *marabouts* in Algeria.'

He shook his head and frowned. 'No, I was born in Paris. What is a *marabout?*'

'I'll tell you about it the next time I come by with some pheasant. Godda go. Bye.'

Brixton sounded promising. But before I could get there, I came down with flu. That Thursday, Tara and Petra's father, Anthony, took them to the theatre. During the interval, Petra said idly to Tara, 'I wonder if Mummy will be well enough to do her sacrifice tomorrow?'

That did it. Anthony phoned me up and swelled his diatribe against voodoo with charges of chronic eccentricity, Bohemian living and flawed motherhood. I didn't point out that voodoo, which is an occult religion practised in the Caribbean and Latin America, was different from the religious magic of the *marabouts* of West Africa. Carping on definition was not going to clarify the issue. By whatever name, I was indulging in a practice that had no scientific basis. More to the point, I was involving myself in *their* supernatural beliefs, not our own, well-trodden Catholic ones.

Why this squeamishness about an offering to a deity? Couldn't Anthony see I was just after a touch of propitiation? Or, if he'd rather, why didn't he consider it an African version of touching wood? I knew a lot of people, all of them sane and logical, who walked round ladders propped up on the pavement. Was this so different? It was the same 'just-in-case' mentality. I might not get the house back if I killed a chicken and gave it to a beggar, but it certainly wasn't going to make things worse. It was worth a try. You never knew. It might work.

Nearly all my friends had responded to my plan with a mixture of discomfort and alarm. Only one was a vegetarian on moral grounds. None were signed up members of the RSPCA. Neither, so they insisted, did they believe in the darker forces of the supernatural. So why were they uneasy?

Kathy had reacted badly to the fetishist's doll and asked if I would remove it from the flat. That I understood. It definitely had an evil aura. I could just see the doll from my bed. It was lying on the floor under the desk where I had tossed it when I was unpacking. There was something bestial about the clotted mass of white feathers and brown blood sticking to its wooden faces. It also threw off a feral odour that wafted up into my nostrils. The metallic smell of stale blood did nothing to help my raging headache.

I felt I couldn't throw the doll away in case of satanic retribution. But at least I could put some distance between us. When I was well enough, I stuffed it into a manila envelope, took it down to the bank and asked for a safe deposit box.

'Do you want to know what the contents are?' I asked. The clerk shook her head. 'What if it's something evil . . . umm . . . dangerous. You know . . . something that's not good for the bank. That you'd rather not have on the premises if you knew what it was.' She forced a tired smile and said it was against regulations to enquire about the contents of safe deposit boxes. It wasn't important. I didn't have much money in my account anyway. But if Natwest suddenly went into receivership, I told myself, I'd know why.

The following Friday I drove down to Brixton.

Funny how you always pick strangers to ask the way. Tony said he was from Paris. He was balding even though I wouldn't have put him past mid-thirties. What was left of his hair was tight and curly. He must have had North African parentage, but as he told me he was French, it would have been rude to probe.

Tony had exceptionally bad teeth. They were so widely spaced, there were gaps between them, and one or two were missing. But there was something appealing about his face. Maybe it was his gentleness shining through. He told me he had come to London to study English. He didn't seem to be doing very well at it. He could barely string a sentence together. Perhaps that was why he walked with me to Brixton market. He was worried I wouldn't understand his directions. Then again, that couldn't have been it because we had conversed in French. Whatever the reason, I never actually invited him to join me. He just did.

At the market I talked to an elderly Arab, who was sitting behind the till of his small grocery store. Licences to slaughter animals had not been issued in London since the Second World War, he said. The only person who still managed to renew his licence every year, 'for ritual purposes', was an old Jewish butcher in Aldgate East. He didn't know the address.

Tony and I wandered down to the butchers. I turned into one where a young black guy was buying meat. I could sense he was African from the wild look in his eyes. His face, however, was leaden. He was focussed on appearing neither overawed by London nor lost in it. I gave him a friendly smile.

'Where are you from?'

'Nigeria.'

'Oh yeah? I'm from Kenya. I've been told there's a butcher in Aldgate East who sells live chickens. Do you know where he is?' Africans like to eat chickens that have been slaughtered on the premises. They taste better and you know what you're getting.

'Yes. Liverpool Street. I go there sometimes.'

I didn't know the place, but Tony did. So he led the way. While we were travelling on the underground, he told me he was a Muslim and worked as a chef at Lucullus, a restaurant in Knightsbridge. I tried to explain to Tony about *marabouts* and somehow got sidetracked into reincarnation. He listened with polite incomprehension. We were an odd couple. Or perhaps we were perfectly matched. The native African professing to be a Frenchman and the white woman claiming to be of Africa.

He was so baffled by my attempts to liken European mediums to fetishists (they were both instruments for channelling the supernatural) that I fell silent. Tony smiled shyly. 'You're too romantic. You are wild, like me. You are the first woman I have ever helped with a sacrifice. I think you're *formidable*.'

We walked from the underground past Petticoat Lane and turned into Wentworth Street. Pedestrians wandered amongst stalls selling clothes, jewellery, fruit and vegetables. Shoved up on the pavement were red and green pushcarts ready to take all the merchandise away when night fell. I bought some tangerines from a man with a weatherbeaten face so that I could enquire about butchers. 'None here, love. Haven't been for ten years.' Then as an afterthought, while he was still shaking his head in denial, 'The only thing they've got is a place for killing chickens. Down there. Second on the left.'

We turned into a small lane and fetched up at what must have once been a warehouse. It was so humid inside, blisters of moisture dotted the brown ceiling of the small entrance area. Through another room I could see crates and crates of brown hens piled on top of each other. Next to them, in a room with a barred entrance, some fearsome white roosters paced the straw-strewn floor. Underlying the odour of dampness was the full-bodied reek of something that was instantly recognisable: warm, bloody flesh and discarded stomach contents. It must have been familiar, too, to the men in business suits and women in coats who stood patiently in line, clutching empty plastic shopping bags. They were all African.

To the right of the entrance was an aperture in the wall so small and low that you had to bend down to converse with the man on the other side. Even then, he was barely visible, mummified as he was by layers of woollen hat and scarf. Woollen mitts left his swollen fingers free to count money.

'What's the name of this place?'

He presented a bulbous red nose and a mouthful of gnarled teeth. 'No name. No address.'

'How long have you been here?'

'We been here hundred years.' His broken English was so heavily accented, it was difficult to understand.

'Is this your place?'

'No, no.' The muffled nose moved back and forth, 'My guvner partner Mrs Thatcher family. Mrs Thatcher, she no Prime Minister now. So she drink. She smoke.' He opened his index and second fingers to make way for an imaginary cigar. 'My guvner, only water.' He beamed at me proudly.

'I want a white hen!' I was shouting. The din of metal scraping, thunking and slamming was tremendous.

'No white hens. Only roosters.'

'That will do.'

'Six pounds, then.' He stabbed at a scrap of paper with his pen and handed it to me. I noticed it bore the address of a law firm on the reverse side. 'Tell them over there. You wait the counter.'

The man he was pointing to was shiny with sweat even though there was no central heating in the place and the door on to the street was open. It had snowed the day before and it was bitterly cold outside. 'Can I watch you do it? This is a sacrifice.'

'Sorry, you can't come in here, luv. You can collect it at the counter. Head, feathers, feet?'

'No feathers. Leave the rest.'

I turned to Tony. 'I can't watch them do it. I hope nothing goes wrong.'

Tony brightened. 'I can do it for you. We'll take it to your flat and kill it there. Then there'll be no mistakes.'

This proposition was not appealing. I shrugged. 'It will be okay.'

When I got to the counter, there was a row of chickens lying on it. Their skin was covered with little bumps where the feathers had been plucked. Each one had a red gash in its neck. Revealed in their nudity, they didn't look very attractive. How was I going to get a beggar to accept this warm bundle of goose bumps? 'I've changed my mind about the head and feet. Can you cut them off?'

A black man with a gold loop in his ear chopped expertly.

'50p more. It's the service charge. There you are, darling. I hope the sacrifice works for you.' He wrapped the bird in newspaper and handed it over. Tony, being a gentleman, carried it for me.

After that I bought a yard of white cloth. No problems there. But the next part wasn't going to be as easy. We had been told that the tramps of the neighbourhood hung out by the Spitalfields Market.

Once again, Tony took the lead. When we had emerged from the underground, the pavements were filled with office workers. Wentworth Street had been busy with shoppers. Now we were in a blindfolded city of empty streets. We strolled at a leisurely pace, absorbing each corner and doorway as if we were tourists. On our left a shuttered convent. Down to the right the Georgian façade of Christ Church. Opposite two men sweeping the cobbles outside the vegetable market, which was closed. And there, beyond it, a large open space.

At the end nearest the market two grey figures stood by a bonfire. One of them was drunk. I could tell by the way he stood, feet braced and swaying slightly as if receiving the swell on an ocean-going yacht. The other man was throwing a vegetable crate into the yellow flames. His face was as round and knobbly as a freshly dug potato and just as dirty. I headed towards him.

'Hello, there! I was wondering if you would do me a favour? There's a chicken here in this bag. I want to give it to you as a present. You see, I've been thrown out of my home. And I don't have anywhere to live, like you. Someone in Africa put a curse on me. Now if I give you this chicken as a present . . . and also some material . . . that's in the bag, too . . . then the curse will go away. Then I'll be able to get my house in Africa back. So would you take it?' He stared with unfocussed eyes. 'Please?' I wheedled. He said nothing.

'What's he going to do with it?' said the other man in a thick Irish accent. He was holding a tin and gently shaking it so the liquid inside sloshed back and forth.

'You can cook it.'

'Where's the stove then?' said the man who looked like a potato.

'I can't even open a tin. You expect me to cook a bloody chicken?' added the Irishman. He walked towards me and put his face inches from mine. A spider's web of red veins lay on his cheeks. Wisps of hair fell across his forehead. He was tall and brawny. Not bad looking at all. A good bath and change of clothes and I could see him charming the ladies in the pub. 'What's all this mumbo jumbo then? I don't believe in it.'

I stared at the flecks of spittle on his lips. 'Look, it's not mumbo jumbo. It's witchcraft. You don't have to believe in it. I just want you to accept my present. Wouldn't you like a good meal?'

'How are you going to cook it then?'

'You mean, if I cook it, you'll take the chicken?'

'Maybe.'

I didn't like this shifting of responsibility. I'd been at countless goat slaughters in the bush where we'd cut whippy branches from *lileshwa* bushes, stripped off the bark and used them to skewer the meat over a fire. But how did you barbecue in a deserted city lot in the rain? It was difficult to concentrate. The drizzle and puddles and the garbage strewn about were distracting. 'Do you have any skewers?'

'Wazzat?'

'We need a briquet,' said Tony in French.

'What about aluminium foil?' I suggested. 'Is there a Sainsbury's round here?'

'We have to gut it,' said Tony. I had visions of hunkering down and chopping the bird up with my Swiss Army penknife.

'Just chuck it on,' said the Irishman.

I protested. 'No, it'll burn to a frazzle.' You'd think I was Julia Child. What did I care? Next I'd be suggesting rosemary.

Suddenly the man who looked like a potato started talking, slowly and with some difficulty. He was hovering between the present and some half-remembered world he had left behind. 'Abroad is different from here. Here when they take your car away you can get it back. If you can't pay the rent on your house, then give them the papers for the house. Then you can get your car back. But this chicken won't help you. Voodoo's no good here. It's different from abroad. It doesn't work here.'

The Irishman looked up at the grey sky, down at the ground and then at me. 'Tell you what. Give me a can of beer and I'll take it.'

'This is a Muslim sacrifice. We can't have any alcohol.'

He squinted at me and looked crafty. 'Money then. Throw a pound on the ground. Throw it at my feet. And I'll just happen to find it and pick it up.' This new-found business instinct pleased him.

'No. That's a bribe. Anyway, you'll use it to buy a pint. '

'What about cigarettes?'

'Well . . . I suppose I could give you a present. But it's not an exchange. It's got nothing to do with the sacrifice.'

The deal struck, he introduced himself as John and we set off in search of a tobacconist. The sun had come out and the cobbled street glistened. Coming towards us were two grey-haired men in pinstripe suits and bowler hats. As they drew abreast, John threw his hands up in the air and danced an Irish jig in their path. 'Yuppies! Yuppies!' he taunted. They pretended not to notice him and walked on.

John was pretty full of himself now that he had an audience to play to and material gain was in sight. He turned to me, jerking his thumb in Tony's direction. 'This your old man?'

'What's he saying?' Tony asked. I told him.

'Tell you one thing, maybe he doesn't speak English, but he knows that

I fancy you.' John winked and laughed hard. Then we all laughed. I was enjoying myself.

We found a tobacconist on the corner. I gave Tony a pound, and he went inside to buy a packet of ten Embassy. He gave them to John, who opened it and took one out.

'Could I have one?' Tony asked.

'My pleasure,' said John with a bow. The two men lit up.

'Now, I'd like to give you a present,' I said. Tony handed me the package and I handed it to John. 'One white rooster. Topped, tailed, plucked and ready to cook. And one yard of white cloth. They're all yours.'

John thrust it under his arm and shoved his hands in his pockets. 'That's some old lady you've got there. She's daft.' He winked and sauntered off. No doubt to do some bartering with a publican.

On the way back, Tony stopped at a wall till and withdrew some cash. Then he handed me a pound. 'That's for the cigarettes. They were a present from me. They have nothing to do with the sacrifice.' I thanked him and gave it to two children of about ten and thirteen who were begging on the steps of the underground.

Tony got out at Green Park. He had to report for his night shift at the restaurant. 'You're sure you'll find your way back to Brixton? You don't need me to take you back?'

'No, I'll be fine.'

'Can I see you again?' he asked hopefully. I doubted our easy companionship would prosper beyond this adventure, but it would have been churlish to withhold my phone number. I wrote it down and handed it to him. He gave me a radiant look. 'My first sacrifice. You are *formidable*.' As the train rolled out, he turned and waved.

Well, I thought to myself, that was a job well done. Now all I could do was sit back and wait to see what happened. It had been a ramshackle sort of day. My best in London so far. I was happy.

The weeks passed. I wrote, worked out at the gym, went out in the evenings. I stopped wearing my winter coat and started playing tennis in shorts. Friends asked if the chicken slaughter had lifted the spell. Had it? I didn't know. Did the end of a run of bad luck signal success? In my heart of hearts, I didn't think so. The conviction imparted in the dim and derelict huts of West Africa had become transparent. I could no longer see what it was I had felt.

Then one day my apathy was jolted. I received an invitation to lunch with my friend the Kenyan minister. His star had risen since we had last met. He was a powerful figure acknowledged to be close to President Moi. He had been in Washington for meetings and was passing through London to collect an award.

He and his bodyguard were waiting for me outside their hotel, two tall men with touches of grey in their hair standing beneath an overcast sky. They wore pinstripe suits and silk shirts from Gieves and Hawkes. They were imposing figures, even in London.

He wanted chops. His bodyguard ordered steak. I had poached salmon. Neither of them felt like wine so I settled for a Campari and soda. It was an excellent lunch lubricated with easy conversation.

He enquired about Tara and Petra and reminisced about his own days at university in England. They were some of his happiest, he said. He told me he loved reading philosophy. Isaiah Berlin was one of his favourites. It was something I hadn't known. He suggested I read philosophy too, starting with Plato before moving on to Aristotle, whose thought was more complicated.

Inevitably, the talk gravitated back to Kenya. I asked if things were going well in his constituency. He wanted to know how SAIDIA was faring. He remembered other Sunday afternoons, he said, when the two of us used to sit on my verandah and sort out Africa's problems over a bottle of chilled white wine.

'I liked your house. It was near the Athi Plains and had leopards.'

'I'm very homesick. When do you think I can come home?'

'Well, you know that business has all blown over now. I am speaking to you as a friend. There were certain parties who fanned the flames. But if you write a letter saying that your children are homesick, I think you will get a pardon. He likes children.'

'What should I do with it? Post it?' I asked ingenuously.

'No, give it to me. I'll see that it gets to him.'

When we parted, he kissed me on the cheek. He had never done that before. He was usually such a formal man.

Patrick Leigh Fermor suggested in his book *The Traveller's Tree* that voodoo was founded on nostalgia. The initiates, in this instance Caribbean slaves, were not seeking to attain higher planes of consciousness. They were warrening back to the African terrain from which they had been rudely plucked. They wanted to regain the womblike intimacy of the place where they had been happy. This was why, he theorised, most of the *Lwas* (spirits) they worshipped bore the names of African rivers and towns rather than African gods. The gestalt of the exile's faith was structured around the longing to return.

I was conscious that I, too, had fallen victim to this absurdity. Would a pardon from Daniel arap Moi be a deliverance or was it a *fata morgana* shimmering in the recesses of my mind? The lifting of my deportation order wasn't the threshold to paradise. Returning to Kenya would merely allow me to work hard and love those around me just as I had done before. Still, given the choice, I wanted to be amongst my family.

They still wrote regularly, charting their victories and defeats. The boys had all left school and had varying degrees of success in finding jobs. Chege had passed his mechanic's course but couldn't find employment with any of the garages. For a while he had a job loading people into *matatus*, the local taxis, but something had gone wrong and he had lost it. Paul, the next eldest brother, was drinking heavily. John, who had dropped out of the secondary school I had sent him to, landed the occasional day of casual labour. Joseph and Peris were working hard at school, but Peris still cried and asked when I was coming home. Chege was desperate for money to feed the family. There was a cynical edge to his letters. All his efforts to push the family beyond subsistence had come to nought.

After several false starts, Mike Eldon had found Peter employment with a tour company. Peter had tremendous tenacity and I knew he would do well. On the domestic front, he had steered a steady course through the swamps of bureaucracy on two occasions: the burial of his aunt and the acquisition of land in the Rift Valley behind the Ngong Hills. He was glowing with pride at his achievements. They had done more to make a man of him than the ritual circumcision that initiates Maasai boys into manhood. The unexpected death of his aunt had coincided with the sudden appearance of his real mother. We had all believed him to be an orphan. Mike, with whom Peter had been living for some time, was not introduced to her. She simply arrived one day, spoke to Peter and went away again. Peter mentioned this in passing but evidently didn't feel the need for further explanation. As far as he was concerned, Mike and I were his father and mother. His real mother, for whatever reason, had not been around while he was growing up. She was not of much interest to him.

I worried for Godfrey. He lived in western Kenya, far away from any of my friends who could keep a watchful eye over him. His father was drinking heavily and had thrown him out of the house. By means of erratic correspondence that chased me from London to Cyprus, we settled for higher education in the form of a teacher training college which I agreed to finance. It seemed the most promising course of action. Kenya didn't have much to offer in the way of work, but there would always be a demand for teachers.

Kipenget's battle to retain her land was being waged with heavy artillery. Kili had sold the house in which she lived and the surrounding acres to a *mzungu*. I could see why the would-be owner coveted the property. It had a magical view that looked across the plains and volcanoes of the Rift Valley. Kipenget had managed to get a stay on the sale by challenging Kili's right to dispose of 'their' land without her permission.

Kili had reacted badly to this challenge and regularly pulled out his bow and arrows and threatened to kill her.

Two of their daughters, Segenun and Minice, were circumcised against their will with Segenun swearing she was of the last generation that would have to suffer this indignity. Meanwhile, Joyce, by now sixteen, gave birth. The father was one of the teachers at school, according to her sisters. Joyce refused to be drawn on the subject. Poor sunny, courageous Kipenget. She seemed destined to tread a path of adversity.

Yet, at a rough guess, she was no worse off than the majority of Africans. In fact, she enjoyed a better lifestyle than many. She owned land (just); her children went to school (though they would probably never find regular salaried employment when they finished); and while they were sometimes hungry, they never actually starved. Even so, like everywhere else on the continent, what little money Kipenget earned from selling Maasai jewellery was buying less. It was the same story across Africa. Rampant inflation hiked prices while salaries remained static year after year. People like Lepias, the Samburu who danced at Bomas of Kenya, rarely got a raise. So he spent three quarters of his wages on food and transport for his town family. It was hardly surprising that he failed to send part of his pay packet to Nolotimy, who struggled on at subsistence level in the bush.

Per capita gross domestic product for Africa actually declined during the second half of the 1980s. For personal income to double to seven hundred dollars a year after a quarter of a century, the GDP would have to maintain a six per cent annual growth rate, according to an analysis prepared for the United Nations' Africa Recovery Programme. Less than sixty dollars a month by 2015 didn't seem much to ask for yet all the signs pointed towards disappointment.

Of the world's thirty-six poorest countries, twenty-nine are south of the Sahara. No black African country has an annual turnover to equal that of Exxon's. None – except Nigeria and Côte d'Ivoire – could make it on to the list of the world's hundred largest corporations.

Shrinking budgets and a continental population growth rate of just over three per cent mean there is less to spend on education and health, which hits the ordinary man and woman where it hurts most. Africa's population is expected to double to over one billion in twenty years' time. Never before has a population grown so fast. The population of school-age children is growing by four million a year. In 1991 the Kenyan government withdrew most of its subsidies for secondary schooling. After much juggling with accounts, the headmaster at Baragoi reluctantly announced he would have to raise the school fees for the following year. He was probably unaware of it, but his decision fell in line with a World Bank policy to levy charges for services rendered. SAIDIA had already introduced this system in Samburu District with the annual health insurance each family paid to the dispensaries. The scheme had worked well, but education was different. It was now beyond the reach of many families.

There was success as well as despondency though. By 1990, twenty-two African countries had achieved their target of immunising three quarters of their children against childhood diseases. Kenya (and Samburu District) was amongst them.

These are setbacks and accomplishments within the conventional framework of development. However, nothing can prepare Africa for the cataclysmic social and economic upheaval that will be caused by AIDS. In Uganda, nearly one out of every eight people (including those who are not sexually active) are seropositive. Visitors have reported travelling through villages populated almost entirely by children. In the worst-hit areas, the prevalence of the epidemic doubles every one to three years. In those parts of the AIDS belt with a three to four per cent population expansion (such as Kenya), the growth rate could become negative thirty years after the introduction of the HIV virus. This same region will lose about one third of its labour force, not to mention a large part of its military, politicians, civil service and professionals. In due course, there may not be enough adults left to grow sufficient food and cash crops or to guide the economy through crisis. Services will break down from a shortage of manpower and money just at a time when they need to be expanded. What will happen to the 10 million children who will be orphaned over the next ten years? Who will tend to the thousands and thousands of dying AIDS patients? The consequences of the rising number of AIDS deaths will be tragic.

Meanwhile, Africa's slide into penury is for a great part due to the venality of its leaders. Moi should have bought buses instead of Airbuses so that people could ride to work instead of walk. As Richard Dowden, Africa editor at *The Independent*, pointed out, politicians don't stop at pocketing the change from state purchases. They pocket the treasury.

The other side of the equation calls for a less selfish attitude in the West. This means more aid and trade and forgiveness of debt. African debt stands at around $270 billion. This is insignificant compared to Latin American debt, but it requires burdensome repayments that take up one third of export earnings. A moratorium would give the continent a head start on economic recovery and could easily be accommodated by the world money markets. Poland was forgiven seventy per cent of its debt to the United States, presumably because the Bush administration saw opportunity for commercial enterprise in a revitalised Polish economy. The same could be done for Africa.

It would also be a wise long-term investment. A sinking continent on the West's periphery will rebound on industrialised economies. A favourable climate for the flow of capital, goods and ideas will nurture growth and therefore further trade and investment. South Africa will play a vital role in this now that it is politically acceptable. It is an economic giant compared to its neighbours. In 1990 South Africa's Gross Domestic Product was $120 billion. The combined GDP for the rest of sub-Saharan Africa was $130 billion. South Africa is looking for export markets and ought to be able to provide competitively priced goods. The alternative to external stimuli is stagnation and a flood of economic refugees heading north as is already happening in France.

During the 1980s, net official development assistance to sub-Saharan Africa averaged thirty dollars a person every year. It was an aid flow without parallel in history. Yet Africa now needs even larger amounts of aid. This is unlikely to happen. In the past, aid was partially motivated by the West's desire to compete with the Soviets and Chinese for political dominion. With the Cold War over, that rationale has fallen away. Africa is in danger of being neglected. Ironically, the tension between capitalists and Marxists held everything in place, for better or for worse. Now that it has been removed, the continent could implode and collapse as in parts of Eastern Europe and the former Soviet Union. This would be disastrous. Conflict, along with corruption, has already dragged Africa down. Over the next decade it could rage like a bushfire, jumping from one country to the next, destroying wantonly. You just have to look at Liberia to see how this doomsday scenario is played out.

Two and a half years after I flew out of the rain-sodden airport in Monrovia, little had changed in Liberia. The capital was under siege from Charles Taylor, who refused to lay down his arms because he still wanted to be president. His rival, Prince Johnson, had behaved in a manner that caused everyone to wonder if he had gone insane. At one point, he took prisoner a negotiating team from Monrovia and force-fed its members on urine and neat rum. Johnson eventually surrendered to the West African peacekeeping force, but the vacuum was filled with the emergence of the United Liberation Movement of Liberia for Democracy, a ragtag group of armed teenagers constantly high on *ganja*. So far, over 60,000 had died as a result of the tribal revenge killing, and the United States was as determined as ever to avoid a direct role in resolving the crisis.

The conflict in Ethiopia had a happier outcome, partially because the EPRDF had a sense of mission that was lacking in Taylor's men. It took place just over a year after I had bid a poignant farewell to Goesh, the TPLF fighter who had guarded me against MiGs and assassins. Under the cover of pre-dawn darkness one morning in May 1990, the EPRDF rolled their tanks through Revolution Square and parked outside the Hilton from where they released a barrage of artillery fire on to the Ghibbi

Palace. The Kalib Shaleka, Mengistu's praetorian guard, threw down their arms and fled. Unfortunately, Mengistu escaped retribution. He had slunk away the previous week, taking a plane to Zimbabwe where he owns a farm. His precipitous flight put paid to the theory proffered by a US diplomat in Addis Ababa that 'Ethiopian tyrants have a tendency to die in their boots'. Westerners, too, had fallen prey to the African habit of endowing the continent's leaders with more courage than they possessed.

In Sherraro, the town where we were bombed by MiGs, they must have been dancing in the daylight (for the first time in years) at news of the EPRDF victory. Sherraro continued to be a Derg target right to the end. Three weeks before the EPRDF swept through the capital, the air force bombed the town yet again, killing and wounding 105 people. Sister Bernadette wasn't around to take part in the celebrations that must have been held in Idga Hamus. She had been transferred back to Dublin. But the woman we had driven to hospital under threat of attack from MiGs was. Bernadette wrote to Peter Sharp to say that against all odds, the woman had survived her caesarean operation.

Ethiopia's new president Meles Zenawi is faced with implementing a transition to democracy. This will be no easy task given the demands for secession from the Oromos, Afars and Somalis. Meles's answer is ethnic democracy, a sort of federalism determined along ethnic lines. It is a far cry from the Albanian Marxism he bandied about Whitehall three years earlier. However, Meles may ultimately have to resort to the undemocratic supression favored by Mengistu if he is to contain the many ethnic liberation movements who continue to view the central government down the barrel of a gun. Eritrea has already seceded, and they would like to follow suit.

In many ways, Ethiopia symbolises the future of Africa. It is poised on a knife edge between cohesive, democratic nationhood and total disintegration. Which way it falls depends on the negotiating abilities of Meles's government, the pressure applied by the West through offering sizeable grants to a unified country, and the sheer bloody-mindedness of the Ethiopians. They have never been a homogeneous society. Ethiopia, and Africa, could leap forward into the untested realm of democracy or retreat into the fallacious security of ethnic or religious nationalism. Clan loyalties created anarchy in Somalia after the fall of its former president, Siad Barre. A civil war between Christian and animist southerners and Muslim northerners brought Sudan to a standstill. Similar ethnic conflicts continue to bubble away elsewhere. The former Belgian colony of Zaire, another country on the brink of chaos, has over 200 different tribes. It was perhaps idealistic to assume they could ever live together in harmony.

The colonial powers, specifically the British and French, engineered many morganatic marriages between tribes who were traditional enemies by drawing up national boundaries that suited Europe rather than Africa. It should also be remembered that much of the human rights abuse, corruption and dictatorial governance was learned at the knees of the British and French. Kenya's detention acts were put in place in colonial times. Moi has never done so, but he could have usefully referred to Britain's Prevention of Terrorism Act to justify his own suppression of political opponents. Neither would Moi or Biwott be able to siphon off development money if Western businessmen didn't engineer the deals. The French connived to perpetuate the rule of monsters such as Bokassa, who created the Central African Empire, in return for arms deals and export contracts whose terms were unfavourable to the African buyers.

Experiments in democracy have followed different paths. Kolingba called elections in 1992 after Centralafricans had held a week-long general strike. Civil servants in the countryside had not been paid for fifteen months. They were annulled and rescheduled for the following year when Kolingba placed fourth in the presidential race. Houphuet-Boigny of Côte d'Ivoire held multi-party elections for the first time and retained his seat. Kerekou of Benin followed suit and made history by becoming the first mainland black African president to be voted out of power. It didn't need a political analyst to decipher the results. Côte d'Ivoire acknowledges civil rights and has a prosperous middle class. Kerekou had turned Benin into a bankrupt and oppressive one-party Marxist state.

Kerekou typified the Old Guard. Leaders had a barnacle mentality towards power because they knew leadership could ultimately lead to the grave by means of a coup. Even after they had amassed sufficient wealth to see their families good for several generations, they clung on because they feared change. Kerekou ruled by dint of personality for nineteen years. His longevity fostered disregard for the country's needs and encouraged arrogance and greed. He never deferred to his ministers and kept shut the safety valve of public expression. He was advised by one trusted confidant, a witch doctor.

The good news is that the distortions of leadership and economic management are now being challenged by the African people themselves. Most francophone countries are seeking pluralism and Western-style government through national conferences that present a consensus of opinion. Westerners call it the round-table formula, but Africans have been doing it for centuries in the shade of large trees with spreading branches.

It is only when the desire for reform comes from within that change will take place as began to happen towards the end of 1990. Over the next year, switches in leadership averaged nearly one a month. It was an unusually high rate of turnover, even for the quicksilver politics of Africa. Some heads of state, such as Doe, were dead. Some, such as Mengistu, had fled. Others, such as Kenneth Kaunda, lost at the polls – he gained only twenty per cent of the votes in Zambia's first multi-party elections. Kaunda, patently honest but a disastrous economist, had reigned since independence in 1964.

His resounding defeat was an encouraging sign for government opponents in Kenya. Moi was still resisting democracy, citing tribal conflagration as the reason for his intransigence. Western donors, encouraged by the United States, suspended a $1 billion aid package at the end of 1991. Thus nudged in the direction of accountable governance, Moi called general elections a year later.

During the runup, 800 were killed and 54,000 left homeless. The violence was instigated by Moi's fellow Kalenjin and sanctioned by the KANU elite. It was Moi's way of saying, "I told you so. Kenya can't handle democracy yet." And he was partly right. Most of the electorate voted along tribal lines. Moi was returned with thirty-six per cent of the vote because the opposition, instead of uniting, had fought amongst themselves and fragmented into three main parties. But Moi no longer had absolute power even though he was still president. There had been a sudden gust of wind and the sands had shifted. It was an old African story.

It is true that democracy is doomed if Africans fail to discern that a strong sense of nationhood is central to pluralism. However, the fear of resurrecting ethnic animosities is an empty argument. Tribal hegemony already existed in Kenya, where Moi's Kalenjin dominated politics and commerce. Tribalism will be erased when economic benefits are spread evenly throughout the country, not when they are hoarded by one group. Homogeneity is created in the melting pot of the cities, through higher education and the growth of a middle class. Africa's new leaders are technocrats, professionals, businessmen and trade unionists who have earned, rather than inherited, their positions. Let's hope that as role models for self-improvement they will transcend tribalism.

At first, Kenyans feared change in case the alternative to Moi was even worse. They shuddered as they looked at their neighbours and clung to the imperfect present. There is risk in change, as I had discovered in my own life. But you cannot achieve without risking something.

The answer to my own dilemma came to me the Monday morning following my meeting with the Kenyan minister, as I was driving through Hyde Park. There was no miraculous solution. For me or for Africa. It was a question of following your best instincts. In Africa's case, it meant letting go of old mind sets, casting adrift the ancestral spirits of the past and assuming collective responsibility for the future.

It was time Africa stopped finding scapegoats for its woes. As for me, it meant sticking to my principles, which were very much the same as those of the new Africa: freedom of expression, the right to choose my own course through life.

When I got back to the flat, I picked up the phone and dialled the number of the hotel where the minister was staying. I was lucky. He was in. 'Hello. It's Mary Anne. I've been thinking about your offer. You know that I long to be home. But I can't accept it. If I do, it will compromise me. And you too. Next month I start the book. There are things which I wouldn't be able to say about Kenya if I was living there. I want to write what I feel to be the truth. You know that. Perhaps when the book's published, if all goes well, we can reconsider. I value your friendship and appreciate what you offered to do for me. Thank you for that. And I'm sorry I have to turn it down.'

'I understand. We'll see how it goes,' he said.

I didn't cry. It didn't even hurt because there was no pain. If you survive change, you are free.

The story was meant to end there, but life is never tidy.

I wrote the book in Cyprus then flew back to London to deliver the manuscript to the publisher. To my surprise and great joy, I found Gabriel was in town. He had come over to talk to donors and raise money for SAIDIA. I arrived on a Saturday morning and discovered I would see him that evening at the annual SAIDIA fund-raising dance. I could hardly contain myself, but it was a bittersweet excitement. It was the second time Gabriel had been to England. Knowing his dislike of large cities and overcast skies, there probably would not be another visit. Would I ever see him again after this? Perhaps not.

We kissed hello and grinned and sat beside each other for much of the evening. It was difficult to talk into the electric frenzy of the bands. On Sunday he came over to the flat. We talked for six hours. First I caught up on the news. Lesepen had died a year ago, passing on his soothsaying powers to his second son. Everyone else was well and sent me their love.

SAIDIA's new dispensary at Lesirikan was nearly finished. It had cost forty thousand dollars to build. There was a laboratory, a pharmacy, a treatment room, a health-education centre, four staff quarters. In all, a complex of nine buildings. That practically doubled the size of Lesirikan. It was a far cry from the days when we used to sleep on the floor of the old, bat-infested dispensary and Mark and Sammy sterilised utensils in a tin bowl set on a charcoal stove.

Equally good news, Gabriel was a married man. His wedding to Anna Maria, a Borana girl of sixteen, had taken place the previous week. Kattra was looking after her during Gabriel's absence. He was longing to rejoin his bride.

'It was about time, Gabriel. You'll be such a good father. How old are you now?'

'I don't know, M.A. Maybe I'm the same age as you.'

'We used to reckon you were about eight years younger. How did you manage to catch up?' Like many Africans, Gabriel had only a vague idea when he was born.

He grinned. 'I'm *mzee* now.'

'Well, I'm *mzee*, too. It will be Tara's turn to get married next.'

Gabriel frowned and looked serious. 'M.A., you know I try to be a good friend to you. I'm sorry that I don't answer your letters. They are very good letters. They are so full of information, they are like novels. I take days to read them. I liked the one about your trip to West Africa to see the witch doctors. It arrived the week after Lekisaat was pushed out.'

I blinked and sat up. 'What? What happened to Lekisaat?'

'The *wazee* petitioned the DC [District Commissioner] at Maralal asking for him to be removed. They didn't want him as their chief any more. So there was a big *baraza* and they voted him out.'

I was astounded. 'I can't believe it. He was so powerful. Has that ever happened before?'

'It's very unusual. I can remember it happening once to a chief in Wamba district. That's not all. Lekisaat lost his land as well. When the land that used to belong to group ranches was allocated to private individuals, nine people shared out the area from Elkortikal to Baragoi amongst themselves. No one knew they'd done it. Then an *mzee* discovered what had happened. The people were very angry because it had been done behind their backs. The District Land Officer came to Lesirikan to review the cases. He held court under a tree. The first case to be heard was Lekisaat's. He said he had been given 2,620 acres by Kowop because it was an *ngoroko* area. He had taken it to protect everyone from the *ngoroko*. The people said the *ngorokos* were no longer a nuisance so they wanted the land back. They let him keep twenty acres. The rest of the land reverted to group ranches. Lekisaat was no longer chief by then so he had to agree. There was nothing he could do.'

'Gabriel . . . that guy in West Africa . . . the one who slaughtered a chicken over me and gave me the doll . . . do you think he was responsible for what happened to Lekisaat?'

Gabriel chuckled in the way he did when something amused him greatly. 'Yes, I think he did.'

'Do you think witchcraft is real?'

Gabriel laughed again. 'Look what happened to Lekisaat.'

All the while I had been clamouring for a pardon from Moi. I hadn't given much thought to Lekisaat. Yet it was the Samburu chief, not the

Kenyan president, who had cast the spell on me. I saw in Lekisaat's downfall an impeccable symmetry. He had stripped me of my standing and home. I had stripped him of his. Africa was certainly full of surprises.

I knew then that in two or three years, maybe five or ten, I would once more stand outside the clinic, tin mug of *chai kienyeji* in hand, as the evening silence licked my face. Life was a safari, and I was heading for the top of a mountain.

Glossary

amwi – gods *Baoulé*
asié-usu – genies *Baoulé*
askari – guard or soldier *Swahili*
banda – hut or bungalow *Swahili*
baraza – meeting *Swahili*
bayé-fwé – sorcerer *Baoulé*
boma – fenced in area in which the herds are kept at night *Samburu*
boubou – flowing gown worn by men *Wolof*
chai kienyeji – local tea *Swahili*
dagaa – small freshwater fish similar to whitebait *Swahili*
debe – container for water or petrol *Swahili*
derg – committee *Amharic*
dukka – shop *Swahili*
dwuhuré – black potion used by poisoners *Baoulé*
fafa – soya beans *Amharic*
ferenji – foreigner *Amharic*
gabbi – man's shawl *Amharic*
ganja – marijuana *Swahili*
gris gris – amulet *French*
harambee – let's pull together *Swahili*
injera – sour unleavened bread made from teff *Amharic*
jallabiya – a cotton robe *Arabic*
kwaheri – goodbye *Swahili*
laibonok – Sambura spiritual leader *Samburu*
lakiradorop – a star known as the Short Star *Samburu*
lakirai – a star known as the Traveller *Samburu*
lebarta – a circumcision song *Samburu*
lepayan lelakir – the nickname for Lesepen, the 'man of the stars' *Samburu*
lmugit – a series of five ceremonies to mark the passage of warriorhood; literally means 'the death of many cattle in one place' *Samburu*
ltarakoi – trees *Samburu*
lugga – dry river bed *Swahili*

Lwa – voodoo god   *Creole*
mandazi – triangular doughnut   *Swahili*
manyatta – homestead   *Samburu*
marabout – Muslim holy man whose magic is a mix of Islam and the occult   *French*
matatu – enclosed pickup used as a taxi   *Swahili*
murran/murrani – warrior/warriors   *Samburu*
mzee/wazee – older person/people or elder/elders   *Swahili*
mzungu – white person   *Swahili*
nataka kwenda choo – I want to go the lavatory   *Swahili*
ndio – yes   *Swahili*
ngoroko – Turkana or Pokot bandit   *Swahili*
nkanyit – honour   *Samburu*
panga – machete   *Swahili*
pole – sorry   *Swahili*
posho – maizemeal   *Swahili*
quienti – edible wild grass seed   *Amharic*
rafiki – friend   *Swahili*
rungu – club   *Swahili*
saen – thick layer of bead necklaces worn by girls who are being courted   *Samburu*
safiri salama – bon voyage   *Swahili*
sewa – home-brewed beer   *Amharic*
shamba – smallholding   *Swahili*
shifta – Somali bandit   *Swahili*
shuka – cloth worn by men wrapped and secured at the waist   *Swahili*
silalei – gum from a member of the Commiphora, Boswellia neglecta, used
   to tip arrows   *Samburu*
simi – broad-bladed sword used for fighting   *Swahili*
sirikan – dried meat   *Swahili*
sorrio – the sacrifice of a grey and black sheep covered in milk and honey   *Samburu*
umerudi – you have returned   *Swahili*
umyen – ancestors   *Baoulé*
viande bucané – dried meat   *French*
wadi – dry water course   *Arabic*
wananchi – the people   *Swahili*
wat – curried meat dish   *Amharic*
wa-wé – the abstract essence that joins the body to the soul   *Baoulé*